MULTIMEDIA
AND
HYPERTEXT

The Internet and Beyond

MULTIMEDIA
AND
HYPERTEXT
The Internet and Beyond

Jakob Nielsen

SunSoft
Mountain View, California

AP PROFESSIONAL

Boston San Diego New York
London Sydney Tokyo Toronto

AP PROFESSIONAL
955 Massachusetts Avenue, Cambridge, MA 02139

An Imprint of ACADEMIC PRESS, INC.
A Division of HARCOURT BRACE & COMPANY

United Kingdom Edition published by
ACADEMIC PRESS LIMITED
24–28 Oval Road, London NW1 7DX

Nielsen, Jakob, 1957-
    Multimedia & Hypertext : the Internet and beyond / Jakob Nielsen.
        p.   cm.
    Includes bibliographical references and index.
    ISBN 0-12-518408-5 (acid-free paper)
    1. Hypertext systems.   I. Title. II. Title: Multimedia and
Hypertext.
QA76.76.H94N543 1995
005.75--dc20   94-44429
                                                            CIP

Printed in the United States of America
  95 96 97 98 IP   9 8 7 6 5 4 3 2 1

Contents

Preface

Why is this a book?

The Preface to my book *Hypertext and Hypermedia* (AP Professional, 1990) asked why a book on hypertext would be published as a paper book. So why do I still insist on writing books? Well, the answer I gave in 1990 still holds, though it will probably not hold that much longer: there are still so many practical disadvantages connected with electronic publishing[1] that I decided to stay with paper a few more years for a long work like this book. Developments on the Internet are moving so fast these days, though, that I would expect a future book to be some form of Internet publication.

One of the main advantages of having this book in a hypertext format would be to provide readers with the possibility of linking directly to supplementary reading material for issues of special interest to each individual reader. Unfortunately this would be mostly impossible to do given current copyright restrictions, since the relevant literature on hypertext has so many different copyright holders that nobody could acquire all the relevant permissions.

Instead I have relied on the traditional form of "dead" links in the form of references to the published literature. The appendix contains an extensive bibliography on hypertext, which is annotated to allow you to determine the relevance of a given reference before you go to the trouble of getting hold of it. References throughout the book point to this bibliography through the standard notation of listing the author's last name and the year of publication in square brackets.

To try to compensate for the lack of a running hypertext, Chapter 2 gives a very detailed case study of one hypertext system. The remaining chapters give examples of several additional hypertext systems, and the book is richly

---

[1] Slower reading speed from computer screens than from paper, problems with showing illustrations across platforms, relative lack of portability of computers, etc.

illustrated to give you an idea of the variety of ways hypertext can be implemented.

There have been three major changes in the hypertext field since *Hypertext and Hypermedia* was published. The first major change is the explosive growth of the Internet from about 300,000 host computers with three million users in 1990 to about four million host computers with about 30 million users in 1995. The Internet and its implications for hypertext are discussed in Chapter 7. The second major change is that home computing finally seems to be happening,[2] with millions of people buying powerful computers[3] with CD-ROM drives and other facilities for hypermedia viewing and with networked features like video-on-demand being made ready for introduction by several high-powered consortia of companies from the computer, telecommunications, and entertainment industries.[4] These events permeate many chapters in the book that have been rewritten to reflect the new emphasis on home computing. The third main change is the information overload inherent as a result of the other two changes. In 1990, we were happy every time we could lay our hands on a new hypertext, but in 1995, we have to fight our way out from under a mountain of online information and unsolicited CD-ROMs received as so much junk mail. The information overload problem is discussed further in Chapter 8.

The home computing and multimedia trends have resulted in so many products that it is impossible to include a complete survey of hypertext products. Instead, coverage of many products has been integrated with the main chapters. As further discussed in the following, one of the main benefits of this book is that it is not product-specific, but instead aims at providing the

---

[2] Home computing was a pipe dream for many years and early home computers were sold only in small quantities that mostly ended up in closets. As an example of the change, it took ten years to sell the first million copies of Microsoft's *Flight Simulator* but only one year (1994) to sell the second million (according to Microsoft VP Patty Stonesifer as quoted in the *Wall Street Journal* November 15, 1994).

[3] In fact, the typical home computer sold in the U.S. these days is more powerful than the typical office computer since companies try to save on data processing costs while consumers want as high multimedia quality as they can get.

[4] The 17.5 million CD-ROM drives sold in 1994 was 170% more than 1993 sales. The number of subscribers to the major home-computing online services (CompuServe, America Online, and Prodigy) increased by 76% in 1994 from 2.9 million to 5.1 million.

reader with broad insights from the diversity of hypermedia designs in the world.

A Multitude of Hypertext and Multimedia

This book is based on many examples of hypertext and multimedia in the form of both systems and applications. There are so many different approaches to hypertext and multimedia that it would be wrong to base a book on a single one. There are many books on the market devoted to a single hypertext system, whether it be Apple's HyperCard, Macromedia's Director, NCSA's Mosaic, or yet some other popular tool. These books have many qualities and can be recommended for readers who own one of these tools, but even if you limit yourself to a single delivery platform I believe you can benefit from an understanding of the wide range of design options that exist across the market.

It would also be wrong for users to base their judgment of hypertext's usefulness for them on the basis of knowing a single example of hypertext. Many people may know a single system because they have seen it reviewed or because it is used by one of their friends. Such first hand information should of course be utilized as *part* of a decision on whether to use hypertext, but it should not be the only input to the decision.

Which hypertext system should you choose? The simple answer is, "That depends," since there is no universally single best hypertext system, no matter what the salespeople might tell you [Nielsen 1989e]. You should consider the size of the information you want to represent in hypertext and whether you want a text-oriented system or a system that is good on graphics. You also have to consider whether your application calls for a multi-user system or whether a single-user system will do. Finally, you have to take usability considerations into account. Some systems are suited for professional users who need a lot of features and who have the time to learn them, whereas other systems are simple enough for naive users. I cannot give you a single recommendation since I have used and designed several different systems myself.

It is important to realize that hypertext is such a broad concept that one hypertext system might well be completely unsuited to a particular application even though the application could be well supported by another hypertext system. Therefore this book aims at providing you with an idea of the multitude of hypertext, so that you will be better able to decide for yourself whether your needs can be served by hypertext and what requirements should be fulfilled to serve these needs *well.*

Acknowledgments

I would like to thank the following for help in writing this book. As always, any errors or omissions are solely my responsibility.

Keith Andrews, Graz University of Technology, Austria
Michael Begeman, Corporate Memory Systems
Peter Brown, University of Kent at Canterbury, U.K.
Alan Buckingham, Dorling Kindersley Multimedia, U.K.
Jesus Bustamante, European Commission Host Organisation, Luxembourg
Ellen C. Campbell, Silicon Graphics, Inc.
Kim Commerato, Lotus Development Corporation
Jeff Conklin, Corporate Memory Systems
Kate Ehrlich, Lotus Development Corporation
Jim Glenn, SunSoft
Nadine Grange, EARN European Academic & Research Network, France
Wendy Hall, University of Southampton, U.K.
Martin Hardee, SunSoft
Lynda Hardman, CWI, The Netherlands
Kyoji Hirata, NEC Corporation, Japan
Keith Instone, Bowling Green State University
Yasuhiro Ishitobi, Fuji Xerox, Japan
Donna L. Jarrett, Corporate Memory Systems
Freddy Jensen, Adobe Systems
Jek Kian Jin, National Computer Board, Singapore
Daniel Jitnah, Monash University, Australia
Kazuhisa Kawai, Toyohashi University of Technology, Japan
Ara Kotchian, University of Maryland
George P. Landow, Brown University
Gunnar Liestøl, University of Oslo, Norway
Catherine Marshall, Texas A&M University
Yoshihiro Masuda, Fuji Xerox, Japan
Michael L. Mauldin, Carnegie Mellon University
Naomi Miyake, Chukyo University, Japan
Elli Mylonas, Brown University
Jafar Nabkel, U S WEST Technologies
Emanuel G. Noik, University of Toronto
Randy Pausch, University of Virginia

Ron Perkins, Interchange Network Company

José M. Prieto, Universidad Complutense de Madrid, Spain

Klaus Reichenberger, GMD Integrated Publication and Information Systems
        Institute, Germany

Thomas C. Rearick, Lotus Development Corporation

W. Scott Reilly, Carnegie Mellon University

Paul Resnick, MIT

Daniel M. Russell, Apple Computer

Darrell Sano, Netscape Communications Corporation

J. Ray Scott, Digital Equipment Corporation

Eviatar Shafrir, Hewlett-Packard Company, User Interaction Design

Ben Shneiderman, University of Maryland

Norbert A. Streitz, GMD Integrated Publication and Information Systems
        Institute, Germany

Joel Tesler, Silicon Graphics

Cathy Thomas, National Physical Laboratory, U.K.

Paula George Tompkins, The SoftAd Group

Martien van Steenbergen, Sun Microsystems, The Netherlands

Adrian Vanzyl, Monash University Medical Informatics, Australia

Tine Wanning, National Museum of Denmark

Michael J. Witbrock, Carnegie Mellon University

Keith Yarwood, SunSoft

Jakob Nielsen

1. Defining Hypertext, Hypermedia, and Multimedia

The simplest way to define hypertext is to contrast it with traditional text like this book. All traditional text, whether in printed form or in computer files, is *sequential,* meaning that there is a single linear sequence defining the order in which the text is to be read. First you read page one. Then you read page two. Then you read page three. And you don't have to be much of a mathematician to generalize the formula which determines what page to read next.

Hypertext is *nonsequential;* there is no single order that determines the sequence in which the text is to be read. Figure 1.1 gives an example. Assume that you start by reading the piece of text marked **A**. Instead of a single next place to go, this hypertext structure has three options for the reader: Go to **B**, **D**, or **E**. Assuming that you decide to go to **B**, you can then decide to go to **C** or to **E**, and from **E** you can go to **D**. Since it was also possible for you to go directly from **A** to **D**, this example shows that there may be several different paths that

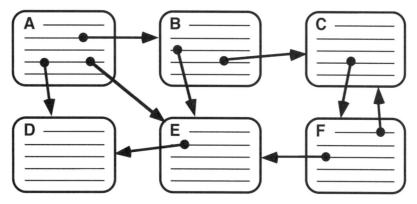

Figure 1.1. *Simplified view of a small hypertext structure having six nodes and nine links.*

connect two elements in a hypertext structure.

Hypertext presents several different options to the readers, and the *individual* reader determines which of them to follow *at the time* of reading the text. This means that the author of the text has set up a number of alternatives for readers to explore rather than a single stream of information.

The same is true of footnotes in traditional printed texts, since readers have to determine upon reaching the footnote marker[1] whether to continue reading the primary stream of text or to branch off to pursue the footnote. Therefore hypertext is sometimes called the "generalized footnote." Another printed form with access structures similar to hypertext is the encyclopedia with its many cross-references.

As can be seen from Figure 1.1, hypertext consists of interlinked pieces of text (or other information). These pieces are illustrated as computer screens in Figure 1.1, but they can also be scrolling windows, files, or smaller bits of information. Each unit of information is called a *node*. Whatever the grain size of these nodes, each of them may have pointers to other units, and these pointers are called *links*. The number of links is normally not fixed in advance but will depend on the content of each node. Some nodes are related to many others and will therefore have many links, while other nodes serve only as destinations for links but have no outgoing links of their own. Sometimes such nodes without further links are called leaf nodes.

Figure 1.1 also shows that the entire hypertext structure forms a network of nodes and links. Readers move about this network in an activity that is often referred to as browsing or navigating, rather than just "reading," to emphasize that users must actively determine the order in which they read the nodes.

A hypertext link connects two nodes and is normally directed in the sense that it points from one node (called the *anchor* node) to another (called the *destination* node). Hypertext links are frequently associated with specific parts of the nodes they connect rather than with the nodes as a whole. In the example in Figure 1.1, we see that the links are anchored at specific locations in the departure node while their destinations are the entire arrival node. A typical application of this feature is to have a link anchored at a certain word in the departure node and then let the user activate the link by clicking on that word.

---

[1] I guess you decided to *read* the footnote this time. But you could as easily have skipped it.

When users follow the links around the hypertext network, they will often have a need to return to some previously visited node. Most hypertext systems support this through a *backtrack* facility. Assume that we are currently located in node **D** in Figure 1.1. If we had arrived at this node via the path **A**→**B**→**E**→**D**, then the backtrack command would take us to node **E** the first time it was issued. A second backtrack command would then take us further back along our path to node **B**. If, on the other hand, we had jumped directly from node **A** to node **D**, then issuing the backtrack command at node **D** would take us to node **A** since that would then be where we came from. This example shows that backtracking is just as dependent on the individual user's movement as is the order in which the nodes were visited in the first place.

Narrower Definitions of Hypertext

Since hypertext has become so popular in recent years, much rides on the exact definition of what constitutes hypertext. Many products are advertised as hypertext without being so according to the common definition presented above. Additionally, many products that are hypertext according to this definition lack important features which might be included in a narrower definition of hypertext.

For example, Frank Halasz from Xerox has put forward the view that a true hypertext system should include an explicit representation of the network structure in its user interface. As shown in Figure 1.1, *any* hypertext will form a network of nodes and links, but in most current systems that network is only present inside the computer. At any given time the user sees only the current node and the links leading out from that node; it is up to the user's imagination to picture how the entire network is structured.

Halasz wants to give the user a dynamic overview showing the structure of this network. Very few current hypertext systems provide such diagrams.[2] The reason the overview diagram needs to be dynamic is that it is normally impossible to draw a graphic representation of the entire hypertext on a computer screen since a hypertext typically contains thousands of nodes. Instead the diagram is displayed in detail only for the local neighborhood surrounding the user's current location, which is often highlighted on the

---

[2] Halasz's own system, NoteCards, is one of the few exceptions. It is discussed further in Chapter 3.

diagram. The various ways of providing an overview are discussed in further detail in Chapter 9.

Almost all current hypertext systems are limited to providing one-directional links like the ones shown in Figure 1.1. This means that the system can show the user the links that have the current node as their departure point but not the ones that have it as their arrival point. In other words, the system will tell you where you can go next but not in what alternative ways you might have arrived at where you are now.

K. Eric Drexler has advocated the use of bidirectional links in hypertext, meaning that the system should also be able to display a list of incoming links. From a computer science perspective it would be almost a trivial task to implement such a feature, but almost none of the current hypertext systems do so.[3]

One example came from Intermedia, which did support bidirectional links. A hypertext structure on Chinese poetry [Kahn 1989b] had links from each poem to the references to those anthologies where it has been reprinted and/or translated. This set-up automatically ensured that each listing for an anthology or a translator had a complete set of links pointing to occurrences of the relevant poems in the Intermedia hypertext.

Drexler has also stated the need for supporting links across various forms of computer network such as local area networks (LANs) and international networks. This step will become necessary if hypertext is ever going to replace the traditional publishing business, since nobody can have all the world's literature stored on their own local computer no matter how big an optical disk they get. Access to remote databases will become a necessity for many future hypertext applications, but many current hypertext systems are limited to working with data stored on a single personal computer. The main exceptions are the World Wide Web which works across the entire Internet and technical documentation systems like Sun's AnswerBook which work across a corporate network.

Many non-hypertext computer techniques may at least match various aspects of the definition of hypertext, but true hypertext should also make users *feel* that they can move freely through the information, according to their own needs. This feeling is hard to define precisely but certainly implies small overhead with respect to using the computer. This means short response times

---

[3] It would just involve updating two lists instead of one every time a new link was added.

Figure 1.2. *Screen from the* Spaceship Warlock *hypermedia adventure. This game combines detailed graphics with a small amount of animation and recorded sound: appropriate music is played in the background to set the mood and the characters speak. This game has proven so popular that a sequel was released in 1995. Copyright © 1991 by Reactor, reprinted by permission.*

so that the text is on the screen as soon as the user asks for it. Small overhead also requires low cognitive load when navigating, so that users do not have to spend their time wondering what the computer will do or how to get it to do what they want.

When asked whether I would view a certain system as hypertext, I would not rely so much on its specific features, command, or data structures, but more on its user interface "look and feel."

Hypermedia: Multimedia Hypertext

The traditional definition of the term "hypertext" implies that it is a system for dealing with plain text. Since many of the current systems actually also include the possibility for working with graphics and various other media, some people prefer using the term *hypermedia,* to stress the multimedia aspects of their system. Personally, I would like to keep using the traditional term "hypertext" for all systems since there does not seem to be any reason to reserve a special term for text-only systems. Therefore I tend to use the two terms *hypertext* and *hypermedia* interchangeably with a preference to sticking to *hypertext.*

As discussed in the next section, being multimedia is not enough for a program to be hypermedia. But it is possible to use quite extravagant multimedia capabilities to good effect as part of a hypermedia system. For example, the Swedish design company *AVICOM* has designed a hypermedia system for a natural history museum in Stockholm called *Naturens Hus* ("the house of nature"). This system includes the more or less traditional hypermedia linking, e.g., maps of the region with photos of the birds living in various areas with recordings of these birds singing. But the hypermedia system also controls a slide projector projecting an image on the very floor where the user is standing. This technique is used to increase the user's sense of immersion in an environment, for instance by turning the floor blue when the system is discussing a geological period when the entire Stockholm region was under water.

In any case, hypertext is a natural technique for supporting multimedia interfaces since it is based on the interlinking of nodes that may contain different media. Typical media in hypermedia nodes are text, graphics, video, and sound.

Graphics can be either scanned images or object-oriented pictures constructed by some computer graphics algorithm. Graphics can be the main form of information in the system as shown in Figure 1.2, they can be used purely as illustration in a system where the links are restricted to the text, or they can be more actively involved with the hypertext aspects of the hypermedia system by also including anchors for hypertext links.

One example of the use of graphics in a hypertext manner is the Drexel Disk from Drexel University in Pennsylvania [Hewett 1987]. For many years, Drexel has required that all its students own a Macintosh computer. This policy makes it possible for faculty to develop courseware and to know that all their students will be able to run it. It also makes it possible for the university to supply introductory information for the freshmen in a hypertext format on the so-called Drexel Disk. This disk contains a lot of information about the university which is interlinked in a hypertext manner. One of the nodes of information is the campus map shown in Figure 1.3.

Whenever the rest of the hypertext mentions some university building, the Drexel Disk allows the student to take a hypertext jump to the campus map to see the location of that building. The campus map also includes links from the individual buildings to descriptions of the departments and the other facilities they house.

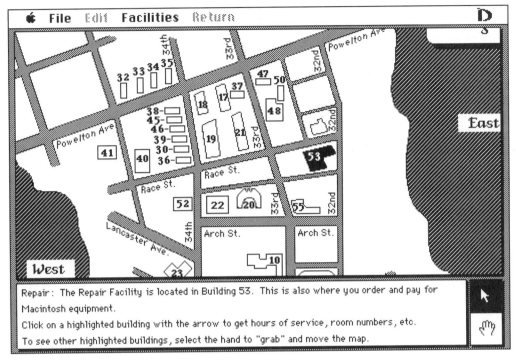

Figure 1.3. *The campus map from the Drexel Disk. Copyright © 1989 by Thomas T. Hewett, reprinted with permission.*

Various moving images in the form of video or animations are also common data types in hypermedia nodes. Figure 1.4 shows an example of use of video to achieve an added sense of realism in the very popular adventure game Myst. Figure 1.5 shows the use of animation to illustrate a movement that might otherwise be very hard to visualize.

One difficulty with representing video in hypertext is the question of how to name links. The most traditional solution has been to use plain text as the hypertext anchor leading to the playing of a piece of video, but that is not a very hyper*media*-like choice.

An alternative solution has been developed at the MIT Media Lab by Hans Peter Brøndmo and Glorianna Davenport [Brøndmo and Davenport 1990] for

Figure 1.4. *Screen from the Myst adventure game [Carroll 1994] showing a combination of a video shot of a live actor and a fixed computer-generated background graphic. Screen shot from Myst® CD-ROM computer game: game and screen shot protected by Copyright © 1993 by Cyan,® all rights reserved, reprinted by permission.*

their *Elastic Charles* project.[4] They represent the link to a video clip by a miniaturized version of the clip or a part of it. Thus their anchors are actually small moving images in their own right called *micons* (moving icons), since users are often able to recognize a piece of film by viewing the movements it contains.

The use of sound in hypertext introduces yet another linkage problem [Catlin and Smith 1988]. It is fairly easy to have a sound as the destination for a

---

[4] The *Elastic Charles* is a hypermedia "magazine" about the Charles River (in Boston/Cambridge); it interconnects several videos about the river filmed by MIT students.

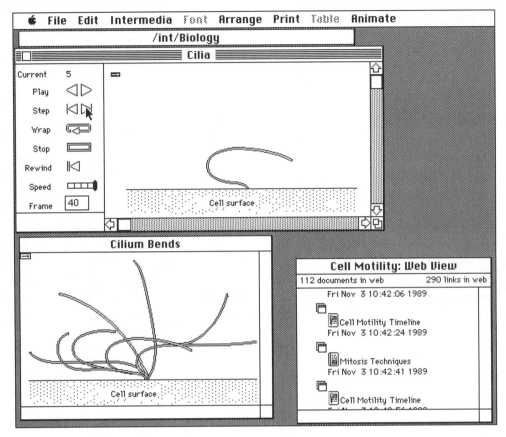

Figure 1.5. *The document "Cilia" (upper left) was created using InterPlay, Intermedia's two-dimensional animation editor. When a link is followed to this document, the animation is automatically triggered to illustrate the movements of the cilia. © 1989 Brown University, reprinted with permission.*

hypertext link; the sound plays when the anchor is activated. But in many applications one also wants to anchor departure points in the sound itself.[5]

For example, some sound-based hypermedia systems like the one shown in Figure 1.6 are used for teaching music theory and link various CD records

---

[5] If the application domain allows a design with unanchored links, a sound-based hypertext can be accessed without any visual support. For example, user navigation could be based on the types of the links from each node rather than their anchor points, allowing the user to activate a link by asking for the link of the desired type [Arons 1991].

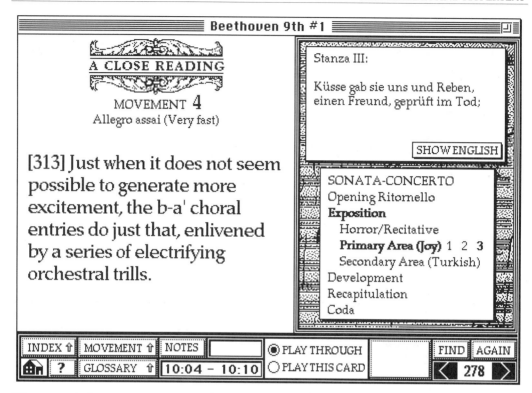

Figure 1.6. *Screen from the hypermedia version of Beethoven's 9th Symphony with comments by Robert Winter published by The Voyager Company, Copyright © 1989 by The Voyager Company, reprinted by permission.*

containing famous works of music to texts analyzing details of the music. As long as the user is satisfied with playing the music, the system can synchronize the display of explanatory text and the text of any vocals.

If the user wants to jump around in the music, the interface design issues become more problematic, and it would be very difficult for the user to annotate a specific piece of music directly. It is unfortunately impossible simply to click on the sound in the same way as one can click on a word or a graphic image. Instead one has to provide the user with a *visual surrogate* representation of the sound on which to click. In the case of music an obvious surrogate would be a picture of the notes of the text of the vocals but for other sounds a less intuitive representation has to be used.

Hypertext is fundamentally different from traditional databases from a user perspective, however. A normal database such as the database of employees in a company has an extremely regular structure defined by a high-level data definition language. All of the data follow this single structure, so we might have ten thousand employee records all of which have the same fields for name, address, salary, telephone extension, etc.

Hypertext and Regular Computer Applications

Upon reading the definition of hypertext in the beginning of this chapter, readers with a training in computer science might have thought, "This is just databases." It is true that hypertext has many similarities to databases, and one does need some form of database at the bottom of a hypertext system actually to store and retrieve the text and other media contained in the nodes.

A hypertext information base has no central definition and no regular structure. We might still have ten thousand nodes in case we have a hypertext for the employees of a company. But now some of the nodes are very extensive, with lots of information, and others are relatively sparse. Some employees may work on projects with co-workers in other divisions, and might therefore have added links from the description of their work to the nodes for those other employees. In general, the structure of a hypertext network is defined as a union of the local decisions made in building each of the individual nodes and links. Each link is put in because it makes sense in terms of the semantic contents of the two nodes it connects and not because of some global decision. This means that a hypertext has great flexibility, which is normally an advantage but can also be a disadvantage.

Another traditional computer application with similarities to hypertext is outliner programs like More. Outliners are normally used to construct the outlines of reports or presentations in a hierarchical manner. They are similar to hypertext in that they connect units of text in a user-defined format. But that format is typically restricted to a strict hierarchy. A chapter heading in an outliner can be viewed as having pointers to the section headings it contains, and these section headings again have pointers to the headings of the subsections they contain. But a chapter heading in an outliner cannot have a pointer to a subsection in *another* chapter even though that subsection may be very relevant to its topic. That limitation is why outliners are not hypertext.

In a similar way, a multiwindow system is also not necessarily hypertext. In fact, some hypertext systems like HyperCard and KMS are not window-based

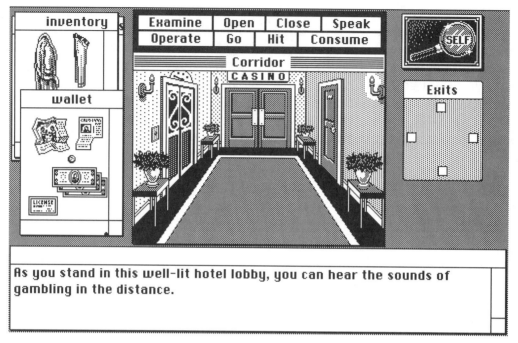

Figure 1.7. *A situation from the* Déjà Vu II: Lost in Las Vegas *graphic adventure game, which is very similar to hypertext in its user interface. Notice how the user can move to other locations in the game by clicking in a first-person navigational view of the corridor (as well as the "Exits" explicit menu of links). Copyright © 1988 by ICOM Simulations, Inc., reprinted with permission.*

at all. A traditional multiwindow editor may allow users to move among several units of information and compare them on the screen, but the users *themselves* must call up the extra windows. The basic concept of hypertext implies that the computer finds the information for the user.

A class of computer systems that are indeed navigation based are adventure games (see the examples in Figures 1.2, 1.4, and 1.7). They can be viewed as hypertext according to some definitions and in a few cases people have actually implemented an adventure game in a hypertext system. I will not classify adventure games as hypertext because they are fundamentally based on making it difficult for the user to navigate to the desired destination and they often hide the clues for the links to other locations in the information space. This is in complete contrast to the requirement for low cognitive overhead in a hypertext user interface.

As mentioned, even though many hypertext systems are also hypermedia systems and include many multimedia effects, the fact that a system is multimedia-based does not make it hypertext. The mixture of text and graphics is not enough in itself. Many multimedia systems are based mostly on displaying various film clips to a passive user who does not get to navigate an information space. Only when users interactively take control of a set of dynamic links among units of information does a system get to be hypertext. It has been said that the difference between multimedia and hypermedia is similar to that between watching a travel film and being a tourist yourself.

One type of multimedia system that is often confused with hypermedia is interactive video. Again, it is certainly possible to use interactive video effects in a hypermedia interface to good effect, but many so-called interactive video systems are not really interactive enough to classify as hypermedia. Nathan Myrhvold, Microsoft's Vice President for advanced technology, calls video on demand "the terminal emulation of the 90s" referring to the way terminal emulators were important applications for early personal computers while holding them back from presenting the advanced user interfaces that became possible with client–server technology.[6] Similarly, video on demand allows users to view movies of their choice (thus adding flexibility compared to a standard cable TV subscription) but limits their experience to the same linear flow of material that characterizes all traditional TV and film productions.

The real issue here is the extent to which the user is allowed to determine the activities of the system. Many interactive video systems reduce the user to the role of a passive television viewer who is only allowed to select video clips from menus. As an example, consider a system that was installed at the THINK exhibition at the IBM Gallery of Science and Art in New York. The system taught various issues surrounding the U.S. Constitution by showing a long alphabetical menu of the issues. The user was limited to selecting an issue from the list, whereupon the system played an appropriate video clip. One of the issues was "piracy," which pointed to a video clip showing, first, traditional

---

[6] This quote from Nathan Myrhvold comes from an interview written by the managing editor of *WIRED* magazine, John Battelle. Interestingly, this article was not published in the printed magazine but only made available through its Internet version. The Wired story on Microsoft can be accessed on the World Wide Web through URL `http://www.wired.com/Hotwired/microsoft/microsoft.html`

pirates from the eighteenth century and then modern aircraft hijackers. The video explained how the language in the Constitution that was originally intended to fight traditional piracy in international waters has been used in recent years to provide the legal underpinning for attempts to prosecute modern terrorists.

The reason this design is not hypertext is that the user had no way to interact with the video clip once it started playing. In other words, the granularity of the interaction was too coarse to provide the user with the feeling of being in control and able to explore an information space. A true hypertext system would have contained links from the overview video to supporting material about the extent of the piracy problem when the Constitution was framed, how pirates were caught and prosecuted, the growth of modern terrorism, and actual legal actions against those terrorists who have been caught.

Of course, it may very well be that the non-hypermedia interactive video interface is the correct solution for a system to teach the U.S. Constitution in a public exhibit space in Manhattan. It is likely that most gallery visitors had a limited interest in the issues and wanted only to see that an IBM screen can display nice color video under computer control. Allowing users more navigational options would have led to a more complicated interface than simply having users select an issue from a long alphabetical list. So perhaps a plain interactive video system was indeed a better design than a real hypermedia system. Even though hypertext is great, it is not a panacea.

The Hype about Hypertext

There is no doubt that hypertext has been "hyped" to a great extent in recent years. Some of the hype in certain advertisements may be overdone but I personally agree that there are good reasons to believe that hypertext is something special.

One of the most important advantages of hypertext is that it is a method for integrating three technologies and industries that have been separate until recently: publishing, computing, and broadcasting in the form of television and film. There have been a few non-hypertext attempts to mix methods among these three industries, such as the "publishing" of videotapes or the use of computing in the editorial departments of newspapers. But, in general, each of the three industries continued with business as usual until the recent "convergence" craze, which has led to mergers of several companies from the three underlying industries.

Hypertext provides the opportunity to publish information structures to the general public in much the same way as books or newspapers are currently published. These information structures would be based primarily on moving images, in the tradition of the film and animation industries, and would be under computer control to allow user interaction.

As an example, consider the NewsPeek system developed at the MIT Media Lab under the direction of Walter Bender. NewsPeek watches the nightly television news for you and records those parts that it knows are of interest to you. You can then browse through the news structures generated by NewsPeek at your convenience.

Systems like NewsPeek can turn the tables of the power structure in journalism. Until now, the general public has been on the bottom of a pyramid populated by journalists and editors, who decide what individual readers and viewers should spend their time on. Computer-based news systems put the power in the hands of the individuals. If you watch one hour of television news every night, you will spend more than twenty thousand hours on this one activity over your lifetime. A computer technology that saves you half of this time is equivalent to a medical breakthrough increasing your life expectancy by two years.

NewsPeek-like systems can gather news from many sources such as broadcast and cable television and various newswire services. They can then integrate this news in a hypertext structure with links among detailed news stories downloaded from *The New York Times*, tables from the Dow Jones service, and film clips from the TV. If a newswire service mentions a topic not covered on the TV news, your computer might link to illustrations it generates itself from a stock of illustrations, for instance maps of the world, stored on a CD-ROM.

All of this news is presented in a format edited by your own computer to match exactly your interests and preferences. For example, the computer might know that you were going on a business trip to Brussels because it had taken care of your airline reservations. It would then give news stories from Belgium higher priority than stories from other countries, and it would present a story about, say, a forecast for a snowstorm in the Brussels area as "front page" material on your personal newspaper.

Scenarios like this are an example of another reason many computer scientists are excited about the potential inherent in hypertext. Even more modest applications of hypertext show that hypertext is fundamentally a *computer* phenomenon, as observed by Gilbert Cockton from Glasgow University. Hypertext can only be done on a computer, whereas most other current applications of computers might just as well be done by hand. You can get only so excited about designing yet another word processor or accounting program, since you are fundamentally doing nothing except making slight improvements to activities that have been conducted almost as well without computers in the past. Hypertext applications, in contrast, make sense only if you have a computer. Except perhaps for presidents, *nobody* gets a personalized newspaper now, but *everybody* will when hypertext gets more established.

The reason people are getting excited about hypertext *now* even though the concept dates back to 1945 is that it can now be implemented with commercially used technology. Many hypertext systems run on small standard Windows machines with no more than 8 MB RAM which have been sold by the millions. Others require high-bandwidth Internet access and/or high-end workstations (which are getting fairly widely used in business), but standard home computers can support a wide range of hypermedia needs.

The computer revolution has resulted in an information explosion where managers risk drowning in detailed data and scientists are buried under a mountain of technical reports. The computer might solve these problems by using artificial intelligence (AI) to manage the complexity of modern society and find exactly those pieces of information that its human user needs. The sad truth is that AI does not have anything like the abilities needed to do this well, and hypertext is also exciting because it is an interaction form relying on *natural* intelligence to address these problems.

A hypertext system works in collaboration with the user, who has the intelligence to understand the semantic contents of the various nodes and determine which of its outgoing links to follow. As an example, Gerri Peper and colleagues from IBM tried implementing a system to support computer network maintenance in two different versions, an expert system and a hypertext system [Peper et al. 1989]. Their experiments are discussed in further detail in Chapter 10, but briefly the result was that the two systems scored about the same on various measures of efficiency but the hypertext system won in the overall comparison because the operators could easily find out how to update the information it contained. In the expert system, the information was coded in a machine-readable knowledge base and required the assistance of special "knowledge engineers" for updates.

A hypertext is under the control of the user, who can customize it by adding links and annotations. Most other computer systems are monolithic and can be modified only by specialists.

Finally, a very important reason for being enthusiastic about hypertext is that it has the potential to save great amounts of money in certain applications. For example, the documentation for an F-18 fighter aircraft is 300,000 pages big [Ventura 1988] and requires 68 cubic feet of storage space when printed on paper. This statistic should be compared with the 0.04 cubic feet the same information takes up when stored on a CD-ROM hypertext.

Not only does hypertext save on the storage space, it also saves on the cost of updating the information. The 300,000 pages of F-18 documentation is not a fixed set of information but changes constantly. Imagine the mailing costs involved in shipping updates to Air Force bases around the world by classified courier service. And imagine the scenes, right out of a slapstick comedy, when every single updated page has to be inserted in the right location in the right binder. Instead, one can just press a new CD-ROM and tell people to destroy the old one.

These savings are one important reason many computer manufacturers now prefer to ship technical documentation in hypertext format. Digital Equipment Corporation has been shipping an online documentation system called BookReader with the full documentation set for VAX/VMS on a CD-ROM since 1989, Hewlett-Packard has a project called LaserROM to convert to a few CD-ROMs the 8,000 *different* documents they ship to their customers every year [Rafeld 1988], Sun customers use AnswerBook as their main way of accessing the online documentation, and some Microsoft is exclusively available in hypertext form and has been eliminated from the printed manuals.

2.   An Example of a Hypertext System

This chapter gives eleven screen shots from a hypertext system I have developed using HyperCard as an implementation tool.[1]

Figure 2.1 is the opening screen of the hypertext system. It includes buttons for getting help and other general information and an option to reset the recorded user history. This screen serves as the "landmark" of the hypertext structure and is accessible from throughout the system by clicking on the "Front cover" icon.

The most prominent graphic on this screen is a picture of a book which is intended to convey a general sense of the nature of the data in this information base. If the user clicks on the name of the author of the book, a new screen will be displayed containing a digitized photo of the author. This facility was of help in the iterative design of this system, since people who had downloaded earlier versions from various computer network services could easily locate the author by sight at conferences to pass on their comments.

The upper right-hand corner of the screen displays a timestamp informing us about the time since we last visited this node in the hypertext system. Since this is the front cover of the book, it thereby also tells us the time since we last used this system.

In this demonstration example, we will assume that we click on the title of the book or on the book cover itself. This action will display Figure 2.2 since the picture of the book itself is the anchor for opening the book. User studies indicate that the use of a book cover and its title as a hypertext anchor is fairly unintuitive for many users. They quickly understand clicking on icons and

---

[1] This chapter is a modified version of parts of my paper "The art of navigating through hypertext," which appeared in *Communications of the ACM* **33**, 3 (March 1990), pp. 296–310, Copyright © 1990 by the Association for Computing Machinery, reprinted with permission.

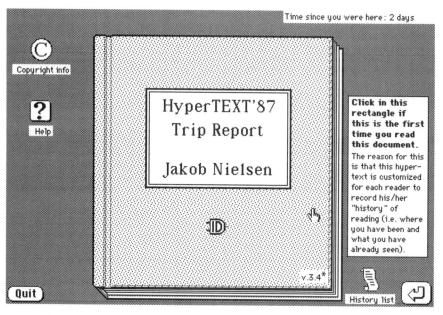

Figure 2.1. *The "home page" front cover node for the hypertext system.*

framed words (like "Quit" in this screen design) but often have to be encouraged to click on a general graphics picture having no specific target indicated. In this case, a special problem is that the normal way to open a book cover is to pull it *up*, while the mechanics of mouse-operated pointers require a push *down*. Because of this observation, the help screen (not shown here) was changed to state explicitly that the book was opened by clicking on it.

Figure 2.2 is the global overview diagram of the contents of the hypertext structure. It serves as a two-dimensional table of contents. The two-dimensional structure was chosen since there is by definition no linear structure of a hypertext: There is no "first" chapter. The layout of the items is intended to suggest their relation: i.e., "Systems" and "Applications" are related, whereas "Definition of 'hypertext'" is a subissue of "Research issues." "Definition of 'hypertext'" is represented directly on the overview map because it is an especially important node in the hypertext network. Users can access the definition node directly throughout the system since the screens of the main text (Figure 2.4 etc.) include this global overview diagram as an active set of hypertext anchors.

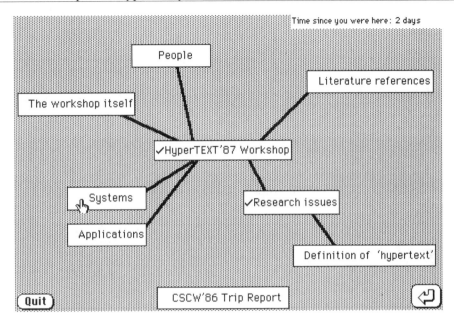

Figure 2.2. *High-level overview diagram.*

The lines between the items are also intended to give an indication of how they are related, since they show that "HyperTEXT'87 Workshop" is the central topic whereas "CSCW'86 Trip Report" is a disconnected topic. In fact, there are hypertext links from some of the nodes in the Hypertext'87 report to some of the nodes in the CSCW'86 report, but these links were judged to be of minor importance and are therefore not represented in this overview diagram.

Checkmarks indicate the nodes that we have visited in previous use of the system (in this case "Research issues").

The more fine-grained overview diagram of hypertext nodes in Figure 2.3 is the local diagram associated with the subject "Hypertext systems," which was chosen from the global overview diagram in Figure 2.2. We click on "Classification of hypertext systems" to display Figure 2.4.

We note that the timestamp in the upper right-hand corner of the screen states that we have "NEVER" been here before. This timestamp is a general facility of the system intended to help readers recognize information they have already seen without having to wonder whether they actually have seen it before.

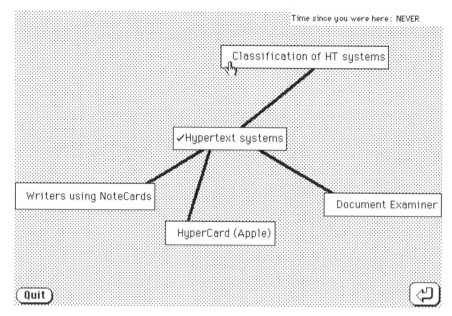

Figure 2.3. *Detailed overview diagram.*

The local overview diagrams have a lighter background color than the global diagram in Figure 2.2. Almost no users notice this difference because they do not see the two colors simultaneously, but the same colors are consistently used in the small-scale overview diagrams in the main text, as shown in Figure 2.4, where they are more noticeable.

Figure 2.4 is a page showing the standard design of the main text of this hypertext. Since this node has more text than can be seen on this one screen, the system follows a book metaphor in allowing readers to page forward to the remaining text by clicking on the right arrow shown at the lower right corner of the book page. Screens other than the first page of a node will also display a left arrow, which pages backward.

The screen design includes small copies of the overview diagrams. All the screens in the main text part of the hypertext system show the same global diagrams; they then display the appropriate local diagram containing the current node. The overview diagrams are active since both of them highlight the user's current location, and they also serve as hypertext anchors. Clicks in the global diagram jump to the corresponding local diagram (e.g., to Figure 2.3

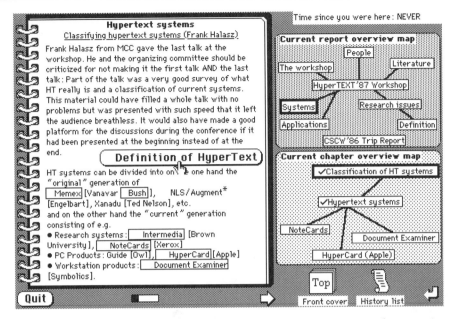

Figure 2.4. *A screen showing a page of information with two levels of overview diagrams. One of the hypertext anchors, "Definition of Hypertext," has been given special status by the layout, so users will often click on it first.*

if "Systems" is clicked), and clicks in the local diagram jump directly to the corresponding node.

On this screen it would be a "good thing" to start by reading the definition of the word hypertext, so we click on that button, which displays Figure 2.5. In general, a problem with hypertext is that it destroys the authority of the author to determine which sections readers need to read first, but in this case we have at least hinted at the recommended reading order by making the anchor for the definition especially prominent.

Some people may think that the need to guide the reader on this screen is an indication that the whole notion of nonsequential text is flawed. If one needs to make certain buttons very large and graphically attractive in order to induce readers to select them first, why bother giving any options at all? The reason is that there are several different classes of readers. Some readers may be experts in the domain of the information base and will know how to navigate it to find the information of specific interest to them. They can certainly do so even though the author has made certain anchors prominent, since readers

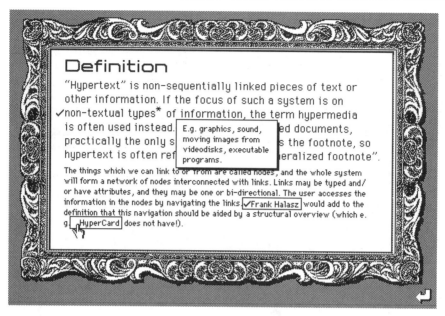

Figure 2.5. *A node with a different graphic design to indicate its status as different from the majority of information in the system.*

retain complete freedom of movement. Other readers, however, may be novices who are more in need of guidance. Instead of forcing people to read in certain ways, our hypertext design allows individual readers to customize their reading to their individual needs and learning styles. But since novices do not yet know the structure of the information space and may have difficulties in understanding the meaning of the terminology, I feel that it is reasonable for the author to provide them with hints.

The graphic design of Figure 2.5 is intended to emphasize its landmark status and to differentiate it from the text of the other nodes. The definition is accessible from all the screens of the main text through its anchor in the global overview diagram.

Just before the screen dump shown here was taken, we clicked on the hypertext anchor "non-textual types" to get the small pop-up annotation giving examples of these types. The pop-up will go away when we click on it or when we leave the screen to go elsewhere. Hypertext anchors for pop-ups are marked on the screen by a raised asterisk, which is intended to invoke the notion of a footnote from traditional books. The asterisk is a different notation

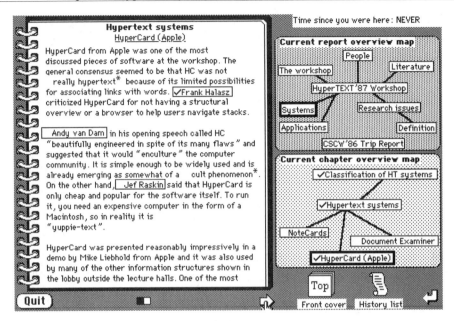

Figure 2.6. *One of the shorter regular hypertext nodes.*

from the boxes used for anchors for hypertext links which jump the user to a new screen; the difference helps users predict the actions of the system in response to their clicks. Versions 1 and 2 of this system had the same box notation for both kinds of link, and users found it very frustrating not to know in advance whether a click would just pop up a small annotation or take them to an entirely different context.

After we clicked on the anchor for the pop-up annotation, the system automatically put a checkmark in front of it to help us remember that we have already seen this annotation if we return to this page later. The system has also put in a checkmark at the anchor marked "Frank Halasz," since we have also seen the destination for that link (it is the screen in Figure 2.4). So let us click on "HyperCard" instead to go to Figure 2.6.

When we arrive at this node, the system puts checkmarks at the hypertext anchors for "Frank Halasz" and "Classification of HT systems," since we have visited the destinations for those links already.

That this screen is part of the node describing Apple's HyperCard system can be seen from the highlighting of that node in the local overview diagram and also by the two headings inside the picture of the book page. The boldfaced heading describes the location in the global overview diagram, and the underlined heading describes the location in the local overview diagram. These two headings are automatically concatenated by the system to form a text string referring to a node in the history list shown in Figure 2.10. In a preliminary design of these headings, the picture of the book page was smaller and the headings were placed outside the book page to indicate that the headings were a kind of computer-generated "state information" and not part of the running text. Even though the early design placed the headings in the same physical location on the screen as the current design, test users did not view the text outside the book page as being a label for the contents of the book page. This failure can be explained by the *gestalt* law of closure, which states that things that are within the same closed region are seen as corresponding [Nielsen 1993a (section 5.1)]. The solution was simply to move the headings into the closure of a larger book page.

The little black and white boxes below the book page form a scroll bar that indicates two things: our relative location within the current node and the size of the node. The length of the scroll bar is proportional to the number of pages in the node, so the scroll bar in Figure 2.4 is longer than the scroll bar in Figure 2.6 because the node visited in Figure 2.4 is bigger than the node we are visiting here. Proportional scroll bars make it possible always to have the "thumb" of the scroll bar (the black box) be the same size, corresponding to the fact that the book pages have a fixed size. The relative size of the thumb compared to the entire scroll bar indicates the proportion of the total text that the user is currently seeing.

The black box indicates our relative position within the node in an analog format. An alternative would have been a digital format (e.g., "page 1 of 2"), but the scroll bar design can also be used as an anchor for direct hypertext jumps to the other pages within the node: When the user clicks in the scroll bar, the system jumps to the page in the node that has the relative location that corresponds to the click.

Here, we see that the current node is quite small and that we are on its first page, so we might decide to look at the rest of the node by clicking on the "right arrow" button. The next page looks similar to this one except that it has a "left arrow" button instead of a "right arrow" button, so it is not shown here. The next page has a hypertext reference to "Vannevar Bush," which we follow to get a reference to this famous author.

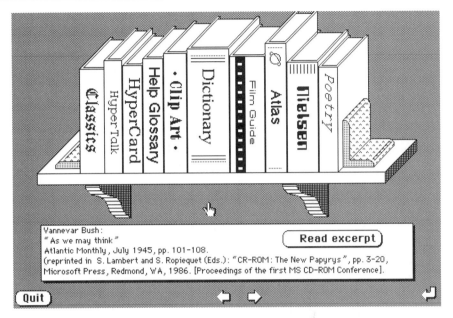

Figure 2.7. *A node from the bibliography section of the hypertext.*

As indicated by the drastically different graphic design, the screen in Figure 2.7 is part of the literature reference section of the information space. The left and right arrows are for moving alphabetically through the reference list. The alphabetical order of authors' last names is an access mechanism with very low semantic meaning, so to utilize hypertext principles, the books on the bookshelf have been designed as hypertext anchors to help users discover literature references. For instance, by clicking on the book marked "Poetry" we can jump to a literature reference about the use of hypertext for teaching poetry.

Some of the book buttons are linked to multiple destinations, one of which is chosen by random. For example, the book marked "Classics" will jump to one of the references considered to be classics in the hypertext field. This randomness was inspired by the "Something Else" feature in the Drexel Disk [Hewett 1987] and should only be used in situations where users are exploring the information space in a browsing mode. In most situations, predictability would of course be the preferred interaction characteristic, and I actually had one user complain that he had spent almost an hour experimenting with the book buttons in a vain attempt to discover the algorithm used to select their

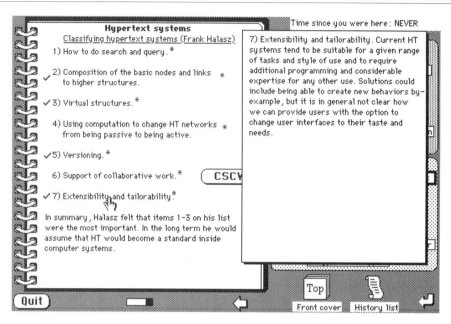

Figure 2.8. *A list of items, each linked to a pop-up node of additional text. Note how the checkmarks make it easy for the user to see what items have already been explored.*

destination. This user was a computer scientist, however, and it is likely that more ordinary users would ascribe the system's behavior to "magic" and not worry too much about it. I do not have enough evidence from my usability studies to decide this design issue for certain; a more detailed study of the effects of randomness in user interfaces would be required. My intuition based on this limited experience suggests that it would actually be better to employ a predictable design. One way of doing so would be to use the Intermedia [Yankelovich et al. 1988a] technique of popping up a menu listing the possible destinations whenever the user activated an anchor linked to multiple destinations.

From the screen in Figure 2.7 we could click on the "Read excerpt" button to see some quotes from the original article by Vannevar Bush. Following automated cross-references to other articles is one of the great benefits of hypertext, but we will not do so in this example for copyright reasons. The copyright problem is exactly one of the worst socioeconomic barriers to realizing the full potential of hypertext. Instead we click several times on the

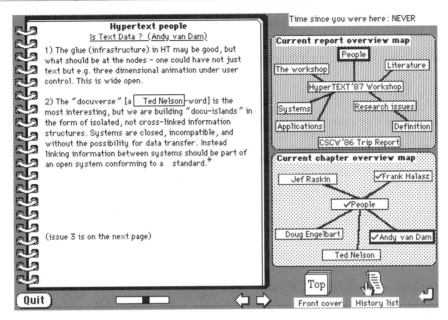

Figure 2.9. *A screen that indicates the problem with context-in-the-small since the user cannot read issue 3 without having to turn the page.*

backtrack ("return") arrow in the lower right corner of the screen, backtracking through the intervening screens until we return to the screen shown in Figure 2.4.

We have backtracked to the screen shown in Figure 2.4 and from there we have read through the rest of the node, ending up on the screen shown in Figure 2.8. This part of the text contains a list of seven issues that are hypertext anchors for pop-up windows. We have already seen issues 2, 3, and 5 (as indicated by the checkmarks put in by the system) and here we have just clicked on the anchor for issue 7.

We can now read the full text describing issue 7 while still being able to see the list outlining the full set of issues. Because of the small screen, the pop-up unfortunately obscures the overview diagrams, but we can always click on it to make it go away.

To get from Figure 2.8 to Figure 2.9 we have wandered a little bit around the hyperspace and finally happened to click on "People" in the global overview diagram and then on "Andy van Dam" in the local overview

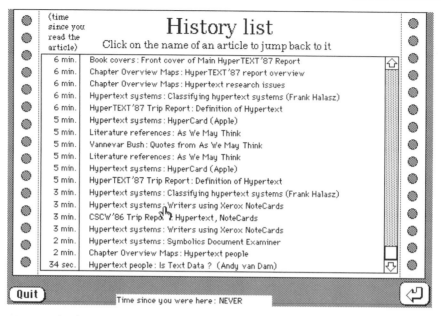

Figure 2.10. *The history list.*

diagram that resulted from that action. We have then read through some of the pages in the node until we came to this list of hypertext research issues.

This design has some problems with "context-in-the-small" since not all the issues can be listed on the same screen. All the text for issue 3 had to be moved to the next page to avoid breaking it up and getting even worse context-in-the-small problems. Originally this screen did not have the extra line "(issue 3 is on the next page)" but usability testing indicated the need for this continuation notice, as many users would otherwise transfer their intuitions from printed books and assume that a screen with a blank bottom half was the end of the current chapter.

From this screen we decide that we do not want to read about Andy van Dam any more but want to return to one of the earlier nodes which we happened upon in our earlier browsing. To do so, we click on the "History list" button.

The history list in Figure 2.10 is a sequential listing of all the nodes we have visited in the hypertext. Each node we have visited is represented on the list, once for every time we have visited it, thus making the list a truly linear mapping of our path through the nodes. For each visit to a node, the history

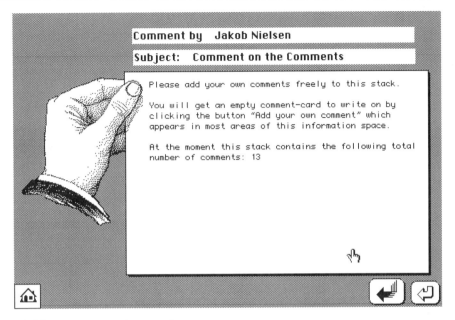

Figure 2.11. *An annotation node.*

list also indicates the time since that visit, because our understanding of different parts of the list will depend quite a lot on whether it shows nodes we have just visited, nodes we visited a few hours ago, or nodes we visited some days (or perhaps years) ago.

Here we could click on the line listing a node to return to it, but we will not do so since this figure concludes the demonstration guided tour of the system.

The first version of this hypertext system allowed readers to add their own annotations to the primary text. Figure 2.11 shows how these annotation pages looked. The graphic design is intended to convey the impression that this is some short added material separate from the main report. A different typeface is used to indicate that the annotations normally will have been written by people other than the author of the main hypertext.

Since a single node in the hypertext could have several associated annotations, a user asking to read annotations would first be taken to a screen showing a menu of the annotations for the current node (not shown here). The user could then choose to read an annotation based on the menu's listing of the authors and subjects.

This screen design has two backtrack arrows, since there are presumably two different ways the user might want to return. (This node has no further hypertext jumps available because the system does not provide a facility for adding annotations to the comments themselves.) The standard return arrow performs the standard backtrack function of returning the user to the departure point for the previous hypertext jump, which in this case is the menu of annotations. An extra arrow to the left of the standard return arrow is an "express return," which returns readers directly to the location from which they jumped to the annotation menu, thus providing a shortcut through the straight backtrack path. In my usability studies, however, almost no test users understood this facility.

3.   The History of Hypertext

Hypertext has a surprisingly rich history compared to most phenomena in the personal computer industry, especially considering that most people had not heard of it until a few years ago.[1] Table 3.1 gives an overview of the history of hypertext; the major events are discussed in more detail in this chapter.

Memex (1945)

Vannevar Bush (1890–1974) is normally considered the "grandfather" of hypertext, since he proposed a system we would now describe as a hypertext system as long ago as 1945. This system, the Memex ("memory extender"), was never implemented, however, but was only described in theory in Bush's papers.

Bush actually developed some of his ideas for the Memex in 1932 and 1933 and finally wrote a draft paper on it in 1939. For various reasons [Nyce and Kahn 1989, 1991] this manuscript was not published until 1945, when it appeared in the *Atlantic Monthly* under the title "As We May Think."

Bush described the Memex as "a sort of mechanized private file and library" and as "a device in which an individual stores his books, records, and communications, and which is mechanized so that it may be consulted with exceeding speed and flexibility." The Memex would store this information on microfilm, which would be kept in the user's desk. This desk was intended to have several microfilm projection positions to enable the user to compare different microfilms, in a manner very similar to the windows that became popular on personal computers more than forty years later.

---

[1] I have been to talks at major conferences where the speakers were ignorant of any hypertext developments preceding the introduction of the WWW.

1945	Vannevar Bush proposes Memex
1965	Ted Nelson coins the word "hypertext"
1967	The Hypertext Editing System and FRESS, Brown University, Andy van Dam
1968	Doug Engelbart demo of NLS system at FJCC
1975	ZOG (now KMS): CMU
1978	Aspen Movie Map, first hypermedia videodisk Andy Lippman, MIT Architecture Machine Group
1984	Filevision from Telos; limited hypermedia database widely available for the Macintosh
1985	Symbolics Document Examiner, Janet Walker
1985	Intermedia, Brown University, Norman Meyrowitz
1986	OWL introduces Guide, first widely available hypertext
1987	Apple introduces HyperCard, Bill Atkinson
1987	Hypertext'87 Workshop, North Carolina
1991	World Wide Web at CERN becomes first global hypertext, Tim Berners-Lee
1992	New York Times Book Review cover story on hypertext fiction
1993	Mosaic anointed Internet killer app, National Center for Supercomputing Applications
1993	A Hard Day's Night becomes the first full-length feature film in hypermedia
1993	Hypermedia encyclopedias sell more copies than print encyclopedias

Table 3.1. *Overview of the history of hypertext*

The Memex would have a scanner to enable the user to input new material, and it would also allow the user to make handwritten marginal notes and comments. But Bush envisaged that

> most of the Memex contents are purchased on microfilm ready for insertion. Books of all sorts, pictures, current periodicals, newspapers, are thus obtained and dropped into place. Business correspondence takes the same path.

Actually we have not yet reached the state of hypertext development where there is a significant amount of preprocessed information for sale that can be integrated with a user's existing hypertext structure.

The main reason Vannevar Bush developed his proposal for the Memex was that he was worried about the explosion of scientific information which made it impossible even for specialists to follow developments in a discipline. Of course, this situation is much worse now, but even in 1945 Bush discussed the need to allow people to find information more easily than was possible on paper. After having described his various ideas for microfilm and projection equipment, he stated that

> All this is conventional, except for the projection forward of present-day mechanisms and gadgetry. It affords an immediate step, however, to associative indexing, the basic idea of which is a provision whereby any item may be caused at will to select immediately and automatically another. This is the essential feature of the memex.[2] The process of tying two items together is the important thing.

Hypertext, in other words!

In addition to the establishment of individual links, Bush wanted the Memex to support the building of trails through the material in the form of a set of links that would combine information of relevance for a specific perspective on a specific topic. He even forecast the establishment of a new profession of "trail blazers,""who find delight in the task of establishing useful trails through the enormous mass of the common record." In current terminology, these trail blazers would be people who add value to published collections of text and other information by providing a web of hypertext links to supplement the basic information. But since we do not even have a market for basic hypertexts yet, we unfortunately have to do without professional trail blazers. Amateur trail blazers have come into existence in recent years in the form of people who list WWW sites they find interesting on their home page.

The building of trails would also be an activity for the ordinary Memex user, and using his microfilm ideas, Bush assumed that such a user might want to photograph a whole trail for friends to put in their Memexes. Again we should note that current technology is not up to Bush's vision, since it is almost impossible to transfer selected subsets of a hypertext structure to another hypertext, especially if the two hypertexts are based on different systems.

---

[2] Bush wrote "memex" with a lowercase m, but since it is now considered the name of a hypertext system, I will write the name "Memex" with an uppercase M.

Vannevar Bush was a famous scientist in his days and was the science advisor to President Roosevelt during the Second World War, when science-based issues like inventing nuclear weapons were of great importance. After "As We May Think" ran in the *Atlantic Monthly*, it caused considerable discussion, and both *Time* and *Life* ran stories on the Memex. *Life* even had an artist draw up illustrations of how the Memex would look and a scenario of its projection positions as the user was completing a link. Doug Engelbart, who later became a pioneer in the development of interactive computing and invented the mouse, got part of his inspiration by reading Bush's article while waiting for a ship home from the Philippines in 1945.

In spite of all this early interest surrounding the Memex it never got built. As hinted above, our current computer technology is still not able to support Bush's vision in its entirety [Meyrowitz 1989b]. We do have computers with most of the Memex functionality but they are based on a completely different technology from the microfilm discussed by Bush.

It is interesting to recall that Bush was one of the pioneering scientists in the development of computer hardware and was famous for such inventions as the MIT Differential Analyzer in 1931. Alan Kay from Apple has suggested that the areas about which we know most may be those where we are most *in*accurate in predicting the future, since we see all the problems inherent in them. Therefore Bush could gladly dream about impossible advances in microfilm technology but he would have been reluctant to publish an article about personal computing since he "knew" that computers were huge things costing millions of dollars.

Augment/NLS (1962–1976)

After Bush's article from 1945, nothing much happened in the hypertext field for twenty years. People were busy improving computers to the point where it would be feasible to use them interactively, but they were so expensive that most funding agencies viewed as completely irresponsible the suggestion that computer resources should be wasted on nonnumeric tasks such as text processing.

In spite of this attitude, Doug Engelbart started work in 1962 on his Augment project, developing computer tools to augment human capabilities and productivity. This project was the first major work in areas like office automation and text processing; in fact the entire project was much more ambitious and broad in scope than the productivity tools we currently enjoy in the professional work environment. The project was conducted at SRI (Stanford Research Institute) with a staff that grew to 45 people.

One part of the Augment project was NLS (for oN-Line System[3]), which had several hypertext features even though it was not developed as a hypertext system. During the Augment project, the researchers stored all their papers, reports, and memos in a shared "journal" facility that enabled them to include cross-references to other work in their own writings. This journal grew to over 100,000 items and is still unique as a hypertext structure for support of real work over an extended time.

In 1968 Engelbart gave a demo of NLS at a special session of the 1968 Fall Joint Computer Conference. Giving this first public demo of many of the basic ideas in interactive computing was something of gamble for the group. Engelbart had to use much of his grant money to obtain special video projectors, run microwave transmission lines between his lab and the conference center, and get other kinds of specialized hardware built, and he would have been in big trouble if the demo had failed. But it worked, and in retrospect spending the money was the right decision; many people have said that it was that demo that got them fired up about inventing interactive computing.

In spite of the successful demo, the government dropped its research support of Engelbart in 1975 at a time when he had more or less invented half the concepts of modern computing.[4] Augment continued as an office automation service but was not really developed further. Engelbart himself is still pushing his original augmentation ideas and a few years ago started the "Bootstrap Project," located at Stanford University.

Xanadu (1965)

The actual word "hypertext" was coined by Ted Nelson in 1965. Nelson was an early hypertext pioneer with his Xanadu system, which he has been developing

---

[3] The reason for the strange acronym was to distinguish the name from that of the oFf-Line System, FLS.

[4] After the Augment project was as good as terminated, several people from Engelbart's staff went on to Xerox PARC and helped invent many of the second half of the concepts of modern computing.

ever since. Parts of Xanadu do work and have been a product from the Xanadu Operating Company since 1990.

The Xanadu *vision* has never been implemented, however, and probably never will be (at least not in the foreseeable future). The basic Xanadu idea is that of a repository for *everything* that anybody has ever written and thereby of a truly universal hypertext. Nelson views hypertext as a literary medium[5] and he believes that "everything is deeply intertwingled" and therefore has to be online together. Robert Glushko [1989b], in contrast, believes that multidocument hypertext is only called for in comparatively few cases where users have explicit tasks that require the combination of information.

If Nelson's vision of having all the world's literature in a single hypertext system is to be fulfilled, it will obviously be impossible to rely on local storage of information in the user's own personal computer. Indeed, Nelson's Xanadu design is based on a combination of back end and local databases, which would enable fast response for most hypertext access since the information used the most by individual users would still be stored on their local computers. Whenever the user activates a link to more exotic information, the front end computer transparently links to the back end repository through the network and retrieves the information.

In Xanadu it is possible to address any substring of any document from any other document. In combination with the distributed storage of information, this capability means that Xanadu includes a scheme for giving a unique address to every single byte in the world if there should be a need for it.

Furthermore, the full Xanadu system will never delete any text, not even when new versions are added to the system, because other readers may have added links to the previous version of the text. This permanent record of all versions makes it possible for other documents to link either with the current version of a document or with a specific version. Frequently one will want to link with the most up-to-date material, as when referring to census statistics or weather forecasts, but in more polemic documents one may want to ensure a reference to a specific version of a position one is arguing against.

The reader of a document linked to a specific version of another document will always have the option of asking the system to display the most current version. This "temporal scrolling" can also be used to show how documents

---

[5] Nelson's main book on hypertext is actually entitled *Literary Machines* (see the section on classics in the bibliography).

have looked in previous versions and can be useful, for instance for version management of software development.

Nelson does realize that this scheme means that billions of new bytes will have to be added to Xanadu every day without the hope of freeing storage by deleting old documents. His comment is, "So what...?" and a reference to the fact that the current load on the telephone system would have been impossible under the traditional technology of human operators connecting every call. The history of computer technology until now does give reason for some optimism with respect to being able to support the Xanadu vision some time in the future.

When everything is online in a single system and when everybody may link with everybody else, there will be tremendous copyright problems if the traditional view of copyright is maintained [Samuelson and Glushko 1991]. Nelson's answer is to abolish the traditional copyright to the extent that information placed in Xanadu will always be available to everybody. This principle may be feasible; the system would still keep track of original authorship and provide royalties to the original author based on the number of bytes seen by each reader.

Publishing an anthology would be a simple matter of creating a new document with some explanatory and combining text and with links to the original documents by other authors who would not need to be contacted for permission. Because of the royalty, everybody would be financially motivated to allow other people to link with their work, since it will be through the links that readers discover material worth reading. Even so, some authors might fear being quoted out of context or having their work misrepresented by other authors. This problem is taken care of in theory in Xanadu because the reader always has the option of asking for the complete text of any document being quoted by a link. In practice, many readers will probably not bother looking at the full text of linked documents, so one might need a mechanism for allowing authors to flag links to their work with an attribute indicating that they believe that the link is misleading.

During some of his early work on Xanadu, Ted Nelson was associated with Brown University (Providence, RI). Since then he has mostly been an independent visionary and author, though he was with Autodesk, Inc. for some time.

Hypertext Editing System (1967) and FRESS (1968)

Even though Xanadu was not even partly implemented until recently, hypertext systems were built at Brown University in the 1960s under the leadership of Andries van Dam. The Hypertext Editing System built in 1967 was the world's first working hypertext system. It ran in a 128K memory partition on a small IBM/360 mainframe and was funded by an IBM research contract.

After the Hypertext Editing System was finished as a research project at Brown University, IBM sold it to the Houston Manned Spacecraft Center, where it was actually used to produce documentation for the Apollo missions.

The second hypertext system was FRESS (File Retrieval and Editing System), which was done at Brown University in 1968 as a follow-up to the Hypertext Editing System and was also implemented on an IBM mainframe. Because of this extremely stable platform, it was actually possible to run a demonstration of this code, more than twenty years old, at the 1989 ACM Hypertext conference.

Both these early hypertext systems had the basic hypertext functionality of linking and jumping to other documents, but most of their user interface was text-based and required indirect user specification of the jumps.

Brown University has been a major player in the hypertext field ever since, with its most prominent effort being the development of the Intermedia system (discussed further later in this chapter).

Aspen Movie Map (1978)

Probably the first hyper*media* system was the *Aspen Movie Map* developed by Andrew Lippman and colleagues at the MIT Architecture Machine Group (which has now merged with other MIT groups to form the Media Lab). Aspen was a surrogate travel application that allowed the user to take a simulated "drive" through the city of Aspen on a computer screen.

The Aspen system was implemented with a set of videodisks containing photographs of all the streets of the city of Aspen, Colorado. Filming was done by mounting four cameras aimed at 90° intervals on a truck that was driven through all the city streets, each camera taking a frame every ten feet (three meters). The hypermedia aspects of the system come from accessing these pictures not as a traditional database ("show me 149 Main Street") but as a linked set of information.

Each photograph was linked to the other relevant photographs a person would see by continuing straight ahead, backing up, or moving to the left or to the right. The user navigated the information space by using a joystick to indicate the desired direction of movement, and the system retrieved the relevant next picture. The resulting feeling was that of driving through the city and being able to turn at will at any intersection. The videodisk player could in theory display the photos as quickly as one frame per 33 millisecond, which would correspond to driving through the streets at 200 mph (330 km/h). To achieve a better simulation of driving, the actual system was slowed down to display successive photos with a speed depending on the user's wishes, but no faster than ten frames/sec., corresponding to a speed of 68 mph (110 km/h).

It was also possible for the user to stop in front of a building and "walk" inside, since many of the buildings in Aspen had been filmed for the videodisk. As a final control, the user could select the time of year for the drive by a "season knob," since the entire town was recorded in both fall and winter.[6] Figures 3.1 and 3.2 show the use of a similar feature in the more recent Ecodisc system. The Ecodisc is an instructional hypertext for learning about ecology by allowing the user to move about a lake and observe its varied habitats [Nielsen 1990e].

The Aspen system used two monitors for its interface, but in a more natural way than the traditional two-screen solution discussed in Chapter 7. One monitor was a regular vertical screen and showed the street images filmed from the truck. This provided users with an *immersive* view of the city and made them feel as if they had entered into the environment. The second screen was horizontal and placed in front of the immersive screen. Used to show a street map, it provided the user with an *overview* of the environment. The user could point to a spot on the map and jump directly to it instead of having to navigate through the streets. The overview map also provided "landmarks" by highlighting the two main streets of the city. This two-screen solution allowed users easily to understand their position relative to these two main streets.

One reason for the availability of funding to build surrogate travel applications in the late 1970s was the successful liberation of hostages from the

---

[6] This concept is somewhat related to the "temporal scrolling" in the Xanadu system described above. But the Aspen season knob is probably easier to understand for users because it relates directly to a well-known concept from the real world even though it provides a functionality that would be impossible in the real world.

Figure 3.1. *View of an area at a lake during the summer from the Ecodisc system. The user can "turn" to look in another direction by clicking the radio buttons in the inner part of the compass rose and can "move" to another location by clicking the arrows in the outer part of the compass rose. Clicking on the snow crystal activates movement in time to the winter view in Figure 3.2. Copyright © 1990 by ESM, Ltd., reprinted by permission.*

Entebbe airport by Israeli troops. Even though these soldiers had never been to Uganda before, they were able to carry through their mission extremely well because they had practiced in a full-scale mockup of the airport that had been built in Israel. Computerized surrogate travel systems might make it possible to train for similar missions in the future without actually having to build entire mockup cities.

It is also possible to imagine that surrogate travel systems like Aspen might be used on a routine basis in the future not just by commando soldiers training for a mission but also by tourists planning their vacations. In the near future, however, the main use of surrogate travel will probably be for educational use; the Palenque system described further in Chapter 4 is a good example.

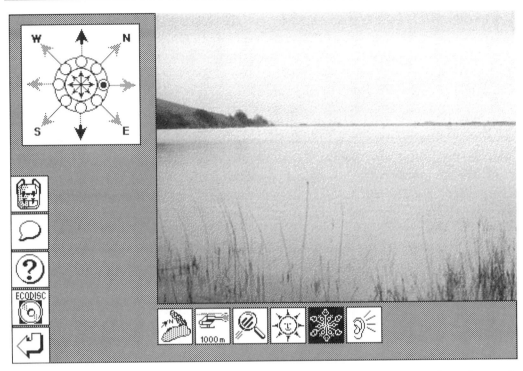

Figure 3.2. *Winter view of the same part of the Ecodisc lake as that shown in Figure 3.1. Unfortunately the two photographs are not perfectly aligned, indicating the need for extreme precision when recording the camera positions and angles in the production of hypermedia with multiple views of the same scenes. Copyright © 1990 by ESM, Ltd., reprinted by permission.*

The Aspen system itself was not really an "application" in the sense that it actually helped anybody accomplish anything. But it was far ahead of its time and of great historical significance in showing the way for future applications. Even now, almost twenty years after the Aspen project was completed, it still stands as one of the more sophisticated hypermedia systems ever built.

As a follow-up to Aspen, the MIT Architecture Machine Group built a more practically oriented system using hypermedia technology to integrate video and computer data. This project was called the *Movie Manual* and involved car and bicycle repair manuals. It is discussed further in Chapter 4.

The *Movie Manual* could use either a regular touch-sensitive computer display or it could project its image on an entire wall in a media room. It had a picture of a car as the table of contents and allowed the user to point to the area that needed repair. The *Movie Manual* would then show its instructions in a mixture of video, annotated images, and ordinary text, allowing the user to customize the screen layout by making the video window larger or smaller. The user could stop the video or play it faster, slower, or backward.

KMS (1983)

KMS probably has the distinction of being the oldest among the currently popular hypertext systems since it is a direct descendant of the ZOG research system developed at Carnegie Mellon University with some development as early as 1972 and as a full-scale project from 1975 [Robertson et al. 1981]. The word ZOG does not mean anything but was chosen because it "is short, easily pronounced and easily remembered." At first, ZOG ran on mainframe computers; it was then moved to PERQ workstations, 28 of which were installed on the aircraft carrier USS *Carl Vinson* in 1983 for a field test of such applications as a maintenance manual for weapons elevators.

KMS is an abbreviation for Knowledge Management System and has been a commercial product since 1983. It runs on Unix workstations and has been used for a large number of applications. KMS is designed to manage fairly large hypertexts with many tens of thousands of nodes and has been designed from the start to work across local area networks.

KMS has a very simple data structure based on a single type of node called the *frame*. A frame can take over the entire workstation screen, but normally the screen is split into two frames, each of which is about as big as a letter-sized page of paper. Users cannot mix small and large nodes and cannot have more than two nodes on the screen at the same time. This might seem limiting at first but proponents of KMS claim that it is much better to use the hypertext navigation mechanism to change the contents of the display than to have to use window management operations to find the desired information among many overlapping windows.

KMS has been optimized for speed of navigation, so the destination frame will normally be displayed "instantaneously" as the user clicks the mouse on an anchor. The time to display a new frame is actually about a half-second, and the designers of KMS claim that there is no real benefit to being faster than that. They tried an experimental system to change the display in 0.05 seconds, but that was so fast that users had trouble noticing whether or not the screen had changed.

If an item on the screen is not linked to another node, then clicking on it will generate an empty frame, making node and link creation seem like a special form of navigation to the user. It is also possible for a click on an item to run a small program written in the special KMS action language. This language is not quite as general as the integrated InterLisp in NoteCards, but it still allows the user to customize KMS for many special applications. See for example the discussion in Chapter 4 of the use of KMS to support the research of a biologist.

KMS does not provide an overview diagram but instead relies on fast navigation and a hierarchical structure of the nodes. Links across the hierarchy are prefixed with an "@" to let users know that they are moving to another part of the information space. Two additional facilities to help users navigate are the landmark status of a special "home" frame, which is directly accessible from any location, and the special ease and global availability of backtracking to the previous node by single-clicking the mouse as long as it points to empty space on the screen.

Hyperties (1983)

Hyperties was started as a research project by Ben Shneiderman [Shneiderman 1987b] at the University of Maryland around 1983. It was originally called TIES as an abbreviation for The Electronic Encyclopedia System, but since that name was trademarked by somebody else, the name was changed to Hyperties to indicate the use of hypertext concepts in the system.

Since 1987 Hyperties has been available as a commercial product on standard PCs from Cognetics Corporation. Research continues at the University of Maryland, where a workstation version has been implemented on Sun workstations.

One of the interesting aspects of the commercial version of Hyperties is that it works with the plain text screen shown in Figure 3.3. It is thus suited for DOS users. Hyperties also works with the main graphics formats on PCs and PS/2s and can display color images if the screen can handle them.

The interaction techniques in Hyperties are extremely simple and allow the interface to be operated without a mouse. Some of the text on the screen is highlighted and the user can activate those anchors either by clicking on them with a mouse, touching if a touch screen is available, or simply by using the arrow keys to move the cursor until it is over the text and then hitting ENTER. Hyperties uses the arrow keys in a special manner called "jump keys," which

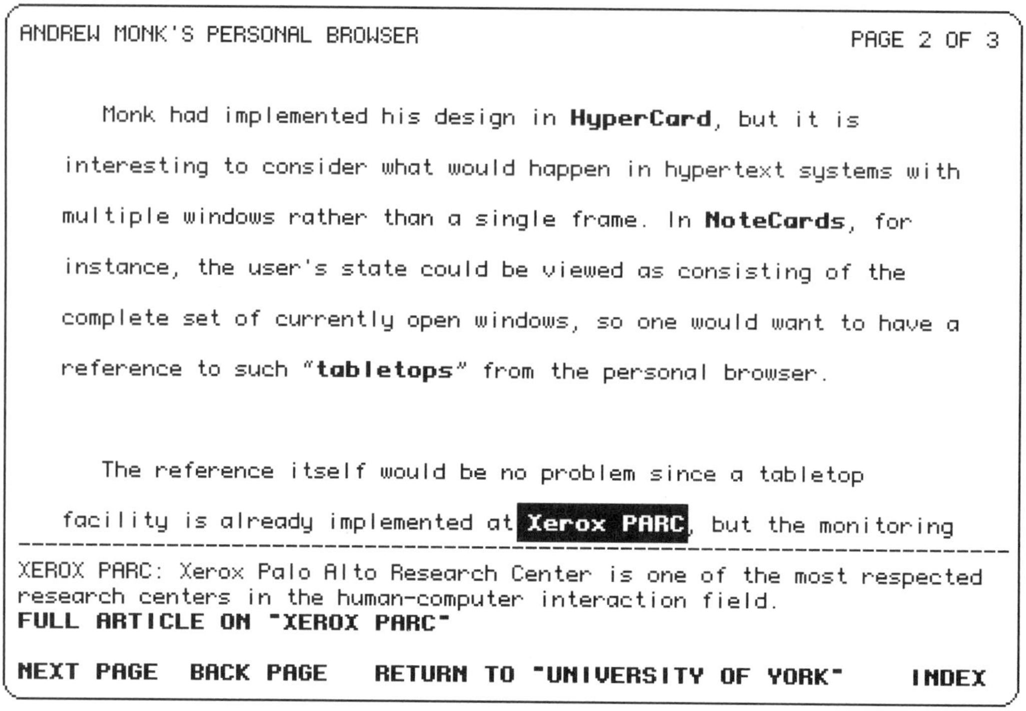

```
╭─────────────────────────────────────────────────────────────────────╮
│  ANDREW MONK'S PERSONAL BROWSER                          PAGE 2 OF 3  │
│                                                                       │
│     Monk had implemented his design in HyperCard, but it is           │
│                                                                       │
│   interesting to consider what would happen in hypertext systems with │
│                                                                       │
│   multiple windows rather than a single frame. In NoteCards, for      │
│                                                                       │
│   instance, the user's state could be viewed as consisting of the     │
│                                                                       │
│   complete set of currently open windows, so one would want to have a │
│                                                                       │
│   reference to such "tabletops" from the personal browser.            │
│                                                                       │
│                                                                       │
│     The reference itself would be no problem since a tabletop         │
│                                                                       │
│   facility is already implemented at ▐Xerox PARC▌, but the monitoring │
│  ─────────────────────────────────────────────────────────────────── │
│  XEROX PARC: Xerox Palo Alto Research Center is one of the most respected │
│  research centers in the human-computer interaction field.            │
│  FULL ARTICLE ON "XEROX PARC"                                         │
│                                                                       │
│  NEXT PAGE   BACK PAGE    RETURN TO "UNIVERSITY OF YORK"      INDEX    │
╰─────────────────────────────────────────────────────────────────────╯
```

Figure 3.3. *An example of a Hyperties screen as it typically looks on a text-only screen on a plain vanilla DOS machine.*

causes the cursor to jump in a single step directly to the next active anchor in the direction of the arrow. This way of using arrow keys has been optimized for hypertext where there are normally only a few areas on the screen that the user can point to and the use of keys has been measured to be slightly faster than the mouse (see Chapter 6).

In the example in Figure 3.3, the user is activating the string "Xerox PARC," which is indicated by inverse video. In the color version of Hyperties it is possible for the user to edit a preference file to determine other types of feedback for selections such as the use of contrasting color.

Instead of taking the user directly to the destination node as almost all other hypertext systems do, Hyperties at first lets the user stay at the same navigational location and displays only a small "definition" at the bottom of the screen. This definition provides the user with a prospective view of what would happen if the link were indeed followed to its destination and it allows the user to see the information in the context of the anchor point. In many cases just seeing the definition is enough. Otherwise the user can of course choose to complete the link.

A Hyperties link points to an entire "article," which may consist of several pages. Users following the link will always be taken to the first page of the article and will have to page through it themselves. This set-up is in contrast to the KMS model, where a link always points to a single page, and to the Intermedia model where a link points to a specific text string within an article. The advantage of the Hyperties model is that authors do not need to specify destinations very precisely. They just indicate the name of the article they want to link to, and the authoring system completes the link.

The same text phrase will always point to the same article in Hyperties, which again simplifies the authoring interface but makes the system less flexible. Many applications call for having different destinations, depending on the context or perhaps on the system's model of the user's level of expertise.

Many of the design choices in Hyperties follow from the original emphasis on applications like museum information systems. These applications need a very simple reading interface without advanced facilities like overview diagrams (which cannot be supported on plain DOS machines anyway). Furthermore, the writers of the hypertexts were museum curators and historians who are mostly not very motivated for learning complex high-technology solutions, so the similarity of the Hyperties authoring facilities to traditional text processing was well suited for the initial users. Now Hyperties is being used for a much wider spectrum of applications.

The commercial version of Hyperties uses a full-screen user interface as shown in Figure 3.3, whereas the research system on the Sun uses a two-frame approach similar to that of KMS.

NoteCards (1985)

NoteCards may be the most famous of the original hypertext research systems because its design was been especially well documented [Halasz et al. 1987]. It was designed at Xerox PARC and is now available as a commercial product.

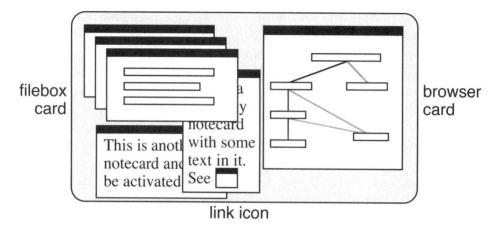

Figure 3.4. *The general layout of a NoteCards screen with the four basic objects: notecards, a link, FileBoxes, and a browser card.*

Originally, NoteCards ran only on the Xerox family of D-machines. These computers are fairly specialized Lisp[7] machines and not in very widespread use outside the research world. Therefore the commercial version of NoteCards was ported to general workstations like the Sun.

One reason for implementing NoteCards on the Xerox Lisp machines was that they provided the powerful InterLisp programming environment. InterLisp made it easy to program a complex system like NoteCards, and it also gave users the option to customize NoteCards to their own special needs since it is fully integrated with the Lisp system. Users who know Lisp can in principle change any aspect of NoteCards and they can implement specialized card types as mentioned below.

NoteCards was built on the four basic kinds of objects shown in Figure 3.4:

• Each node is a single *notecard* that can be opened as a window on the screen. These cards are not really "cards" in the HyperCard sense of having a fixed size but are really standard resizeable windows. Users can have as many notecards open on the screen as they want but quickly risk facing the "messy desktop" problem if they open too many. The notecards can have different

_____

[7] Lisp is a programming language characterized by having a huge number of parentheses (making it hard to read) and great flexibility (making it one of the preferred languages for artificial intelligence research).

types depending on the data they contain. The simplest card types are plain text or graphics but there are at least 50 specialized types of cards for individual applications that need special data structures. For example a legal application might need notecards containing forms for court decisions with fields for the standard units of information (defendant, plaintiff, etc.).

• The *links* are typed connections between cards. Links can be displayed as a small link icon as in Figure 3.4 or they can be shown as a box with the title of their destination card. Users open the destination card in a new window on the screen by clicking on the link icon with the mouse. The link type is a label chosen by the user to specify the relation between the departure card and the destination card for the link. To continue the legal example, lawyers might want one type of link to court decisions supporting their own position and another type of link to decisions that refute their position.

• The third kind of object is the *browser* card, which contains a structural overview diagram of the notecards and links. As shown in Figure 3.4, the different link types are indicated by different line patterns in the browser, thus giving the user an indication of the connection among the nodes. The browser card is an active overview diagram and allows users to edit the underlying hypertext nodes and links by carrying out operations on the boxes and lines in the browser. The user can also go to a card by clicking on the box representing it. The layout of the browser card is computed by system and therefore reflects the changing structure of the hypertext as users add or delete nodes and links.

• The fourth kind of object is the *FileBox,* which is used for hierarchical nesting of notecards. Each notecard is listed in exactly one FileBox. Actually, the FileBox is a special-purpose notecard, so FileBoxes can contain other FileBoxes and it is possible to construct links from other cards to a FileBox.

In one case users customized NoteCards so extensively that the result may be said to be a new system. The Instructional Design Environment (IDE) developed at Xerox PARC [Jordan et al. 1989] is built on top of NoteCards but provides a new user interface to help courseware developers construct hypertext structures semi-automatically. IDE supports structure accelerators that speed up hypertext construction by allowing the user to generate an entire set of nodes and links from a template with a single action.

The standard version of NoteCards has been used for several years both within Xerox and at customer locations. One of the interesting early empirical studies of the actual use of NoteCards was a longitudinal study [Monty and Moran 1986] of a history graduate student who used the system to write a research paper over a period of seven months. This user did not use links across the FileBox hierarchy very much, but that result may not be generalized to other users. The important aspect of the study is that it investigated the behavior of the test subject for an extended period of time and observed the use of the system for a fairly large task.

Symbolics Document Examiner (1985)

The early hypertext systems can best be classified as proof-of-concept systems showing that hypertext was not just a wild idea but could actually be implemented on computers. Even though some systems, like Engelbart's NLS and the early Brown University systems, were used for real work, that use was mostly in-house at the same institutions where the systems were designed.

In contrast, the Symbolics Document Examiner [Walker 1987] was designed as a real product for users of the Symbolics workstations. The project started in 1982 and shipped in 1985, making it the first hypertext system to see real-world use. The Document Examiner was a hypertext interface to the online documentation for the Symbolics workstation, and people got it and used it because it was the best way to get information about the Symbolics, not because it was a hypertext system as such.

The Symbolics manual also existed in an 8,000-page printed version. This information was represented in a 10,000 nodes hypertext with 23,000 links taking up a total of ten megabytes storage space. This hypertext would still be considered fairly large today and was possible in 1985 only because the Symbolics workstation was a very powerful personal computer. To produce all this hypertext, the technical writers at Symbolics used a special writing interface called Concordia, which is discussed further in Chapter 11.

The information in the 8,000-page manual was modularized according to an analysis of the users' probable information needs. The basic principle was to have a node for any piece of information that a user might want.

Furthermore, the design goal for the user interface was to be as simple as possible and not scare users off. Since hypertext was not yet a popular concept in 1985, this goal meant using a book metaphor for the interface instead of trying to get users to use network-based navigation principles. The information was divided into "chapters" and "sections" and had a table of contents. Furthermore, users could insert "bookmarks" at nodes they wanted to return to later.

To assess the usability of the Symbolics Document Examiner, the designers conducted a survey of 24 users. Two of them did prefer the printed version of the manual, but half used only the hypertext version and eight had not even taken off the shrinkwrap of the printed manual [Walker et al. 1989]. These users were engineers and they were using advanced artificial intelligence workstations, so they might have been more motivated to use high-technology solutions than ordinary users are.

Intermedia (1985)

Intermedia was a highly integrated hypertext environment developed at Brown University over several years [Yankelovich et al. 1988a; Haan et al. 1992]. It ran on the Macintosh but unfortunately only under Apple's version of the Unix operating system. Since most Macintosh buyers do not want to touch Unix, that choice of operating system severely restricted the practical utility of Intermedia and may have been a cause of its eventual failure.

Intermedia was based on the scrolling window model, like Guide and NoteCards, but otherwise it followed a different philosophy from the other systems discussed in this chapter. The core of Intermedia was a linking protocol defining the way other applications should link to and from Intermedia documents [Meyrowitz 1986]. It was possible to write new specialized hypertext applications and have them integrated into the existing Intermedia framework, since all the existing Intermedia applications would already know how to interact with the new one [Haan et al. 1992].

The links in Intermedia were highly based on the idea of connecting two anchors rather than two nodes. The links were bidirectional so that there was no difference between departure anchors and destination anchors. When a user activated a link from one of its anchors, the system would open a window with the document containing the other anchor and scroll that window until the anchor became visible. Thus Intermedia authors were encouraged to construct fairly long documents, since they could easily link to specific points in the documents.

Intermedia had two kinds of overview diagram as shown in Figure 3.5. The *web view* was constructed automatically by the system, and overview documents like the *Mitosis OV* document in the figure were constructed manually by the author using a drawing package and only by convention have a common layout with the name of the topic in the center and related concepts in a circle around it.

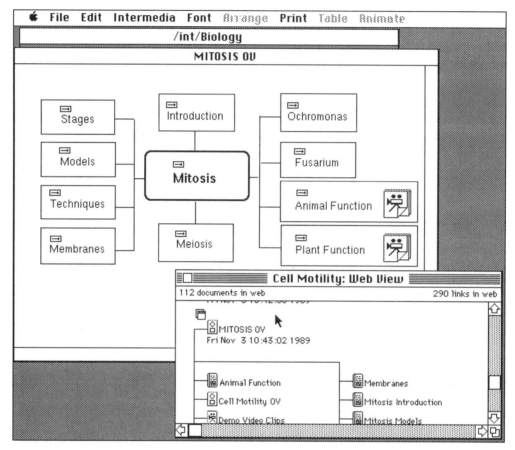

Figure 3.5. *An Intermedia web view. The InterDraw document called Mitosis OV is open. Each arrow icon in the overview diagram indicates the existence of one or more links. These connections are dynamically represented in the "Cell Motility: Web View" document. The web view is individual to each user and is saved from session to session. One of its functions is to provide the user with a path showing which documents he or she has opened, when they were opened, and how the document was reached (by following a link, opening the document from the desktop, and so on). The figure also illustrates another function of the web view: For the current document (the document most recently activated), the web view provides users with a map of where they can go next, thus allowing them to preview links and follow only those that they want to see. Copyright © 1989 by Brown University, reprinted with permission.*

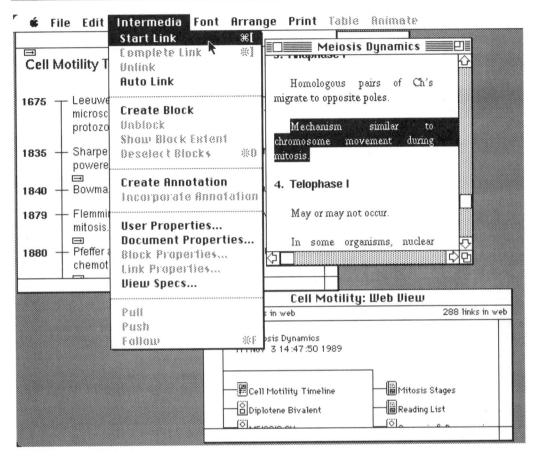

Figure 3.6. *To create a link in Intermedia, the user may select any portion of a document and choose the "Start Link" command. The link creation interface was modeled after the Macintosh cut/copy/paste paradigm; thus, the user may perform any number of intermediate actions and the link will remain pending until the user selects the other anchor for the link and activates the "Complete Link" command. Copyright © 1989 by Brown University, reprinted with permission.*

A typical Intermedia hypertext for a given course would contain many such overview documents, one for each of the central concepts in the course material.

Intermedia was designed for educational use on the university level and was used to teach several courses in both humanities and natural sciences. There is no reason why it could not be used for many of the other hypertext applications listed in Chapter 4, but the educational origin has had some impact on the design. For example, the Intermedia model assumes that several users (i.e., students) will access the same set of hypertext documents (i.e., course readings) and make their own annotations and new links. Therefore Intermedia stores separate files with links for each user in the form of so-called webs. Figure 3.6 shows the creation of a link in Intermedia. When the user has selected the other anchor for the link (for example the event listed under 1879 in the InterVal timeline) and has activated the "Complete Link" command, the new link will be added to the user's web.

Unfortunately, the funding agencies that had been supporting the development of Intermedia decided to discontinue funding the project in 1991, so even though Intermedia was the most promising educational hypertext system in the early 1990s, it does not exist any more.

Guide (1986)

Guide was the first popular commercial hypertext system [Brown 1987] when it was released for the Macintosh in 1986. Soon thereafter it was also released for the IBM PC, and was the first hypertext system that was available on both platforms. The user interface looked exactly the same on the two computers. Recent versions of Guide have been restricted to the Windows platform.

Peter Brown started Guide as a research project at the University of Kent in the U.K. in 1982, and he had the first version running on PERQ workstations in 1983. In 1984 the company Office Workstations Ltd. (OWL) got interested in the program and decided to release it as a commercial product. They made several changes to the prototype, including some that were necessary to get the user interface to conform to the Macintosh user interface.

Peter Brown continues to conduct research in hypertext using the Unix version of Guide that is maintained at the university [Brown 1992]. It is also used for some consulting projects in industry. If nothing else is stated, my use of the term "Guide" will refer to the commercial version on the IBM PC and the Macintosh and not to the Unix workstation version, since there are several differences between them.

Guide is similar to NoteCards in being based on scrolling text windows instead of fixed frames. But whereas the links in NoteCards refer to other cards,

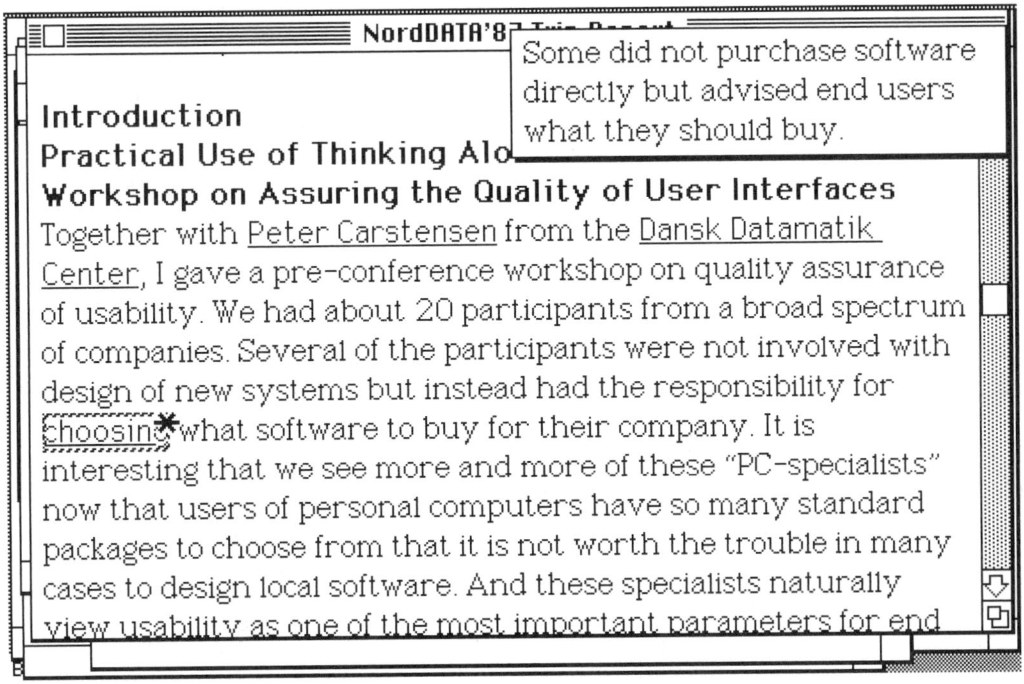

Figure 3.7. *A typical Guide screen where the user is pressing down the mouse button over the anchor for a pop-up note, which is temporarily displayed in the small window at the top right of the screen.*

links in Guide often just scroll the window to a new position to reveal a destination contained within a single file. Link anchors are associated with text strings and move over the screen as the user scrolls or edits the text. This approach is in contrast to, say, HyperCard, where anchors are fixed graphic regions on the screen. Guide does include support for graphic links, but they seem somewhat less natural to work with in the Guide user interface, and graphics have to be imported from external drawing programs.

Guide supported three different forms for hypertext link: Replacements, pop-ups, and jumps.

The *replacement buttons* were used for in-line expansion of the text of the anchor to a new and normally larger text in a concept that is sometimes called stretchtext.[8] Replacement buttons formed a hierarchical structure of text and were useful for representing text in the manner of a traditional textbook with chapters, sections, and subsections. Typically, the initial display would show all the chapter headings and users would then expand the one chapter in which they were interested by replacing the chapter heading with the list of sections in the chapter. They could then further replace the section that interested them the most with its list of subsections, and so on. While making these replacements, the user continuously had the other chapter headings available (perhaps by scrolling the window a little) and thereby preserved context. The reverse action of a replacement was to close the expanded text and have it re-replaced with the original text.

The replacement button existed in a variation called *inquiry replacement,* which was used to list several options and have the user choose one. When the user clicked on a replacement button that was part of an inquiry, that button would expand, and the other buttons in the inquiry would be removed from the screen until the user closed the expansion again. This interface was useful for multiple-choice type applications, like a repair manual where the user was asked to click on the type of equipment that needs repair. The explanation for the selected type was expanded and the other, irrelevant types would be hidden.

The second type of hypertext was small pop-up windows provided by clicking *note buttons* as shown in Figure 3.7. This facility was useful for footnote-type annotations, which are closely connected to the information in the main window. The pop-up was displayed only as long as the user held the mouse button down over the note button, implying that the "backtrack" command consisted simply of letting the mouse button go. This type of user interface is sometimes called a "spring loaded mode" because users are in the mode only as long as they continue to activate a dialogue element that will revert to normal as soon as it is released. The pop-ups are modes, nevertheless, since they make it impossible for the user to perform other actions (e.g., making a copy of the text in the pop-up window) as long as they are displayed.

---

[8] The "stretchtext" term is probably due to Ted Nelson. Similar concepts were found in Augment and several early text editors at Xerox PARC.

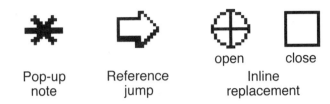

Pop-up note   Reference jump   open   close   Inline replacement

Figure 3.8. *Guide used varying cursor shapes to indicate the type of hypertext action available to the user.*

The third form for hypertext in Guide was the *reference button,* which was used to jump to another location in the hypertext. To get back to the departure point, users had to click a special backtrack icon.

The three different kinds of hypertext in Guide were revealed to the user by changing the shape of the cursor, as shown in Figure 3.8 One might have imagined that this fairly extensive set of different types of hypertext in a single small system would confuse users, but our field studies [Nielsen and Lyngbæk 1990] showed that users had no problems distinguishing among the three kinds of button.

As further discussed in Chapter 10, we also found that users liked the note button for pop-ups best and that the reference button for jumps got the worst ratings. It is interesting to consider that the reference button is exactly the feature that was not included in the "cleanly designed" research prototype of Guide but was added for the commercial release [Brown 1987]. It is of course impossible to say from our data whether the reference button was rated relatively poorly because it was not integrated nicely into the overall design or because `gotos` are just harmful in general.

Version 2 of Guide introduced a fourth type of button called the *command button,* which executes a script in the special-purpose Genesis language when clicked. Genesis was not a general programming language like HyperCard's HyperTalk, however, and was typically only used to access a videodisk to play a specified set of frames.

HyperCard (1987)

It is important to note that the designer of HyperCard, Bill Atkinson, has admitted that it was not really a hypertext product from the beginning. He originally built HyperCard as a graphic programming environment and many of the applications built into HyperCard actually have nothing to do with hypertext. Even so, HyperCard was probably the most famous hypertext product in the world in the late 1980s.

There are several reasons for HyperCard's popularity. A very pragmatic one is that it was bundled free with every Macintosh sold by Apple from 1987 to 1992. You could not beat that price, and the fact that it came automatically with the machine also meant that it was introduced to a large number of people who would otherwise never have dreamt of getting a hypertext system. Even after Apple started selling HyperCard as a traditional product, they still supplied a HyperCard reader for free with every Macintosh sold, meaning that HyperCard developers were ensured of their market.

The second reason for HyperCard's popularity is that it includes a general programming language called HyperTalk, which is fairly easy to learn. My experiments indicate that people with some previous programming experience can learn HyperTalk programming in as little as two days [Nielsen et al. 1991a]. Furthermore, this programming language is quite powerful with respect to prototyping graphic user interfaces. It is not very well suited for implementing larger software systems needing maintenance over periods of several years, however.

HyperCard is a good match for many of the innovative things people want to experiment with in the hypertext field. It is easy to learn, it can produce aesthetically pleasing screen designs, and it allows fast prototyping of new design ideas. One of my own hypertext systems, described in Chapter 2, was implemented in HyperCard. HyperTalk makes HyperCard well suited for experiments with computational hypertext where information is generated at read-time under program control.

As the name implies, HyperCard is strongly based on the card metaphor. It is a frame-based system like KMS but mostly based on a much smaller frame size. Most HyperCard stacks are restricted to the size of the original small Macintosh screen even if the user has a larger screen. This is to make sure that all HyperCard designs will run on all Macintosh machines, thereby ensuring a reasonably wide distribution for HyperCard products. Version 1 of HyperCard enforced the card size restriction without exceptions, but the newer version 2 has made it possible to take advantage of larger screens.

The basic node object in HyperCard is the card, and a collection of cards is called a *stack*. The main hypertext support is the ability to construct rectangular buttons on the screen and associate a HyperTalk program with them. This program will often just contain a single line of code written by the user in the form of a `goto` statement to achieve a hypertext jump. Buttons are normally activated when the user clicks on them, but one of the flexible aspects of HyperCard is that it allows actions to be taken also in the case of other events, such as when the cursor enters the rectangular region, or even when a specified time period has passed without any user activity.

The main advantage of the HyperCard approach of implementing hypertext jumps as program language statements is that links do not need to be hardwired. Anything you can compute can be used as the destination for a link.

In addition to the basic jumps to other cards, HyperCard can at least simulate pop-ups like the ones in Guide by the use of special `show` and `hide` commands. The designer can determine that a specific text field should normally be hidden from the user but that it will be made visible when the user clicks some button. The end result of these manipulations will be very similar to the Guide pop-ups.

HyperCard does have one serious problem compared to Guide, however, and that is the question of having hypertext anchors associated with text strings. In Guide these "sticky buttons" are the standard, allowing users to edit the text as much as they like and still keep their hypertext links so long as they do not delete the anchor strings. In HyperCard, an anchor is normally associated with a text string by placing the rectangular region of a button at the same location of the screen as the text string. But this anchoring method means big trouble if the user ever edits the text, since it is sure to change the physical location of the anchor string on the screen.

Figure 3.10 gives a simplified view of how I implemented the hypertext design from Figure 3.9 in HyperCard. First the general graphic design of the nodes was drawn as a background object that would be inherited by all the nodes in its class. This design included the picture of a book and the global overview diagram (since it would be unchanged for all nodes). The background design also included an empty placeholder field for the text to be added in the individual nodes.

For each individual node I then added a foreground layer with the text of the node and some graphics. The foreground graphics included the local overview diagram (since it would be different from node to node) and the heavy rectangles used to highlight the current location in the local and global overview diagrams. Since HyperCard displays all the levels as a single image on the screen, following the same principle as when an animation artist

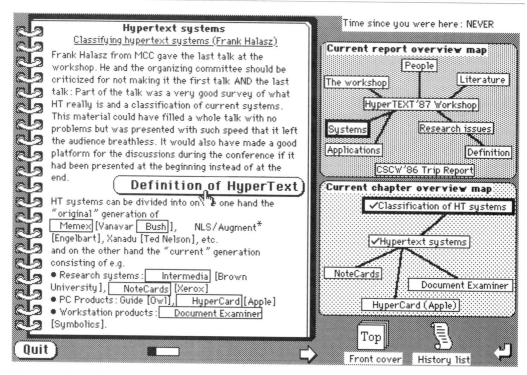

Figure 3.9. *An example of a screen implemented in HyperCard. Figure 3.10 gives a general idea of how this design was implemented.*

photographs a pile of acetates, the user would never know that the visual appearance of the global overview diagram was created by a combination of a fixed background image and a changing foreground rectangle.

Finally, I added a set of buttons to each individual node to achieve the hypertext links. Some of these buttons were for the local overview diagram and were placed over the corresponding graphics, whereas other buttons were anchors associated with text strings in the foreground layer and had to be carefully positioned over the relevant text. Actually, the complete screen contains even more buttons since there are also some global buttons that are common for all nodes and are therefore placed in the background level. They are not shown specifically here.

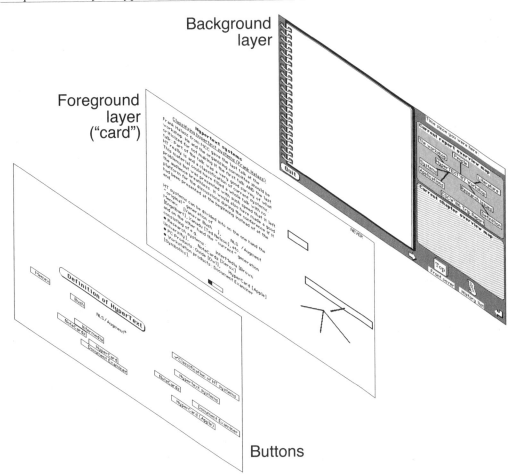

Figure 3.10. *A simplified view of the HyperCard implementation of the hypertext design in Figure 3.9. The background level contains graphics that are common for several nodes, whereas the foreground level contains the text and graphics that are specific for the individual node. Finally, the designer has placed several buttons on top of the text and graphics.*

HyperCard has several competitors, including SuperCard, Plus, and MetaCard. SuperCard has integrated facilities for dealing with color and several variable-sized windows at the same time and also allows object-oriented graphics of non-rectangular shapes to act as buttons. Plus is available both for the Macintosh and for the IBM PC (under Microsoft Windows as well as OS/2), affording cross-platform compatibility of its file format. MetaCard runs on workstations using X Windows, thus expanding the range of platforms on which the basic HyperCard type of hypertext can be used. Several other limitations have not been addressed by these competing products, however.

Some of these unsolved problems are not all that conceptually difficult, and one could imagine that HyperCard would address them in a possible version 3. This is true of the missing sticky buttons and the slow execution speed of HyperTalk programs.[9] Other problems are harder to address since they conflict with the basic nature of HyperCard. These include issues such as changing the programming language to be completely object-oriented and more maintainable and designing advanced hypertext features or multiuser access.

Interestingly, HyperCard's early success was not just due to its conceptual structure or the power of the underlying system. A major reason many people started authoring their own HyperCard stacks was the inclusion of a "construction kit" of graphical user interface elements with the basic system. I can't begin to count the times I have seen people using the picture of a man thinking in front of a computer that was included with the original HyperCard. More important, instead of just providing square boxes for buttons and hoping that people would fill them in with their own icons, HyperCard shipped with a large collection of pointing hands, turning arrows, and other appropriate designs that could be used as building blocks for new user interfaces. The attractiveness of these sample and template materials made many of the early HyperCard stacks look pretty good and helped build critical mass. I would definitely advise developers of future systems to include plenty of GUI widgets and pre-designed graphics.

Hypertext Grows Up

Symbolics Document Examiner was an example of hypertext meeting the real world since it saw real use by real customers. But the Symbolics was a fairly specialized artificial intelligence workstation and was very expensive when the Document Examiner was first introduced. So even though it counts as the first real-world use of hypertext, it was not a widely distributed and known system.

---

[9] Just changing from an interpreted language to a compiled one (as was partly done in version 2 of HyperCard) should do the trick.

Several hypertext systems were announced in 1985 and saw widespread use in the late 1980s and early 1990s, including NoteCards from Xerox and Intermedia from Brown University.

In contrast, when Office Workstations Limited (OWL) introduced Guide in 1986, it was as a commercial product. Guide was the first widely available hypertext to run on ordinary personal computers of the type people have in their homes or offices. To some extent the release of Guide could be said to mark the transition of hypertext from an exotic research concept to a "real world" computer technique for use in actual applications.

The final step to "realworldness" came when Apple introduced HyperCard in 1987. A nice product in its own right, its real significance was to be found in the marketing concept of giving away the program (or later a reader) for free with every Macintosh sold after 1987.

An event that really marked the graduation of hypertext from a pet project of a few fanatics to widespread popularity was the first ACM[10] conference on hypertext, Hypertext'87, held at the University of North Carolina on November 13–15, 1987. Almost everybody who had been active in the hypertext field was there, all the way from the original pioneers (except Vannevar Bush) to this author. Unfortunately the conference organizers had completely underestimated the growing interest in hypertext and had to turn away about half of the 500 people who wanted to attend the conference. Even so, we were crammed into two auditoriums that were connected by video transmission, and people had to sit on the floor. For those people who were lucky enough to get in, this was a great conference with plenty of opportunity to meet everybody in the field and to see the richness of ongoing hypertext research and development.

History repeated itself when the first open conference on hypertext in Europe was held in 1989. This was the Hypertext'2 conference in York in the U.K. on June 29–30, 1989. The reason this conference was called Hypertext'2 was that there had been a first, closed conference in Aberdeen the year before. Again the organizers had underestimated the growth of the field and had facilities to accommodate only 250 people. But 500 wanted to come, so half had to be turned away.

---

[10] ACM = Association for Computing Machinery, the oldest and probably most prestigious organization for computer professionals in the world.

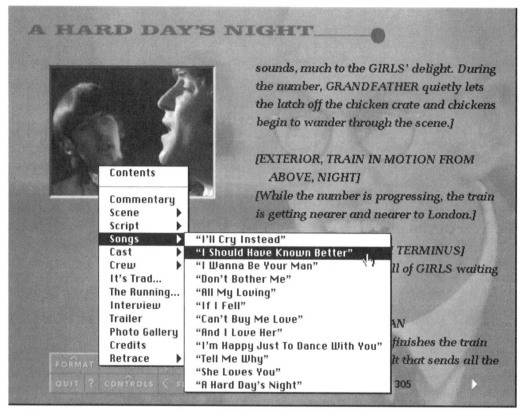

Figure 3.11. *Screen from the CD-ROM edition of the Beatles film* A Hard Day's Night. *The film itself is playing in the upper left window and the rest of the screen updates to show the part of the original script that corresponds to the scene currently playing. Pop-up controls allow the user to move directly to various scenes or songs and to view related films. Copyright © 1964 by Proscenium Films, 1993 by The Voyager Company, reprinted by permission.*

The year 1989 also saw the birth of the first scientific journal devoted to hypertext, *Hypermedia*, published by Taylor Graham. It is discussed further in the bibliography.

In the mid-1990s, hypermedia systems came to the attention of the larger public through the proliferation of CD-ROMs. For example, the first full-length feature film in hypermedia form was shipped on a CD-ROM in 1993 when the Voyager Company released the Beatles film *A Hard Day's Night*. In 1993, compression technology was still primitive enough to make this something of a feat, and the only reason it was possible is that *A Hard Day's Night* is a rather short film and was filmed in black-and-white. Figure 3.11 shows a screen from this hypermedia production. The Voyager Company released a large number of other titles throughout the 1990s and proved that it had become possible to launch a successful publishing company by concentrating on shipping hypertext.

A final event in the mid-1990s was the extremely rapid growth of hypertext on the Internet, spearheaded by the specification of the World Wide Web by Tim Berners-Lee and colleagues at CERN (the European Center for Nuclear Physics Research in Geneva, Switzerland). Almost immediately after its introduction by the National Center for Supercomputing Applications (NCSA) in January 1993, Mosaic became the most popular browser for the WWW and the growth of Internet hypertext accelerated even more. See Chapter 7 for a more extended treatment of hypertext over the Internet.

It is interesting to contemplate the fact that Mosaic and the WWW more or less succeeded in establishing a universal hypertext system in just three years, even though Ted Nelson could not get his Xanadu system accepted in thirty years of trying. One major reason for this difference is doubtless that the WWW projects were paid for by the taxpayers (the European taxpayers in the case of CERN and the American taxpayers in the case of NCSA). It always makes it easier to sell a product when the cost is $0. Even so, there are also other reasons why WWW succeeded where Xanadu failed. The most important differences are the open systems nature of the WWW and its ability to be backwards compatible with legacy data. The WWW designers compromised and designed their system to work with the Internet through open standards with capabilities matching the kind of data that was available on the net at the time of the launch. These compromises ensured the success of the WWW but also hampered its ability to provide all the features one would ideally want in a hypertext system. The specification of the WWW's underlying hypertext markup language (HTML) has been through three versions in the first four years after the introduction of the system and it is still not ideal. There is no doubt that this reliance on iterative design and evolutionary change is better than waiting for the revolution that never comes. After all, if the choice is between perfection and nothing, then nothing wins every time. We should be grateful to the WWW designers for offering us a third choice.[11]

In conclusion, we can say that hypertext was conceived in 1945, born in the 1960s, slowly nurtured in the 1970s, and finally entered the real world in the 1980s with an especially rapid growth after 1985, culminating in a fully established field during 1989. We now have several real-world systems that anybody can buy in their local computer store (or get for free bundled with their computer); we have successful conferences and a journal; and most important of all, we have many examples of actual use of hypertext for real projects. These examples are the subject of the next chapter.

---

[11] Note that the WWW really *is* far from ideal. I present some of my critiques in Chapter 7, but I should emphasize that I fundamentally admire the WWW and its designers.

4.   Applications of Hypertext

As Pat Wright [1989] observes, the variety of hypertext is similar to the diversity of printed material. To use her example, children's pop-up books, railroad timetables, and the instructions for operating a washing machine are all very different types of print. Different applications call for different kinds of hypertext support, and this chapter reviews some of the current applications of hypertext.

Not all applications should be done in hypertext. To determine whether an application is suited for hypertext, Ben Shneiderman [1989] has proposed what he calls the **three golden rules** of hypertext:

- A large body of information is organized into numerous fragments.
- The fragments relate to each other.
- The user needs only a small fraction at any time.

If the information is small or all one object, it should be displayed as a whole. This would also be true if the user needed to access all of the information at the same time. If the various parts of the information are totally unrelated (e.g., the telephone numbers in the white pages) then a database would be more appropriate than a hypertext as the organizing principle.

Computer Applications

Since hypertext is a computer medium, it is natural to use it in connection with computer-oriented applications. The fourth golden rule of hypertext might be stated "do *not* use hypertext if the application requires the user to be away from the computer." Using hypertext for computer applications completely eliminates any conflict with this rule since the user will already be at the screen anyway.

Besides the actual applications of hypertext discussed below, hypertext can also be used to prototype the user interface for almost any other computer program [Nielsen 1989a], because most initial prototyping consists of linking together screen designs and presenting them to the user in an order determined by simple user actions. Extremely simple prototypes can be constructed in any hypertext system just linking together screen designs in the appropriate order. As the prototyping work advances beyond the storyboard stage, the need for more application functionality increases, but computational hypertext systems with access to a programming language can still be of use in many cases. HyperCard has been used frequently for this purpose.

Online Documentation

Online documentation may be the most natural of all hypertext applications; it was the purpose of the first real-world hypertext application, the Symbolics Document Examiner (see Chapter 3).

"Nielsen's first law of computer manuals" states that users do not read manuals, period [Nielsen 1993a (section 5.10)]. The second law is that when a user wants to read the manual anyway, then one can be sure that the user is in big trouble. Because of the first law, users will often not be able to find the manual when they finally need it, since somebody else may have borrowed the manual or it may have become lost in general. This situation does not happen with an online manual, which is always present on the computer. Rob Lippincott from Lotus Development Corp. talks about the need for "just-in-time learning" that allows users to learn *what* they need *when* they need it.

Since no user wants to read the entire manual anyway, users also require good access tools to help them retrieve the sections of the manual that are relevant to their current needs. Hypertext is the obvious method for helping users in this situation, and many recent software packages have been delivered with online manuals or online help systems in hypertext form. For example, Macintosh System 7.5 and Microsoft Office 4.0 both ship with limited printed manuals that refer users to check the online hypertext information for detailed instructions. Figure 4.1 shows an example of an interface for online help [Nabkel and Shafrir 1995].

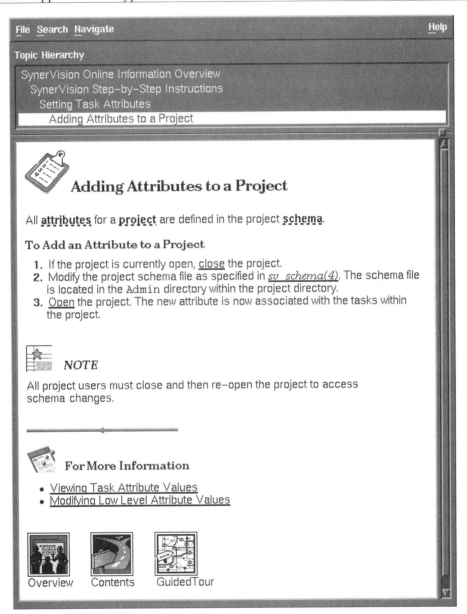

Figure 4.1. *HP's SynerVision online help. User interface by Jafar Nabkel (Software Engineering Systems Division, Hewlett-Packard Company) and Eviatar Shafrir (User Interaction Design, Hewlett-Packard Company). Copyright © 1993 by Hewlett-Packard Company, reprinted by permission.*

User Assistance

Users need more information than can be found in manuals. In fact, a study by Robert L. Mack of the IBM User Interface Institute and myself showed that business professionals rated traditional reference manuals as the second worst out of twelve methods for initial learning about computer systems.[1]

Hypertext provides a mechanism for integrating several forms of user assistance, including the online manual, an introductory tutorial, an online help system, and even the error messages. Because users only get error messages when they are in some kind of trouble, the error messages are a prime candidate for providing users with assistance. The traditional perspective implicit in such classic error messages as ILLEGAL COMMAND - JOB ABORTED was that the user must have been criminally stupid to make a mistake, but luckily that perspective has mostly been abandoned in modern user interfaces [Ehrlich and Rohn 1994].

In an integrated user-assistance facility based on hypertext, it would be possible for the user to link from an error message to the location in the help system that gives further assistance on the problem. If the user's difficulty was not the error situation in general but a single incomprehensible word in the message, it would be possible to link from that word to the location in the online manual where it was defined. And if the user wanted further assistance than could be provided by the help system or the manual, it would be possible to link further, to the appropriate location in the tutorial component, to get a computer-aided instruction lesson.

This type of integrated user assistance does not exist in current computer systems, but we are seeing hypertext applied to individual components in the user-assistance field. For example, the Sun386i workstation had its online help system implemented as a hypertext [Campagnoni and Ehrlich 1989] and most computer systems in recent years have shipped with hypertext help systems and sometimes even hypertext online documentation.

OpenWindows had a feature called spot help that allowed users to press the HELP key on the keyboard at any time. Spot help would take a snapshot of the part of the screen surrounding the user's cursor and would display the bitmap in a dialog box with an explanation of the user interface element being

---

[1] R. L. Mack and J. Nielsen: "Software integration in the professional work environment: Observations on requirements, usage, and interface issues," *Technical Report* **RC-12677**, IBM T.J. Watson Research Center, Yorktown Heights, NY 10598, April 1987.

pointed to. Thus, spot help provided an implicit hypertext link between all objects in the graphical user interface and their help information. The dialog box furthermore provided a MORE button with a link to more detailed information, adding some degree of integration.

Software Engineering

During the software development lifecycle, a large number of specification and implementation documents are produced, and hypertext has great potential for providing links among them [Cybulski and Reed 1992]. For example, it would be possible to start from a requirements document and link to that part of the design specification that meets a given requirement. One could then link from the design specification to the actual code to see how that design is implemented; or one could follow the links in the reverse direction, starting from the source code to see what customer requirements lay behind a certain code element.

To benefit fully from this form of hypertext links among the various documents in the software lifecycle, a development organization would need to follow a software engineering methodology supported by an integrated set of computerized tools in a complete CASE (Computer Aided Software Engineering) environment. One such system is the Dynamic Design project at Tektronix [Bigelow 1988], which supports version control for various reports, documents, and code objects by using the Neptune hypertext abstract machine [Delisle and Schwartz 1987].

It is also possible to use hypertext in a less lifecycle-oriented approach by including linking facilities in structure-oriented editors for program code. For example, it is possible to click on a variable to get to see its definition and associated comments, or to link from a procedure call to opening a window with the text of the procedure. The Smalltalk code browser links related pieces of code in somewhat this manner.

Since much of the software engineering process is spent on designing systems rather than simply hacking code, there is also interest in specialized tools to support the design phase of the lifecycle. One interesting system was gIBIS (graphical Issue Based Information System) from MCC (Microelectronics and Computer Technology Corporation) in Austin, Texas [Conklin and Begeman 1988]. gIBIS was part of the Design Journal project, which aimed to capture the rationale for a software design.

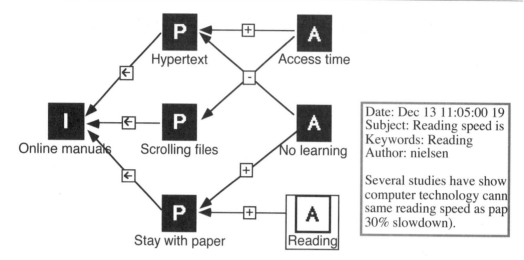

Figure 4.2. *An issue network similar to those used in gIBIS. The "issue" is how to do online manuals, and there are three positions: Use hypertext, use a traditional scrolling text file, and avoid online manuals completely by staying with paper. Several arguments have been posted, and the user has selected the "Reading" argument, which brings its full text up in the text window. The real gIBIS screen is in color and has much larger windows both for the diagram and for the text window. Note that the links are typed as indicated by the small icons showing, for example, that the reading speed argument supports the position of staying with paper.*

Since software design is usually a collaborative process involving many people, gIBIS was a multiuser hypertext system. It was based on a theoretical model of the design process as a conversation among "stakeholders" who bring their respective expertise and viewpoints to bear on a number of design issues. The participants in the design process argue about these issues by suggesting positions (ways to resolve the issue) and arguments for and against those positions. All of this was represented in a hypertext structure with three types of nodes: issues, positions, and arguments. The "g" in gIBIS came from the graphic representation of the hypertext network as shown in Figure 4.2. The overview diagram gave the user an idea of the design rationale at a glance and also provides access to the underlying full text.

Originally, gIBIS was designed for use on Sun workstations with color screens and it therefore used color to indicate the types of nodes and links in the network overview diagram. At first, users were allowed to customize the

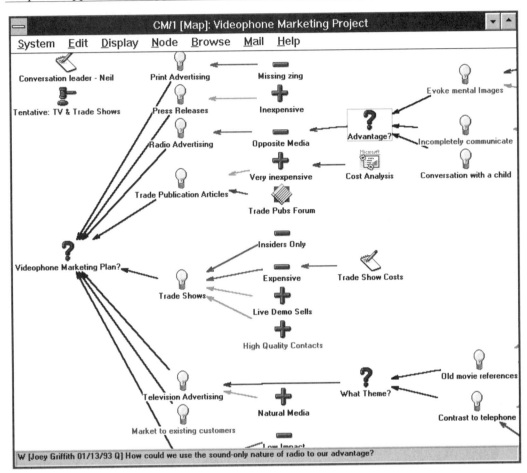

Figure 4.3. *An argumentation map in the CM/1 system. Copyright © 1994 by Corporate Memory Systems, Inc., reprinted by permission.*

assignment of colors, but later versions of gIBIS were based on standardized use of color, making it possible for users to learn quickly the type mappings for the most commonly used nodes and links. Type identification then became a rapid, unconscious activity. gIBIS also ran on monochrome displays and then used the iconic representation of types shown in Figure 4.2.

Jeff Conklin and colleagues who invented gIBIS later formed a company to market the ideas from gIBIS in a form suited for personal computers. Figure 4.3 shows an example of their CM/1 system with question-mark icons for issues, light-bulb icons for positions, and plus/minus icons for the arguments.

Additional icons mark nodes that have been imported from external applications such as the cost analysis.

Operating Systems

Finally, hypertext has the potential for revolutionizing the user interface to personal computers in general in order to arrive at a task-integrated working environment. Current personal computers are fundamentally based on a file paradigm, where the user manipulates discrete (but large) units of information in the form of files. Each file can typically be found only in a single location in the file system, and it is typically best suited for use by a single application program.

This model had a good fit with early personal computers, which were rather small and limited in many ways. They operated only on a few data types (often text and numbers); each user used only a small number of applications because they were difficult to learn; and the file storage was limited by the capacity of small hard disks. Modern personal computers are intended for multimedia data, and they support sufficiently user friendly interfaces to allow users to learn and use many different applications.[2] Furthermore, they are often connected to large hard disks (I have a 2.1 GB disk on my home computer), optical disks, or network-based servers, and therefore have to access a large number of files.

Most current file systems organize files in a hierarchy and require the user to navigate through multiple levels of nested subdirectories to reach the relevant files. Users often forget where they have stored a certain piece of information and are restricted mostly to searches based on filenames. Some add-on products like Lotus Magellan do exist and can help users find files on the basis of a full text search, but they are still fairly primitive compared with the navigation facilities offered by the best hypertext systems.

---

[2] One reason users are now able to use more applications is that the user interfaces are getting consistent. Users can transfer their skills from one program to the next, which therefore becomes easier to learn. See J. Nielsen (Ed.), *Coordinating User Interfaces for Consistency*, Academic Press, ISBN 0-12-518400-X.

It would be possible to extend future operating systems[3] with a system-based hypertext service somewhat like the Sun Link Service [Pearl 1989], or the hypertext support built into the Penpoint operating system for pen computers [Meyrowitz 1991]. Such extensions allow different applications to link transparently to information generated by other applications and stored elsewhere on the computer. Users only need to establish the connection between two work items once and are then freed from having to navigate manually. Hypertext links can take the user from one piece of information to the next, thereby avoiding the need for the user to drop into the file system. Users can concentrate on their tasks and have the computer integrate its applications and data to fit those tasks.

Business Applications

This section concentrates on "mainstream business," but quite frankly there are not yet all that many business applications of hypertext in place to be used every day for real profit. But there are potential applications that are currently being investigated by several companies, and there are also some systems in real use. Also, many of the applications mentioned under other headings are "real business" examples; the software and entertainment industries, for example, are just as dependent on profits as everybody else.

Repair and Other Manuals

The MIT *Movie Manual* discussed in Chapter 3 is an example of a repair manual done in hypertext. It contains descriptions of how to repair cars and bicycles linked to video clips of mechanics performing the various operations and even to video segments showing typical mistakes and what could go wrong during certain operations.

One memorable sequence, which I still recall from seeing it in 1983, is a video clip showing what would happen if certain nuts were loosened too rapidly. The film shows the oil pan slipping and discharging its contents all over the head of the poor mechanic. After having seen this sequence, you use your wrench cautiously for a long time.

---

[3] Even if a hypertext service is not embedded as part of the operating system, it might still be possible to provide cross-application hypertext links between applications that agree to support a hypertext protocol [Hall et al. 1992; Kacmar and Leggett 1991].

The *Movie Manual* was suited for both experienced and novice mechanics. One facility for the novice was an explanation of the tools used in the repair procedure. Each time a tool was mentioned there was a hypertext link to a picture of the tool and a description of how the tool was used. A true novice could even watch a film of an experienced mechanic using the tool to observe how the expert would handle the tool. Of course these links would never be followed by experienced mechanics, but they were very useful for do-it-yourself people.

The IGD (Interactive Graphical Documents) System [Feiner et al. 1982] is an early hypertext manual for repair of electronic equipment produced at Brown University with support from the U.S. Navy. It is highly based on graphically *showing* the technicians how to repair things, rather than on describing the same material in textual form.

These early repair manuals include some options for having the system model the user as being, for instance, a novice or an expert repair technician. It would also be possible to have the hypertext links depend on information about the outside world. In a system like IGD for repair of electronic equipment on warships, there might be some cases where a given piece of equipment could be repaired in two different ways: a careful and generally recommended way, and a quick-and-dirty way. The link that displayed a description of the repair procedure would then depend on the system's knowledge of the status of the ship. If it was in no particular danger, then the careful repair procedure would be accessed, but if the ship was under attack, the system would naturally display the fastest possible repair procedure. This dynamic reconfiguration of a repair manual is one of the great advantages of hypertext compared to traditional printed works, which would have to display every single option to the technician, and would thereby be more complex and require increased user literacy.

Many car companies are supplying instructions to mechanics in hypertext form (often on CD-ROM), because there are so many different models and spare parts that the distribution of complete sets of regular manuals is becoming unfeasible.

Dictionaries and Reference Books

Several dictionaries and large reference works have been converted from a traditional paper form to a hypertext format but so far we have seen no major project trying to generate a hypertext dictionary from scratch except for the

a b c d e f g h i j k l m n o p q r s t u v w x y z

dog

 A dog is a furry
animal with a tail
that wags. Dogs are
usually kept as pets.

  Dog words

Pets

Surprise me   Backtrack   Games   Quick search   Options   Quit

Figure 4.4. *Entry from* My First Incredible, Amazing Dictionary. *For pure enjoyment, the user can click on the picture of the dog to have it replaced by another kind of dog. Note the hypertext links to "dog words" and to other pets, as well as the links to other words from the definition. All these features encourage the child to explore the dictionary and learn new words. Copyright © 1994 by Dorling Kindersley, reprinted by permission.*

children's dictionary shown in Figure 4.4. Two of the conversion projects (the *Manual of Medical Therapeutics* and the *Oxford English Dictionary*) are described in further detail in Chapter 12.

Figure 4.5 shows a hypertext version [Fox 1992] of a famous reference work in the user interface field: the design guidelines collected by Sid L. Smith and Jane N. Mosier from the MITRE Corporation. This single reference work has actually been converted into several other hypertext forms, including one commercial product for the IBM PC called NaviText SAM [Perlman 1989], a

HyperCard version from Bond University in Australia (BRUIT-SAM),[4] and a Japanese translation implemented in a fourth-generation language by a group coordinated by Hiroshi Tamura of the Kyoto Institute for Technology. Unfortunately, so far nobody has conducted a comparative experiment to assess the usability of these different conversions of the same underlying text.

The DRUID system shown here is only a prototype of a fairly ambitious design that will include support for many steps in the usability engineering lifecycle. For example the system is intended to provide support for using the hypertext as a checklist for design and evaluation. DRUID allows users to select and weight the importance of relevant guidelines for a system design, and also allows users to rate the compliance with those selected guidelines.

Even the prototype DRUID system includes all the guidelines of the printed report with the appropriate hypertext links. It turns out that user interface design guidelines are heavily interlinked because they often complement (or even contradict) one another. In Figure 4.5 we are reading about the need to allow users to edit a command before they have submitted it for execution. This guideline is linked to four other relevant guidelines, and we have here clicked on the reference to guideline 6.0–10, resulting in a preview of that guideline on the bottom line of the screen. If we wanted to study the guideline on "user review and editing of entries" we could click on the "show" button to follow that link to its destination. The guideline on user review and editing further states that in the case of error, the user should be allowed to fix the problem by editing the erroneous input instead of being required to reenter everything (which might introduce new errors). It is obviously relevant for any system designer who is reading about command editing also to know what to do in the case of an error, so this hypertext link is very well placed.

The guideline in Figure 4.5 also has literature references to a U.S. military standard (MS) and to a scientific paper from the journal *Human Factors*. These links are unfortunately not all that useful in the current version of the hypertext since they take the user only to the relevant bibliographic reference. In the next version of DRUID, the links to the military standard will be made "live" and actually take the user to the full text of the relevant sections of MIL-STD-1472D. Such "multi-document hypertext" [Glushko 1989b] can

---

[4] BRUIT-SAM can be downloaded by anonymous FTP from kirk.bu.oz.au [131.244.1.1] in the /pub/Mac directory.

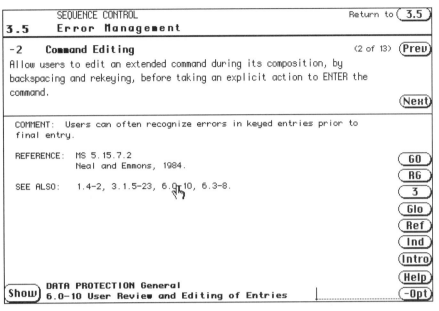

```
          SEQUENCE CONTROL                       Return to ( 3.5 )
   3.5     Error Management

   -2    Command Editing                          (2 of 13) (Prev)
   Allow users to edit an extended command during its composition, by
   backspacing and rekeying, before taking an explicit action to ENTER the
   command.
                                                             (Next)

      COMMENT:   Users can often recognize errors in keyed entries prior to
      final entry.

      REFERENCE:   MS 5.15.7.2
                   Neal and Emmons, 1984.                    ( GO )
                                                             ( RG )
      SEE ALSO:    1.4-2, 3.1.5-23, 6.0-10, 6.3-8.          (  3  )
                                                             (Glo )
                                                             (Ref )
                                                             (Ind )
                                                             (Intro)
                                                             (Help)
  (Show)  DATA PROTECTION General
          6.0-10 User Review and Editing of Entries    |···    (-Opt)
```

Figure 4.5. *A screen from the DRUID (Dynamic Rules for User Interface Design) hypertext version of a major compendium of user interface design guidelines. Copyright © 1989 The MITRE Corporation, reprinted with permission.*

significantly increase the utility of hypertext. For the foreseeable future users will probably have to acquire the rest of the references from their library in the traditional way.

The Electronic Whole Earth Catalog was a CD-ROM version of the printed *Whole Earth Catalog*. The main difference between the printed and CD-ROM versions was that the CD-ROM contained a large number of digitized sound clips of the various records reviewed in the catalog. The CD-ROM seemed to contain the same illustrations as the printed version, albeit using the somewhat poorer resolution of scanned Macintosh screen images.

The sound clips were a major advantage of the electronic version, but it also had better search options than the printed book. For example, when I was interested in buying a quotation dictionary, I wanted to read reviews of this kind of book and so tried to look up "quotation" in the index of the printed book. That word was not in the index, but using the full text search capabilities of the electronic version, I found a review of *Bartlett's Familiar Quotations*, which had been listed under **B** in the printed index. In a printed index, you have to know what to look for to a much larger extent than you do in a hypertext work.

The Electronic Whole Earth Catalog was a fairly big hypertext with its 9,742 nodes taking up a total of 413 megabytes. Most of this storage space was used for the sounds, however, with only 34 megabytes needed to store the main parts of the hypertext. A hypertext using all the storage space on the CD-ROM for text would be a much larger and more complex work, like encyclopedias which takes up 20–30 volumes in their printed form. Encyclopedia CDs typically have about thirty thousand entries plus ten to twenty thousand illustrations, a few hundred animation and videosequences, and a few hours hour of audio.

Clearly one of the biggest advantages of hypertext encyclopedias and dictionaries, compared to a printed work, is that they can show moving images and play sound. For example, Microsoft Bookshelf contains a dictionary with sound recordings of how the words are actually pronounced. As another example, HarperColins Interactive's *American Sign Language Dictionary* on CD-ROM contains video slips of 2,181 signs. Printed dictionaries for deaf users portray hand and facial gestures through line drawings with arrows to show movement, so multimedia dictionaries are clearly a superior format for communicating this dynamic language. Also, the computer format has added benefits such as the ability for less experienced users to view a sign at much slower speeds than normal conversation.

Auditing

Auditing is another natural application for hypertext because it is based on relating information from various sources and checking for consistency. The audit task includes gathering and producing large numbers of documents and linking them together to substantiate the accuracy of the information they contain. A huge amount of information gets distilled into a single financial statement, so links are needed between the conclusions and the source data. Furthermore, the audit of an international company involves a large audit team distributed over several countries, leading to several advantages for various forms of computer support like electronic mail and hypertext links among documents produced in different areas of the world.

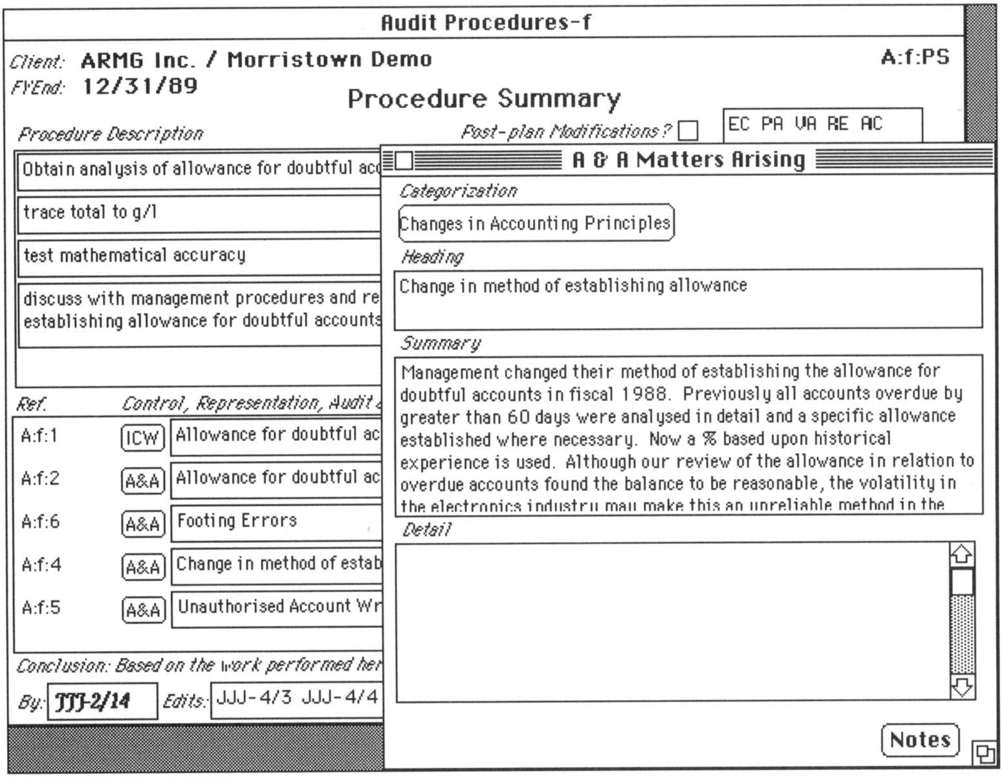

Figure 4.6. *A Procedure Summary Form has fields for the most important information for the audit procedure. The list of potential issues has links to supporting evidence (on the left) and to windows with room for further detail (here the user has clicked on "Change in methods of establishing allowance" to see its description window). The description window provides further detail and also shows that this auditing issue has been categorized under "Changes in Accounting Principles." This classification makes it possible to construct summary reports elsewhere in the system and thus show all the issues in a category. This figure illustrates a prototyping effort, which does not necessarily reflect current or future audit methodology or practice. Copyright © 1989 by Price Waterhouse Technology Centre, reprinted with permission.*

Studies conducted by the Price Waterhouse Audit Research and Technology Group indicate that approximately 30% of the time spent on an audit is dedicated to producing, relating, and reviewing "Audit Working Papers." This figure does not even take into account the time spent obtaining

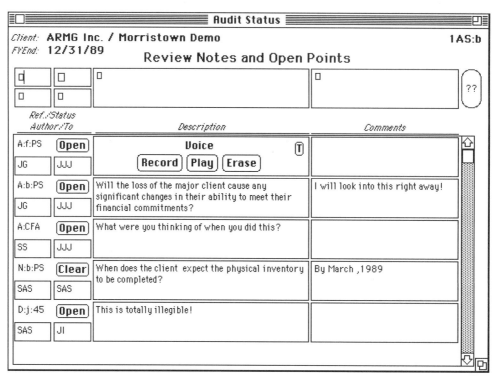

Figure 4.7. *Review Notes can help large audit teams manage and coordinate activities by providing the ability to view the same information from several perspectives. This window gives an overview of issues that remain to be resolved and has hypertext links to the underlying documents. This figure illustrates a prototyping effort which does not necessarily reflect current or future audit methodology or practice. Copyright © 1989 by Price Waterhouse Technology Centre, reprinted with permission.*

the information. Therefore a good hypertext system for auditing support has the potential to reduce the time needed to conduct an effective audit, and Figures 4.6 and 4.7 illustrate a prototyping effort that the Price Waterhouse Technology Centre in Menlo Park started to investigate these possibilities [De Young 1989].

The hypertext system links the information produced during the audit process and makes it possible to track information from, say, a final financial statement back to where it originated. It is possible to scan original documents from the client, and it might conceivably be possible in the future to link directly into the client's own computer system. Since the linking structure is so important for the issues raised during the audit process, the auditors need to take personal responsibility for the establishment of links. In a traditional, paper-based audit this responsibility is sometimes noted manually by adding initials to references to other documents, but the hypertext system can automatically timestamp every new or changed link and record the name of the user.

One difference between auditing and many other hypertext applications is that the presentation of the information used in auditing has been fairly standardized over a long period of time. Because less flexibility is needed in an auditing hypertext, the form filling paradigm is a natural user interface as shown by the figures.

The well-structured nature of the auditing hypertext makes it possible for the system to provide automatic access to higher-level reports computed on the basis of the hypertext network. The system can automatically construct lists of all issues of a certain type or all issues handled by a certain auditor. As an example of another coordination tool, Figure 4.7 shows a management report for keeping track of the status of the work in large teams of auditors.

A high degree of standardization can be observed not just in the structure of auditing procedures and reports but also in the very language of the reports. Therefore there are substantial advantages in being able to *reuse* portions of the language in reports from previous audits of the same client or of another client with a similar type of business. A hypertext system would facilitate such reuse by making the appropriate earlier documents easily available in online versions for copying and editing.

Law

Hypertext has two main applications in the legal field. The first is to support legal research and is mainly used by professional lawyers. The second is support of legal document creation and management and is used by both lawyers and people who wish to avoid paying legal fees.

Legal texts are filled with cross-references and are therefore well suited for hypertext support. Typically, a lawyer's brief might refer to several court rulings, each of which would refer to further rulings and to the applicable statutes. Having each of these references available online saves the lawyer much time in researching the law. A special aspect of law is that new statutes or higher court rulings may invalidate earlier decisions, meaning that something may be legal one day but illegal the next. This time-varying nature of the law has two consequences for legal hypertext systems. The first is that a lawyer who accesses one of these overruled cases had better be informed that it is no longer valid law. Legal information services achieve this purpose by inserting bidirectional links from the new law to any earlier nodes referring to the same issue. Lawyers can then follow the links in the opposite direction in a process known as Shepardizing after the printed books that originally supplied these inverse links. The second implication is that lawyers will sometimes need temporal scrolling of the law to discover what the rules were at some earlier point in time when the action under consideration took place. For example, if a client is taken to court over an old income tax return, the defense should be based on the tax rules for the year in question.

Any major legal case involves a myriad of documents and case management systems are appearing to allow lawyers direct access to specific documents from their computers. These systems have many similarities with the auditing systems discussed in the previous section and allow the lawyers to annotate individual documents and to create links between related documents.

Many legal documents consist of large amounts of boilerplate text combined with a few customized words and phrases. Since lawyers typically charge large fees to produce these documents, many people have started using computer software to help them assemble individualized legal documents from stored writing samples. One such user is the large telephone company Nynex which uses its Contract Drafting System to produce tailored contracts for large purchase contracts [France 1994]. Nynex estimates that each contract can be produced by the purchasing manager in about half an hour. Before the computer system was introduced, similar contracts required four hours of the manager's time, two attorney hours, and four hours of word processing, so the system saves substantial resources. Nynex estimates that it is saving about $200,000 per year just from this elimination of overhead labor. Additionally, the system may lead to better deals because it allows the purchasing department to act more quickly. With the traditional system, it frequently took ten iterations between the purchasing department and the legal department to get a contract right, leading to purchasing delays of four to six weeks.

The Nynex Contract Drafting System asks the purchasing manager about 25 to 35 questions (depending on the complexity of the deal) and pulls appropriate clauses from its supply of boilerplate. In some ways, the system can be thought of as a simple expert system since the specific questions asked later in the dialogue will depend on the user's answer to earlier questions. Simple questions like "what is the name of the supplier?" result in direct text substitution, whereas questions like "how long will the contract last?" may lead to use of different kinds of contracts and different follow-up questions. The system goes down a decision tree, following rules that were developed by experienced lawyers.

A final legal application is the use of multimedia visualizations by trial lawyers to illustrate their version of events during a trial. Since visualizations are so compelling, juries can often be convinced that something really happened because they *saw* it happen (on the computer).

Trade Shows, Product Catalogs, and Advertising

Many kinds of advertising and communication to customers can be improved by hypertext. Right now hypertext has a novelty value, which is an advantage in itself in some types of advertising. For example you can attract attention at trade shows by having a computer with hypertext information about your products.

Hypertext can also be used to provide information about an entire trade show and help people find those exhibitors that would interest them.

In the long term, the novelty value of hypertext will of course disappear and one will have to rely on the intrinsic advantages of hypertext in an advertising context. One of these advantages is the general ability of hypertext to provide access to large amounts of information but to show the user only those small parts that interest him or her. This property of hypertext is important for applications like product catalogs. A hypertext product catalog can reduce the complexity of choosing among a large number of options by showing only those that are relevant for the individual customer. It can also offer help in placing the order and might even place it by an online connection to the vendor. A hypertext catalog could also include an option to remember what products the user ordered the previous time, thus making them especially easy to reorder.

Having a hypertext product catalog could be a tremendous asset for direct marketing people if they could gain access to data about how customers have used the hypertext.[5] For example the system could record how many times a specific user clicked on links related to the price of products and special savings

---

[5] In some countries it may be illegal to collect such data without the user's knowledge.

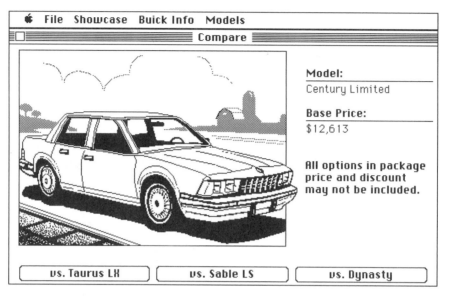

Figure 4.8. *A screen from a 1988 SoftAd for Buick. Copyright © 1988 by The SoftAd Group, Inc., reprinted with permission.*

options as compared to how many times the same user clicked on links related to advanced features of the product or descriptions of luxury options. This somewhat simpleminded example shows how the hypertext system could provide the basis for a market segmentation down to the level of the individual customer. The next hypertext catalog sent to the customer could be tailored to have more prominent links of the type that customer had shown an interest in.

Traditional types of advertising are certainly possible in hypertext, either by sending customers a disk or by making promotional materials available on the Internet. For example, the Norwegian company Arctic Adventours organizes Arctic expeditions for tourists and has designed a hypertext version of their travel catalog.[6] Internet delivery makes perfect sense for this kind of specialized product where enthusiasts will spread the word. Since it is easy to send one's friends a one-line URL-hypertext link to an interesting travel brochure, a company like Arctic Adventours may generate substantial word-of-mouth advertising by having linkable information available on the Internet.

---

[6] URL http://www.oslonett.no/data/adv/AA/AA.html

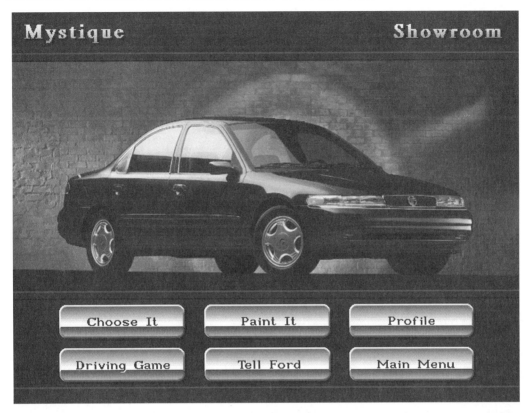

Figure 4.9. *Screen for the Ford Mystique in the 1995 Ford Simulator hypertext. The user can see the car in different colors by clicking the "Paint It" button. Copyright © 1994 by The SoftAd Group, Inc., reprinted by permission.*

As further discussed in Chapter 7, Internet advertising is often used to pay for interesting, but free, services on the net that are accessed by many users. Through hypertext, those users who are interested in a specific offer (like Arctic travel) can link to more detailed information without the need to clutter up the main part of the service. Compared with paper publishing, where a majority of the pages in many newspapers consist of advertising (see Table 8.1 for an example of a Sunday issue of *The New York Times* that contained 62% advertising), hypertext provides great potential for saving resources while actually making *more* advertising content available to those readers who express an interest in a certain ad and follow its link to the supplementary materials.

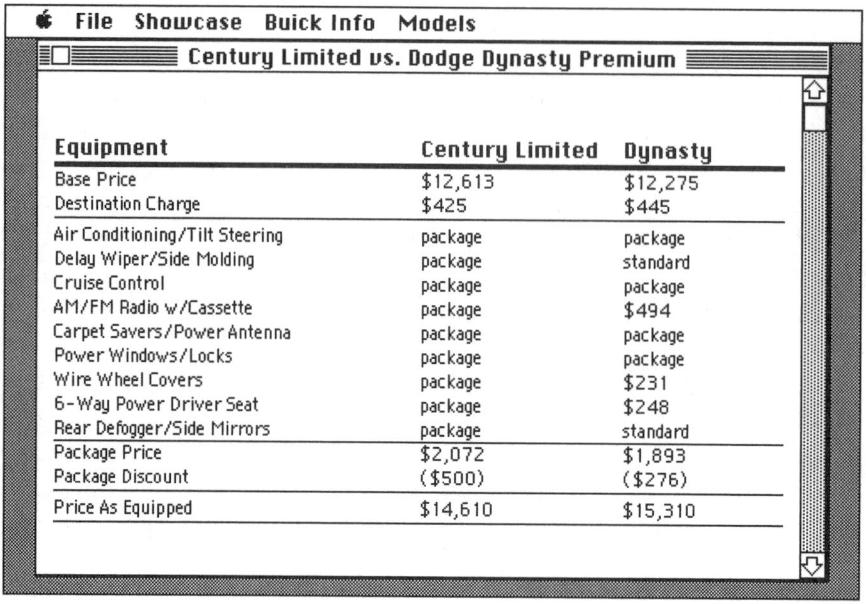

Equipment	Century Limited	Dynasty
Base Price	$12,613	$12,275
Destination Charge	$425	$445
Air Conditioning/Tilt Steering	package	package
Delay Wiper/Side Molding	package	standard
Cruise Control	package	package
AM/FM Radio w./Cassette	package	$494
Carpet Savers/Power Antenna	package	package
Power Windows/Locks	package	package
Wire Wheel Covers	package	$231
6-Way Power Driver Seat	package	$248
Rear Defogger/Side Mirrors	package	standard
Package Price	$2,072	$1,893
Package Discount	($500)	($276)
Price As Equipped	$14,610	$15,310

File Showcase Buick Info Models
Century Limited vs. Dodge Dynasty Premium

Figure 4.10. *A comparison screen from the 1988 Buick SoftAd generated by clicking on the "vs. Dynasty" button in Figure 4.8. Copyright © 1988 by The SoftAd Group, Inc., reprinted with permission.*

Hypertext advertising can also benefit from other properties of the computer medium. For example, Buick has released their car catalog in hypertext form for several years and has included driving simulations and other games to attract attention. Figure 4.8 shows a screen from an early version of Buick's electronic advertising. In a hypertext form for comparative advertising, this screen allows the user to compare the Buick cars with several competing alternatives. Users can click on the one other car they might consider buying instead and then see a detailed comparison like that in Figure 4.10. This example again uses hypertext to manage complexity. A printed catalog would have had to compare all the cars in a single confusing table.

Figure 4.9 shows a more recent electronic ad from Ford with essentially the same underlying design as Figure 4.8. Notice the considerably higher "production values" possible when using color graphics. Not only does the car look better, it also becomes possible for the user to interactively choose the color of the car.

In the marketing field, the bottom line is considerably more interesting than theoretical speculations about information complexity. And hypertext does sell. The manager of Buick Motor Division's electronic product information department, Nancy J. Newell, was quoted in *Business Week* on October 9, 1989 as saying that 12% of those who bought cars after receiving the Buick disk ended up picking a Buick. This rate was about double their usual market share. In a television commercial that was tested in the New York market in November 1994 Toyota offered to send potential customers information either in a brochure or on a disk. Sixty percent of the people who called requested the disk.

Online shopping is still in its infancy. In 1993 Americans bought $200 million worth of goods through online shopping. Considering that 3.3 million American homes had online connectivity that year, the average spending per home was only about $60. Compare this amount with the $70 billion spent per year in the U. S. on non-online mail order. This is about $700 per household or more than ten times as much as the (presumably richer than average) online-connected households spent on online shopping. The two main reasons for the low spending on online shopping are probably that the selection of goods available online was much smaller than represented in a typical holiday season's worth of mail order catalogs and that the user interfaces for online ordering often are very clunky. Both problems are being addressed vigorously with the explosion in home computing and the Internet that started around 1994 and some industry analysis estimate that online shopping in the U. S. should reach $100 billion per year around the year 2005.[7] Some of the reasons for optimism regarding online sales are the surveys showing that consumers find many kinds of shopping boring (especially weekly grocery shopping for packaged staples) and that fear of crime is causing many Americans to prefer to stay at home.[8]

---

[7] Retail sales in the U. S. are more than $2 trillion per year, so a 5% market share for online shopping will be enough to meet the analysis' predictions.

[8] Note that the surveys showing consumer boredom and fear of crime were conducted in the United States. Companies wanting to sell in other countries are well advised to investigate the factors driving those countries' consumers. For example, Japan is a low-crime country, so fear of muggings would not be a factor in keeping people at home. Instead, Japanese consumers might be motivated by the ability of online shopping to deliver high-quality goods at significantly lower prices than they are used to or by the possibility of avoiding a long commute.

Advertising on the Internet poses special problems since the users normally pay (in some way) to receive the messages. On the one hand, advertising can be used to finance services that would otherwise not be available freely on the net, but on the other hand unethical advertisers can easily flood the users' mailboxes with undesired ads by use of irrelevant mailing lists and newsgroups. Martin Nisenholtz, who is a senior vice president of Ogilvy & Mather Direct, proposed six guidelines for ethical online advertising in a July 1994 article in *Advertising Age*:

• Don't send intrusive messages: no one should receive advertising by electronic mail unless he or she has asked to receive it.

• Don't sell consumer data without the explicit permission of the user. The way people use their computer and navigate the Internet should not be disclosed to others.

• Advertising should appear only in newsgroups and mailing lists that are related to the product or service being sold.

• Conduct promotions and direct selling only under full disclosure. Users should be able to review the exact rules of an offer before responding.

• Conduct consumer research only with the user's informed consent. Users should be told the consequences of answering a market research questionnaire.

• Never use communications software to conceal functions. For example, do not scan the user's harddisk for competing software and mail off the results as part of a registration procedure without permission.

Intellectual Applications

I do not want to imply that business and education are not intellectual activities, but there seems to be a third category of applications that are less immediate in nature and more oriented towards the scholarly approach. In fact, many of these "intellectual" applications are actually used quite a lot in business.

Idea Organization and Brainstorm Support

Some hypertext enthusiasts claim that hypertext is the most natural way to organize human ideas because its semantic network-like structure matches the human brain. That may or may not be true, but even if hypertext should not be the optimal way to organize human thoughts it is still much better than the linear text format used by word processors. The one way humans certainly do *not* work when they are, say, writing a book is to start by getting the idea for what to write on page one, then moving on to getting the idea for page two, and going on like that until they finally end by getting the idea for the last page.

We have already discussed gIBIS as a tool for organizing the discussions of software designers (see Figure 4.2). NoteCards from Xerox [Halasz et al. 1987] is another famous hypertext system built mainly to be used as an idea organizer.

Because hypertext allows the coordination of many disparate pieces of text, it can also be used to organize the ideas of groups of people. Doing so was part of the basic design of gIBIS but was originally not possible in NoteCards. Subsequent versions of NoteCards did include support for asynchronous cooperative work. Besides regular multiauthor support, hypertext can also help coordinate ideas by its basic capability for having any user add new annotations and links to any node. For example, the Intermedia InterNote service shown in Figure 5.5 allows an author to make a hypertext available to a larger group and to collect their comments as annotations.

Figure 4.11 shows an example of the use of hypertexted argumentation structures in the cooperative SEPIA system developed at the German research institute GMD-IPSI [Streitz et al. 1992] to support synchronous as well as asynchronous collaboration. In the figure the user haake is working as a single user in the SEPIA planning space on structuring the problem of making decisions about designing the parliamentary area in Berlin, where the capital of Germany will be moved from the current location in Bonn. This results in requirements on the design of the plenary building ("issue") for the parliament. The example illustrates cooperative work in a committee that is split between Bonn and Berlin, opening up the problem of a distributed environment.

There are three positions in the argument. The node labeled "small solution" suggests using the old existing Reichstag building as it is, i.e., without the dome that burned in the 1930s. Haake is working on the node "big solution" which refers to restoring the dome on top of the Reichstag. The third position is "new building." During the session, haake has been joined by users streitz and geissler (as shown in the current users list) in the argumentation space where they are in a loosely coupled mode [Haake and Wilson 1992]. Streitz is working on the node with the title "No building should be higher than the Reichstag building" (a statement made by the German Chancellor Kohl) which—in combination with the "big solution"—results in the claim that higher buildings would possible in the area if a dome

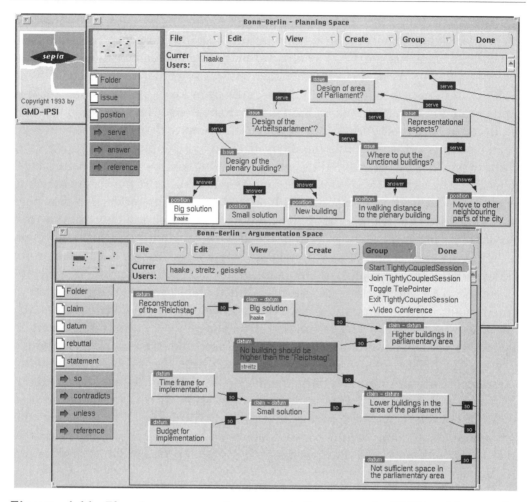

Figure 4.11. *Planning space and argumentation space in SEPIA with complex hypermedia structures representing design alternatives and their rationale. This screendump was taken from the user* haake's *workstation. Copyright ©* *1993 by GMD-IPSI, reprinted by permission.*

was added to the Reichstag. Note how SEPIA uses typed nodes and links to represent the different aspects of an argument.

Figure 4.11 is the view from haake's workstation and the nodes this user is editing are therefore highlighted in a lighter color (yellow on a color screen), whereas nodes used by others are highlighted in a darker color (red on a color screen). For example, the user `streitz` is accessing the "No building" node in Figure 4.11. This figure is an example of SEPIA's loosely coupled mode where a user cannot see what the other users are doing but only what nodes they are currently editing. For closer collaboration in real time, it is preferable for the users to know exactly what everybody is doing and to be able to exchange comments over the computer network. To enter this mode from Figure 4.11, `Haake` is opening the "group" menu in order to start a tightly coupled session with the other two users, resulting in Figure 4.12.

Figure 4.12 shows the view from the workstation of the user `streitz` after the three users have entered the tightly coupled mode where each can see what the other is doing. `Streitz` is working on a node of type datum with the title "No building should be higher...," which now has a light color (because we are seeing the view from his workstation) while user `haake` opened the content of the node of type "claim-datum" with the title "Big Solution" (now shown dark). For showing and editing the content of this node, the user is using an integrated shared drawing tool (WSCRAWL) displaying the old Reichstag building as it looks now in Berlin (the "small solution"). User `geissler` has added a schematic drawing of the former dome and—using a telepointer as indicated by the userid—is showing the other users how the big solution (restoring the old dome on top of it) would look. In the upper window, `streitz` has started to turn on his telepointer in order to show something to `haake` (whose telepointer is already on).

A tightly coupled mode implies strong WYSIWIS (What You See Is What I See), i.e., all the users' computers display identical areas of a much larger network structure (there is a roaming box in the upper left corner of the window for a full overview over all nodes) and scrolling is coupled. In loosely coupled mode, only certain areas are seen by all depending on who navigates where (each user has full control over his/her window of that space) but all are made aware if somebody else is navigating in this space. Change from individual/single mode to loosely coupled mode can happen by navigating in the space. The fact that a user has entered a SEPIA space where another user was already working is indicated by the sound of a door bell. In addition to sharing workspaces at different levels and in different clusters/spaces with different people, SEPIA also supports video and audio conferences among those coworkers who are in tightly coupled mode in order to complement pointing and editing by voice and face communication. In other words, the hypertext system has been integrated with desktop video conferencing.

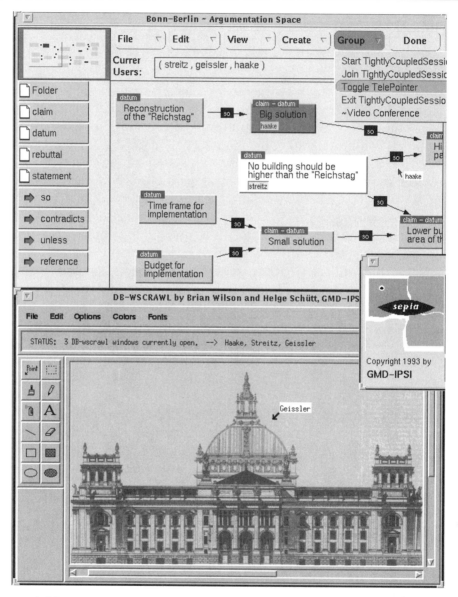

Figure 4.12. *Cooperative SEPIA with three users in "tightly coupled" collaboration mode in the argumentation space sharing views at the network level of typed nodes and links (upper window) and at the node-content level (lower window). This screendump was taken from the user* `streitz's` *workstation. Copyright © 1993 by GMD-IPSI, reprinted by permission.*

SEPIA is intended to support the situation where the collaborators are located in different rooms (possibly in different cities or countries). For really tight collaboration people normally prefer to meet physically in a single room. Physically proximate reality (PPR) is still superior to any kind of computer-supported or virtual reality (VR). Figure 4.13 shows a meeting room at GMD-IPSI in Germany equipped with computers to allow people to access and develop their hypermedia documents during a meeting [Streitz et al. 1994]. The software connecting the LiveBoard (an interactive electronic whiteboard [Elrod et al. 1992]) with the workstations is called DOLPHIN.

In the meeting room, most users sit around a table equipped with workstations. One user works with a cordless pen at the LiveBoard, an interactive electronic whiteboard displaying a page of DOLPHIN. Since users want to discuss and create material as a group, DOLPHIN supports this cooperative process by providing a shared public workspace displayed on the LiveBoard. It can be accessed and edited from the workstations as well as with the pen while standing in front of it. Figure 4.14 shows a screendump from one of the workstations. The upper window is the DOLPHIN "meeting space," which is shared by all users and displayed on the LiveBoard. The user is also accessing a private SEPIA argumentation space in the lower window.

Since there are users at both the workstations and the electronic whiteboard, DOLPHIN provides ways of integrating the two. Before the screendump in Figure 4.14 was taken, one user had scribbled several notes on the LiveBoard. These words are shown in "ink" (unrecognized pixels) since the system does not yet perform handwriting recognition. Some of the scribbles, e.g. the word "Building," were turned into hypermedia nodes (gray boxes) by gesture operations carried out with the pen at the LiveBoard. Other text was typed in from the users around the table using their keyboard (e.g., the node "New building"). Some of these were also transformed in hypermedia nodes and then connected by links, again using a simple gesture operation. The whole area of DOLPHIN can be used to annotate the hypermedia nodes and links, etc.

Before a meeting, a user might have prepared an argumentation structure with SEPIA to emphasize a point that the user wants to make in the meeting. In the meeting, the user can access the prepared structure in his or her private space and copy it into the public space of DOLPHIN to make it visible to all meeting participants. Subsequently, this argumentation structure could be connected via links with other DOLPHIN nodes. The meeting space will

Figure 4.13. *Meeting room at GMD-IPSI in Germany equipped with a Xerox LiveBoard (electronic whiteboard) and with individual workstations mounted in the table. The LiveBoard is showing hypertext nodes that are networked to information in the participants' workstations. Copyright © 1994 by Norbert Streitz, reprinted by permission.*

eventually exhibit coexistence and transformation of more informal (handwritten scribbles, etc.) and more formal (typed nodes and links) structures in the same space. After the meeting it will be possible to transfer DOLPHIN structures into SEPIA spaces and use them there. For example, general hypermedia nodes like "building" in Figure 4.14 could be transformed into argumentation type nodes of a given type and used in future work back in the office.

Collaboration can also take place via electronic mail or computer conferences which can be enhanced by hypertext mechanisms. The basic principle of computer conferences and most electronic mail is that several participants write messages with comments on previous messages by other

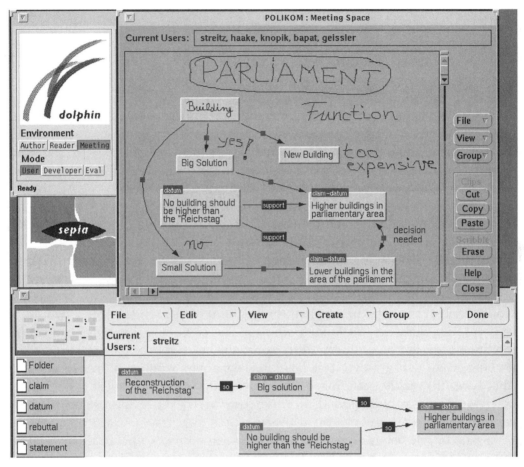

Figure 4.14. *View of the "public" meeting space of DOLPHIN shared by five users in the upper right window. The lower window is an argumentation space from SEPIA used as the "private" space of an individual user. Copyright © 1993 by GMD-IPSI, reprinted by permission.*

participants, making these communication media well suited for hypertext support [Jackson and Yankelovich 1991]. The HyperNews system from the Technical University of Denmark (see Figure 8.11) is a hypertext interface for such a conferencing environment for the Internet netnews. Hypertext links connect a message both forward and backward in time with all those other messages in the same stream of comments.

Journalism

In addition to the long-term possibility of having newspapers and television news in an integrated hypermedia system (see Chapter 1), it is also possible to use hypertext in the current way of doing journalism. Much of a journalist's work is of course plain gathering of information and writing of stories, and the hypertext mechanisms for idea organization discussed above should be able to help.

For the collection of information it would also be possible to use large hypertext collections of previously published news material. Newspapers like *The New York Times* and the *San Jose Mercury News* already provide information services with online access to databases with "old news," but the information is currently not in hypertext form. Many other newspapers still use traditional files of paper clippings and good journalists are able to flip through such files at an amazing speed. They have learned to recognize cues from the typography and layout of the clippings and are able to classify an article without having to read it. For example, a certain layout and typography would be recognized as being from the London *Times* while another would be recognizably from the *National Enquirer*. The same size letters in a headline might be used in one publication to signal the start of World War Three while it could mean that a movie star has knocked down a police officer in another. This type of quickly recognizable signal to support a journalist's skill-based behavior needs to be included in a hypertext news retrieval system if it is to compete with a simple pile of press clippings.

Radio or television reporters can also use hypertext to provide background information during a broadcast. For example, ABC produced a hypertext with about 10,000 nodes for its coverage of the U.S. presidential election in 1988 to allow its anchor Peter Jennings fast access to relevant information. Having a well-linked hypertext instead of traditional cueing cards allows a broadcast commentator to have more "that reminds me of" remarks.

In an interesting twist, ABC reused much of their 1988 hypertext material in producing an educational hypertext in 1989 called *The '88 Vote*. In addition to the hypertext material it also contains film clips from the Presidential campaign and key commercials from both candidates. This combined hypermedia package was released by ABC News InterActive.

Research

Obviously research to a large extent consists of idea generation and writing, so hypertext tools for supporting those activities can also be used to support researchers. Here I will mention a few examples of applying hypertext to the domains studied by the research.

John L. Schnase from Texas A&M University has written a biology paper in KMS [Schnase and Leggett 1989]. The paper describes an individual energetics model for Cassin's Sparrow (*Aimophila cassinii*), which is a common bird in the west Texas mesquite-grasslands. The goal of the research was to account for the energy expenditure of individual birds over 24-hour periods.

The hypertext structure developed for the research contains all the raw data collected from field observations of the activities of male and female Cassin's Sparrows. It also contains the programs necessary to perform various simulations on the basis of the data. The program to simulate the male birds was written within the KMS action language, which made it possible to run the simulation entirely within KMS. Unfortunately the version of KMS used (6B1) had very poor support for arithmetic expressions and also ran very slowly.[9] Therefore the program to simulate female birds was written in the traditional C programming language.

The C program was still kept within the hypertext structure, so that it was possible to have it cross-referenced with the main paper. When a simulation was to be performed, the KMS action language was utilized to write the C program and the raw data to Unix files and to start the calculations in Unix. The output from the C program was then reimported into KMS by action language statements, so that the user never had to leave the hypertext structure. Because of this use of computational hypertext, it was possible to have a single integrated personal environment for scientific knowledge work that simplified the personal information management problem for the researcher.

Another advantage of having the paper in hypertext format is that it was possible to send it to other biologists by electronic mail and thereby bypass the delay of two to three years posed by a traditional journal. Unfortunately this distribution mechanism does not reach all biologists, so the paper was still

---

[9] The current version of KMS has solved many of these problems.

submitted to a traditional biology journal. This goal made it necessary to use the system to produce a linearized version of the paper, but the project showed that the hypertext system could support the entire traditional scientific process from the storage and collection of field data over the formulation of models and theories to the production of a camera-ready report. The only research step that had to be done without hypertext support was the collection of field data in the Texas grasslands since KMS does not run on any kind of portable computer.

In addition to these attempts to construct scientific communicative material entirely in hypertext, there is also the possibility of converting traditional journal articles to hypertext [Egan et al. 1991]. One such experiment was the "Hypertext on Hypertext" project from the Association for Computing Machinery, which converted one issue of the *Communications of the ACM* journal to hypertext in several different formats [Alschuler 1989]. A more ambitious project is underway at Loughborough University in the United Kingdom to convert eight volumes of the journal *Behaviour and Information Technology* into Guide [McKnight et al. 1990] for possible later publication as a CD-ROM. This larger project takes advantage of the tendency for papers in a given scientific journal to contain many references to other papers in earlier issues in the same journal, by converting these references to hypertext links. Its goal is to make reading the hypertext journal a much more dynamic experience and to increase the likelihood that readers will actually check the references.

Projects to convert traditional journal papers to hypertext might miss some of the opportunities for taking advantage of the new medium. Except for automated references and better search mechanisms, a hypertext version of a traditional paper would not really offer any advantages over a printed version and would suffer the disadvantages associated with forcing users to read large amounts of text from computer screens.

It is likely that the main advantage of hypertext will come from constructing new types of scientific communications which could take advantage of the new opportunities. Scientific "papers" in hypertext would come close to the biology and acoustics examples discussed here by including substantial additional detail which would be suppressed by traditional journal publication. Most readers would not bother following the links to those details, but they would be there for those specialists who might need to do so. Research publications in hypertext would present readers with a "virtual laboratory" and access to much richer representations of the original source data.

Yet another kind of research is the linguistic and theological studies of the Bible which are now being made possible by hypertext. The basic research problem is that the Bible exists in many different versions due to changing translation methods and the various scrolls and manuscripts found by archaeologists. Serious study of the Bible therefore requires the reader to compare several different versions of the same text, a task eminently suited for hypertext. OWL has developed a modified version of Guide called CDWord for the Dallas Theological Seminary, which can maintain access to several manuscript versions and scroll them in parallel such that the same part of the text is always displayed in all manuscript versions no matter which of them is used as the basis for jumps or searches.

As a matter of fact, the Bible, Torah, Koran, and other religious manuscripts can be viewed as some of the earliest examples of the hypertext principles. Many medieval manuscripts were heavily annotated by monks, rabbis, and scholars who devoted substantial time to developing linking structures between the basic documents of their respective religions and more or less canonical interpretations and elaborations such as the Talmud.

Educational Applications

Many of the applications discussed in other sections of this chapter actually have an educational slant. This is, for instance, true of the manuals that teach how to repair things and the hypertext versions of journals, dictionaries, etc.

Even so, there have been many hypertext systems produced specifically for educational use. Hypertext is well suited for open learning applications where the student is allowed freedom of action and encouraged to take the initiative. For example, the *Interactive NOVA* hypertext (see Figure 9.8) allows the student to browse through a large set of biology information and see those parts that interest the student or make sense in the context of a current assignment. On the other hand, hypertext may be less well suited for the drill-and-practice type learning that is still necessary in some situations.

One specialized educational hypertext was the Palenque system from Bank Street College of Education [Wilson 1988]. The purpose of the Palenque system was to teach Mexican archaeology to children in the eight- to fourteen-year age range by letting them take a tour of the Palenque ruins. The system was implemented in DVI (Digital Video Interactive) on a CD-ROM and allowed surrogate travel among the ruins in a practical application of the methods pioneered by the MIT Aspen *Movie Map* project discussed in Chapter 3.

The CD-ROM contains a large number of photographs of the Palenque site, and the user can move among them in the "traditional" surrogate travel style. Because of the digital image processing it is also possible to provide continuous panning around a 360° panoramic view as if the user was turning in a circle. In addition to the simulated visit to the ruins, the Palenque system also included a museum with "theme rooms" about the Mayas and the rainforest. As users "walked" around the ruins or "visited" the museum, they had a simulated camera and scrapbook available to construct their own personalized record of their experience.

As an example of how a computer system can sometimes provide an experience richer than real life, the Palenque system included a "magic flashlight" that allowed users to dissolve their surrogate travel view of a building to old photographs of how the same ruin looked before it was restored and even to reconstructions of how the building might have looked in the days of the Mayas.

Palenque was intended to teach children, though it has been great fun for adult users also. In contrast, the Shakespeare project at Stanford University [Friedlander 1988] was explicitly aimed at university level students in drama theory. The hypertext contained film clips from plays like *Hamlet* and *Macbeth* and links between corresponding scenes in the different films, to illustrate how the same play has been interpreted by different directors and actors. There were also links between the film clips and hypertext nodes with analyses by various theoreticians of the texts and the performances.

Furthermore, the Shakespeare project included a simulation facility called TheaterGame where students could stage their own interpretations of the plays from a database of hundreds of costumed actors and props. While they went through the activities in TheaterGame, the students could jump to hypertext tutorials about unfamiliar concepts, or they could browse a library of annotated examples.

A different kind of educational use of hypertext is to support the teacher's side of the process. John Leggett from Texas A&M University experimented with hypertext support for teachers as part of a course he taught on hypertext [Leggett et al. 1989]. This was probably the first university level course on hypertext. Students were asked to turn in their assignments on the KMS hypertext system at Texas A&M and Leggett graded and annotated them on the system.[10] Since KMS is a multiuser system, Leggett could return the reports to the students on the system and include cross references from one student to another: "See how XX did it...."

Foreign Languages

The linking abilities of hypertext are ideal for the learning of foreign languages. Hypertext can provide automatic access to dictionaries through implicit links from any text, as shown in the Intermedia system in Figure 4.15. A student who does not know English very well might still be able to understand material in Intermedia because of its ability to link to an explanation of any word. As further discussed in the following section on the classics, hypertext also enables students to view two parallel versions of the same text: An original version and a translation.

The *Video Linguist* is a hypermedia system that teaches a language by showing clips of television broadcasts from a country speaking that language. For example, French lessons might show a sports broadcast from the Tour de France. The advantages of this approach are that TV shows are fun and motivating (and often well produced) and that they teach the culture of the country in addition to the language. One major problem with learning languages is that native speakers of many languages tend to speak in a very agitated and fast manner which makes their utterances hard to understand for foreigners. But of course the goal of learning French is to understand the way the language is actually spoken in France and not the way a teacher may speak it in class. Therefore the Video Linguist initially plays the original sound track from the broadcast version of the show. If there is a part of the sound track that students do not understand, they can utilize the hypertext facilities and link to a version where the same words spoken more slowly. If they still don't understand it, they can follow a link to a version where each word is spoken v-e-r-y s-l-o-w-l-y and clearly. Students can also link to subtitles in French (normally not displayed in order to encourage attention to the spoken language) and to an English translation. A final hypertext feature in the Video Linguist allows the student to click on any word in the subtitles and get its dictionary definition. Unfortunately, these translations come up in separate windows that have to be explicitly dismissed, even though a better solution would have been to minimize the user's overhead in viewing the dictionary

---

[10] See also [Brown 1990] for a discussion of grading criteria for hypertext essays.

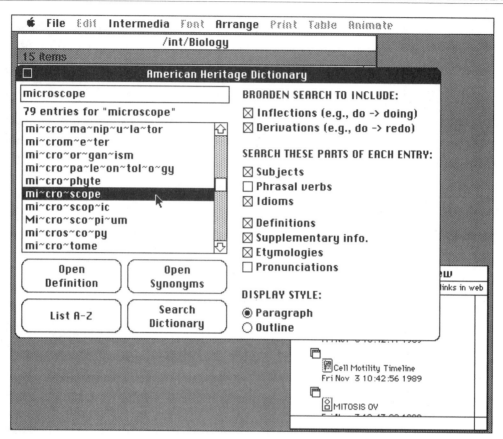

Figure 4.15. *The IRIS InterLex Server, adds dictionary and thesaurus support to Intermedia. A user may search either Houghton-Mifflin's American Heritage Dictionary or Roget's Thesaurus II for the definition or synonyms for a specified word. Users can broaden or narrow the scope of the search by turning "inflections" and "derivations" on or off. They can search only the subject fields, or any combination of the other six fields. Both the dictionary and thesaurus lookup are accessible directly from the desktop; the user can just select the word and choose either the "lookup" or "thesaurus" menu command. Copyright © 1989 by Brown University, reprinted with permission.*

by showing it in a pop-up field that would disappear automatically when the user let go of the mouse button.

À la Recontre de Philippe from MIT's Project Athena [Hodges et al. 1989] teaches French by a role-playing simulation where the student must help a

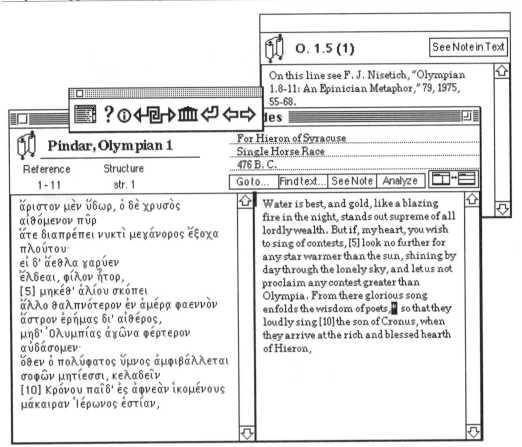

Figure 4.16. *A screen from Perseus showing two versions of a poem by Pindar. Copyright © 1989 by the President and Fellows of Harvard University and the Annenberg/CPB Project, reprinted with permission.*

Parisian named Philippe find a new apartment. In one instance they have to relay a message to him from an answering machine. In order to do so, they obviously have to understand the message. In addition to traditional facilities for replaying video sequences, the Philippe system allows students to add subtitles in either French or English if they need them, and it also has hypertext links to a glossary and to cultural notes with backup information about idiomatic expressions or historical locations. The hypertext advantage is that each student can utilize as much of this material as needed or desired by that student.

Classics

Classical Greek literature and culture is a natural application for a CD-ROM, because the chief disadvantage of a read-only device is almost irrelevant. It does not matter so much that the CD-ROM cannot be updated because there is not any new classical Greek literature being written.[11] The Perseus project [Crane 1987, 1988; Marchionini and Crane 1994; Mylonas 1992] at Harvard University is a major attempt to provide hypertext support for the study of ancient Greek literature, history, and archaeology. The Perseus CD-ROM gives hypertext access to large amounts of original source text in Greek and also provides several facilities to help students understand the text, including the parallel translation shown in Figure 4.16.

Furthermore, the Perseus disk contains hypertext versions of some scholarly articles and encyclopedia articles that interpret the original Greek sources. These secondary writings often contain extensive references to the primary sources that can be automated as hypertext links. This system has the potential to change completely the way students approach the learning of classical Greek culture. When a textbook may have as many as 25 source references on every page, there is little chance that the student will actually go to a traditional library and find all the dusty volumes on the top shelf. In a hypertext, however, the sources are a single click away, and while students still may not pursue all 25 citations, they will no longer have to accept most of the textbook author's statements uncritically. The trend for students to move their focus of attention in the direction of the original Greek sources is also reinforced by translation tools such as automatic morphology analysis[12] and dictionary lookup.

As shown in Figure 4.17, Perseus contains more than text [Mylonas and Heath 1990]. It has photographs of temples and other architecture and illustrations of archaeological objects. The thumbnail browser provides an overview that allows the user fast access to the various views. In many cases, one actually gets a better image of the artwork by looking at the photos on the computer than by looking at the original work of art since it may be small or

---

[11] Actually, the interpretations and opinions of how Greek literature is read and how exactly the text should appear *do* change. So the read-only nature of the CD-ROM can still be a disadvantage, although it is used in the Perseus project because of its huge storage space.

[12] Determining the grammatical role of words in a sentence to understand, for instance, which word is the object and which is the subject.

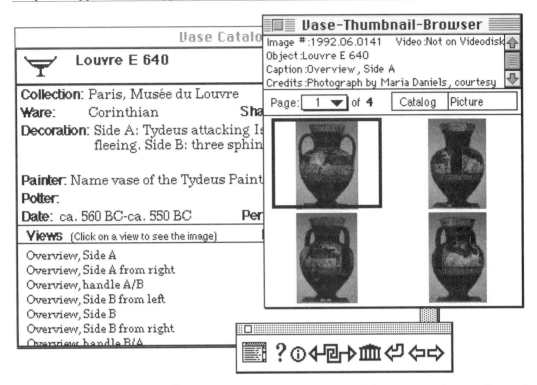

Figure 4.17. *Part of the vase catalog in Perseus. Users can view enlarged details of the artwork or see color photographs of the vases displayed on a separate monitor. Copyright © 1989 by the President and Fellows of Harvard University and the Annenberg/CPB Project, reprinted with permission.*

poorly lit in a museum. The hypertext nature of Perseus enables the different parts of the system to enhance one another. For example, the *Bacchae* of Euripides can be appreciated better when one can link to vase paintings of satyrs. Similarly, the histories of Herodotus and Thucydides are clearer when illustrated with maps and photographs of the places they mention.

The current version of Perseus is implemented in HyperCard on Macintosh computers. But classicists have a long-term perspective and are prepared to move on to another platform if a better one becomes available several years from now. A hypertext version of classical Greek literature can be used for many more years than the lifetime of a computer system. Because of this "diachronic" perspective [Crane 1990], all text elements and hypertext links have been coded in a machine-independent format using a set of SGML

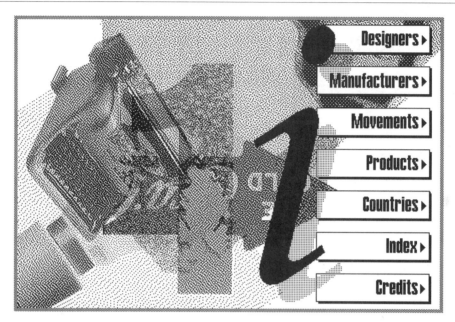

Figure 4.18. *The front screen of the London Design Museum information hypertext. Screen layout copyright © 1989 by Cognitive Applications, contents copyright © 1989 by the Design Museum, reprinted by permission.*

markup tags. Images are stored in resolution-independent formats like PostScript to allow them to be displayed on other types of computer screens in the future. These standard SGML and PostScript files are then converted once more by an automatic process to a HyperCard format when they are included in the distributed version of Perseus.

The first edition of Perseus appeared in 1991 on a single CD-ROM and a laserdisk and the second edition was released in 1994 (now on several CD-ROMs). The Perseus database will grow and change in future releases, since it is being produced in stages. Successive versions of Perseus are planned to have more and better information on it.

Museums

A special case of educational hypertext is the museum information system [Bearman 1991] since most people do not go to museums specifically to study. It is impossible to present museum-goers with all the relevant information about the exhibits in a printed form; that would scare them away. The difficulty

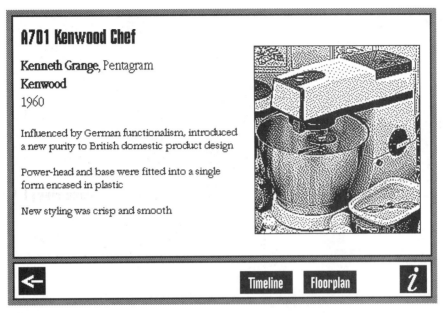

Figure 4.19. *A "product screen" from the London Design Museum. Clicking on "floorplan" takes the user to a screen with the location of the product highlighted. This node also has links to a historical overview ("timeline"), and to information about the manufacturer and designer. Clicking on the "i" will take the user back to the first screen from any other node in the hypertext. Screen layout copyright © 1989 by Cognitive Applications, contents copyright © 1989 by the Design Museum, reprinted by permission.*

of knowing the extent of a hypertext information space is actually an advantage in this application.

The Getty Museum has produced an electronic version of its illuminated medieval manuscripts to allow their visitors the sense of paging through the books even though the originals are much too fragile to be handled by the public. The traditional way to exhibit medieval manuscripts has been to display a single two-page spread in a glass case, but that method removes the individual illustration from its context as part of the telling of a story. The electronic medium allows the user access to the full sequence of illustrations.

These examples have been minor additions to existing museum resources, but the Design Museum in London has based its entire information system around a hypertext. Figure 4.18 shows the front screen, which welcomes the user and allows access to various forms of information about modern design.

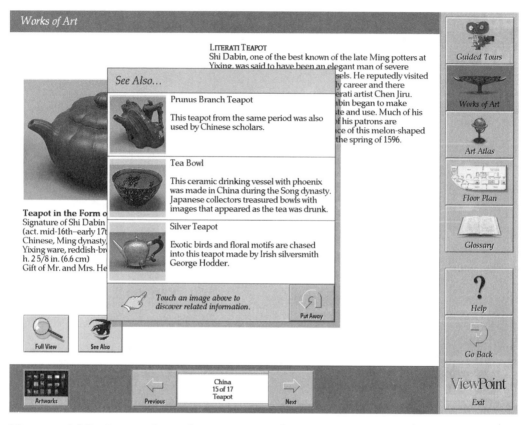

Figure 4.20. *Screen from the ViewPoint hypertext accessed in the Chinese art gallery of the Seattle Art Museum. Copyright © 1992 by Continuum Productions Corporations, Developed with the Seattle Art Museum, reprinted by permission.*

Users can access information about various design movements like Bauhaus or Functionalism or they can access the information starting with countries or manufacturers. They can also look at individual designers or products. All of this material is of course connected with hypertext links; visitors who might have started with accessing the screen about the Kenwood Chef in Figure 4.19 because they once owned one themselves could end up reading about other products of the same period and the underlying theoretical design movement defining the look of the 1960s.

Museum systems require "walk-up-and-use" usability in the sense that users will not be willing to go through a special initial period of training to be able to use the system. Simple designs without too many fancy navigational options are suited for this application. The need to pull the museum-goer into the hypertext information space also impels the use of very attractive initial displays (welcome screens) like Figure 4.18.

By installing hypertext kiosks in the galleries, museums can encourage visitors to explore connections between the objects in their collections that are not immediately apparent due to the physical nature of the building. For example, Figure 4.20 shows a screen from the ViewPoint hypertext system that users may see while visiting the gallery for Chinese art in the Seattle Art Museum. The basic node shows a Chinese teapot and gives more information about it than can comfortably be written on its physical label. By clicking on the "See Also" button, the user gets a list of other objects in the museum, including additional items associated with tea in China but also with an image of an Irish silver teapot. This Irish teapot is exhibited in a completely different part of the museum and museumgoers would never see the two teapots next to each other, but the hypertext system allows people to explore similarities in form and functionality and differences in decoration and style across the two cultures. By clicking on the miniatures, the user can follow the hypertext link to further information about the Irish teapot and may be encouraged to look it up on the floor plan and go see it.

Some museums have taken advantage of the Internet to deliver online versions of their exhibition catalogs or to present guided tours through parts of their collections. Figure 4.21 shows an online version of the catalog for an exhibition in Singapore. By providing access to their collections over the Internet, museums can communicate with more people than they otherwise would. To some extent, the Internet versions of museum exhibits can help attract people to visit the physical museum, by generating additional publicity and by giving people more information than would be found in a typical poster or newspaper ad. On the other hand, some museum curators fear that Internet distribution of too wide parts of their holdings would keep people from actually going to the museum. The outcome of this dilemma remains to be seen but one should remember that coffee-table books have been available for many years with much better reproductions of paintings than we are likely to see on computer screens for several more years, and people still feel that there is something special about seeing the original *Mona Lisa*.

Figure 4.21. *Internet version of the catalog for the* Raffles Reviewed: 175 Years Later *exhibition on Sir Stamford Raffles (URL* http://www.ncb.gov.sg/nhb/raffles/intro.html*) organized by the National Heritage Board of Singapore. Notice how the node about the English East India Company has a hypertext link to the Dutch East India Company. The anchor is displayed in a different color, indicating that the user has already seen the destination document. Copyright © 1994 by the National Heritage Board and National Computer Board, Singapore, reprinted by permission.*

The ultimate user interface for a museum hypertext would be to provide links from the exhibited objects themselves to any additional information. In his automated tour guide project, Ben Bederson suggests using an augmented reality approach to museum hypertexts [Bederson and Druin 1995]. Augmented reality is almost the opposite of virtual reality: instead of embedding the user within an artificial 3-D world of computer graphics, augmented reality starts with the existing physical world and lets the user stay connected to reality while superimposing (e.g., from a projector) computer information onto the objects near the user. In the automated tour guides project, a museum visitor can walk through a series of galleries in any order and hear descriptions of individual exhibits simply by stopping in front of them. When the viewer walks away from a piece, the description stops.

Entertainment and Leisure Applications

Hypertext provides several opportunities for pure enjoyment. Unfortunately there has been very little research conducted in this area, possibly because funding agencies may find it frivolous to study how to have fun. But there has still been some pioneering research as well as the first few commercial examples.

Tourist Guides

Tourist information achieves a good match with the "golden rules" of hypertext since tourists typically want to read only a small part of the information available about a given city or country. Furthermore the information can reasonably easily be divided into nodes for each attraction, tourist service, historical era, or geographical location. The problem with traditional tourist guides is that they need to structure all this information according to a single principle, whereas the tourist has multiple varying needs.

Most tourist guides structure their information according to the type of information and have separate chapters on hotels, restaurants, shopping, and museums and sights. In contrast, ACCESS guides [Wurman 1989] are structured according to the geography of each city and describe everything in a given neighborhood on the same page. The advantage of the ACCESS approach is that it is easy to find a place to eat lunch after a visit to the British Museum, but the disadvantage is that it is hard to find the best place in London to buy science

Figure 4.22. *The welcome screen for the* Glasgow Online *tourist information system. Copyright © 1989 by the University of Strathclyde Department of Information Science, reprinted with permission.*

fiction books. I personally often buy both the ACCESS guide to a city and a more traditional guide book.

Glasgow Online [Baird and Percival 1989] is a hypertext tourist guide that combines the best of both types of guide. The front screen of the system (see Figure 4.22) has the traditional subject-oriented view of the city and allows the user to find, say, a hotel in a certain price range. From the description of the hotel, the user can jump to a map of Glasgow with a highlighted icon for the chosen hotel. The user can then click on other icons in the neighborhood to see what other facilities are nearby.

Tourist information systems have the problem that they should be usable by visitors from foreign countries [Baird 1990], who may not speak the local language. The designers of *Glasgow Online* have not completely solved that problem, but they have addressed it by extensive use of icons and graphics and by conducting usability tests with foreign users.

Tourist guides should ideally be portable since large parts of a tourist's information needs do not become apparent until the tourist hits the streets.

Traditional personal computers do have laptop versions that would be capable of displaying standard hypertexts as portable devices. A business traveler might bring a laptop for other reasons and might benefit from loading it with a travel guide in addition to, say, a PowerPoint presentation or some business reports that need to be edited. A leisure tourist would probably find a traditional laptop computer to be too large and heavy to carry but might be willing to carry a PDA (personal digital assistant). Currently, there is not much software available for PDAs, but one of the few exceptions is the Fodor's tourist series of tourist guides for the Apple Newton. The fact that a hypertext tourist guide was one of the first ten commercial applications to become available for the Newton is an indication of the potential for the genre once PDAs become more prevalent.

Libraries

Some library applications are for the retrieval of technical or scientific information and are very similar to the applications discussed above under dictionaries or to the information retrieval techniques discussed in Chapter 8. Also, libraries certainly need to include electronic publications like hypertext, if they want to keep up with modern technology. In the future, a "library" might well be a computer network service rather than a building.

The Book House is a library system using hypertext techniques to help users find books without the limitations of traditional information retrieval. In contrast to most computer systems for libraries, which are intended for the retrieval of technical literature, the Book House is intended for average citizens who use public libraries to borrow fiction.

The Book House project [Pejtersen 1989] was conducted in cooperation among Risø National Laboratory, Jutland Telephone, RC Computer Inc., the Royal Art Academy, and the Royal School of Librarianship in Denmark under the leadership of Annelise Mark Pejtersen. The system was field tested at the Hjortespring Library with good results.

The user interface of the Book House is based on a building metaphor somewhat like a real library.[13] The first choice upon entering the building is whether to enter a room with books for children, a room with books for adults, or a room with books for everybody. After having made this choice, the user will see the "strategy selection room" shown in Figure 4.23. In our illustration

---

[13] One indication of the building metaphor is that the icons at the top of each screen for returning to previous states depict the relevant rooms.

Figure 4.23. *The main room in the Book House. Users select their search strategy by clicking on one of the four library patrons. Copyright © 1989 by Annelise Mark Pejtersen, reprinted by permission.*

we have chosen to search for books for adults, so the people shown looking at the books are adults. The illustrations in the children's section show drawings of children instead.

Because people have many different ways of finding books, the Book House supports four different search strategies, which can be selected in the strategy selection room by clicking on one of the four areas of the room in Figure 4.23. The simplest strategy is the random browsing used by the man on the right. Users who click at this part of the room are taken directly into the database of books at a random location. The woman in the left part of the room is performing a search by analogy by looking through the shelves for a book similar to one already read. Users who select this strategy will be prompted to select the book they have already read and the system will then present a list of similar books ordered by similarity rating.

The woman looking at a set of pictures is engaged in a browsing strategy whereby she is looking at pictures to find something that may interest her. Users who select this strategy are presented with several screens of icons, each

Figure 4.24. *Book House icons, used for the browsing strategy. Users might click on the card game icon to browse books about gambling and card playing. Each icon represents several themes, and the exact meaning depends on whether the user has been identified to the system as a child or an adult. Copyright © 1989 by Annelise Mark Pejtersen, reprinted by permission.*

of which represents a set of search terms that can be selected by clicking. This process frees the user from having to generate search terms and may also give rise to potentially new perspectives on perhaps vaguely perceived needs. The search terms associated with each icon have been determined by empirical user testing.

For example, the icon showing a handshake (in the middle of Figure 4.24) could be viewed as a Dane shaking hands with a foreigner and might therefore represent the abstract concept of aid to developing countries. But it could also be seen as simply representing "friendship." Instead of trying to come up with icons to represent all index terms uniquely, the solution was to assign each icon several meanings and have the 108 icons in the system cover more than 1000 terms. The exact terms associated with each icon further differ depending on whether the user is a child or an adult.

Figure 4.25. *The desk objects used to represent different kinds of analytic search in the Book House. For example, the user could click on the movie poster to search for books by their plot and theme, or they could click on the reading glasses to search for books at a given reading level. Copyright © 1989 by Annelise Mark Pejtersen, reprinted by permission.*

These icons have been designed for the user's national cultural context. For example, all Danes would recognize the icon for prehistoric settings as a Neolithic dolmen (lower left of Figure 4.24). A corresponding British system might have used an image of Stonehenge while other countries would have to use yet other icons.

The man at the desk is performing an analytic search and has access to twelve classification dimensions as represented by the following graphic elements in Figure 4.25:

- Movie poster: Plot and theme.
- Book cover: Physical appearance of the book (e.g., picture and color of cover).
- Drawers with hearts, weapons, and animals: Genre.
- Busts: Main characters, name and age.
- Globe: Place (geographical environment).

- Landscape through the window: Setting (social, professional, and geographical environment).
- Glasses: Readability of the text.
- Clock: Time period.
- Theater masks: Emotional experience (e.g. exciting or humorous).
- Picture of a writer: The author's intention of cognition/information.
- Index cards: Search by name of author or search by title (two different search dimensions).

By combining several of these classification dimensions, users can find, for instance, romance novels set in seventeenth century France.

In addition to providing several search strategies, the Book House also utilizes hypertext principles to allow users to change strategies by jumping back to the strategy selection room or by linking to books "similar" to the one currently on the screen, no matter how it was retrieved.

From field testing of the Book House it turns out that regular library users do indeed use many different strategies. Using the analytical classifications accounted for 31% of the searches, while picture browsing was second most popular with 27%. Search by analogy accounted for 23% of the searches, and 20% of searches were performed with random browsing. Users liked the system very much: 95% were satisfied with the interface and 84% were satisfied with the search results.

Another example of a library application is providing public access to archives of historical documents. For example, the State Library of New South Wales in Sydney, Australia, contains large amounts of old convict records from the settlement of the colony 200 years ago, and many modern Australians visit the library to discover what crimes their ancestors committed that caused them to be deported. Currently this genealogical search requires people to wade through mounds of old documents and follow the links to past generations by hand. Most of this material would be an obvious candidate for hypertext access, however, since the information is interlinked to a great extent. One problem would be the need to represent the form of the original records and not just their content since they have considerable "romantic" attributes. The right ambiance might be created by scanning in images of the original pages and combining them with handwriting recognition to generate a machine-readable representation for automatic construction of hypertext links.

Unfortunately current computer technology cannot read the handwriting of eighteenth century Royal Navy officers, and there are several other technical obstacles to implementing a hypertext system for the convict records. These problems will probably be solved in the next ten years or so, and one could well envisage additional library services that would result from having the records on hypertext. For example, computer networks would make it possible to bring the library to the users rather than having them come to the library, a feature that would be a considerable advantage in a country as large as Australia. It would likewise be possible to use the original records in teaching the national heritage, even in schools in the outback, and to give all students the feeling of exploring original sources.

Interactive Fiction

As further described in Chapter 10, I got very negative replies when I asked a group of computer science students whether they would like to read fiction online. They only gave online fiction a rating of 0.5 on a scale from zero to four (with two as the neutral point). But that survey asked people who had not had actual experience with reading online fiction and who would therefore have a hard time imagining the potential advantages of *interactive* fiction as opposed to purely *online* traditional fiction.

My personal view is that there is very little to be gained from converting traditional forms of fiction to the online medium. As long as you are just reading a regular novel with a single stream of action, you are much better off reading a printed book. Only when new forms of fiction are invented will we gain any benefit from putting them on hypertext. The reader needs to be able to interact with the fictional universe instead of just being in a page-turning mode.

One possibility for online fiction would be the "shared universe" type of story that has recently become popular in the science fiction genre. The basic idea is that several authors write stories set in the same fictional universe with the same general background and many of the same characters. One could potentially collect several hundred such stories together in a hypertext on a single CD-ROM and let readers pursue the type of plot and character each of them found interesting. Such an online fiction project would fit the three golden rules of having many smaller plot elements that were interlinked and were enjoyable for readers who read only a few such elements.

The commercial feasibility of this type of shared online fiction is problematic, however. Hundreds of authors would need to write stories that would have to be coordinated and interlinked, but buyers would not be willing to pay much more for the CD-ROM than perhaps five times the price of a regular novel, since each of them would only read a small part of the total text. Maybe doing a "shared universe" hypertext CD-ROM would be an idea for a collaborative project for a large group of students taking classes in creative writing?

It is also possible to have interactive fiction in works by a single author [Howell 1990]. The Storyspace system from the University of North Carolina is a hypertext system specifically designed for writing and reading interactive fiction. Probably the most famous work written in the Storyspace system is *Afternoon, A Story* by Michael Joyce (1987). *Afternoon* consists of 539 nodes and 915 links, enough to form a reasonably complex hyperspace for the story. The actual story does not have a traditional plot but is more in the nature of a number of snapshots of an underlying fictional construction, which readers discover as they read more and more snapshots. The *Dictionary of the Khazars: A Lexicon Novel in 100,000 Words* by Milorad Pavic (1988) is an example of this kind of "trackless expanse" [Moulthrop 1989] implemented in a traditional printed book. It is a collection of encyclopedic articles about a Central European people whom the reader gradually gets to know by reading various "dictionary" entries. There is no narrative as such in the book.

Interactive fictions in the form of simulated worlds[14] are some of the most popular hypertexts for children. One example is *Inigo Gets Out* (see Figures 9.18 and 9.19), which children find very enjoyable. In a longitudinal study of a single five-year-old boy we have found that he continues viewing/reading/navigating/using/playing with the story even after several months, as well as showing it to other children when they visit. The language does not yet have a single good word for the activity of going through a hypertext like *Inigo Gets Out* since it is completely nonverbal.

A larger nonverbal interactive fiction for children ("of all ages") is *The Manhole* (see Figures 4.26 and 4.27), which contains 753 nodes and takes up 23 megabytes on a CD-ROM.[15] It takes place in a fantasy world with talking

---

[14] In future systems, these simulated worlds will most likely be displayed in virtual reality, but currently they mostly use two-dimensional user interfaces or simulated 3-D on flat screens.

[15] *The Manhole* was reissued in a second edition in 1994 under the title "*The Manhole CD-ROM Masterpiece Edition*" with color screens and better sound effects. The new CD-ROM contained 200 MB of data. To get an idea of the changes, compare Figure 4.26 and 4.28. The new edition has several distinct improvements like the use of morphing to transform objects to other objects, but I

Figure 4.26. *Screen from* The Manhole *showing the user's view after having moved to the top of a tower in the woods. Users will see this screen after having been through some previous screens showing a winding stairway leading to the top of the tower. Because of this movement and the presence of the flamingo on the top of the tower, users initially view the tower as a traditional building, but further movement will reveal something else (see Figure 4.27). Copyright © 1988 by Cyan, reprinted with permission.*

animals and dragons where magic bean stalks grow into the sky. The fantasy world is displayed to the user in a first-person perspective (i.e., graphically showing what you would actually see if you were positioned at the current location in the world), and users move through the world by clicking on the place they want to go.

Figures 4.26 and 4.27 show an example of navigation that violates traditional expectations. This "magical" movement in the world of an

---

personally feel that the original black-and-white interface had more charm and was a better fit with the story.

Figure 4.27. *Screen from* The Manhole *showing an example of a magical dimension: When users move to the objects seen outside the tower in Figure 4.26, they get to this screen where it is revealed that the tower has been magically transformed to a rook on a chess board (this visual pun is actually better in Danish where a chess rook is called a tårn ("tower") so that the pun also becomes verbal). Copyright © 1988 by Cyan, reprinted with permission.*

interactive fiction adds spice to the experience of using the system and is probably good in a system having entertainment as its main purpose. It also seems to make it harder to acquire a conceptual model of the navigation space, however, so it would probably not be suited for more work-oriented situations.

The Manhole is not completely nonverbal but contains messages from various characters to the user. These messages are printed on the screen in cartoon-like speech-bubbles and are also read out loud by the system using good quality sound and some interesting voice characterizations. There are four main characters with whom the user interacts: An elephant who paddles the user around in a small boat, a dragon, a walrus, and a rabbit. Each character has a tone of voice consistent with the way it behaves (e.g., the walrus is lazy

Figure 4.28. *The image corresponding to Figure 4.27 in the revised color version: Screen shot fromThe Manhole CD-ROM Masterpiece Edition. CD-ROM computer game: game and screen shot protected by Copyright © 1994 by Cyan, Inc.® All rights reserved, reprinted by permission.*

and the dragon is a hip dude). Other sound effects, including both music and various naturalistic sounds, are also used to good effect so this is a true hypermedia system.

The main experience of viewing/navigating/reading/(whatever we want to call it) *The Manhole* is again not that of following a traditional plot or narrative. Instead the hypertext provides a fictional space in which readers construct their own stories as they move through it. The experience is somewhat like an exploration, but it is distinctly more relaxed than the feeling one gets from exploring adventure games (see the example in Figure 1.2), where the user is set a specific goal and is under continuous pressure to achieve it or "die."

Harry McMahon and Bill O'Neill from the University of Ulster have tried placing a few Macintoshes with sound and image digitizers in an elementary school to get the pupils to create their own interactive fictions. Of course, most of these stories are fairly simple—such as "The teddy bear went for a walk in the forest and met another teddy bear" (a seven-year-old's creation)—and were shown over a sequential series of screens like a cartoon strip.

More advanced designs use a facility called bubbles where the children can first draw their cards and then choose from various shapes of comics-like speech- and thought-balloons to add to the image. The interesting idea is that it is possible to add multiple bubbles to each card whereupon they will be displayed to the reader one at a time. In this way, it is possible for the child to generate a dialogue between characters in the story. It is even possible to contrast what the characters *say* with what they *think*. For example, in a story about a mouse about to be killed, the mouse asked for a last wish: to sing a song. This wish is spoken out loud (placed in a speech-balloon), but the mouse's thought (placed in a thought-balloon) is "I am not as stupid as I look." The next speech-balloon revealed that the mouse had chosen to sing the well-known song about bottles on a wall (falling down one at a time), but starting with, "A thousand million green bottles sitting on a wall...." So this smart mouse will survive for some time to come.

Most of these stories were basically linear in nature and do not really have all that much to do with the concept of hypertext. McMahon and O'Neill have on purpose avoided introducing commercial hyperstories (such as *Inigo Gets Out* or *The Manhole*) to the children in order to be able to observe the natural evolution of their approach to the new medium of interactive fiction. It actually did happen that a few ten-year-olds discovered the hypertext principle on their own. They were creating a story about a person who was visiting an alien world and was captured by the aliens. He was offered a job by the alien boss and thought to himself, "Should I try to escape?" or "Should I take the job?" The reader could click on either of these two thought balloons to proceed with the story. McMahon has remarked that an interesting aspect of this story design was that the pupils had had to change their perspective on writing. Originally they thought of creating a story as they went through it (writing for the writer, as it were), but in this new situation, they had to consider what the reader could do and would want to do, so they had to change their perspective to writing for readers.

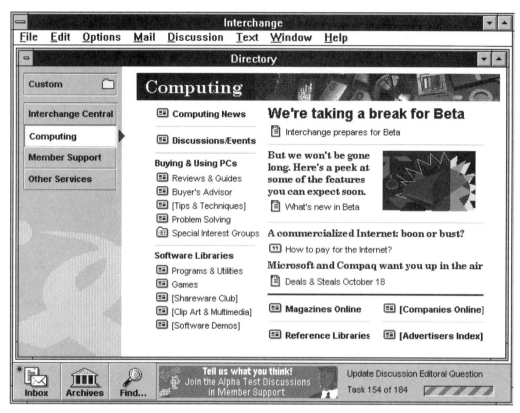

Figure 4.29. *The Interchange online service provides a selection of computer magazine articles and other news. Copyright © 1994 by the Interchange Network Company, reprinted by permission.*

News, Newspapers, and Magazines

News delivery is an obvious candidate for online services since events can be reported as they occur instead of having to wait for the scheduled publication time of a newspaper or magazine. Most large newspapers have online versions where their articles can be accessed around the clock. Some added value derives from search capabilities where one can find, for example, all news stories about a certain company over the last month before deciding whether to invest in it or how to solicit it as a customer. As further discussed in Chapter 8, information filtering can be used to design personalized electronic newspapers with exactly those newsstories that are of interest to the individual reader.

Figure 4.29 shows a screen from the Interchange online service which provides access to articles from many computer magazines as well as discussion groups and the ability to download software [Perkins 1995]. The ability to link between articles from several magazines is a value-added feature of the hypertext versions of the magazines, as is the discussions between the subscribers. As further discussed in Chapter 8, even the discussions between readers is a value-added feature for the hypermedia versions of the magazines: if somebody is reading, say, an article about an upgrade to a spreadsheet application, that person is likely to be interested in the experience other readers have had when installing the upgrade.

Interchange has a multitasking software architecture. This allows the user to have multiple activities going on simultaneously. For example, the system can download new articles on subscribed topics without keeping the user from following hypertext links from the article currently on the screen.

Sex

Given human nature, it should come as no surprise that most new media are used for various sexual, erotic, and pornographic purposes. When home video players were first introduced, very few major film studios wanted to release their films in VCR format for the small home market, and for the first several years VCR revenues were dominated by pornographic films. In fact, industry lore has it that one of the reasons the VHS format won over the technically superior Betamax format was the higher availability of porn videos on VHS tapes. Similarly, the telephone, photography, the written word, and even cave paintings have all been used as pornographic media.

Following along the lines of these earlier media, the hypermedia market has seen a large number of sexually and pornographic products, with interactive experiences like *Virtual Valerie* topping the CD-ROM bestseller lists.[16] According to reviews, these early pornographic multimedia productions are not sufficiently erotic and suffer from poor image quality and limited interactivity, so it is likely that they mostly sell due to their novelty value. Over the long term, the dynamic and user-controlled nature of hypermedia should offer great potential for this particular application and it should be

---

[16] Version 2.0 of the Virtual Valerie CD-ROM sold 30,000 copies in the first two weeks after its release in November 1994 according to Mike Saenz who is president of the vendor, Reactor.

Newsgroup	Number of Readers	Monthly Postings
news.announce.newusers	700,000	37
alt.sex	600,000	4,867
news.answers	550,000	1,584
rec.humor.funny	470,000	48
alt.sex.stories	440,000	2,283
alt.binaries.pictures.erotica	410,000	8,772
misc.forsale	410,000	5,385
rec.arts.erotica	400,000	60
misc.jobs.offered	380,000	8,992
rec.humor	370,000	3,954

Table 4.1. *List of the top-ten newsgroups on the network news with respect to number of readers world wide at the end of 1994 based on data from Brian Reid's Usenet survey. At that time, the Internet had about 30 million users, 7.1 million of whom were reading at least one newsgroup. In total, about 3.2 million articles were posted to the 12,500 or so active newsgroups that month according to UUnet traffic statistics.*

possible to design interactive experiences that are more powerful than those offered by static media.

Current technology essentially makes advanced user interfaces useless for pornographic purposes, but that does not stop people from speculating on future possibilities in more or less sensationalist ways. Noted virtual reality researcher Randy Pausch from the University of Virginia says that he has been asked questions about virtual sex or virtual pornography by every single member of the press that ever interviewed him with the exception of a reporter from *Reader's Digest* [Pausch et al. 1993].

The early-market dominance of sex in new media is demonstrated by the Internet network news. As shown in Table 4.1, four of the ten most widely read netnews groups are about sex:

  • alt.sex is for general discussions about sex
  • alt.sex.stories distributes fiction with pronounced sexual content
  • alt.binaries.pictures.erotica contains digitized photographs of an erotic nature
    • rec.arts.erotica also distributes fictionwith sexual content, but is edited

Moderated newsgroups like rec.arts.erotica are edited by a human who reads all submitted postings and only passes those through that meet editorial quality criteria. Comparing the number of monthly postings from alt.sex.stories (2,283) and rec.arts.erotica (60) may indicate that the quality of the posted stories is not always very high given that only 3% of them were good enough to pass an editor's scrutiny. Similarly, the moderated group rec.humor.funny carried only 1% of the jokes in the unmoderated group rec.humor.

There is no doubt that the current dominance of the sex newsgroups is partly due to the fact that the Internet still has a very large proportion of its users among undergraduate college students, with many more male than female users. Over time, the sex groups may grow more slowly than overall net growth as the pool of users becomes more diversified and representative of the population at large. As a comparison, remember that pornographic films dominated early sales of videotapes for home VCRs but that the best-selling videos these days are Disney animations (though, of course, there is still a large market for porn videos as evidenced by the shelf-space allocation of most video rental stores).

A final aspect of computerized erotica is that it may overcome censorship barriers. Many countries employ armies of customs inspectors to paint over the offending parts of pictures in imported publications, but digitized pornography can circumvent the censors in the disguise of, for example, the least significant digits of a large spreadsheet.

5.   The Architecture of Hypertext Systems

In theory one can distinguish three levels of a hypertext system [Campbell and Goodman 1988]:

- Presentation level: user interface
- Hypertext Abstract Machine (HAM) level: nodes and links
- Database level: storage, shared data, and network access

Actually, very few current hypertext systems follow this model in their internal structure; most are a more or less confused mix of features. Even so, the model shows interesting directions for the future and is important for standardization work. The following sections describe each of the levels in further detail, starting at the bottom.

The Database Level

The database level is at the bottom of the three-level model and deals with all the traditional issues of information storage that do not really have anything specifically to do with hypertext. It is necessary to store large amounts of information on various computer storage devices like hard disks, optical disks, etc., and it may be necessary to keep some of the information stored on remote servers accessed through a network. No matter how the information is stored it should be possible to retrieve a specified small chunk of it in a very short time. This sounds very much like a specification for a database, which is what it is.

Furthermore, the database level should handle other traditional database issues, like multiuser access to the information, and various security considerations, including backup. Ultimately it will be the database level's responsibility to enforce the access controls which may be defined at the upper levels of the architecture.

As far as the database level is concerned, the hypertext nodes and links are just data objects with no particular meaning. Each of them forms a unit that only one user can modify at the same time and that takes up so many bits of storage space. In real life, it may be advantageous for the database level to know a little bit more about its data objects in order to enable it to manage its storage space most efficiently and provide faster response. But in any case the hypertext field would do well in taking advantage of the extensive work and experience in the traditional database field for the design and implementation of the database level.

The Hypertext Abstract Machine (HAM) Level

The HAM sits in the middle of the sandwich between the database and user interface levels. This center is where the hypertext system determines the basic nature of its nodes and links and where it maintains the relation among them. See the discussion below about the range of design choices regarding nodes and links. The HAM would have knowledge of the form of the nodes and links and would know what attributes were related to each. For example, a node might have an "owner" attribute that specified the user who created it and who has to authorize updates, or it could have a version number. Links might be typed as in NoteCards, or they might be plain pointers as in Guide.

The HAM is the best candidate for standardization of import-export formats for hypertexts, since the database level has to be heavily machine dependent in its storage format and the user interface level is highly different from one hypertext system to the next. This leaves only the HAM, and since we do need the ability to transfer information from one hypertext system to the other, we have to come up with an interchange format at this level. One current example of a HAM-level standard is HyTime (the ISO standard for *hypermedia/time*-based document structuring) [Newcomb et al. 1991; DeRose and Durand 1994].

Interchanging hypertexts is more difficult than simply interchanging the component data in the nodes, even though there are also problems with the less standardized data formats for non-ASCII information like graphics and video clips. The problem is that hypertext interchange also requires the transfer of linking information. It should be possible to transfer the basic links (i.e., the "A points to B" type information), but large parts of the linking information may be lost.

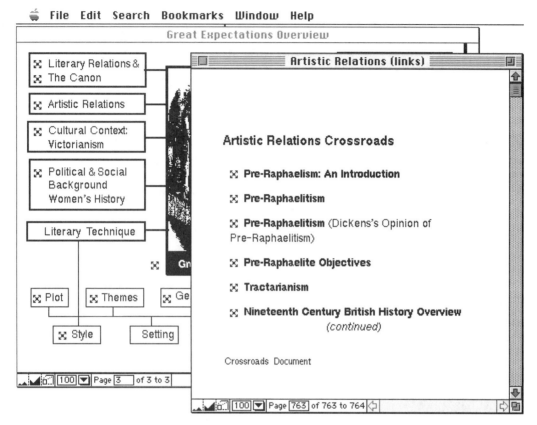

Figure 5.1. *So-called crossroads document used to represent one-to-many links in the WorldView version of the* Dickens Web. *Copyright © 1992–94 by Paul Kahn, George P. Landow, and Brown University, reprinted by permission.*

For example, some hypertext systems like Intermedia have links that point to specific text strings in the destination node, whereas other systems like Hyperties only point to the destination node as a complete entity. A transfer of a hypertext from Intermedia to Hyperties would therefore lose important aspects of the linking information but should still be possible in principle.[1] Of

---

[1] If we were to transfer a hypertext structure from Hyperties to Intermedia there would be no way to come up with a sensible substring for the destination anchor because the Hyperties author would not have considered that option when writing the hypertext. We would probably have to come up with a dummy anchor in the beginning of the destination node just to keep the Intermedia system happy.

course if the transfer had been from Intermedia to Guide (which does have anchored link destinations), then we would want the transfer to keep the information about the destination substring so that it could be highlighted on arrival. The difficulty is that we would like to achieve both of these results with a single interchange format.

Kahn and Landow [1992] report on their experience in transferring the *Dickens Web* (a hypertext about Charles Dickens) from Intermedia where it was originally developed to two other hypertext systems: Eastgate System's Storyspace and Interleaf's WorldView. One of the major problems was that the "fat" one-to-many links in Intermedia could not be transferred to WorldView since it only had traditional one-to-one hypertext links. As an alternative, Kahn and Landow came up with "crossroads" documents like the one shown in Figure 5.1.

A crossroads documents serves as a waystation between the original departure anchor and the original destination anchors. The original link is replaced by a link from the departure anchor to the crossroads document as well as however many links it take to connect the crossroads document to all the original destination anchors. This example shows how awkward it can be to move hypertexts between systems if they do not share fundamental concepts as to the structure of the hypertext.

Work on the definition of hypertext interchange formats was initially started through informal meetings of the so-called Dexter Group, consisting of many of the designers of the early hypertext systems.[2] Since the hypertext standardization workshop in January 1990, work on hypertext reference models has continued through more formal activities at the U.S. National Institute of Standards and Technology.

This work has resulted in more detailed architectural models than the simple three-level model discussed here [Halasz and Schwartz 1990, 1994; Grønbæk and Trigg 1992, 1994] and also in some preliminary success in transferring hypertext information from NoteCards to HyperCard.[3] Figure 5.2 shows the relation between the Dexter model and the model used in this book.

---

[2] The Dexter Group is named after the inn in New Hampshire where it had its first meeting. The two meetings that resulted in the reference model were organized by Jan Walker and John Leggett and funded primarily by Digital Equipment Corporation and Texas A&M University.

[3] Both NoteCards and HyperCard are frame-based hypertext engines, where the information is displayed on fixed cards. It would presumably be harder to transfer between hypertext systems

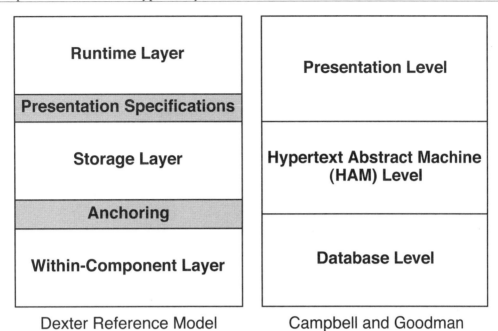

Figure 5.2. *Comparing the Dexter reference model to the three-level model proposed by Campbell and Goodman [1988] and used in this book. There are some terminology differences, such as the use of the word "storage" in the Dexter model to refer to the representation of the abstract hypertext network, but otherwise the main difference is the explicit discussion in the Dexter model of the interfaces between the levels, especially with respect to anchors.*

The User Interface Level

The user interface deals with the presentation of the information in the HAM, including such issues as what commands should be made available to the user, how to show nodes and links, and whether to include overview diagrams or not.

Let us assume that the HAM level of a hypertext defines the links as being typed. The user interface level might decide not to display that information at

with different architectures, such as, for example, a transfer from a window-based system like Guide with its long scrolling texts to a frame-based system. See the discussion of frame-based vs. window-based hypertext in the following section on Nodes.

all to some novice users and to make typing information available only in an authoring mode. The very distinction between reading and writing is one of the basic user interface issues.

Let us now assume that the user interface level does want to display the link typing to the user. It might want to do so by changing the shape of the cursor, as Guide does (see Figure 3.8), or by having a special notation for various forms for anchors. It could also decide to display typing information in an overview diagram. If it had a color display available, it might choose to show each link type in a different color, whereas on a monochrome display it would have to use different representations, such as different line patterns (like NoteCards), small icons (like CM/1, see Figure 4.3), or by using words to label the lines.

Actually, this decision cannot be made at the user interface level in isolation without considering the likely form of the data in the HAM. If the hypertext will have only a few link types, then colors or line patterns are suitable choices, but human ability to understand and distinguish such an encoding is limited to about seven different values. Icons could support hypertexts with somewhat more link types, but a hypertext with hundreds of link types would probably require the use of the type names in the interface.

Nodes

Nodes are the fundamental unit of hypertext, but there is no agreement as to what really constitutes a "node." The main distinction is between frame-based systems and window-based systems.

Frames take up a specific amount of space on the computer screen no matter how much information they contain. Typical examples are the KMS frames and the HyperCard cards. Often the size of the frame is defined as the size of the computer screen, but that determination may not hold in all systems. Since the frame has a fixed size, the user may have to split a given amount of information over several frames if it cannot fit into one. The advantage of frames is that all user navigation takes place using whatever hypertext mechanisms are provided by the system.

In contrast, window-based systems require the user to use a scrolling mechanism in addition to the hypertext mechanisms to get the desired part of the node to show in the window. Because the system can display only a (potentially small) part of the node through the window at any given time, the node may be as large as needed, and the need for potential unnatural distribution of text over several nodes is eliminated. Guide and Intermedia are typical window-based systems.

A great disadvantage of window-based hypertexts is that the hypertext designer has no control over how the node will appear when the user reads it since it can be scrolled in many ways. The advantage is that windows may be of different size depending on the importance and nature of information they hold. One can imagine a window-based system that did away with scrolling and thus kept most of the advantages of both display formats.

The real world is not quite as simple as the clear distinction between frames and windows. HyperCard is mostly frame-based but includes the possibility for having scrolling text fields as part of a card. Hyperties uses a full-screen display without scrolling but instead requires the user to page back and forth through a sequence of screens in case the node is too big to fit on a single screen.

Most current hypertext systems provide fixed information in the nodes as written by the original author. In computational hypertext systems like KMS and HyperCard (with an embedded programming language) or NoteCards (with an interface to a programming language), it is possible to have *computed nodes* generated for the reader by the system. An example is a node with the current weather forecast retrieved from an online service like the American Prodigy or the French Minitel. Computing a node on the fly by executing a program obviously involves the risk of Trojan horses leading to virus infection or other problems. The problem is minimized when the program is executed on a remote server that is restricted to transmitting the resulting data to the user's computer. If the code has to execute on the user's computer precautions will need to be taken in the form of virus scanners. There are also efforts under way for constructing safe programming languages that can be interpreted inside a protective shell that ensures that no permanent damage can be done to the user's system.

If one has a certain amount of information to communicate, one issue is whether it should be split into many small nodes or kept in a rather small number of larger nodes. Kreitzberg and Shneiderman [1988] report on a small experiment to investigate this issue, wherein they split the same text into either 46 articles of between 4 and 83 lines or 5 articles of between 104 to 150 lines in Hyperties. The result was that users could answer questions significantly faster in the information base with many small nodes (125 sec. vs. 178 sec. per answer). One reason for this result is probably that Hyperties is one of the hypertext systems that links to the beginning of an article and not to the location within an article where the information of interest for the departure point is located. Because of this feature, Hyperties is most easily operated with small, focused nodes dealing with precisely one issue so that there can be no doubt about what part of the node a link points to.

Links

Links are the other fundamental unit of hypertext besides nodes. Links are almost always anchored at their departure point to provide the user with some explicit object to activate in order to follow the link. The result of activating the anchor is to follow the link to its destination node. Most often, this anchoring takes the form of "embedded menus" where part of the primary text or graphics does double duty as being both information in itself and being the link anchor. It is also possible to have the hypertext anchors listed as separate menus, but that somehow seems to reduce the "hypertext feel" of a design, and a study by Vora et al. [1994] found that users performed 26% faster when the anchors were part of the main text.

Most links are explicit in the sense that they have been defined by somebody as connecting the departure node with the destination node. Some systems also provide *implicit* links, which are not defined as such but follow from various properties of the information. A classic example of implicit links is the automatic glossary lookup possible in Intermedia (see Figure 4.15). The InterLex server provides a link from any word in any Intermedia document to the definition of that word in the dictionary, but it would obviously be ridiculous to have to store all these links explicitly. Only when the user requests the definition of a word does the system need to find the destination for the link.

The StrathTutor system [Kibby and Mayes 1989] provided another kind of implicit link. The hypertext author was not expected to provide links between nodes but was instead asked to define a set of relevant attributes for each node and for areas of interest in the node. These attributes were keywords taken from a predefined restricted vocabulary. The areas of interest were called "hotspots" and served a purpose similar to anchors in other hypertext systems. When the user activated a hotspot, the system would view the user's interests as being defined by the combination of the attributes (keywords) from the current node and the selected hotspot. StrathTutor therefore linked to a new node having the highest overlap between its own attributes and this set of attributes. Kibby and Mayes claimed that this form for distributed specification of hypertext connections was the only way one could manage the authoring of really big hypertexts.

The StrathTutor links were an example of *computed links* determined by the system while the reader is reading, instead of being statically determined in advance by the author. Another example of computed links is a link from a tourist guide like *Glasgow Online* to the train schedule, where the system could link to the listing for the next train out of Glasgow for each destination.

A hypertext link has two ends. Even if a link is not bidirectional[4] there may still be a need to anchor it explicitly at the destination node. Most frame-based hypertext systems only have links that point to an entire node, but when the destination is large, it is an advantage for the user to have the system point out the relevant information more precisely. See for example how the Drexel Disk highlights Building 53 because the user jumped to the campus map in Figure 1.3 from a description of the repair facility (which is located in that building).

In general, a hypertext design should tell the user *why* the destination for a link was an interesting place to jump to by relating it to the point of departure and following a set of conventions for the "rhetoric of arrival" [Landow 1989a].

Given that the hypertext is based on explicit links, the next issue is whether or not to make the anchors especially prominent on the screen compared with the rest of the node. In a *sparse* hypertext, where maybe less than 10% of the information serves as anchors, it is probably a good idea to visually emphasize the anchors. This is just a special case of the general user interface guideline of letting the user know what options are available in a dialogue. In a *rich* hypertext, where almost everything is linked to something, the best advice would be to remove any special emphasis on the anchors. After all, if everything is highlighted, then nothing is really highlighted anyway.

It is possible to use the Guide method of providing feedback by changing the shape of the cursor when it is over an anchor (see Figure 3.8). But that method should still be supplemented with some visual indication of the location of the anchors since users will otherwise be reduced to playing mine sweeper with the mouse to discover the active areas of the screen.

Unfortunately the highlighting of anchors conflicts with the use of emphasis in the running text. Traditionally writers have used typographical

---

[4] See the discussion of directional versus bidirectional links in Chapter 1.

notation like *italics* or **boldfaced** type to indicate various forms for emphasis or special purpose text like quotations, and we would like to keep these capabilities for hypertext authors. But many current hypertext systems use the same or similar notation to indicate hypertext anchors also. This can unfortunately be very confusing to users unless the author has used a *style guide* to provide consistent notation for anchors and running emphasis. One solution to this problem may be the invention of special typographical cues for hypertext links [Evenson et al. 1989] and the gradual emergence of conventions for hypertext notation.

Most current hypertext systems have plain links, which are just connections between two nodes (and possibly anchors). The advantage of that approach is of course the simplicity of both authoring and reading. There is nothing to do with links except to follow them, and that one action can be achieved by a click of the mouse.

Alternatively, a link can be tagged with keywords or semantic attributes such as the name of the creator or the date it was created. These tags allow one to reduce the complexity of a hypertext through filter queries like, "Show all links created after March 23, 1995" or "Hide all links by so-and-so" (if we think that that person's contributions are rubbish).

Links can also be typed to distinguish among different forms of relationship between nodes. Trigg [1983] presents a very elaborate taxonomy of 75 different link types, including abstraction, example, formalization, application, rewrite, simplification, refutation, support, and data.

In addition to the standard links connecting two nodes, some hypertext systems also have "super-links" to connect a larger number of nodes. There are several possibilities for dealing with having a single anchor connected to several destinations. The two simplest options are either to show a menu of the links or to go to all the destinations at the same time. Intermedia uses the menu option and allows users to choose only a single destination. This approach requires good names for the links or destination nodes in order for users to be able to understand their options. Some users of NoteCards have implemented a "fat link" type that opens windows on the screen for all the destination nodes.

The alternative way to deal with multiple destinations would be to have the system choose for the user in some way. The choice could be based on the system's model of the user's needs or some other estimate of the best

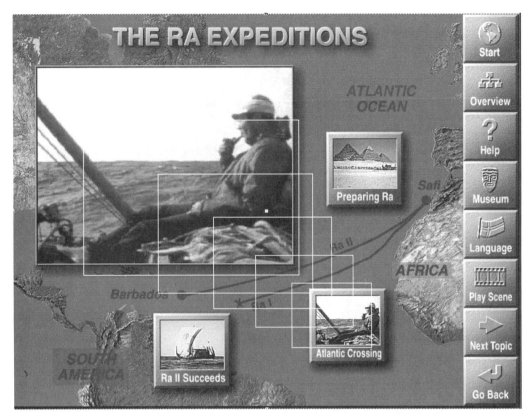

Figure 5.3. *The Kon-Tiki system generates a video footnote by zooming the large video image to an icon. Copyright © 1993 by The Kon-Tiki Museum, reprinted by permission.*

destination, or it could simply be random, as in the example discussed towards the end of Chapter 2.

Link anchors present special problems for layered hypertext architectures like the model presented in the beginning of this chapter. In principle, links belong at the hypertext abstract machine level, but the location of the anchor in the node is dependent on the storage structure for the node media. In a text-only node, an anchor position can be described as a substring ("characters 25–37"), whereas an anchor in a film clip needs both substring information ("film frames 517–724") and a graphic location ("the rectangle [(10,10);(20,20)]").[5] Therefore the actual anchoring of the link cannot be handled by the hypertext abstract machine. The solution in the Dexter model [Halasz and Schwartz 1990] is to define an explicit interface between the hypertext abstract machine (called "storage layer" in their model) and the database level (called "within-component layer" in their model) as shown in Figure 5.2. Anchors become indirect pointers and the anchoring interface provides a translation between anchor identifiers in the hypertext abstract machine and actual anchor values in the node data.

Gunnar Liestøl and Per Siljubergsåsen have designed a user interface for the Kon-Tiki Museum in Norway that uses an interesting way of indicating links in video materials [Liestøl 1994]. The museum has large amounts of films recorded in connection with Thor Heyerdahl's expeditions, and the design challenge was how to represent the links between the video clips and other information such as text, maps, and photographs.

To get a device pointing out of a video sequence, the designers borrowed[6] a convention from the Macintosh user interface guidelines: when documents are opened or closed on the Mac, the relationship between the document and the icon representing it is visualized by an animated rectangle zooming between the two positions. Similarly, the main video area in the Kon-Tiki system "throws off" miniature pictures that zoom down from the video to rest on the screen as "video footnotes" that can be clicked for further information about that part of the video.

Annotations

A special link type is the annotation link to a small, additional amount of information. The reading of an annotation typically takes the form of a temporary excursion from the primary material to which the reader returns after having finished with the annotation. Annotations are quite similar to footnotes in traditional text and can be implemented, for instance, as Guide pop-up windows that disappear as soon as the user releases the mouse button.

---

[5] Some dynamic anchors may be even harder to specify: Try encoding the anchors in a video of a football game to allow the user to click on a player at any time to link to that player's name and statistics.

[6] Michael Arent [Vertelney et al. 1990] uses the term "interface slang" for this approach to borrowing elements of an established interaction vocabulary for other, though related, uses.

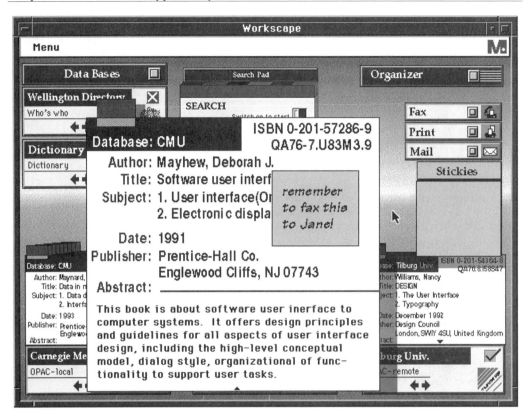

Figure 5.4. *Use of sticky-notes to represent annotations. To add an annotation, the user tears off a sticky-note from the pile to the right and places it on the object that needs a comment. Every time this object is displayed in the future, the sticky-note will be there (until the user removes it). Copyright © 1994 by J. Ray Scott, Digital Equipment Corporation, reprinted by permission.*

Alternatively, as shown in Figure 5.4, annotations can be floating "stickies" (almost always shown in yellow windoids in homage to 3M's Post-It notes [Lucas and Schneider 1994; Scott 1994]), or they can be accessed through an icon.

Hypertext writers can use annotations in the same way they would use footnotes in traditional text with the exception that hypertext annotations are less intrusive because they are not shown unless the reader asks for them. The most interesting use of annotations in hypertext is for the readers, however. Many hypertext systems allow readers to add new links to the primary material even if they do not always allow the reader to change the original nodes and

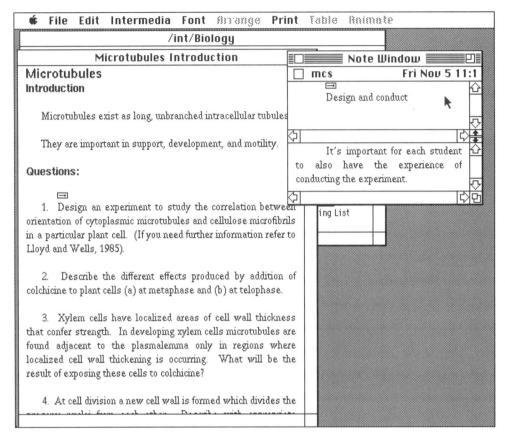

Figure 5.5. *The InterNote service within IRIS Intermedia provides a quick facility for annotating documents of any type. The top frame of the note window (right) contains the annotator's suggestion of a change in wording. The bottom frame explains the reason for the suggestion. The author of the "Microtubules Introduction" document may now choose to incorporate the change by selecting the marker at either end of the link that connects the note to the document and choosing the "Incorporate Annotation" command. © 1989 by Brown University, reprinted with permission.*

links, and readers can use these facilities to customize the information space to their own needs. For example, readers of a hypertext medical handbook [Frisse 1988a] might want to supplement the generic description of a drug in the handbook with an annotation stating the brand name normally prescribed at their hospital.

One system that does provide an annotation facility is Intermedia, as shown in Figure 5.5. Other systems like Hyperties do not allow readers to annotate but reserve all options to change the information space for the authors. In the case of Hyperties, one reason for refusing readers the right to add information is that the system was originally designed for museum information systems where one may in fact not want random users to alter the content of the hypertext. Another reason was the desire for an extremely simple user interface to Hyperties: Having a smaller number of options available to the user means that there is less to learn.

Finally, users can annotate a hypertext by adding various forms of highlighting [Nielsen 1986], such as the use of various colors to emphasize text of special importance to a particular user [Irler and Barbieri 1990]. One product that supports highlighting is Folio. Even though individualized highlighting does not really constitute a form of link, information gathered from highlighting (possibly from multiple users) can be used in filtering the hypertext to show only important information or to search the hypertext for nodes that had previously been highlighted.

Hypertext Engines

Many hypertext systems are really hypertext engines that can display many different hypertext documents. Other hypertext systems are built specifically to display a single document and can therefore provide a much richer interaction with respect to the content of that particular document.

Besides the obvious advantage of not having to program a new application, the use of hypertext engines also has the advantage that they provide a user interface common to many documents. Users who already know how to use Guide, for example, can immediately start to read the next Guide document without any training.

Some hypertext systems like Guide and Hyperties are truly plain engines. The author just pours text into them and they take care of everything else. For example, a pop-up window in Guide *always* appears in the top right corner of the screen. The author does not have to make any user interface decisions except for a few low-level formatting details such as where to break paragraphs. Considering that most people are poor user interface designers, this may well be an advantage.

Other hypertext engines allow the hypertext designer to customize the user interface to a document within a certain framework. HyperCard is a prime example of such a system since it allows the designer to move fields around and add all sorts of background graphics. Even so, the designer is constrained by the basic HyperCard framework of being a frame-based system with a fixed size monochrome card. There are certain user interface facilities available in a kind of construction kit for the designer, but it is not possible to add new interaction techniques.

Actually it *is* possible to extend the framework of HyperCard, but only by leaving its built-in HyperTalk programming language behind and programming so-called external commands (XCMDs) in a traditional programming language like C. NoteCards is extensible because it is integrated with InterLisp, but it also provides several simpler possibilities for hypertext designers to customize their interfaces to the needs of their individual documents [Trigg et al. 1987].

HyperCard not only allows hypertext authors to customize the user interface of their hypertext documents, it *requires* them to do so. HyperCard has no default document design but in principle presents the author with a blank screen where it is necessary to define the placement of text fields before anything can be written.

Finally, some hypertext documents are implemented as specialized applications. These include the Drexel Disk (see Figure 1.3) and Palenque (see Chapter 4). These specialized applications can achieve an exact match between the hypertext system and the needs of the document. For example, for the children exploring the Mexican jungle, Palenque has special features in the form of a filmed television personality who pops up from time to time to introduce new discoveries. The designers of Palenque added this guide character to the interface after having interviewed children about how they would like to explore Maya ruins in the Mexican jungle. And they certainly did not want to do so *alone*.

Open Hypertext

Most hypertext researchers work with systems that are specifically designed as hypertext systems. Most *users*, on the other hand, work with systems that assist them in performing all kinds of tasks, from simple spreadsheet calculations to complex domain-specific work like analysis of seismic data from oil exploration sites. The conflict between these two perspectives on the world will definitely never be resolved by having the majority of users convert to using a hypertext tool and give up on their other software tools. A more promising approach is called open hypertext and is aimed at integrating hypertext capabilities with the rest of the user's software environment. The key notion is to let each application work with the data it is optimized for and have some way for the applications to communicate with a shared hypertext mechanism that handles the links across applications (and possibly even within applications).

Engelbart [1990] defines three levels of interoperability for open hypertext: interoperability in an individual's information space (e.g., linking from a phone list to a set of notes), interoperability in a group's information space (e.g., from one person's file space to a colleague's), and interoperability across groups (e.g., linking from the marketing organization to the manufacturing or product development organizations). The latter case is an example of interoperability across knowledge domains since the different groups are likely to use very different applications for their specialized work.

This section will mostly concern the first level of interoperability: the ability to link between information objects in different applications. The remaining two levels are in the nature of computer-supported cooperative work and involve networking and groupware software to a larger extent than they involve hypertext as such. Interoperability across group and companies can partly be supported by the World Wide Web and other Internet mechanisms discussed further in Chapter 7.

The typical method for supplying open hypertext is to remove the hypertext level from the applications and provide a single hypertext service for everything on the user's computer. The hypertext service will need to keep track of what information is moved where, and it can then communicate with the applications using message passing to indicate, for example, that they should open a certain document and scroll it to a certain location. The link information is typically stored in a database that is separate from the primary documents and is maintained by the hypertext service rather than the user's applications. The reasons for this separation is that the link information may exist in formats that are incompatible with some of the applications and that one does not want the user to have to see these internal data structures.

The Microcosm project [Davis et al. 1992, 1994; Hill and Hall 1994] defined three degrees of application-support for open hypertext: fully aware, partly aware, and unaware applications, where the term "aware" refers to the extent to which the application knows about hypertext and the possibility of links between its data and other applications. Figure 5.6 shows fully Microcosm-

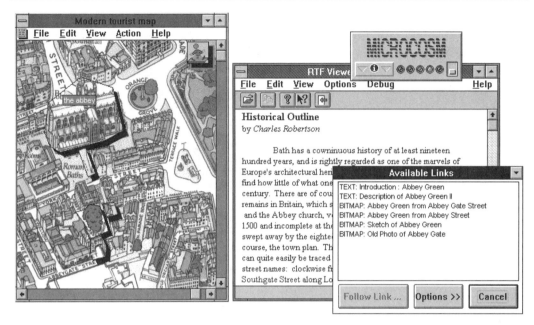

Figure 5.6. *Fully aware Microcosm viewers. The image viewer shows part of a city map with super-imposed "buttons" on top of the bitmap data for display purposes. The text viewer is based on RTF (rich text format). These viewers have been launched as a result of the user selecting items from the available links box, which is showing links available from the source anchor "Abbey Green." Copyright © 1994 by the Microcosm Group, University of Southampton, U.K., reprinted by permission.*

aware applications and the way Microcosm supports links between, say, a graphics application and a word processor. When a fully aware application opens a document, it sends a message to Microcosm to find out whether the document contains any links, and if so, it can display the anchors as buttons and make the user interface more appealing and intuitive to use. When the user activates an anchor, the fully aware application will know that a hypertext link should be followed, and it can ask the Microcosm service to do so. As the user edits the information in the source document, a fully aware application can inform Microcosm if link anchors have been added, moved, or deleted, and Microcosm can thus get the necessary information to maintain the link database.

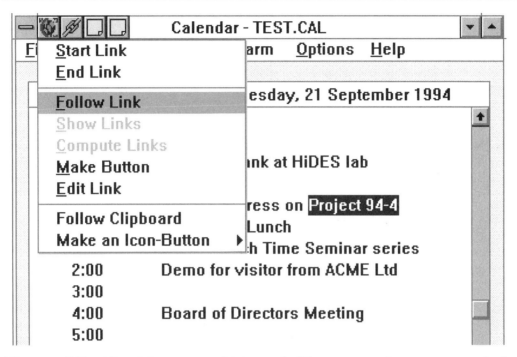

Figure 5.7. *The Microcosm Universal Viewer running on top of the Microsoft Calendar program which is completely unaware of Microcosm. The Universal Viewer acts as a shim between Microcosm and unaware applications, displaying the menus and any relevant buttons on the application's title bar, and allows the user to make selections within the application for making or following links. Copyright © 1994 by the Microcosm Group, University of Southampton, U.K., reprinted by permission.*

The main problem with fully aware applications is that they have to be customized for the particular open hypertext model employed by the user. In this case, Microcosm was used, but several other open hypertext systems exist (and more can be expected in the future), so it is not realistic to expect all applications to be modified to work with all hypertext services.

Partly aware viewers are those that have some kind of programmability that allows them to be extended with an action menu with the commands needed to interact with the hypertext service. Many popular applications, including Microsoft Word and most spreadsheet packages, come with a scripting facility (e.g., Visual Basic) that can be used for this purpose. The partly aware viewers typically do not allow anchors to be marked as buttons since they control their own user interface and the way they want to show their data on the screen. Thus, users are relegated to selecting objects in the application using its normal selection mechanism and then issuing hypertext commands such as "Follow Link" from the Microcosm menu.

In an unaware application, the hypertext commands cannot even be represented as menu commands but must be supplied through a modification of the window system or some other level of the underlying operating system. Figure 5.7 shows how the Microcosm Universal Viewer can attach itself to the title bar of a window and thus be accessed in the context of the application running in that window even though the application knows nothing about Microcosm. When the Microcosm service is activated through the menu on the titlebar, it reads the current selection in the window and compares it with its database of anchors or other hypertext objects, after which Microcosm can take the appropriate action (e.g., open another window with the destination of a link, even if that destination is in another application).

Applications that are partly aware or unaware of the hypertext service will not know to inform the hypertext service as the user edits information that may contain hypertext links. Therefore, the hypertext service will need some other mechanism to update its link database to ensure link integrity. This problem cannot be solved fully in all cases since users may have modified the document too much to allow the hypertext anchors to be located. Remember that the document itself is typically not allowed to contain any anchor markup in order to keep it compatible with the original application datastructures. The typical solution to the problem of the moving anchors is to remember the location of the anchor before the document was edited and then to search for a location as close as possible with the same text (or other data) as the anchor. Of course, if the user edited the anchor itself or if it was moved too much, then this approach will fail.

Integrating Hypertext Ideas into Other Environments

A final architectural observation is that hypertext does not really need to involve a full-fledged set of features. It is possible to utilize a smaller number of ideas from hypertext and integrate them into other computer systems without making them full hypertext systems [Frisse and Cousins 1992].

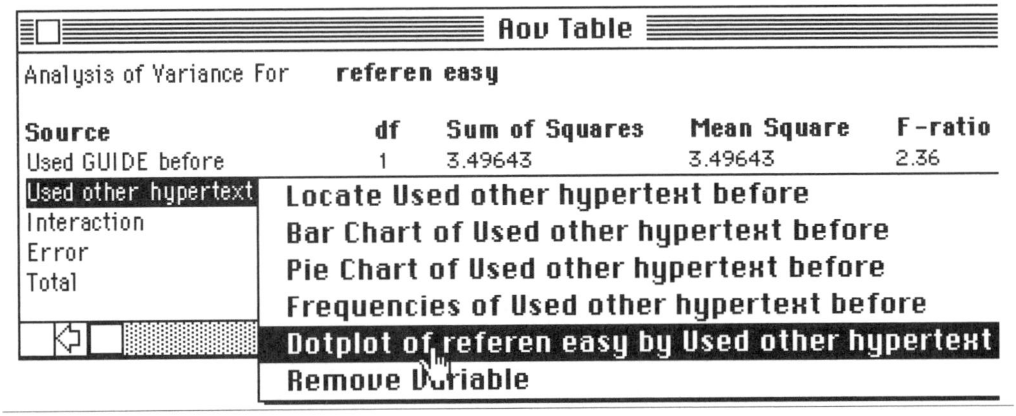

Figure 5.8. *A HyperView pop-up menu from the statistics program Data Desk Professional. The user is looking at a table containing an analysis of variance and has indicated a special interest in one of the variables. The pop-up menu now allows the user to open windows with additional statistical analyses and graphs that are especially relevant given this context.*

For example, the statistics package Data Desk Professional from Odesta has a facility called HyperView which is shown in Figure 5.8. HyperViews allow the user direct access from one statistical analysis to a small number of other analyses that are relevant given the user's current context. Based on its knowledge of statistics, the program "knows" what other statistical analyses people normally want if they have an interest in the selected variable in the context given by the existing table.

The result of making a choice from the menu in Figure 5.8 is to jump to a new window containing the desired analysis or graph. Of course the system has to calculate the content of that window first so the real result is just to activate the statistics package with a given command and a given set of parameters. But to the user it *feels* like a hypertext-like navigation between connected windows. It is also a great practical advantage of the HyperView facility that it reduces the need for the user to find the correct command among the large set of statistical analyses available in the program and that it automatically specifies the correct parameters.

6. Hardware Support for Hypertext

Hypertext needs to run on a computer and is therefore highly dependent on the available hardware technology. Many of the complaints people have against hypertext applications are not really directed against the very principle of hypertext or the user interfaces of existing hypertext systems but are based on deficiencies in the current generation of computer hardware.

For example, there are many hypertext applications, such as tourist guides, which would only really make sense if hypertext systems could be as portable as a paperback book. One quite good hypertext with travel information, called *Business Class*, got poor reviews in the personal computer magazines exactly because of this problem.

In a field study of hypertext I conducted [Nielsen and Lyngbæk 1990], 33% of the users complained about the very fact that the hardware was not as convenient as paper. Typical comments were "I don't want to have to stay with the computer. I often read reports on the train or at home" or "I have to make a conscious effort to read it and first boot up the Macintosh, while with paper less planning is needed."

Because of this problem, many hypertext researchers dream of the day computers get so small that they are actually as portable as books. Alan Kay discussed this concept several years ago [Kay and Goldberg 1977] and called it the *dynabook* ("dynamic book"). There is actually a commercial product out now called "DynaBook" based on a CD-ROM reader, but it is not nearly what Kay imagined.

Problems with the Computer Screen

One practical problem with many present computer screens is that they cannot show the video images that form an important part of many hypermedia interfaces in sufficiently good quality. This problem is only temporary since add-on video cards have been designed for all the important brands of personal computers to allow them to display live video on the screen integrated with computer generated text and graphics.

Unfortunately these video cards and color screens of sufficiently high quality are still too expensive for many applications, and some systems therefore use a "two-screen solution." One screen is used to display color video images, while another screen is a standard computer screen showing computer text and graphics and accepting user input via the mouse.

Even though it can be a practical necessity, the two-screen solution is poor from the usability perspective since it requires users to divide their attention between two screens. Also it prevents integration between the computer generated graphics and the video image because they have to be shown on separate screens. The single-screen solution allows better possibilities for dynamically adding annotations and outline drawings to video images and for having users activate image areas by the mouse.

Some computer users still have monochrome screens, but the more common problem is to have color screens that are limited to 256 colors. This number of colors is insufficient to show high-resolution photographs without dithering (approximating additional colors by alternating colors for each pixel) and the resulting loss of quality. Even worse, many hypermedia applications involve the display of multiple photos or color graphics on a single screen, meaning that the available 256 colors in an 8-bit color map have to be shared instead of being optimized for the individual illustration. Because of these many problems, it is highly recommended to use 16-bit video cards (or even better, full 24-bit color that can display millions of colors) for multimedia applications.

Reading Speed from Screens

The two-screen problem will disappear by itself as the cost of single-screen solutions drops, but hypertext by its very nature needs to be read from a computer screen, and it will therefore always be relevant to consider the actual speed with which people can read from screens. Several scientific studies have compared the reading speed from screens with the reading speed from paper, and they have generally found that screens are about 30% slower. For example, Wright and Lickorish [1983] had users proofread text which appeared on either a traditional computer display or on paper. The time to proofread two texts was

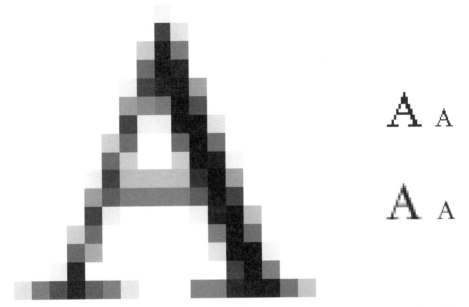

Figure 6.1. *An example of **anti-aliasing:** The "jaggies" in the A have been smoothed over by the use of gray pixels. The characters on the right show the effect of using anti-aliasing: The top As have not been anti-aliased, while the bottom As use the gray pixels shown in the left figure. Try looking at the figure from a distance to see how the anti-aliased letters look better.*

quite a lot slower on the screen than on paper (29 min. vs. 21 min.). Gould et al. [1984] got a similar result on a similar test.

Gould et al. [1987] tested a more advanced type of computer display in the form of an IBM 5080 display which had 91 points per inch and displayed anti-aliased fonts. As shown in Figure 6.1, anti-aliasing is a computer graphics technique used to smooth over "jaggies" by the use of grayscales instead of the traditional black-and-white only pixels. Gould et al. had people proofread texts from this advanced screen and from paper and found that they had practically the same reading speed (204 words per minute vs. 206 words per minute) and the same accuracy in finding the spelling errors in the text (79% vs. 81%). The small differences were not statistically significant, so one might interpret the result as showing the same performance on an anti-aliased screen as on paper. Unfortunately, anti-aliasing is not used in the present generation of computer displays.

Wilkinson and Robinshaw [1987] tested the error rates of subjects doing proofreading from screens and from paper. During the first ten minutes of the experiment, screens did somewhat worse than paper (error rate 25% vs. 22%) but they did much worse after subjects had been proofreading continuously for 50 minutes (error rates 39% vs. 25%). This difference shows that people get tired more easily when reading from computer screens than when reading from paper.

Because of these results hypertext designers have to take care that users are not required to read too much text on the screen. Even though the plain reading speed is slower from present screens, overall user performance with a hypertext system can still be better than with paper if the hypertext system allows the user to find the relevant text faster and makes it possible to extract the relevant information without having to read as much.

Screen Size

Bigger screens allow users to see more hypertext material at the same time and allow room for various extra user interface features such as permanently shown overview diagrams. Shneiderman [1987a] had users read a hypertext on the Jewish Holocaust in Austria in order to answer questions about it. Users who used a screen displaying 34 lines of hypertext at a time performed slightly faster than users who could only see 18 lines (8.6 min. vs. 9.8 min.), but the difference was not statistically significant, probably because only 12 subjects were used. The 34-line display would correspond to approximately 432 pixels, and 18 lines would correspond to 240 pixels on a graphics display. The same research group also conducted experiments with subjects reading program text from various screen sizes using ordinary text editors [Reisel and Shneiderman 1987]. For a 22-line display (288 pixels), answering the questions took 9.2 min., for a 60-line display (744 pixels), it took 7.9 min., and for a 120-line display (1464 pixels) it took 6.6 min. All these experiments confirm the common belief that bigger is better when it comes to computer screens.

Hansen and Haas [1988] tested the effect of screen size on a more active use of computers in the form of letter-writing. They compared a full-page workstation display, which could hold 47 lines of text, with a small window on the same workstation, which could hold 22 lines of text corresponding to 80 columns of fixed-width characters. Both conditions used proportionally spaced characters. The subjects wrote with about the same writing speed (20 vs. 21 words per min.) but wrote longer letters on the larger screen (353 words vs.

292), and the quality of the letters as rated by an English teacher was higher on the larger screen (11 vs. 8 on a 16-point scale). So people tend to write longer texts when they use bigger screens, but they also write better texts.

Color Coding

Color might be a solution to the problems users have in remembering where in lengthy texts they have previously read something. An experiment conducted by Wright and Lickorish [1988] showed that, when reading one set of printed documents on colored paper, users were able to answer questions about the texts they had read in 51 secs.; but they needed 60 secs. when using texts printed on single-colored paper. In a follow-up experiment with another set of texts, it turned out that the color-coded paper was slower, and two sets of online text were also found to be slower than monochrome online text. The authors speculate that color might work better as borders or strips or if it was assigned by the readers rather than by the writers (as in highlighting, cf. [Nielsen 1986]).

Pointing Devices

Almost all current hypertext systems are used with a mouse as the pointing device. Several human factors studies of computer interfaces in general have shown that the mouse is a good pointing device, and it has certainly seen wide use in recent years.

Ewing et al. [1986] compared the mouse with a special use of the keyboard arrow keys for activating hypertext anchors in Hyperties. This special use of the arrow keys has them jump the cursor in a single step to the hypertext anchor that is nearest to the previous cursor location in the direction indicated by the arrow key pushed by the user. It turned out that the mouse was somewhat slower than this special use of the arrow keys (3.3 min. vs. 2.8 min. for anchors that are close by and 3.5 min. vs. 3.3 min. for anchors farther away).

For some hypertext applications, such as information kiosks, the mouse is too fragile to be used. In these situations it is common to use a touch screen as the pointing device instead. Touch screens are not used in the standard protected office environment because having to raise their arms quickly becomes tiresome for users and because the touch screens are normally less precise than the mouse.

The simplest implementations of touch screens emulate the mouse and can therefore be used with any hypertext system without any need to change the software.

Touch screens can, however, be used in several different ways to activate hypertext anchors. Potter et al. [1989] tested several such strategies for activating anchors in Hyperties, including the *land-on* strategy, which activates a point on the screen the moment the user touches that point (similar to a `mouseDown` event in mouse-driven interfaces); and the *take-off* strategy, which activates the point which the user last touched when the hand is taken off the screen (similar to `mouseUp` events). Users performed about the same with these two strategies but had a tendency to be slightly slower with the take-off screens. Error rates were significantly lower with the take-off strategy since users could see what they had selected before lifting their fingers.

Potter et al. also tested a touch screen strategy called *first-contact,* which activates the first selectable area on the screen entered by the user's finger. If the user touches down on a selectable area, the result is the same as the land-on strategy, but if the user touches down on a blank area, nothing is selected until the user's finger has moved to the first active region on the screen (similar to a combination of `mouseEnter` and `mouseWithin` events in a mouse system). There was no statistically significant difference between the first-contact and the take-off strategies in this experiment done with Hyperties, even though fairly large and significant differences had been found in an earlier experiment [Potter et al. 1988] on selection in a traditional text environment. In the earlier, non-hypertext experiment, subjects had to select targets that were two characters in width and were separated by a two character space. For such a task, the first-contact strategy gave rise to a lot more errors but was somewhat faster than the lift-off strategy where users could see what they were selecting. In Hyperties, however, the anchors are typically whole words which are far apart on the screen so users have a much smaller risk of touching something by mistake and they don't need to rely as much on the feedback. The different outcome of these two experiments shows the importance of conducting usability tests of as high a validity as possible with regard to the actual final use of whatever is being tested. For selecting hypertext anchors, the first-contact and take-off strategies performed about the same, so the take-off strategy might be chosen by a designer because it is the simplest to explain to users. But for a text editing application, one should choose the first-contact strategy.

Can Text-Only Computers Be Used for Hypertext?

Many people may wonder whether hypertext will run only on modern personal computers such the Macintosh, Windows, or on high-end professional workstations. Hyperties is one hypertext system that proved it was possible to have hypertext even on the old "plain vanilla" IBM PC personal computers without graphics capabilities. Many other hypertext systems will work on minimally configured personal computers running DOS.

The only real requirement for hypertext is to have some possibility for the user to point to an item on the screen and activate it.[1] This activation is most frequently done with a mouse, but if one does not have a true pointing device available, the same action can be performed by using the arrow keys to position the cursor on the desired word and then hitting ENTER.

It is thus possible to have hypertext even on dumb terminals connected to mainframe computers. Of course, the response time requirements inherent in hypertext make hypertext unfeasible on timeshared computers unless they have sufficient capacity for subsecond response times.

In any case, only fairly primitive hypertext interfaces will work on a text-only screen. The more advanced methods for improved navigation orientation, discussed in the next chapter, require some kind of graphic support, and many applications of hypertext also work much better if there is a windowing system available. It must be said that large-scale hypertext use is naturally matched to the capabilities of the modern, graphic personal computers and workstations.

Mainframes are rapidly being replaced by personal computers, workstations, and client–server solutions in the so-called "rightsizing" movement. Some people will nonetheless have to use legacy systems with old text-based terminals for years to come, and they can still get some of the advantages of hypertext, for instance in their online help systems.

One should also not completely discard the use of mainframe computers as a part of a hypertext architecture. Mainframes are good for handling the large databases one would need for really big hypertexts, and they could also serve as host computers for distributed hypertexts accessed cooperatively by many users. This type of host computer should serve only as a backend repository,

---

[1] As a matter of fact, some limited types of hypertext can even be supported with line-oriented interfaces [Wahlen and Patrick 1989], which rely completely on commands typed by the user.

however, whereas the user interface should run on local personal computers with graphic capabilities.

CD-ROM as a Storage Device

A special hardware problem is the storage space needed for the multimedia in hypermedia. For example, a single color television image takes up 105 kilobytes of storage, meaning that a minute of live video would take almost 200 megabytes. This obviously makes it impossible to deliver any form of hypermedia material with lots of video on traditional computer disks.

We have to turn to optical storage devices such as CD-ROM[2] to get room for these huge amounts of data. A CD-ROM disk[3] is physically the same as an audio CD, but instead of storing music it stores computer data. The similarity to audio CDs gives access to a great economy of scale for CD-ROMs since they can be pressed on the same factories that supply the huge world market for audio CDs. Thus a CD-ROM can be produced for about 90 cents plus a one-time fee of $500 for the master disk used in pressing the disks.[4]

The CD-ROM players have certain similarities to home CD players but are more expensive since they do have to contain special electronics and be faster at nonsequential access to the tracks on the disk. After all, when listening to Mozart you almost never jump around on the disk so an audio player can be optimized to read the tracks one after another. But as mentioned in Chapter 1, the entire idea behind hypertext is to read the data nonsequentially.

---

[2] Compact Disk-Read Only Memory. For more information about CD-ROM, see [Sherman 1994] and the alt.cd-rom FAQ (frequently asked questions) document that is posted monthly to the Usenet newsgroups alt.cd-rom and news.answers.

[3] "C" or "K"? There is no agreement about whether to spell it disc or disk. I have chosen to follow the spelling used by the *IEEE Spectrum* magazine and use "k." A less serious argument is that my own first name is spelled with a "k" but often misspelled with a "c" so I tend to like people who spell words with "k"s.

[4] Compare the cost of CD-ROM duplication with the cost of floppy disk duplication, where a normal price is about 51 cents per high-density 3.5" disk that can hold between 1.4 and 2 MB. Thus, if you want to distribute more information than will fit on a single floppy, CD-ROM is cheaper. Packaging can add as much as 25 cents to the price of a CD-ROM if using "jewel boxes," but cheaper packaging is available and one will also benefit from the lower postage needed to ship a CD compared with stacks of floppies.

The reason CD-ROMs are called *ROMs* is that they are a read-only storage device. This means that the individual user cannot change the contents of the disk. Actually, some writeable optical disks exist but they are mainly used for applications like data backup and prototyping of CD-ROMs intended for eventual mass manufacturing. For many hypertext applications it is actually fine to have the basic data stored on a read-only medium. Users can still be allowed to add links and annotations which could be stored on the user's traditional magnetic computer disk since it is most likely that user additions would be very small compared with the basic data and would therefore fit on a smaller disk. This is done in the Voyager Company's series of Expanded Books on CD-ROM (e.g., Don Norman's *Defending Human Attributes in the Age of the Machine*). The Voyager display engine and similar hypertext system simply merge the data from the harddisk and the CD-ROM whenever they need to display it to the user, so the user never knows the difference.

A CD-ROM disk can store around 630 megabytes of data, which is equivalent to between 500 and 1000 standard textbooks or novels as long as we are talking text-only books. But as just mentioned, we also want to include other media with much greater storage requirements.

Actually, even a CD-ROM is not really large enough to hold the amounts of multimedia data we want for our hypermedia applications if the data are just stored in a plain uncompressed format. But compression can often yield room for significantly more data. For example it has been possible to store the entire Canadian telephone directory on a single CD-ROM even though it takes up 2 giga[5] characters in its plain text form and therefore should require four CD-ROMs instead of one. But because so many people have the same names it was possible to compress the data by a factor of four. For example, instead of storing five characters for every person named "Smith" one could just store a one-byte code indicating that the person has "name # 1" or something like that.

For multimedia data it is possible to achieve even greater compression factors. For color images, one can take advantage of the fact that they often contain large surfaces with a single color or with only small variations in color shades, and that therefore a smaller amount of information is needed to store

---

[5] Giga = thousand mega = thousand million = a (U.S.) billion.

each pixel.[6] For moving images (film) it is possible to achieve yet another degree of compression since two sequential movie frames are almost always close to identical. The actor may have moved a little, but the background stays the same.

As a result of various ingenious compression schemes it has proven possible to store a full hour of video on a CD that originally could store only an hour of less-demanding sound. There is an international standard for the physical CD-ROM format since it is the same as the audio CD format. There is also an international standard called "High Sierra" format, or ISO 9660, for the storage of plain data on CD-ROMs, but there are unfortunately several standards for the compressed data, including MPEG and QuickTime.

CD-ROM drives have become widely available in recent years as the price has dropped. Market estimates indicate that the number of CD-ROM drives in the United States grew from slightly more than a million in 1990 to about ten million in 1994. In 1994, about a third of all personal computers came with a CD-ROM drive, and it is expected that about half of all personal computers sold in 1995 will have CD-ROM drives.

Originally, CD-ROM drives used the same data transfer speed as audio-CD players. Transfer rates of 150 kilobytes per second are sufficient for good sound quality but only allows for very jerky videos and for very slow hypertext jumps in a rich multimedia interface. Therefore, 300 kilobyte per second have become the absolute minimum transfer rate assumed by most hypermedia authors, and so-called double-speed CD-ROM drives have completely replaced the original "single-speed" drives. Even double-speed drives are actually too slow to support the kind of hypermedia needed to provide a satisfying experience, so it is safe to predict that "quad-speed" drives capable of transferring data at a speed of 600 kilobytes per second will take over and be the minimum hardware needed to play the next generation of CD-ROMs starting, maybe, in mid-1995 or early 1996.

Single-speed CD-ROM drives were introduced[7] in quantity in 1988, double-speed drives became the norm for advanced users in 1993, and quad-speed drives were the desired hardware in 1995. In other words, the time to double

---

[6] Pixel = picture element (the dots making up a digitized image). Sometimes referred to as a pel.

[7] Of course, CD-ROM drives had been available before 1988 (the first Philips drives were demonstrated in 1984), but until the introduction of the AppleCD with a decent SCSI interface in 1988 they were special-purpose devices and not in common use even among hypertext enthusiasts.

the speed of CD-ROM access for high-end users was five years for the first doubling and two years for the second. There are at least two more speed-doubling generations of CD-ROM drives ahead. In January 1995 Peripheral Land Inc. introduced the QuickCD drive with fifteen times the sustained speed of a single-speed drive (2.25 MB/s) and even faster speeds for shorter bursts of data. Since the technology already exists in high-end equipment, we can thus predict that 16-speed CD-ROM drives will be the norm by the year 1999 (and possibly even sooner), corresponding to a two year interval for each additional doubling of the transfer speed. These drives will have about four times the data transfer rates of the T3 lines that are currently the fastest way to connect to the Internet.

In the slightly longer term, the standard CD-ROMs with 630 MB will be replaced by a new storage standard capable of storing three or four gigabytes on the same platter. This will happen if for no other reason that the fact that a 16-speed drive will suck all the data off a standard CD-ROM in less than five minutes, meaning that users will crave larger capacity disks. Sony is promoting a format that stores 3.7 GB and is backwards compatible in the sense that the new drives would be capable of reading the old disks. Toshiba has a competing format that stores 4.8 GB on a CD but requires players that would probably not be able to read old CDs. Both formats will eventually be able to double their capacity by using double-sides CDs in the case of Toshiba or two layers of encoded surface in the case of Sony. It is impossible to predict which of these two formats will win, but both offer the potential of storing a full-length feature film (up to 135 minutes of video) with a picture quality that is better than videotape, so there is no doubt that they represent a major step forward in CD-ROM technology.

Comparing CD-ROMs with the Internet as a way to access data, CD-ROMs have a major advantage in access speeds. A double-speed CD-ROM drive delivers data about 150 times as fast as a modem and about twenty times faster than ISDN (currently the fastest connection to the Internet for home users), and the highest-end CD-ROM drives deliver data almost four times as fast as a T3 line (currently the fastest connection to the Internet for business users). On the other hand, a CD-ROM contains much less data than the Internet. In the beginning of 1995 there was probably about 13 terabytes of information available on the World Wide Web,[8] or about 20,000 times as much as will fit on a CD-ROM, and about 40 TB of information on the entire Internet (or 63,000 CD-ROMs). Due to the fast growth of the Internet, I would expext the Internet to offer between 100,000 times and 500,000 times as much information as a CD-ROM in the year 2000, even given the coming large-capacity CD-ROMs. Since each has its advantages, I would expect both CD-ROMs and the Internet to continue for several years as hypermedia data sources.

---

[8] The estimate of 13 TB on the WWW was derived as follows: The Lycos index server had indexed 248,291 documents at the end of 1994 with a total of 1.6 TB of data (or 6 KB per document). Lycos had 1.5 million URLs in its database (most of which had not been indexed yet) and had not achieved full coverage of the WWW, so the entire WWW probably contained about 2 million documents at the end of 1994. Extrapolating these figures gives 13 TB for the entire WWW. In fact, this estimate is probably conservative since Lycos does not index image, audio, and video files which often are larger than text files.

7. Hypertext on the Internet

The Internet is the name for the interconnected set of computer networks around the world. Most companies and other organizations have internal networks that connect their computers with each other and with printers and servers. These internal computer networks allow users to share files, to access databases and other client–server applications, to exchange electronic mail, and to gain many of the other benefits that come from connecting multiple computers and peripherals. Internal networks only take you so far, though, since some applications require access to outside computers. Two classic examples are electronic mail and electronic document interchange where one normally wants the ability to communicate with people in other companies through their computers. The Internet was designed to solve this problem by promoting a few technical standards that would allow computers and networks from all the many different vendors to talk together. Thus, when one refers to a computer "being on the Internet," one normally means that it is connected to an internal network that has a gateway connection to one of the Internet backbone networks.

Backbones are high-capacity networks that carry traffic between individual sites and span entire countries or parts of the world. One of the most famous backbone nets is the NSFnet which is sponsored by the National Science Foundation in the United States and connects many research-oriented sites to the Internet. The backbone nets are again interconnected to form the full Internet. Thus, the Internet is not really a single net. Rather, it is a combination of the many backbone nets, their interconnections, and the very large number of internal networks in various organizations.

The Internet has grown dramatically in recent years [Claffy et al. 1994]. Table 7.1 shows the growth rates[1] of the Internet toward the end of 1994; the

---

[1] The growth rates shown in Table 7.1 refer to annualized growth at the rate experienced during the last months of 1994. The actual growth during the full year of 1994 was not necessarily the

	Annualized Growth Rate	Days Needed to Double
Number of host computers connected to the Internet	85%	411
Amount of data flowing through the NSFnet backbone net	121%	320
Amount of data accessed through the World Wide Web	2,136%	81
Number of servers on the World Wide Web	679%	123

Table 7.1. *Growth rates estimated for the Internet at the end of 1994. See also Figure 7.1 for longer-term trends.*

amazing fact is that very similar growth rates have been recorded for several years. For example, traffic over the NSFnet backbone grew by 124% in 1992, by 117% in 1993, and by 117% in 1994. As shown in the table, overall traffic (amount of data flowing through the net as measured by the NSFnet backbone) doubled about every 320 days or more than once per year, and the number of servers (computers that offered information to others) on the World Wide Web doubled almost every three months.

The best estimate is that the number of users with access to the Internet was around 30 million at the end of 1994. Nobody knows for sure how many users are on the Internet because of its distributed nature.[2] The only solid fact is that about four million computers are attached to the Internet through a direct connection. The estimate of 30 million users comes from a guess that each directly connected computer corresponds to maybe seven or eight users on the average, but of course the exact number is not known. In many cases, people have personal computers with Internet connections, meaning that their computer would have one, or at most two, users. In other cases, a directly connected computer might be the host machine for a large online service like

---

same since the growth rates varied during the year. Traitionally, there is a decline in traffic during the Holiday season (the Internet usually carries about 2% less data in December than in November).

[2] It may seem strange that nobody knows the extent of the most important development in the computing field in this decade, but the Internet does not have a centralized authority to keep track of it or to plan its growth. In fact, several analysis believe that the distributed nature of the Internet has been a major contributor to its success and its ability to adjust quickly to changing technology and user needs. In contrast, most countries' centrally planned "information superhighway" projects have been failures except for France's Minitel project, which gave away terminals and was very liberal in recruiting information providers. Minitel has been a great success with more than 6 million users and 18,000 services in 1993.

America Online with more than a million subscribers, some proportion of whom would be using the Internet. At Sun Microsystems, the 13,000 employees access the Internet through a small number of highly secure computers called firewalls that are used to guard against intrusion by crackers, so a count of computers on the open Internet would only see a few computers from Sun even though these computers were linked over the internal corporate network to thousands of workstations with thousands of Internet users.

Another problem with estimating the size of the Internet is that it is debatable what constitutes "access" to the Internet. Some purists would require a user to have full abilities to use all services on the Internet before they will count that person as a "net.user" even though that definition would mean that most computer users in security-conscious companies would not be counted because their firewalls would prevent access to insecure services. Using the purist definition, the Internet might have had as little as five million users in 1994. On the other hand, a more liberal definition might be that a person is "using" the Internet if that person is sending or receiving data to/from the net. Under that definition, anybody using an email service with a gateway[3] to the Internet would be an Internet user, and the Internet might have had between fifty and a hundred million potential users in 1994, even though most of the users of company-internal email systems would probably not have figured out how to route their email through the gateway to the Internet.

In spite of the statistical difficulty in measuring the number of Internet users, most authorities agree that the number is about doubling every year since both the number of machines attached to the net and the amount of network traffic double every year. Given exponential growth, it almost doesn't matter what the initial number is: the number of users will eventually get big enough. The only question is whether the number of users will get huge soon or very soon. If the trend continues, the number of users will reach one billion in the year 2000 if the number of users at the end of 1994 was 30 million. If the

---

[3] Even though gatewayed email is the most primitive class of Internet access, it is still very useful. As an example, I recently managed the design briefings for the CHI'95 conference on user interfaces. Of the 15 presenters and session chairs, only one did not have a gateway between the Internet and that person's company, but having to communicate with that one person by alternative means was almost twice as much work for me and my administrative assistant as the total effort of communicating with the 14 people who could be reached through the Internet.

number of users at the end of 1994 was only 5 million, the one billion mark will be reached in the year 2002 instead. In other words, the seemingly large difference in current estimates of the size of the Internet under different definitions will at most result in a difference in two years with respect to when companies should make various investments to get on the net with their respective products and services. Of course, two years do matter in investment terms, and there is good reason for companies to pay fat consulting fees to Internet experts to get advice on exactly what to do when, but in the long term, the answer will be the same.

The reason I picked one billion as the number of users to look at in the previous paragraph is simple: this number constitutes approximately the entire population in the industrialized world and is therefore the maximum number of users of the Internet in the foreseeable future. In a longer-term perspective, the group of countries with large numbers of potential users will increase as a result of changes like the $1 trillion infrastructure investment[4] expected by the Asian Development Bank for non-Japanese Asia during 1995–2004.

It is probably too aggressive to assume that the entire population will be Internet users in the year 2000 or 2002. Trends represented by systems like KidLink and SeniorNet no doubt help promote computer literacy and network use among people outside the workforce but there will still be infants, very old people, and illiterates who are not going to become Internet users. Therefore, the growth rate of the Internet will *have* to slow down in the coming years, but I would definitely not be surprised if we reach half a billion Internet users very shortly after the year 2000, distributed with maybe 200 million users in the United States alone, 150 million in Europe, and 150 million in the industrialized part of Asia. By the year 2010 I would expect a billion users: 250 million in the U.S. and Canada, 50 million in Latin America, 250 million in Europe, and 450 million across much of Asia.

Currently, the Internet is dominated by American users. The fact that the Internet is a successor to the Arpanet (an early computer net sponsored by the U.S. Defense Advanced Research Planning Agency) no doubt provides a major historical explanation for this phenomenon. A second explanation can be

---

[4] OK, "only" $150 billion of these investments are expected to go for telecommunications, but that should still be enough to upgrade the networks significantly given the falling costs of the necessary equipment.

Country	Currency Exchange Rate: $1.00 Equals	Monthly Subscription Fee	Usage Charge Per Hour	Cost of Local Telephone Call per Hour	Annual Cost of Internet Usage
Denmark	5.98 Kroner	$20.90	$5.89	$1.61	$1,600.80
Denmark (IBM)	5.98 Kroner	$16.72	$5.02	$1.61	$1,213.32
Japan	96.9 Yen	$49.54	20 hours free	$2.06	$965.28
Germany	1.52 Mark	$26.32	None	$0.76	$452.64
United Kingdom	0.63 Pound	$18.65	None	None	$223.80
United States	1.00 Dollar	$17.50	None	None	$210.00

Table 7.2. *Estimate of the cost in various countries of using the Internet from an individual account for fifteen off-peak hours per month. The estimates reflect quotes from respected access providers at the end of 1994 and evening local telephone charges from low-cost telephone companies in major cities. Internet service from IBM Denmark is only valid for OS/2 Warp users and includes three free hours per month. All costs have been converted into U.S. dollars at the exchange rates listed in the table.*

gleaned from Table 7.2, which shows the cost of home Internet usage. Currently, using the Internet is between two and eight times as expensive in other countries than in the U.S. The main exception is the U.K. where costs approximate those in the U.S. because of the British government's early decision to set its telecommunications industry free.

Another interesting observation from Table 7.2 is the way IBM uses the high rates of public Internet access in Denmark to entice customers to buy their OS/2 Warp system by offering comparatively cheap access through IBM's own world-wide datanet. From a user perspective, using and buying a computer really includes hardware, software, and online services (of which the Internet is the most important). The distinction between the three components of computation should not concern users who want to buy *solutions* and not technology for its own sake. Thus, the ability of international computer companies to offer cheap and easy service connectivity may well prove a major selling point for their systems in coming years. After all, saving almost $400 per year on Internet usage might be reason enough for a Danish computer user to buy an OS/2 system instead of a competing platform.

Having realized this connection between system purchases and online services, Microsoft will offer the Microsoft Network as an integrated part of

Windows 95. Many representatives of competing online services (e.g., America Online) are complaining that Microsoft is using the large sales of its operating system to build market share for its online service, but it may well turn out that the opposite effect is as important: having a good online service can be a way of getting people to buy your system. Certainly, their deeply integrated Internet access mechanisms are one of the strong selling points for Unix systems.

Accessing Hypertext Through the Internet

The Internet provides many services, with some of the most popular being electronic mail, file transfer, video broadcasts of current events over the MBone [Eriksson 1994], and the ability to run software on other computers than your own and still get the results displayed on your own screen. The Internet can also be used for hypertext and this use has seen very dramatic growth since 1992. As shown in Figure 7.1, the use of the Internet for hypertext (the bottom three curves) has grown much faster than the Internet overall (the upper two curves).

There are many reasons for the popularity of hypertext on the Internet. First, the traditional user interfaces to the Internet have been very difficult to use [Kellogg and Richards 1995] and required users to understand a line-oriented command language with many obscure abbreviations and confusing options. The alternative approach of having the computer display the options and allowing the user to click on pictures or natural-language descriptions of the information is much more intuitive for new users. As the Internet continues to approximately double in size every year, the user population is changing from the original hard core of system wizards to less technically inclined users, so it is no surprise that they prefer easier user interfaces.

Information providers also have incentives to make their information available over the Internet. This is indeed happening at a rapid pace as indicated by the bottom curve in Figure 7.1, which shows the number of services providing information over the World Wide Web. One reason to put information on the Internet is simply to attract the attention of a large number of well-educated users. For example, Sun Microsystems has a set of Sun SITE™ servers around the world that are accessed by about 140,000 Internet users a day.

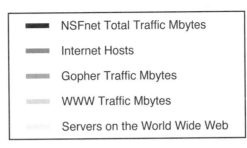

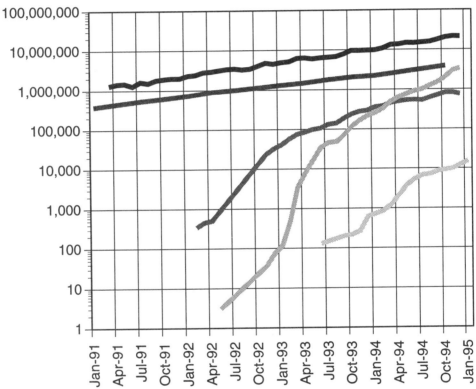

Figure 7.1. *Plot showing various indicators of the growth of the Internet. The two lines showing number of hosts (on the entire Internet and the number of hosts serving the World Wide Web) are for the entire Internet and the lines showing net traffic are for the NSFnet backbone, which is only a subset of the Internet. Traffic measures are in megabytes per month. Note that the scale showing traffic and host growth is logarithmic: the Internet has grown so rapidly that it would be impossible to illustrate with a linear scale.*

Another reason is that the Internet is a very cheap method of providing certain forms of information. In the computer industry, the median cost of servicing a customer support call is about $23 [Nielsen 1993a] and the cost goes up to $75 if it becomes necessary to ship a package with a software bug fix to the customer. Thus, computer companies can save large amounts of money if customers can answer their own questions by accessing hypertext information over the net and if they can download the bug fixes themselves instead of having them shipped physically.

Paying for Information

Some of the information on the Internet is pretty frivolous: for example it is possible to connect to coffee makers at several university break rooms around the world and learn whether they are full or empty. There was also a fellow in Norway who provided a digitized audioclip of his dog barking to disprove the popular saying that "on the Internet, nobody knows you're a dog."[5] Even so, much of the information on the Internet is very useful, and more useful information can be expected in the future when it becomes possible to charge users for their information usage.

Currently, there are only two possibilities for making information available over the Internet: either you restrict access to paying customers who have an established account with you and who have been given a special password or you let anybody in. Of course, the main benefit of providing information over the Internet is to attract a wide audience and it is much too cumbersome to set up accounts for potential users in advance. Also, much information access is due to rapidly changing needs and users would not have accounts with those information providers they suddenly need to access.

As an example, Encyclopedia Britannica has an Internet service where people can search and retrieve online versions of the text for $20 per month. This may sound like a cheap subscription fee compared with the purchase price for this very expensive publication, but in reality many people are likely to need only one or two articles per month. Of course, the value of information

---

[5] This saying is mostly true, though. On the Internet, other users really *don't* know whether you might be a dog since all they see with current technology is what you type on your keyboard. Of course, network technology is changing rapidly and several companies have projects aimed at providing video telephony over the Internet [Tang and Rua 1994], meaning that any dogs will be flushed out pretty soon. (By the way, the saying "on the Internet, nobody knows you're a dog" was a line in a cartoon by P. Steiner printed in *The New Yorker* July 5, 1993, p. 61.)

can be calculated in numerous ways, and $10 for an Encyclopedia Britannica article is no doubt cheap if it provides the information needed for a major report or business project the user is working on. On the other hand, many people who might be willing to pay, say, $1 for every article would refuse to sign up for the service unless they expect to be very heavy users. In other words, by using a subscription service, the information provider has priced itself out of the market for most users.

I am expecting some kind of "NetCash" to become popular very soon since the continued growth of the Internet depends heavily on it. Several projects are underway to provide NetCash [S. Levy 1994], and a few early systems started operating in 1994, though they did not gain sufficiently wide acceptance to satisfy most users' payment needs.

Real cash has several interesting properties that should be replicated on the Internet. First, and most important, it is not necessary to set up special arrangements in advance to pay cash. Given that I have enough bills in the local currency, I can walk into any shop anywhere in the world and buy any good that is for sale, even if nobody in the shop has seen me before and even if they will never see me again. Of course, the fact that you usually need to have local currency is a downside of cash,[6] and an international system like the Internet should operate with a payment system that is independent of the countries in which the buyer and the seller are located. The second advantage of cash is that the overhead in conducting a transaction is minimal. If I give somebody a ten-dollar bill, they immediately recognize it for what it is and allow me to get ten dollars worth of goods without further discussion. I can carry around money in my wallet without having to worry about its weight or size (at least as long as I am using bills and not coins) and it only takes me a few seconds to hand over the money as payment when I buy something. The third main advantage of cash is its anonymity, meaning that I can buy something without having to fear that it gets registered in some government database even though I am using currency issued by the government. In contrast, if I use a credit card, the credit card company usually needs to record where I have shopped in order to provide the monthly statement.

At a minimum, it should be possible to set up payment systems on the Internet that can be used without prior agreements and that involve

---

[6] Besides the lack of a world-wide currency, the main disadvantage of cash is its tendency to invite crime (all the way from bank robbers to pickpockets).

minimum overhead. These two properties are necessary for users to be able to pay for a small piece of information that they may want to download in a matter of seconds from a remote server. The most likely mechanism for NetCash will involve some form of third party who registers the transaction and debits the users account for the amount at the same time as the information provider's account is credited. It would requiring $n{\times}m$ contracts for n users to pay m information providers if every user and every information provider had to set up agreements with each other, but it would only require $n{+}m$ contracts if the users and the information providers could agree on a single third party to handle their payments. Privacy concerns might initially be addressed by requiring users to trust the payment service but it should soon be possible to use various forms of encryption to provide guaranteed anonymity.

Once a payment service gets established on the Internet, we will likely see an explosion in the amount of high-quality content that is made available over the net. We can hope that pricing structures are established to encourage high-volume use since the Internet is well suited to mass distribution of information. Having low prices but high volume is a way for the information providers to generate large profits without having to worry about copyright and unauthorized copies of their material. If I could buy a piece of information for five cents I might not bother storing a copy; I would just retrieve it again if I needed it a second time. And I would certainly not bother pirating the information. In other words, the main value-added from the information providers would be their search mechanisms and the guarantee of being able to find high-quality information whenever needed and not so much the information itself. In a rapidly changing world, the actual information will quickly lose much of its value anyway: very few people use yesterday's newspaper for anything but wrapping fish.

At the time of this writing, none of the NetCash schemes are widely accepted, and most Internet services are funded by the information provider as an act of kindness (or to save them money as in the case of customer support information discussed earlier). Some information is funded by advertisers who pay in order to get users to look at their name (and possibly follow the hypertext links to their own Internet server with additional promotional materials). A prime example of advertising-supported Internet hypertexts is O'Reilly & Associates' GNN (Global Network Navigator), which is an electronic magazine. Similarly, Oslonett's information about Norway is funded by local advertisers such as an Arctic tour company (`http://www.oslonett.no/html/adv/advertisers.html`).

Flash Crowds

One of the potential problems with Internet hypertext is that millions of users from all over the world have the capability of accessing the same server at the same time. Normally this does not happen because people have different needs and interests, so most of the time it is possible to design the capacity of a hypertext server to match the demand: a popular hypertext service will run on a powerful computer with a high-bandwidth connection to the Internet and a more specialized service will run on a smaller computer with a slower connection.

Unfortunately, sometimes large masses of Internet users suddenly decide to link to the same site within a short amount of time. Typically, an Internet flash crowd[7] happens when somebody provides information about an event that is highly publicized around the world. For example, the Norwegian Oslonett provided updated results and event photographs from the 1994 Winter Olympics in Lillehammer and received 1.3 million requests for information during the 18 days of the Olympics, corresponding to almost one request per second. Requests came from users in 42 of the 64 countries that had Internet connections in 1994. Because of this huge load, Oslonett had to get relief from Sun Microsystems, which established a so-called mirror server to handle about half a million requests from users in the United States, meaning that the Norwegian server "only" had to handle 800,000 requests.[8]

Similar, though so far smaller, flash crowds gather when new hot hypermedia services are first described on the "What's New" page at the National Center for Supercomputing Applications (see Figure 7.2).

---

[7] I got the term "flash crowd" from a 1973 science fiction short story with that title by Larry Niven. The story concerns teleportation and what will happen when people can travel to anywhere in the world as easily as making a telephone call (their own body flows down the wire, so to speak). Of course, millions of people immediately teleport to any location that is mentioned in the news and the police get unheard of problems with crowd control.

[8] Even though flash crowds are temporary, one must still plan for the long-term effects of server popularity. During December 1994 (almost a year after the event), the North American mirror server still had to service 774 users wanting information about the Lillehammer Winter Olympics.

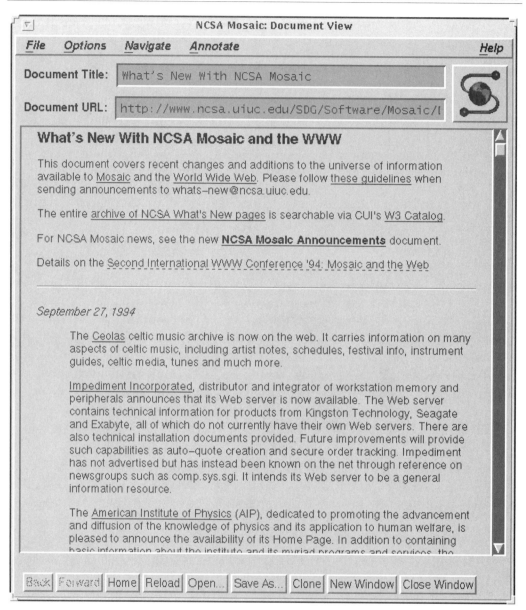

Figure 7.2. *Example of entries from the "What's New With NCSA Mosaic" hypertext page edited at the National Center for Supercomputing Applications. Of course, this text changes all the time. Copyright © 1994 by the National Center for Supercomputing Applications, reprinted by permission.*

A system can go for a long time with a small number of users who access it based on word-of-mouth, but when a link to the service is included on a widely read list of good stuff a small server can quickly become overwhelmed by the many users who want to check it out within a day or two. The "What's New" page is a prime example of a "meta-service" that help users find other good services. Index servers like the one shown in Figure 7.5 and 7.6 are another example of meta-services, though they are less likely to cause flash crowds.

Mirror servers are computers that store an exact copy of the information from some other computer. Thus, people can connect to either computer and find the same information, meaning that the risk of crowding at the main site is reduced. Typically, the mirror server is updated ("mirrored") every night, though more frequent updates are possible for rapidly changing information.

Two of the main problems with mirror servers as solutions to flash crowds are that they are normally not set up until well after the original server becomes overloaded (because it takes some time to recognize the phenomenon and to negotiate space on the mirror) and that users have to know about the mirror server in order to connect to it.

An alternative solution is the use of *cache servers*. A cache server stores a local copy of any information that has recently been requested by users in its neighborhood and if other users request the same information, the cache server gives them its own copy instead of fetching a new copy over the net. For example, Sun Microsystems has an internal hypertext system called SunWeb with information of interest to employees. If a lot of users in Sun Germany decide to look up a certain engineering white paper from headquarters in California, only the first of the requests will generate trans-Atlantic network traffic since Sun's German cache server can handle the subsequent requests.

The downsides of cache servers are that they don't reduce load if users access many different files and that they need a protocol to ensure that updated versions of the information get propagated.

Tim Berners-Lee has mentioned[9] that one of the primary goals in the initial design of the World Wide Web was scalability, meaning that the system should continue to work as it grew larger and more heavily used. Unfortunately, the designers' initial concept of scalability was oriented toward the number of hypertext objects present on the Internet, and the system was

---

[9] In his keynote presentation at the WWW conference in Chicago, October 18, 1994.

designed to allow individual servers to work equally well, no matter how many other servers were added to the Internet. Thus, each server would be independent of all the other servers and would not be burdened with maintaining, say, an overview diagram of the full set of information. As use of the Internet and the Web grew, it became apparent that scalability was not just a matter of handling increased numbers of servers but also of handling increased numbers of users, and mirror and cache servers have therefore become steadily more popular.

The World Wide Web and Mosaic

The most widely used system for hypertext access over the Internet is the World Wide Web (normally abbreviated WWW, sometimes abbreviated W3) [Berners-Lee et al. 1994]. The WWW uses a client–server architecture for distributed hypertext that can be accessed over the Internet. Essentially, the WWW follows the three-level architecture for hypertext systems recommended in Chapter 5. The lowest level, the database level, consists of the Internet and all those computers around the world that choose to supply materials to others over the WWW. These computers act as servers and, in principle, the user need not care where they are located, what types of hardware or software they use, or what internal storage mechanism they use for the data. All the servers provide their data to the client software in a standardized format called HTML (hypertext markup language) through a standard communication protocol called HTTP (hypertext transfer protocol). This combination of HTML and HTTP constitutes the hypertext abstract machine and is the only point at which client and server computers need to agree.

The user can use a variety of software running on a variety of computers as long as they talk HTTP and understand HTML-formatted files. The true benefit of a shared standard is that any of these front-end client computers and client software can connect to any of the back-end servers, no matter whether they are mainframes, Unix workstations, or personal computers.

The presentation level of the model is handled by the client viewer running on the user's machine. One of the great aspects of the WWW is that many different viewers are available to handle different user needs and capabilities. The most famous WWW viewer at the time of this writing was Mosaic as shown in Figure 7.2. NCSA Mosaic™ has a graphical user interface and was developed by the National Center for Supercomputing Applications at the University of Illinois at Urbane-Champaign in 1993. Versions are available for most workstations running X Windows, for the Macintosh, and for Windows. An unsupported version is also available for the Amiga.[10]

Many other WWW viewers are available even though it is a common mistake for people to equate the WWW and Mosaic. In fact, the WWW is the name for the underlying architecture, infrastructure, and the information content made available over the Internet. Mosaic is the name of one specific piece of software that can be used to view information acquired from the WWW. The second-most famous viewer is Lynx which is shown in Figure 7.4. Lynx is a text-only viewer intended for people with terminal emulators capable of supporting a standard VT100 terminal session with connection to the Internet.

Figures 7.3 and 7.4 both show the same hypertext node, the home page of the European Community *I'M EUROPE* service. The information displayed by the two viewers was downloaded from a European Community server in Luxembourg (note in Figure 7.3 that the document's URL field indicates that it is stored on a server in the .lu domain). Figure 7.8 shows the actual information received from the server in an encoded format which the two viewers decode in the manner most appropriate for their respective display formats.

The original WWW viewer from CERN even works over line-oriented telnet connections, meaning that it does not require VT100 support. It can be used from mainframe computers and essentially any computer that can communicate with the rest of the world.

In August 1994, *WIRED* magazine analyzed the 20,920 connections that were made to their Web server over a two-week period (about one per minute). 73% of the connections came from users using Mosaic, indicating the overwhelming dominance of this program in 1994. The distribution of the Mosaic users across platforms was 42% X Windows, 33% Microsoft Windows, 24% Macintosh, and 0.3% Amiga.

---

[10] Mosaic exists in several different version, including the original NCSA Mosaic and commercial products like Netscape from the Netscape Communications Corporation, AIR Mosaic from Spry, and Enhanced Mosaic from Spyglass. Several other products like WebExplorer from IBM are also very similar to Mosaic. At the time of this writing, the productized versions offer distinct advantages over NCSA Mosaic, but they are all based on fundamentally the same user interface and the same hypertext model. Thus, this chapter will use the term "Mosaic" to refer to the shared properties of all the versions.

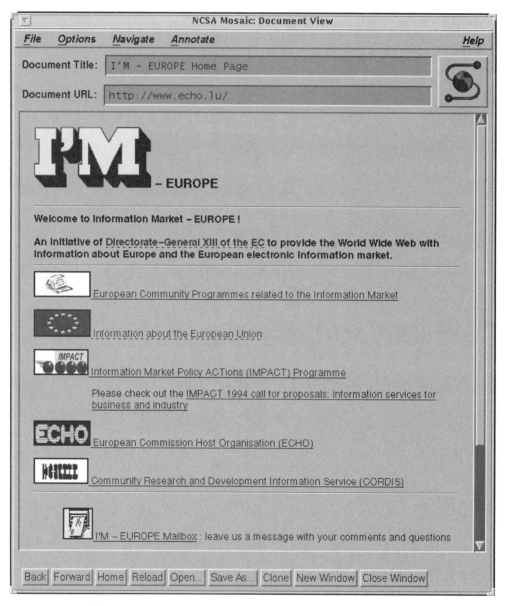

Figure 7.3. *The home page of the European Community information service I'M EUROPE. Copyright © 1994 by the European Commission Host Organisation (ECHO), reprinted by permission.*

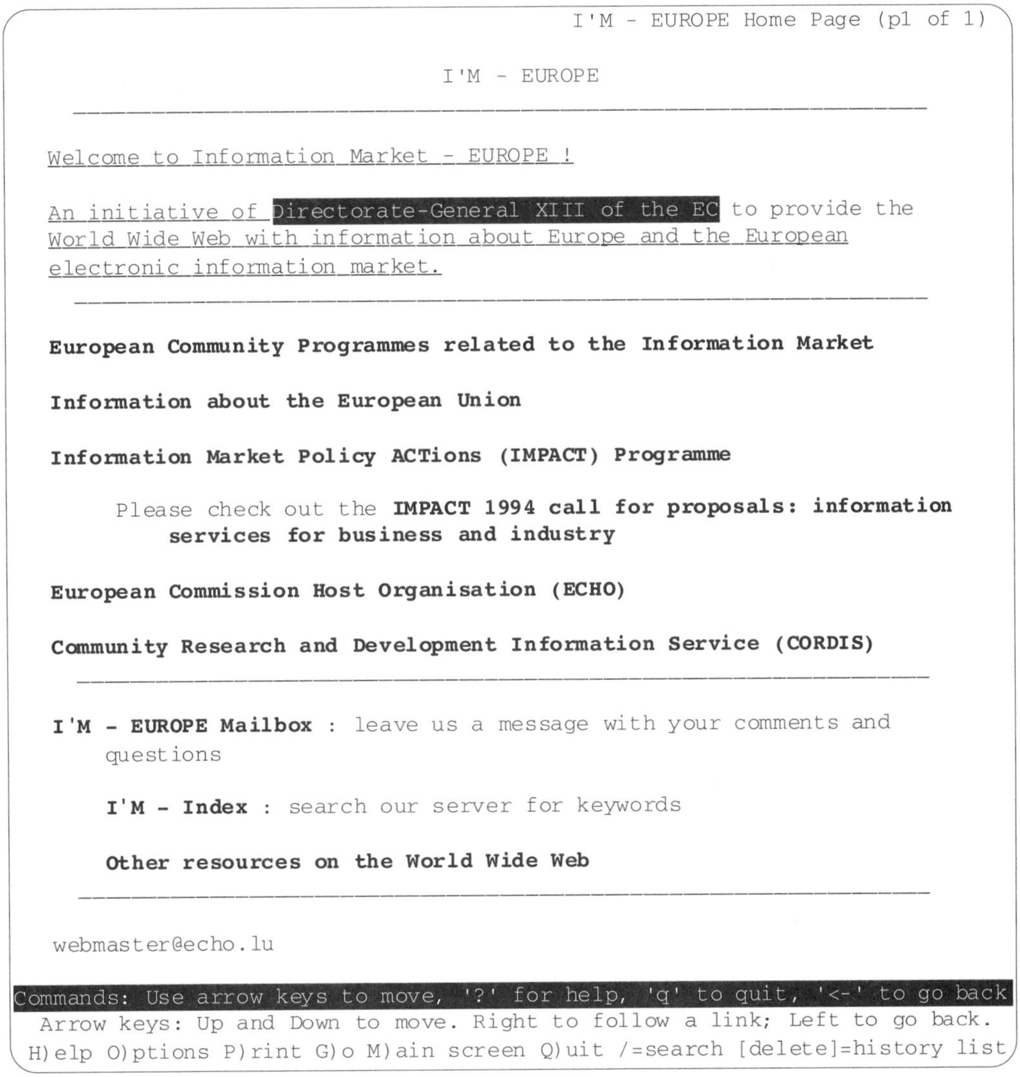

```
                                    I'M - EUROPE Home Page (p1 of 1)

                        I'M - EUROPE
    _____

    Welcome to Information Market - EUROPE !

    An initiative of Directorate-General XIII of the EC to provide the
    World Wide Web with information about Europe and the European
    electronic information market.
    _____


    European Community Programmes related to the Information Market

    Information about the European Union

    Information Market Policy ACTions (IMPACT) Programme

         Please check out the IMPACT 1994 call for proposals: information
              services for business and industry

    European Commission Host Organisation (ECHO)

    Community Research and Development Information Service (CORDIS)
    _____


    I'M - EUROPE Mailbox : leave us a message with your comments and
         questions

         I'M - Index : search our server for keywords

         Other resources on the World Wide Web
    _____


    webmaster@echo.lu

 Commands: Use arrow keys to move, '?' for help, 'q' to quit, '<-' to go back
  Arrow keys: Up and Down to move. Right to follow a link; Left to go back.
 H)elp O)ptions P)rint G)o M)ain screen Q)uit /=search [delete]=history list
```

Figure 7.4. *The* I'M EUROPE *home page viewed from the text-only Lynx browser displaying in a VT100 terminal emulator window. Copyright © 1994 by the European Commission Host Organisation (ECHO), reprinted by permission.*

The second-most popular Web browser after Mosaic was Lynx, with 14% of the connections. The only other browser with more than one percent of the connections was MacWeb at 3%. There is thus no doubt that Mosaic was the most popular WWW browser at the time when the Web was growing the most.

Popularity is fickle on the Internet, however. Just four months later, Mosaic had been replaced as the most popular browser by Netscape which was released in December 1994 (though beta versions had been circulated on the Internet for a few months). Statistics gathered in the week before Christmas 1994 indicated that 64% of the WWW connections were made by Netscape users, 21% by Mosaic users, 7% by Lynx users, and 3% by IBM WebExplorer users. MacWeb had dropped below 1% of the users. Of course, since Netscape is essentially an enhanced version of Mosaic, another way of looking at the data is that Mosaic and related products increased their market share from 73% to 85% in four months and that the number two, Lynx, got its market share cut in half.

Comparing Figures 7.3 and 7.4, the first obvious difference is that Mosaic can display illustrations whereas the text-only browser obviously can't. In Mosaic, anchor points for links are indicated by underlining. Solid underlines indicate links that the user has not followed yet whereas stippled underlines indicate links to destinations that the user has already seen. Mosaic keeps track of which nodes the user has seen in a database stored on the user's machine.

Given the distributed nature of the Internet, the underlying WWW would be hard pressed to provide this service (a popular hypertext node might have to record millions of names of users that had accessed it), but the user's own machine can easily handle the task of showing new and previously visited links differently since this is purely a matter of user interface presentation. On a color monitor the two kinds of links are also shown in different colors and again, this is a matter of user interface presentation and can be changed by the users to suit their individual preferences.

In Mosaic, users activate an anchor by clicking on it with the mouse. In Lynx, no mouse is available, and users activate an anchor by hitting enter while it is highlighted. This means that Lynx has the concept of "the current anchor" which is absent from Mosaic and many other browsers. In Figure 7.4, the current anchor is highlighted in inverse video and the remaining anchors are shown in boldface. The line-mode browser from CERN indicates anchors by numbers and requires users to activate a link by typing in its number. Thus, link activation is also a matter of user interface presentation.

A final difference between the two browsers is their support of text formatting. Since Mosaic has a graphical user interface, it can use different typefaces for different kinds of text. For example, headings can be shown in a larger font and emphasis might be indicated by *italics*. Lynx has to make do with the smaller set of font changes supported by the VT100 terminal and can use underlining, boldfacing, and inverse video.

Even though several browsers exist for the WWW, there is no doubt that the introduction of Mosaic in 1993 caused the tremendous growth of the WWW shown in Figure 7.1. The WWW had grown a very impressive 28,600% in 1992 when it was supported by a variety of text-oriented browsers and a few experimental graphical user interfaces, but growth exploded to an almost incomprehensible 289,000% in 1993 when Mosaic was released. The improved user interface made all the difference and Mosaic became the "killer app" of the Internet in the sense that many people started using the net just to use this one application.

Figure 7.1 also reveals another indication of the importance of good user interfaces. One of the curves in the figure shows the growth of use of Gopher and even though Gopher started out being used much more than the WWW, eventually the WWW overtook Gopher and became the largest service. Gopher is another approach to hypertext over the Internet but it uses a less interesting menu-based interaction style. Gopher users basically see a list of available topics, and after selecting one of them, they get a new menu of whatever their selection pointed to. Eventually, a Gopher user will reach a leaf node that actually contains some information and not just lists of other nodes. Gopher's interaction style is much easier than the traditional Internet Unix commands, so it was fairly popular in 1991 and 1992 as shown in Figure 7.1. Now, however, the WWW has user interfaces (notably the various flavors of Mosaic) with much higher usability, and the WWW has outgrown Gopher. Considering the normal importance in the computer industry of being first and gaining initial market share dominance, it is very impressive that the WWW surpassed Gopher in March 1994 despite the fact that Gopher was used 439 times as much as the WWW as recently as December 1992. This change in market share definitely proves the importance of good user interfaces.

As shown in Figures 7.3 and 7.4, the WWW uses a concept called home pages as the top nodes of an organization's hypertext. In principle, every other user on the Internet can establish links into any specific node on the WWW, but since these nodes are stored on other peoples' computers, there is no guarantee that they will be there in the future. The home pages are more stable since everybody has one. The home pages are often used to present a high-level overview of an organization or an individual user with links to more in-depth information. Often, home pages also link to other home pages of related organizations or individuals.

Strengths and Weaknesses of Mosaic

Despite its many advantages, Mosaic also has several important weaknesses, and since many of these weaknesses are reflections of some of its greatest strengths, it is worth looking more closely at the five main limitations of Mosaic. Some of these problems will doubtless be addressed in future releases, but many of them are inherent in the basic way the system is constructed.

The first great strength of Mosaic is that it runs on all the important platforms (Unix, Macintosh, Windows) and that it is compatible with other systems for most remaining computers (e.g., mainframes that are supported by text-only browsers like Lynx). Because of this cross-platform compatibility, Mosaic has a large enough pool of users to be attractive for information providers. In fact, Mosaic can piggyback onto the user pool of the entire WWW, meaning that the critical mass for many applications can be reached sooner than it might be by the user population of any individual application. The WWW is also an open system in the sense that people can stop using Mosaic and change to a competing product any time they like without having to change the format of their hypertext data or without having to give up on accessing any outside hypertext servers they have found through Mosaic. Many users prefer open systems over proprietary systems because they don't have to fear being locked into a single vendor or a single technology that may become obsolete.

The dark side of cross-platform compatibility is that Mosaic cannot be optimal for any single platform. Information providers putting their data up on the WWW have to consider the still sizable proportion of users with text-only browsers, meaning that they cannot design their hypermedia presentations to take full advantage of a graphical user interface. Information providers cannot design information that would be great on some specific platform if users on other platforms would suffer or be unable to access their information. Even on the browser side, cross-platform compatibility means sub-optimal user interfaces because the software cannot be designed to be fully integrated with other applications or system-supported capabilities on any individual platform without starting to deviate too much across platforms. Similarly, the code is normally not as optimized for speed as it would be for an application that was developed solely for a single platform.

The second strength of Mosaic is that it relies on third-party players to display any kind of advanced multimedia node. Mosaic itself can only display text and small bitmapped images. Any sounds, animations, video, PostScript files, or other advanced formats get displayed by having Mosaic start up another application that can display the format in question. The advantage of this approach is that Mosaic can handle all possible datatypes as long as the user has acquired some software that can play back the data. For the most common datatypes, shareware players exist for all major platforms, so it is typically easy for users to get the playback software they need to view most multimedia nodes. When a new datatype such as QuickTime VR is introduced, players typically become available for the major platforms fairly rapidly and users can then start to view the files without waiting for the Mosaic developers to upgrade the system.

The main downside of the reliance on external players for advanced datatypes is that all the hypertext linking capabilities are lost the minute a node is received in one of the externally supported datatypes. When Mosaic spawns an external player, it gives up control over the display of the node and users cannot follow any links from that node on. This again means that Mosaic is incapable of supporting hypermedia features in time-varying media. It would not be able, for example, to play a Mozart symphony and allow the user to link from certain parts of the music to explanations of the composition or to the way another conductor had interpreted the same movement.

The third strength and weakness of Mosaic is the fact that the WWW works over the Internet and can access thousands of computers around the world. Mostly, it is a benefit to be able to get information from far away without having to set up special accounts, and it is an advantage that one can link from, say, an American ornithology database to the server at the Royal Society for the Protection of Birds in Britain that again contains a link to Australia for retrieval of digitized sounds of Australian bird calls. This can happen even if the Australian biologists never bothered telling anybody in the U.S. about their bird sound project.

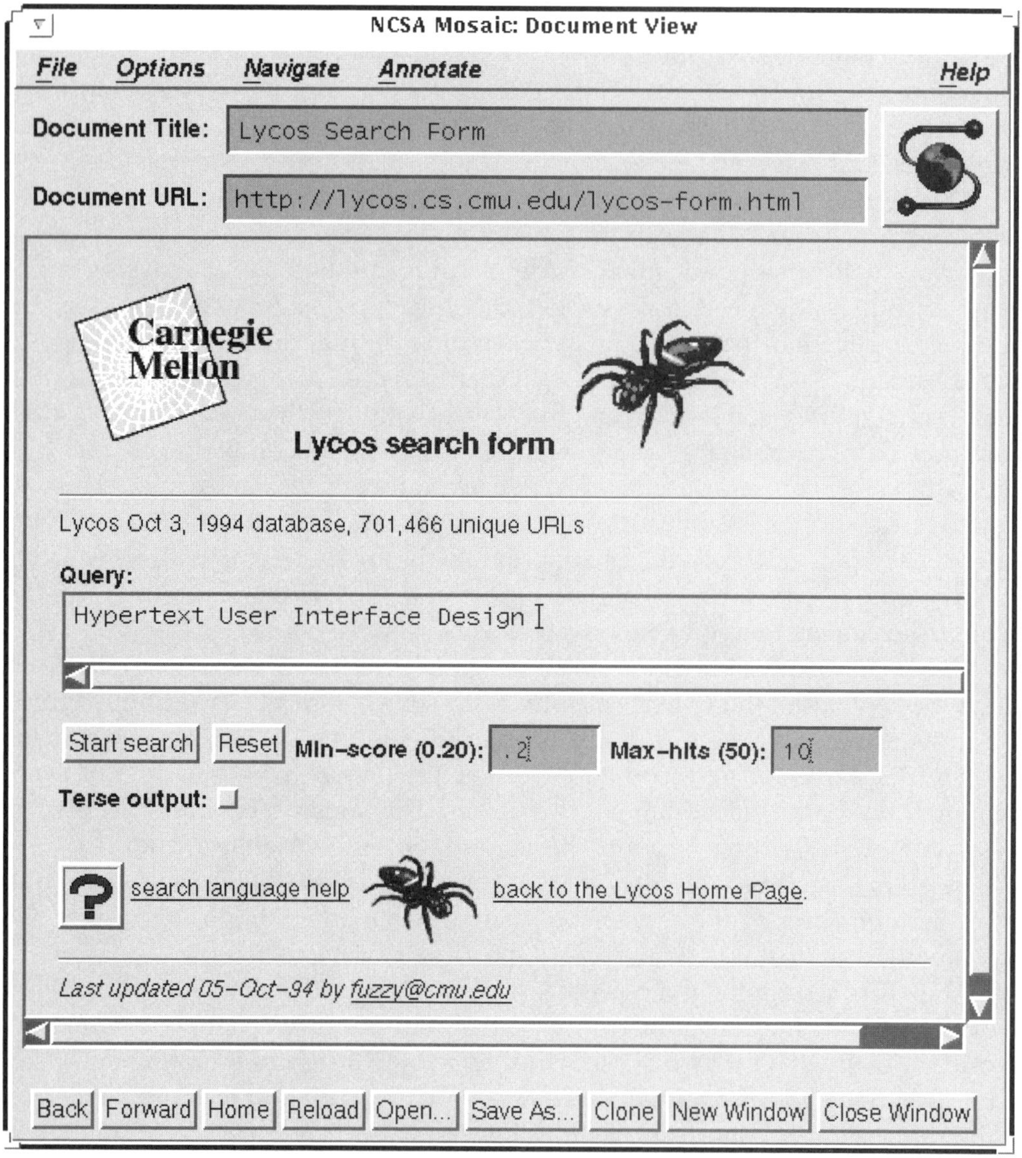

Figure 7.5. *The search form on the Lycos WWW index server. Here, the user has entered a search for the terms "hypertext user interface design." Note, by the way, that a four-word query is somewhat unrepresentative since experience shows that about 90% of searchers use no more than one or two terms. Copyright © 1994 by Michael L. Mauldin, reprinted by permission.*

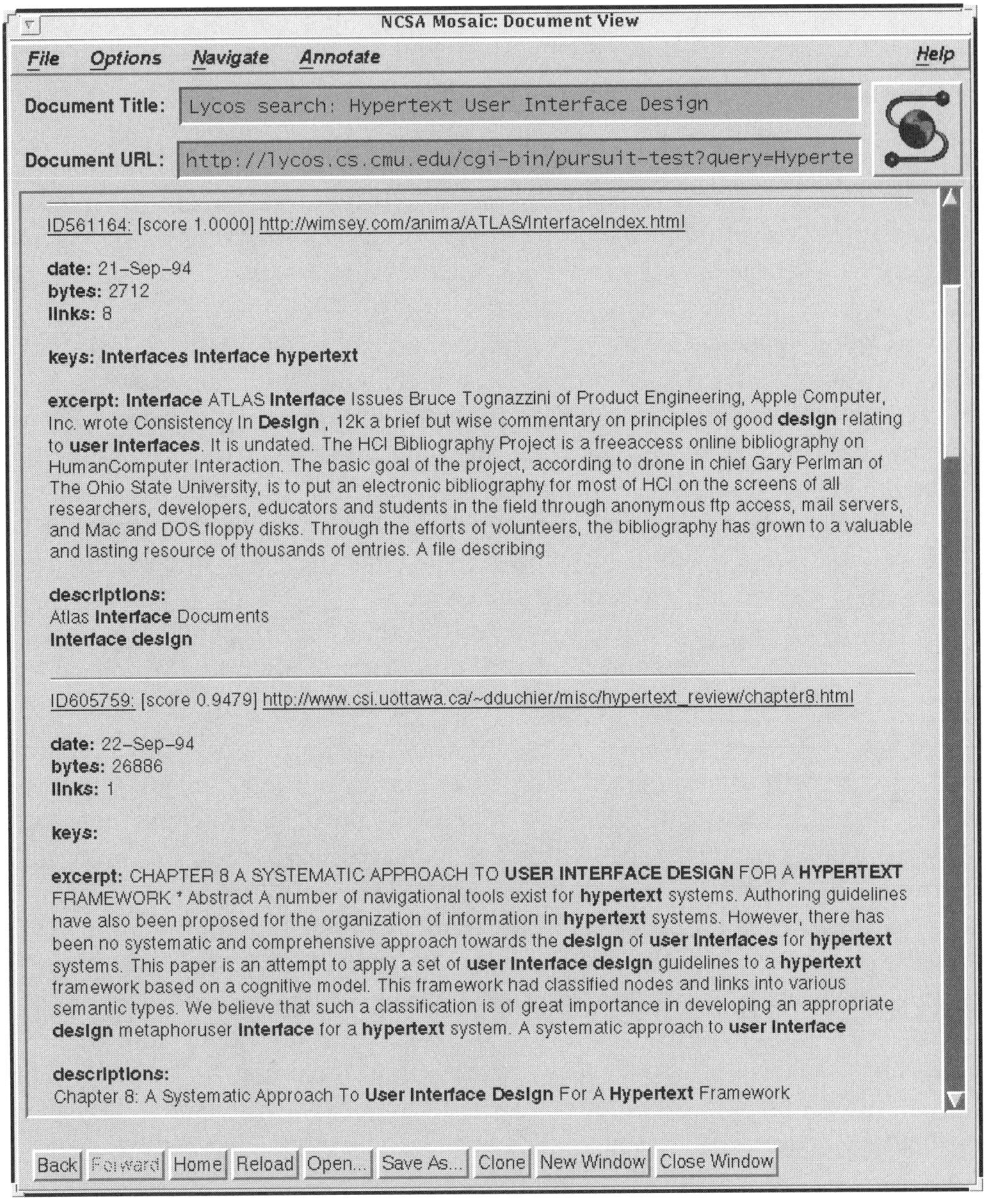

NCSA Mosaic: Document View

File   *Options*   *Navigate*   *Annotate*   *Help*

Document Title: Lycos search: Hypertext User Interface Design

Document URL: http://lycos.cs.cmu.edu/cgi-bin/pursuit-test?query=Hyperte

---

ID561164: [score 1.0000] http://wimsey.com/anima/ATLAS/InterfaceIndex.html

date: 21–Sep–94
bytes: 2712
links: 8

keys: Interfaces Interface hypertext

excerpt: Interface ATLAS **Interface** Issues Bruce Tognazzini of Product Engineering, Apple Computer, Inc. wrote Consistency In **Design** , 12k a brief but wise commentary on principles of good **design** relating to **user Interfaces**. It is undated. The HCI Bibliography Project is a freeaccess online bibliography on HumanComputer Interaction. The basic goal of the project, according to drone in chief Gary Perlman of The Ohio State University, is to put an electronic bibliography for most of HCI on the screens of all researchers, developers, educators and students in the field through anonymous ftp access, mail servers, and Mac and DOS floppy disks. Through the efforts of volunteers, the bibliography has grown to a valuable and lasting resource of thousands of entries. A file describing

descriptions:
Atlas **Interface** Documents
Interface design

ID605759: [score 0.9479] http://www.csi.uottawa.ca/~dduchier/misc/hypertext_review/chapter8.html

date: 22–Sep–94
bytes: 26886
links: 1

keys:

excerpt: CHAPTER 8 A SYSTEMATIC APPROACH TO **USER INTERFACE DESIGN** FOR A **HYPERTEXT** FRAMEWORK * Abstract A number of navigational tools exist for **hypertext** systems. Authoring guidelines have also been proposed for the organization of information in **hypertext** systems. However, there has been no systematic and comprehensive approach towards the **design** of **user Interfaces** for **hypertext** systems. This paper is an attempt to apply a set of **user Interface design** guidelines to a **hypertext** framework based on a cognitive model. This framework had classified nodes and links into various semantic types. We believe that such a classification is of great importance in developing an appropriate **design** metaphoruser **Interface** for a **hypertext** system. A systematic approach to **user Interface**

descriptions:
Chapter 8: A Systematic Approach To **User Interface Design** For A **Hypertext** Framework

Back | Forward | Home | Reload | Open... | Save As... | Clone | New Window | Close Window

Figure 7.6. *The search result screen from the Lycos query in Figure 7.5. Note how the user's search terms are highlighted in the file summaries. Copyright © 1994 by Michael L. Mauldin, reprinted by permission.*

The downside of the international and distributed nature of the Internet is that there is no structure to the overall hyperspace, no consistency in the design of the individual hypertext nodes, and no way of searching the full set of information to know what it contains and how to get to specific information one needs.

Even though the WWW itself has no search features, several people have designed index servers that wander the Web to retrieve a copy of all available information. A prime example is Lycos as shown in Figures 7.5 and 7.6. These index servers typically build some kind of index of the information they have seen and allow users to search the index and get a list of links pointing to nodes with matching information. The problem with the index servers is that they are not an integrated part of the user interface and that they vary tremendously in the quality of their user interface and the extent of their database. Normally, users have no idea of the scope of their searches (e.g., what parts of the Internet are covered in the database). Also, in the long term, it will not be feasible for a system with millions of users to rely on searches being carried out on individual researchers' workstations.

Lycos was already getting accessed 200,000 times per day in December 1994. The growth rate of Lycos usage from mid-August to mid-December 1994 corresponded to an annual growth of 130 million percent. This number is skewed by a few weeks in October with very rapid growth,[11] but almost all weeks saw growth at annualized rates of at least a million percent. Given that the annualized growth rate of the WWW was "only" a thousand percent or less in the same period, the growth of Lycos usage clearly indicates an extreme user need for good search tools. As an aside, it is doubtful whether the extreme growth rates recorded for Lycos could be found anywhere but on the Internet.

Because of the decentralized nature of the WWW, no single unified overview diagram is available, although several servers include lists of many of the most important sites. Users can construct their own overview diagrams of sites they have visited. An experimental system for doing so is the KJ-Editor (shown in Figure 7.7), developed by Kazuhisha Kawai at the Toyohashi University of Technology, Japan, and Hajime Ohiwa at Keio University, Japan.

---

[11] During the single month of October 1994, Lycos usage increased by 836%, corresponding to an annualized growth rate of 27 trillion percent.

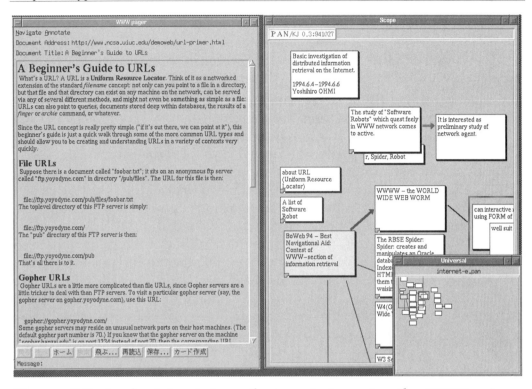

Figure 7.7. *In the left window, the user is browsing the WWW using a traditional single-page viewer. The right window contains an overview diagram in the KJ-Editor. The overview diagram is constructed by the user who for each page visited in the WWW browser can decide whether to add it to the map window. Copyright © 1994 by Hajime Ohiwa and Kazuhisa Kawai, reprinted by permission.*

The fourth strength of Mosaic is that it has a simple point-and-click graphical user interface that allows users to navigate the Internet without knowing anything about networking and without having to learn any advanced commands or options. When a new user starts up Mosaic it begins by displaying its default home page which can be the home page of the user's organization if it has been defined and otherwise the home page of the Mosaic project at the National Center for Supercomputing Applications. The initial home page typically contains links to a number of interesting hypertexts that again contain further links, and soon the new user has visited scores of servers on several continents without ever having done anything but clicking on some words or pictures that seemed interesting.

The downside of its simplicity is that Mosaic does not support advanced graphical user interface interaction techniques. The dialogue model is extremely primitive with a single window[12] In a throwback to the mainframe era, the dialogue is asynchronous, meaning that the host computer does not react to the user's actions in a window until the user moves on to the next node by activating a link. After the introduction of forms support in Mosaic version 2, the user interface does support some simple forms of user manipulation locally in a window. For example, users can fill in text fields and select options from radio buttons, but these actions do not take effect until the user transmits them to the remote server.

Also, the current interface only supports a subset of the commonly used GUI widgets though this is not so much a fundamental limitation as it is a matter of development resources. Because of the primitive user interface model, many information providers have taken to including bitmapped pictures of more advanced user interfaces, and in principle, Mosaic can display pictures of anything, meaning that the range of user interface options for information providers is extremely large. Unfortunately, the bitmaps are ultimately no more than bitmaps and the user gets no local feedback when interacting with them. The only thing the user can do is to click somewhere on the bitmap, but the system does not provide feedback in the form of highlighting, and the user cannot use direct manipulation interaction techniques like drag-and-drop.

The fifth strength and weakness of Mosaic is its tremendous growth as shown in Figure 7.1. It is a strength that so many users are starting to use Mosaic for so many purposes because that means a rapid exploration of the various ways of designing hypertexts for delivery over the WWW. It is also reassuring that the user base is getting large enough to support many commercial versions that will add more features and capabilities as the need for them becomes known.

---

[12] It is possible to run multiple Mosaic sessions with their own windows, but the windows do not communicate and thus cannot be used to support advanced hypertext features that would require the coordination of the content of several windows. For example, a "tabletop" style guided tour [Trigg 1988] where one window is used to comment on the content of another window as the user moves through a hypertext would require tighter coordination between windows than the Mosaic model provides.

One downside of the rapid growth is that Mosaic is being used for many things for which it is ill suited. For example, Mosaic is being used for user interface prototyping despite its very limited range of interaction techniques as just discussed. People are also using Mosaic to present technical documentation in situations where the documentation is essentially stable and could be made available through a less dynamic hypertext system that provided better search capabilities.

Another problem with the many users of Mosaic-style browsers and the many WWW servers is that it is getting more and more difficult to change the underlying protocols, formats, and other standards because of the installed base. When the first few versions of Mosaic were released, they introduced several changes to the way WWW information was encoded (e.g., use of embedded graphics and forms), but doing so was acceptable since the WWW had very few users who would be inconvenienced. Also, the early changes were fairly easy to make backward compatible with the earlier standards, but as the complexity of the WWW grows it will become steadily more difficult to upgrade it without breaking something.

A final downside of the rapid growth of the WWW is that every new server seems to be experimenting with a new user interface or a new way of organizing its data. Users cannot build up expectations for what to expect or rely on conventions to guide their navigational behavior. Web interface, thy name is Inconsistency.

HTML

The encoding used for information exchange over the WWW is referred to as HTML, meaning Hypertext Markup Language [Graham 1995]. An example of a HTML-formatted file is shown in Figure 7.8. HTML is a form of SGML (Standardized General Markup Language), meaning that the text is marked up according to its meaning and not according to its physical display on the screen.

Each viewer has a stylesheet that translates between the HTML tags and the most appropriate way of displaying the information in their user interface. For example, the author of the I'M EUROPE home page wanted the words "Welcome to Information Market - EUROPE !" to be displayed prominently. This is indicated by embedding these words (and the next few lines of the welcome message) within the HTML tag `<strong>` and `</strong>`.

```
<htmlplus>
 <head>
  <title>I'M - EUROPE Home Page</title>
 </head>
 <body>
   <h1><IMG align=bottom SRC="icons/imnew.gif" ALT="I'M">  -  EUROPE
   </h1><hr>
<strong>
Welcome to Information Market - EUROPE !
<p>
An initiative of
<a href="/dg13/en/dg13tasks.html">Directorate-General XIII of the EC</a> to provide the World
Wide Web with information about Europe and the European electronic information
market.</strong><hr>


<a href="/programmes/en/programmesindex.html"><IMG SRC="icons/infoprogsmall.gif" ALT="">
European Community Programmes related to the Information Market</a><p>
<a href="/eudocs/en/eudocshome.html"><IMG SRC="icons/EUlogomedium.gif" ALT="">
Information about the European Union</a><p>
<a href="/impact/en/impacthome.html"><IMG SRC="icons/impactsmall.gif" ALT=""> Information
Market Policy ACTions (IMPACT) Programme</a><p>
<ul>
<ul>
 Please check out the <a href="/impact/en/cfp.html">IMPACT 1994 call for proposals: information
services for business and industry</a><p>
</ul>
</ul>
<a href="/echo/en/menuecho.html"><IMG SRC="icons/echosmall.gif" ALT="">    European
Commission Host Organisation (ECHO)</a><p>
<a href="/cordis/en/cordishome.html"><IMG SRC="icons/cordissmall.gif" ALT=""> Community
Research and Development Information Service (CORDIS)</a>
<hr>
<ul>
<a href="/mailim.html"><img src=/icons/mbox.gif alt=""> I'M - EUROPE Mailbox</a> : leave us a
message with your comments and questions<p>
<a href="/cgi/ice-form.pl"><img src=/icons/searchsmall.gif alt=""> I'M - Index</a> : search our
server for keywords<p>
<a href="other/otherhome.html"><img src=/icons/websmall.gif alt=""> Other resources on the World
Wide Web</a>
</ul>
<hr>
<addr>webmaster@echo.lu</addr>
</body>
</htmlplus>
```

Figure 7.8. *The HTML file that generated the two views of the* I'M EUROPE *home page in Figures 7.3 and 7.4. Copyright © 1994 by the European Commission Host Organisation (ECHO), reprinted by permission.*

As shown in Figure 7.3, Mosaic shows "strong" text in boldface, and as shown in Figure 7.4, Lynx shows it underlined. One could build a WWW browser for blind users that would read the text rather than displaying it, and such a browser might treat "strong" text to being read in a special tone of voice or by a more authoritative speaker.

It would also be possible for users with a small screen to get all text displayed in a smaller font, with the system choosing appropriate fonts for each kind of text rather than just uniformly making everything smaller by the same percentage (which might render footnotes unreadable), and it would be possible for users with weak eyesight to get the system to display the information in a larger font.

Compare these advantages of content-oriented markup with the traditional display-oriented formatting used in many word processors. The author of the I'M EUROPE home page could have specified that the welcome message should have been displayed in, say, 14 point Helvetica bold, but there would have been no way for the system to treat this text differently from any other text in the same font even if that text had a very different meaning. For example, 14 point Helvetica bold might also be used for second-level headings, and the interface for blind users might want to treat headings in a special manner, for example by reading a list of them in the beginning to give the user the understanding of the structure of the document which a seeing user would gain from glancing at the page. If the text was marked up in HTML, the tags `<h2>` and `</h2>` would be used to mark a second level header, and the system would have no problems in distinguishing that from text marked `<strong>`.

HTML follows the syntax of SGML in using tags that are indicated by angle brackets `<>`. All tags come in two versions, a start tag that is just the name of the tag in angle brackets and an end tag that starts with a slash (/) after the opening angle bracket. Thus, the title of the I'M EUROPE home page is encoded as `<title>I'M - EUROPE Home Page</title>`. As can be seen from Figures 7.3 and 7.4, Mosaic puts the document title in the upper left of its window an Lynx puts the document title in the upper right. In both cases, the browsers can utilize the fact that they know the titles of the documents to use the titles as the node names in their history lists and bookmark lists (called the "hotlist" in Mosaic) to allow users to easily return to the documents. Again, this would have been difficult if the browsers had needed to pick out a relevant name from a file that was formatted with text fonts for display purposes only.

The main exception for the need for a closing tag to indicate the end of a certain form of text is the paragraph marker <P>, where it is assumed that the beginning of one paragraph implicitly marks the end of the previous paragraph, if any. Line feeds are not significant in HTML, because the browsers are supposed to format the text in the manner that makes the most sense to their circumstances. For example, most WWW viewers word wrap the text according to the user's current specification of the window width, meaning that line breaks occur in different places on each user's screen.

Simple HTML tags just indicate the meaning of the text they enclose. More advanced tags include attributes. The syntax for a tag with attributes is the opening angle bracket followed by the tag name followed by one or more attributes of the form `attribute_name=value` followed by the closing angle bracket. The most common use of attributes is to specify the insertion of images and possible alternative text to be used if the image is unavailable (either due to a transmission problem or because the HTML file is being viewed in a text-only browser).

As an example, consider the following element from the I'M EUROPE home page: `<IMG align=bottom SRC="icons/imnew.gif" ALT="I'M">`. The term `IMG` immediately after the open bracket indicates that we are dealing with an image tag that will specify an illustration for the document. The tag has three attributes, specifying the alignment and the source of the image as well as an alternative text string to be used if the image cannot be displayed. The source of the image is given as a file name in the `icons` directory. In Figure 7.3 the `imnew.gif` image was retrieved and in Figure 7.4 the alternative text, `I'M`, was displayed instead.

HTML supports hypertext through anchor tags. The text between the anchor start tag <A> and the anchor end tag </A> constitutes the actual anchor that the user can activate by clicking or some other means defined by the browser. The result of activating the anchor is defined by its attributes, the two most important of which are the `HREF` hypertext reference and the `NAME` attribute for defining the named destination of a link.

An example from the I'M EUROPE home page is this anchor (note that the capitalization of tag names and attributes is not considered significant):

```
<a href="/echo/en/menuecho.html"><IMG
SRC="icons/echosmall.gif" ALT="">      European Commission Host
Organisation (ECHO)</a>
```

This is an anchor with one attribute: a hypertext reference to the address of a destination node to be retrieved if the user activates this anchor. The destination node is `/echo/en/menuecho.html`. The fact that the destination node is given as a filename without a machine name or other access mechanism means that it is to be interpreted as a file from the same machine as the one from which the page was originally retrieved. The anchor-start and anchor-end tags surround a piece of HTML that specifies an image to be retrieved if possible (but no alternative text to be displayed if the image cannot be shown) as well as some regular text. This means that the anchor will be activated if the user clicks on either the image or somewhere in the text string.

A `NAME` attribute in an anchor defines a destination point that can be referred to by an incoming hypertext link that wants to go to a specific part of a document and not just to the top. To go to a named anchor, the departure anchor would have a HREF attribute that consisted of the address of the document followed by a number sign # and the desired name.

The hypertext references are given in a notation called URL for Uniform Resource Locator. A URL[13] has three components: the access method by which the client can retrieve the information object, the Internet address of the server where the object is stored, and the address of the object in that server's file space. For example, information about the WWW project is available in a hypertext node with the URL `http://info.cern.ch/hypertext/WWW /TheProject.html`. The word before the colon indicates the protocol (transfer method) used to access the information, in this case HTTP. HTTP stands for Hypertext Transfer Protocol and is the main method by which WWW clients communicate with their servers. WWW also supports alternative access methods like gopher and FTP (File Transfer Protocol) for more primitive straight file retrieval. One of the reasons for the early success of the WWW was its ability to access information that was already available on the Internet in other formats without being restricted to information in its own format. In the "early days" (just two years before the WWW took over the Internet), users could get attracted to using the WWW without having to give up on accessing information in other formats. Backward data compatibility is often important for the acceptance of new hypertext systems because people often have large amounts of data that cannot easily be converted to the new format.

---

[13] "URL" is normally pronounced "you-are-ell" and not "earl."

The second component of the URL is the address of the server. Here, `info.cern.ch` is the name of the `info` machine at CERN in Switzerland. `.ch` is the Internet domain for Switzerland—each country has a two letter abbreviation, though addresses in the U.S. often omit the ".us" domain and are referred to by a three-letter domain like `.com` (companies), `.edu` (educational institutions), `.gov` (Federal government), etc. The two slashes between the access method and the machine name indicate that the URL does indeed include a machine name. Often, relative URLs are used that refer to information stored on the same machine as that from which the document in which they are contained was originally retrieved. In that case, the URL is simplified and no machine name is given.

Finally, the third component of the URL is the file name of the destination node. In principle, it is problematic to have to encode the exact machine names and file locations with subdirectory paths in a URL since this information often changes as machines are moved around, upgraded, or otherwise reconfigured. Therefore, the WWW is moving toward a solution based on a naming service and so-called URNs (Universal Resource Names) that will be address-independent.

A final feature of HTML is the ability to encode the full ISO Latin 1 character set within an ASCII file, meaning that it is possible to represent the main European languages without any special treatment. The non-English characters are specified by an ampersand followed by a mnemonic for the desired character and a semicolon. Thus, for example, the Swedish word smörgåsbord would be represented in HTML as `sm&ouml;rg&aring;sbord`.

It will be apparent from the examples in this section that HTML is a fairly simple markup language. It is therefore easy for people to write HTML files for distribution over the WWW, and this simplicity of authoring has been one of the factors in the success and growth of the WWW. In fact, during the first years most HTML files were hand-edited with a human author inserting the appropriate tags manually. Early support for automated HTML construction included macros for the emacs editor that automatically matched start and end tags. For example, to indicate emphasis, the author could select some text and automatically have the editor wrap it in `<EM>` and `</EM>` tags, thus eliminating the risk of forgetting or misspelling the end tag. Manually authored HTML often has tag errors, and a common indication of a manually authored WWW page is the case where *the entire end of a paragraph is rendered as emphasized text and not just the few words that were intended. Inspecting the HTML markup often reveals that the author had forgotten the slash in the end tag or had misspelled it.*

Due to the popularity of the WWW, several authoring tools have emerged that allow WYSIWYG (what you see is what you get) editing where the author can rapidly shift between seeing the text as it would be formatted in various popular browsers and seeing it with the markup tags in place. There are also several conversion tools available to help transform traditional files written in word processors like FrameMaker and Microsoft Word into HTML files for the Web. These conversion tools rely on the paragraph styles used in these word processors and thus work best if the author has been meticulous in the use of styles. For example, if all chapter headings are formatted as "Heading1" paragraphs, it is a simple matter to convert them to <H1> marked text.

The basic HTML facilities discussed so far are all part of the original specification of HTML, which is often referred to as HTML level 1. This specification is available from:

```
http://info.cern.ch/hypertext/WWW/MarkUp/HTML.html
```

Most WWW browsers also support the slightly more advanced HTML level 2 format. The main change from level 1 to level 2 is the provision of forms to allow users slightly more interaction features than simple link activation by anchor clicking. Figure 7.9 shows an example of the use of forms on the WWW to support an interactive art exhibition. Each of the pictures in the hypertext node has a pop-up menu associated with it which the user can change to vote on how much he or she likes that picture. There is also a set of radio buttons across the bottom of the page for the user to indicate how much he or she enjoyed the experience as a whole.

When the user clicks on the "continue" button, the WWW browser connects back to the server and transmits the user's choices to the host program. In this particular example, the remote software will tally the statistics of how many users liked which pictures. After enough users have connected to the art exhibit, the system will know what pictures were "best" and it will use a genetic algorithm to generate additional pictures that share some properties with the ones that got high votes. Typically, a new generation is "born" every day and users can connect back to the exhibit later to see how the pictures have changed as a result of their votes.

Note: You will only be able to view this exhibit properly if you are using a browser with forms support and a colour display

International Interactive Genetic Art, Generation 13

When you have finished saying how much you like the pictures, press here to
criticise .

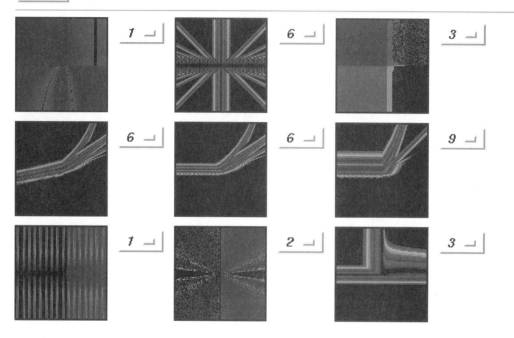

Click here for voting help and more information about this project.

How much did you enjoy participating in this performance?:

∨ 1 ∨ 2 ∨ 3 ∨ 4 ∨ 5 ∨ 6 ∧ 7 ∨ 8 ∨ 9

Interactive art by wsr@cs.cmu.edu. Mosaic user interface by witbrock@cs.cmu.edu.

Figure 7.9. *Screen from an art exhibition on the Internet. with pictures generated by the users working with the computer. Users can vote on the various pictures and the next exhibition will contain pictures similar to the ones that were liked the most. The system automatically generates new pictures to look like the ones with the highest scores. To connect to this exhibit, go to* hhtp://porsche.boltz.cs.cmu.edu:8001/htbin/mjwgenform. *Copyright © 1993, 1994 by W. Scott Reilly and Michael J. Witbrock, reprinted by permission.*

The term "genetic algorithm" refers to the way this approach ensures the survival of the fittest by producing more pictures of the kinds that are liked and killing off those that are not liked. For each new "generation," the algorithm introduces some random mutation in the form of new (and possibly radically different) way of drawing the pictures, and some proportion of these new ideas are good enough to survive and pass on their "genes" (that is, attribute values) to subsequent pictures.

The interactive art exhibit is a somewhat unusual application of the forms capability of HTML level 2, but I am showing it because it is an example of a new use of computers that is enabled by the Internet.

A more traditional example of HTML forms is seen in the pizza ordering system from Pizza Hut (at `http://www.pizzahut.com/`). Users who connect to Pizza Hut's server are asked to enter their address and telephone number in text fields that are transmitted back to Pizza Hut's computer. Users can then click on pictures of various pizza offerings and toppings and select their desired choice. At the time of this writing, actual pizza delivery does not take place until a Pizza Hut employee has called the user back to verify that the order is genuine and not a hoax. This additional step is an obvious waste of resources but is necessitated by the lack of secure communication over the WWW. By the time you read this, I would expect secure versions of Mosaic and other WWW browsers to have become available, and these systems should enable Pizza Hut to use a computerized authentication scheme to verify that the person ordering a pizza is in fact whom he or she claims to be.

The HTML level 2 specification is available from:

`http://www.hal.com/users/connolly/html-spec/HTML_TOC.html`

HTML level 3 (also known as HTML+) adds further features like support for tables. HTML level 3 also includes the ability for the hypertext author to specify that certain links should be represented as footnotes or pop-up notes. Considering that pop-ups are one of the most useful features of single-machine hypertext systems, this addition has great potential for improving the usability of the WWW. The specification of HTML level 3 is available from:

`http://info.cern.ch/hypertext/WWW/MarkUp/HTMLPlus/htmlplus_1.html`
`http://www.w3.org/hypertext/WWW/MarkUp/html3-dtd.txt`

Information about HTML style sheets can be found in:

`http://info.cern.ch/hypertext/WWW/Style/`

Hyper-G and Harmony

Even though it is currently the most famous, the WWW is not the only hypertext system to operate across the Internet. Another promising project is called Hyper-G, developed by the Institute for Information Processing and Computer Supported New Media (IICM) at Graz University of Technology in Austria [Andrews and Kappe 1994, Fenn and Maurer, 1994]. The most interesting Hyper-G client is the Unix/X11 viewer called Harmony; other clients are available for PC/Windows (Amadeus) and Unix text-only terminals (hgtv), and a Macintosh client is under development. Just as with the WWW, one should distinguish between the fundamental hypertext architecture and distribution system on the one hand (WWW and Hyper-G) and the user interface presentation on the other hand (Mosaic and Harmony). The terminal client can be tried out by establishing a telnet connection: "`telnet -1 info info.tu-graz.ac.at.`"

Hyper-G is based on a client–server model where the client program connects to a single server for the duration of the user's hypermedia session. The WWW client–server model involves repeated connections to servers for every additional hypertext link that is traversed. Even if all the hypertext nodes are stored on the same server, the WWW model involves establishing a new connection for each node that is accessed. The advantage of the WWW model is that connections have low overhead since the server will not need to keep track of its users. After all, if they want anything else, they will just make another connection. On the other hand, the lack of session support means that the WWW cannot support interaction styles that require the server to know who the user is and what the user has been doing.

Even though the user connects to a single Hyper-G server, that server can access Hyper-G documents from remote servers as needed, so users are not denied the freedom to roam the full Internet. Hyper-G supports several levels of user authentication, from anonymous to fully identified. The commercial WWW browsers will have to provide some form of user authentication and payment methods, but the basic WWW architecture does not support that well. Hyper-G also provides several different levels of access rights for users, meaning that one can make certain documents available to everybody in the world and other documents available to, say, registered customers, association members, or other groups or individuals.

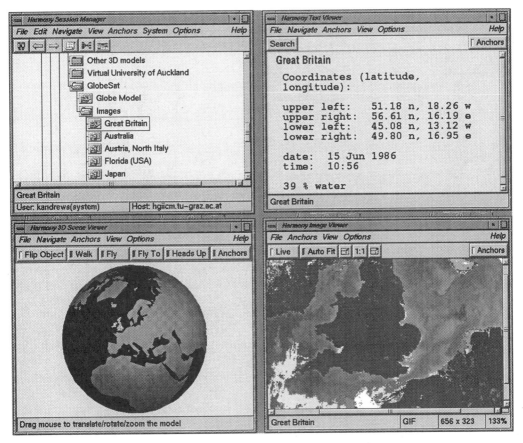

Figure 7.10. *The Hyper-G viewer Harmony. The lower windows show the Harmony scene viewer in action. The GlobeSat dataset uses a 3D model of the earth to provide quick point-and-click access to satellite images. The model may be rotated, zoomed, etc., allowing users full hypertext capabilities even with this fairly complicated data view. Copyright © 1994 by IICM, Graz University of Technology, Austria, reprinted by permission. Further information about Hyper-G and Harmony can be obtained by anonymous FTP from* `ftp.iicm.tu-graz.ac.at` *in directory pub/Hyper-G.*

Hyper-G also has a much richer data model than the WWW. On the WWW, hypertext nodes are considered as individual objects without any structure, but Hyper-G supports a hierarchical structure of documents into collections, which may themselves belong to other collections. Hyper-G also

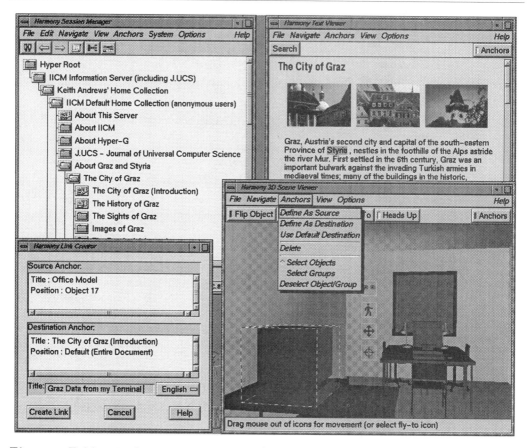

Figure 7.11. *Definition of an anchor in a three-dimensional scene in Harmony. Copyright © 1994 by IICM, Graz University of Technology, Austria, reprinted by permission. Further information about Hyper-G and Harmony can be obtained by anonymous FTP from* `ftp.iicm.tu-graz.ac.at` *in directory pub/Hyper-G.*

provides full-text search and allows users to view the search results in the context of the collection hierarchy. An important distinction between Hyper-G and WWW is that Hyper-G stores links in a separate database (like Intermedia did). This is why Hyper-G can have links in arbitrary media, generate "local map" link overviews, maintain link consistency, etc.

When a document or collection is visited, its location within the collection structure is automatically displayed in the Session Manager's collection

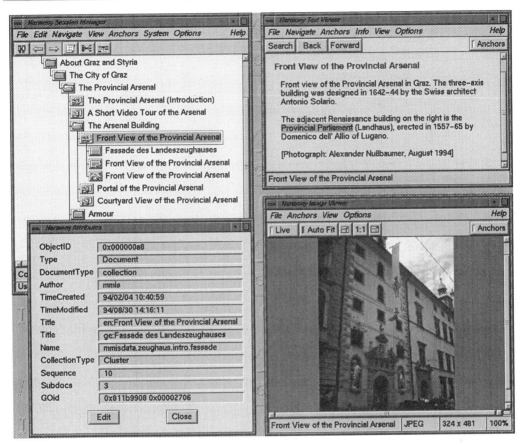

Figure 7.12. *Attribute window for part of a composite node in Harmony. Copyright © 1994 by IICM, Graz University of Technology, Austria, reprinted by permission. Further information about Hyper-G and Harmony can be obtained by anonymous FTP from* `ftp.iicm.tu-graz.ac.at` *in directory pub/Hyper-G.*

browser (by opening up the path to it), regardless of whether the object was reached as the result of a search, by following a hyperlink, or via the local map. This feature of Harmony is a powerful instrument in the fight against disorientation because users can orient themselves with reference to a fixed structural framework.

The main Hyper-G viewer, Harmony, provides full integration of several advanced media types beyond text, meaning that it is a true hypermedia browser. Figure 7.10 shows an example where the Harmony user is selecting hypertext anchors on a rotating globe in order to retrieve satellite images. Figure 7.11 shows an example of link creation in a three-dimensional viewer. The user has selected the object representing a terminal and is about to define it as the source anchor for a new link. The selection is shown by a wireframe bounding box (or rather, a bounding cube) in the viewer.

Having three-dimensional hypertext nodes introduces the special problem that users will need navigation controls to move about within the node itself [Andrews and Pichler 1994]. Of course, navigation controls are also needed for traditional scrolling windows, but because users are so familiar with those controls from their everyday use of the window system, the navigation within a scrolling window rarely presents a special burden on the user.

Figure 7.11 shows 3-D navigational controls embedded within the image window. The icons represent eyes (partly overlapped by the pull-down menu) that are used to "turn the user's head" in the image, a walking person that is used to move the view forward or backward in the horizontal plane, and the arrows are used for sideways and vertical motion. Finally, the cross-hairs are used to control flying through the 3-D space. The actual flight path from the user's current view to the one indicated when a flying operation is initiated is followed at logarithmic speed, meaning that movement is rapid initially but slows down as the destination is approached. Logarithmic movement along the flight path helps minimize the user's sense of disorientation or abrupt movement and still allows fast changes of scene [Mackinlay et al. 1990].

Hyper-G has a rich attribute model for its nodes and supports composite nodes with many different views. These composite nodes are referred to as "clusters" in Hyper-G. Figure 7.12 shows an example of a node about the Provincial Arsenal with three components: an English description, a German description, and a photo. Figure 7.12 also shows a window with the attributes for the photo, including the author, creation and modification date, and captions in multiple languages.

Hyper-G explicitly supports multilingual user interfaces and allows the user to choose one or more preferred languages. The Harmony viewer displays its user interface in the user's first preference and any retrieved nodes are displayed in the best match between the user's language preference and the languages used in the node. For example, Figure 7.13 shows a Harmony view of a composite node while English was specified as the user's first language and

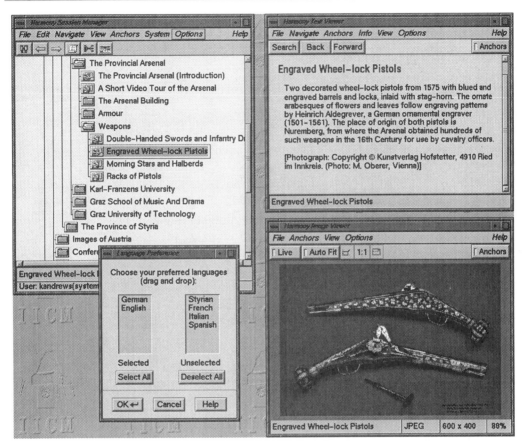

Figure 7.13. *View of a composite node in Harmony while English is specified as the user's first language. The language preference dialog box can be used to rank order the chosen languages and specify what languages the user never wants to see. Copyright © 1994 by IICM, Graz University of Technology, Austria, reprinted by permission. Further information about Hyper-G and Harmony can be obtained by anonymous FTP from* `ftp.iicm.tu-graz.ac.at` *in directory pub/Hyper-G.*

German was specified as the second. If the user switched language preference to make German the first language, the view would change to that in Figure 7.14.

Note in Figure 7.14 how Harmony's user interface (menus, buttons, information fields, etc.) has changed to German. The text component of the composite node is available in both English and German on the server, so the

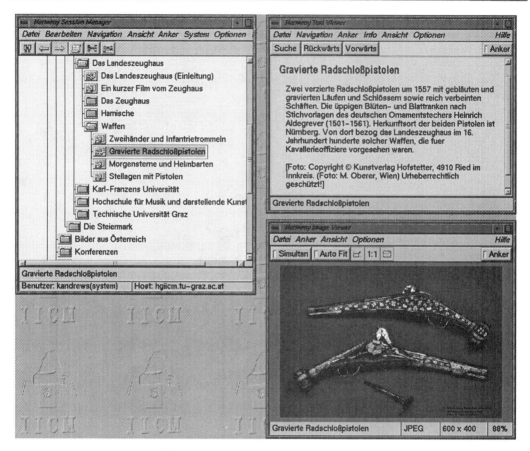

Figure 7.14. *View of the same composite Harmony node as the one shown in Figure 7.13. Now, German has been chosen as the first language. Copyright © 1994 by IICM, Graz University of Technology, Austria, reprinted by permission. Further information about Hyper-G and Harmony can be obtained by anonymous FTP from* `ftp.iicm.tu-graz.ac.at` *in directory pub/Hyper-G.*

text window is also changed to German. In general, Hyper-G supports not just multilingual text nodes but also multilingual figure captions and other hypermedia elements (see the attribute window in Figure 7.12). In the example in Figure 7.14 all information is available in German, but if some were not, it would be displayed in English since the user had specified English as a second language.

The ability to support multiple languages is of obvious importance to hypertext accessed through the Internet with users from all over the world. During the early years of Internet hypertext, most users were technically sophisticated users who had some training in English due to their computer science or engineering degrees. As the user population gets broader and starts including more non-technical people and less highly educated people, additional languages will become necessary.

The Norwegian Oslonett service has an interesting approach to providing multiple languages over the WWW which otherwise does not support multilingual hypertext. When a request for a node comes in over the WWW, the Oslonett server simply looks at the address of the computer sending the request, and if it is located in the .no domain (.no for Norway) then the answer is sent in Norwegian. If the requesting computer is located elsewhere, the information is sent in English. This solution works most of the time but it will fail in the case of an expatriate Norwegian or a foreign visitor using a computer in Norway, so explicit language support in the underlying hypertext architecture is still to be preferred.

International use is not just of importance on the Internet. Hypertext productions for the mass market and for educational use in elementary schools will also need to present text and spoken narration in the language of the user. One example of a multilingual CD-ROM is the Ecodisc, which is an educational application teaching ecology by presenting a large number of images about a lake and its habitats.

See Figure 7.15 for the language choice screen and Figure 7.16 for an example of a narration screen. Almost the entire user interface exists on the disk in nine major European languages (English, French, German, Spanish, Italian, Danish, Swedish, Norwegian, and Dutch). Considering the difficulties inherent in international user interfaces, this is a major accomplishment. Only very few user interfaces are available simultaneously in this many languages. Most translated user interfaces ship in single-language version where the user has to select a language at the time of purchase[14] but the Ecodisc allows the individual user to choose a language at the time of use.

---

[14] In fact, normally the user does not even get a selection of languages since software is sold in a single language per country even when many other translations exist.

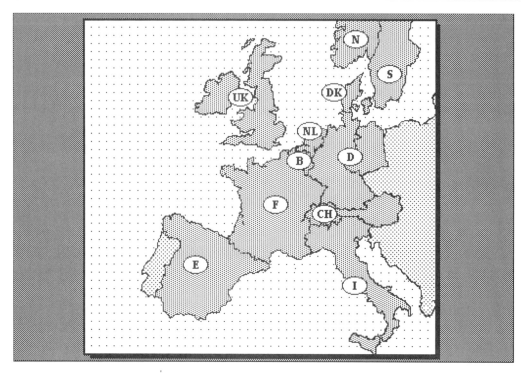

Figure 7.15. *The language choice screen from the Ecodisc. The user selects a language from this screen before starting to use the system and it is also always possible for the user to change language in the middle of a session by returning to this screen. Copyright © 1990 by ESM, Ltd., reprinted by permission.*

On the Ecodisc, the images and screen design remain constant whereas text fields, command names, and the audio narration all change to reflect the language chosen by the individual user. This makes it possible to have nine different interfaces on the same disk and the user can change language at any time. I have tested the English and Danish interfaces in detail and found them to be equivalent, with the Danish translation being of high quality.

Half-Dead Hypertext and the Electronic Business Card

The most compelling examples of Internet hypertext are definitely those where the users immediately get the nodes they request. Normally, the links are "live" in the sense that the computer will display the destination node as soon as the user has activated a link (for example by clicking on a word or a button).

Figure 7.16. *Screen showing the naturalist talking about the lake in the Ecodisc. The presentation uses a sequence of still images that are synchronized with the spoken narration. The naturalist's actual words are played back over the sound track in the language chosen by the user in Figure 7.15, and because still pictures are used rather than live video, the same images can be used for all languages. Copyright © 1990 by ESM, Ltd., reprinted by permission.*

Indeed, the response time for the display of the destination node is critical for the user's feeling of navigating an information space freely.

Not all interlinked information is live, however. The prime example is obviously non-computerized cross-references like those found in an encyclopedia. I will refer to such links as "dead" since it will do no good to try to activate them. The link itself has no action associated with it, and the human user will have to do the work to find the information referred to by the link.

Hypertext systems sometimes have dead links in cases where they have to refer to material that is not included in the hypertext itself. A good example is *Making It Macintosh*, which is a CD-ROM hypermedia presentation of the interaction techniques used in the Apple Macintosh interface standard [Alben et al. 1994]. *Making It Macintosh* contains short descriptions and animated illustrations of the user interface techniques but relies on references to the printed *Macintosh Human Interface Guidelines* for further detail and exact definitions. For example, the node on "Feedback for time-consuming processes" has dead links that appear in a see-also list as follows: "the pointing device: page 270" and "menu behavior: page 55". Note how the provision of page numbers makes the dead links fairly easy to follow. *Making It Macintosh* does contain some live links; the node on "Feedback for time-consuming processes" has live see-also links to the nodes for feedback after menu selections and the cancel vs. stop buttons. Thus, it is possible to combine links of different degrees of liveliness.

A third class of hypertext links in addition to the fully live links and the user-burdening dead links might be called "half-dead links." Half-dead hypertext is characterized by links where the computer ultimately brings the information to the user but where the user also has to do some work to bring the connection about. One example could be a link to material stored on a CD-ROM or laserdisk that was not presently mounted. Having the user activate the link would not display the destination but rather the computer would generate a request for the user to locate the appropriate storage medium and mount it.

Another example of half-dead hypertext is the FasTrak service operated by *The New York Times* during a period of 1994. Using FasTrak, job seekers stored their resumes in a database at the *Times*. Employers who wanted to utilize the system to get faster response from these job seekers could print a FasTrak code in their classified job ads, after which interested applicants could call up the service and enter their code to establish a link between the job ad and their resume. The next day, the employer was sent a disk with all the resumes, meaning that the newly generated links were not really live hypertext links but of the half-dead nature discussed here. Unfortunately, cost considerations led the *Times* to cancel the FasTrak service and there is no doubt that such a service would work much better over the Internet than over a proprietary net where applicants had to access it through a cumbersome push-button telephone interface and where the employers got their applications by disk and not online.

In general, there can be no doubt that live hypertext is to be preferred from a usability perspective since it puts as much of the burden as possible on the computer. Specifically, when the information is brought to the user automatically, the user will feel encouraged to browse more freely and will be allowed to concentrate on the content of the material and not on secondary issues like where and how the information can be accessed.

On the other hand, pragmatic considerations may sometimes make dead or half-dead hypertext acceptable (or ever preferable) when one needs to refer to material that cannot easily be included as live hypertext in the current collection of online information due to copyright restrictions, limited storage space, or other problems. Even in situations where live hypertext might be feasible, it may sometimes be preferable from a usability perspective to move to a half-dead solution. Consider, for example, a World Wide Web link to an MPEG file of a hundred megabytes or so that is stored at the other end of an overloaded Internet connection with a bandwidth of maybe only 14400 baud or so. Instead of blindly starting to download the movie when the user clicks on an anchor pointing to it, the system might interrupt the user and indicate the expected delay before the film can be shown. If offered the choice, the user might prefer to have the system download the film overnight and have it available for showing the next day, thus making the link pretty well half-dead.

Half-dead hypertext may also support a kind of subscription service that is otherwise normally implemented by agents. For example, a half-dead link may point to a node that has not yet been created, and users may activate that link as an indication that they want to get a copy of the information once it becomes available. Staying with the metaphor, such links might be called "unborn links" and one application could be the case where a user knows that a certain project is under way and wants to sign up to get a copy of the project report when it gets written. Note that this particular type of half-dead hypertext is different from regular subscription services where one gets a continuous stream of information (e.g., weekly progress reports). It is also different from the traditional forms of computed hypertext where link activation causes an updated version of certain information to be displayed. This latter form of hypertext is based on live links from the user's perspective since the destination is displayed as soon as it is requested (assuming that the computations are not too time consuming).

In the future, many business professionals may be carrying "personal digital assistants" (PDAs) with them as they go to meetings, conferences, etc. One possible use for these PDAs is to exchange electronic business cards through infrared beaming or some other mechanism for wireless data transfer.

Currently business professionals often exchange little cardboard business cards when they meet. These business cards serve several purposes, including two that are of special interest for the electronic business card project: Business cards provide people with a record of whom they have met, and business cards serve as dead links to those other people, making it possible to reach them by phone, fax, paper mail, and sometimes email.

If the PDAs of all attendees in a meeting automatically exchanged electronic business cards, people would have a record of the other participants without having to explicitly collect little pieces of paper and having to keep track of them. Of course, there are some privacy concerns that will need to be addressed, and one could imagine people instructing their PDAs only to send out their electronic business card under certain circumstances or to certain recipients. In general, though, many advantages could be realized if the electronic business cards were to be exchanged automatically since they would serve as a kind of "readwear" [Hill et al. 1992], meaning that the user would have zero overhead in generating or receiving the electronic business cards. For example, one could collect electronic business cards from all meetings and not just from meetings with outside visitors. Such lists of automatically collected electronic business cards could be used for obvious applications like the circulation of minutes or follow-up notes to all meeting participants. A collection of such lists could be used to statistically construct groups of people with related interests (people who tend to go to the same meetings, talks, and events) without the need for explicit human intervention or maintenance.

One interesting property of the electronic business card is that it can serve as a half-dead hypertext link to the person whose card it is. Due to realistic limitations of wireless transmission bandwidth as well as the storage capacity on the recipient's PDA, an electronic business card will never contain all the available machine-readable information about its originator. Instead, it will contain hypertext links, and the recipient will then need to connect to the net to retrieve further information if needed. One can in fact imagine that a single electronic business card that is broadcast to all participants in a meeting would contain links that granted different levels of access privileges to different categories of recipient. For example, only people who were already on a list of approved friends might be allowed to link to the originator's calendar system to schedule a meeting.

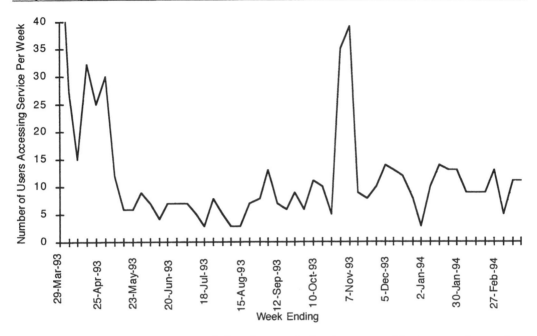

Figure 7.17. *Weekly usage of the electronic business card in terms of number of different users that week. The electronic business card had 86 users the first week.*

The electronic business card is a link to a hypertext with further information about its originator. Typical information that might be available would include scanned photographs, videos, and other personal information. Some people might want to enable access to information about their private lives, like their hobbies or scanned drawings made by their children. For a researcher, the electronic business card could also link to a repository of that person's papers, and for a salesperson, the electronic business card might link to a product catalog with prices, promotional animations, direct order entry services, etc. In general, the type of information accessed through an electronic business card would be highly dependent on the originator's job and interests. For research purposes, I established an electronic business card for myself for a period of one year, March 1993 to March 1994 [Nielsen 1995b]. Users could send email to my electronic business card server to receive copies of my articles and information about my work and whereabouts.[15]

Figure 7.17 shows the number of users who accessed my prototype electronic business card server during the 52 weeks it was in service. As one might expect, the server saw extensive use right after it was introduced as I announced it to my colleagues. After the first few weeks, usage was reasonably constant with the exception of a peak at late October and early November 1993. This peak was due to the fact that I was presenting a seminar in London. The seminar announcement had been circulated to a mailing list of seven hundred people with an interest in human–computer interaction and included a reference to my electronic business card to supplement the traditional speaker's bio. In addition to this seminar announcement, the electronic business card was also mentioned in my talks and papers at the *INTERCHI'93* conference in early May 1993, and the server did see extensive use during the following weeks.

In the beginning, there was naturally not much repeat traffic since all users were accessing the electronic business card for the first time. For the first three months of 1994, the proportion of repeat users has been fairly steady at around 25%. Most users only used the electronic business card once. 88% of the users issued all their logged commands within a single week. Only 8% of the users accessed the server in two different weeks, and only 4% of the users accessed the server in three or more different weeks.

The electronic business card was used by 556 users from around the world during its one-year period of operation. The largest number of users were located in the United States, with 337 users in the U.S. and Canada compared with 213 users in the rest of the world. Interestingly, the largest number of commands were issued by users in countries outside North America, with 934 commands originating in the U.S. and Canada and 1,165 commands originating from the rest of the world. Combining the statistics for number of users and number of commands results in the finding that the average number of commands per user was much greater for users outside the U.S. and Canada than for users in the U.S. and Canada, with American and Canadian

---

[15] In an example of computational hypertext, the electronic business card server would check how recently I had read my electronic mail and use that information as a basis for telling users whether I was likely to be in the office.

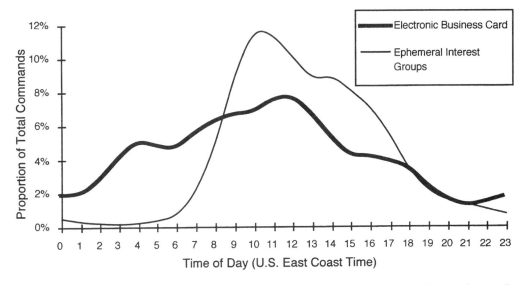

Figure 7.18. *Comparison of the hourly usage of two systems throughout the day: commands received by the electronic business card server (which was accessed by users world-wide) and postings to the ephemeral interest group system (which was essentially only accessed by users in New Jersey).*

users issuing an average of 2.77 commands each and users in the rest of the world issuing an average of 5.47 commands each.

This result may just indicate that people who are further away from a given locus of information have larger needs for rapid, electronically disseminated information of that information. However, given the many studies showing that most electronic communication occurs between people who are geographically proximate, the fact that distant users used the service the most bears some further consideration. One interpretation is that the electronic business card was used mostly as a half-dead hypertext service to provide access to certain units of information. It was used very little as a device to get personal information about its owner. In other words, based on the limited evidence from a single experiment, it would seem that our original ideas of people using the electronic business card as a way to stay informed about its originator were overblown. Instead, people wanted to get information for their own purposes.

Because of the highly international use of the electronic business card server, its load was fairly evenly distributed throughout the day as shown in

Figure 7.18. For comparison, the figure also shows the distribution of the load on the ephemeral interest group system [Brothers et al. 1992], which was an experimental communication system used in a single location (Bellcore in New Jersey). It is clear from the figure that the ephemeral interest group system had very little use from around midnight to seven o'clock in the morning and that it experienced very heavy traffic around ten o'clock in the morning (when people started their computer and entered new comments into the system). Since a large proportion of the cost of computer and network systems is constant and depends only on the peak load that has to be supported and not on the amount of off-peak load, Figure 7.18 shows that hypertext systems with world-wide appeal may have an attractive load distribution profile and reduce the flash-crowd phenomenon.

The electronic business card server provided users with a list of popular nodes that listed both recently popular nodes and nodes that had been popular throughout the year. Usage statistics showed some evidence for locality of reference with respect to node access: the correlation between the number of times a node was accessed during any given week and the number of times it had been accessed the previous week was $r=.45$, whereas the correlation between access in a given week and overall access throughout the year was only $r=.24$.

8.   Coping with Information Overload

Michael Lesk once wrote a paper called "What To Do When There's Too Much Information" [Lesk 1989]. Lesk was dealing with a hypertext system with 800,000 objects which is certainly larger than most current systems, but future systems will have to deal with at least that many objects and possibly more. Consider that the number of objects available over the WWW was probably at least two million in the beginning of 1995 and that the Library of Congress holds more than 100 million publications. On the WWW, the millions of objects are not registered in any single place, so no single user interface has to deal with that many objects, but in return, the user has no way of truly taking advantage of the full amount of information because it is not being managed and presented in any way.

As shown in Figure 7.1, the Internet is about doubling every year. The amount of data transmitted over the Usenet netnews is growing by about 181% per year according to statistics from UUnet (a major netnews hub). The actual number of articles transmitted is "only" growing by 132%, and the discrepancy between these two numbers can probably be explained by the growing popularity of transmitting long messages with executable programs and digitized images.[1] Also, the number of newsgroups to which these messages get posted is growing by 52% per year, meaning that individual newsgroups do not see quite as rapid growth. Even so, individual newsgroups do grow. For example, `alt.hypertext` had an annual growth rate of 77% in number of messages posted from 1992 to 1994 and `comp.human-factors` had an annual

---

[1] At the end of 1994, about 100,000 netnews articles were posted per day, and 48% of the total number of bytes transmitted were due to articles that were 16 kB or more. In the beginning of 1994, only 40,000 articles were posted per day, and only 33% of the transmitted data were due to articles that were 16 kB or more.

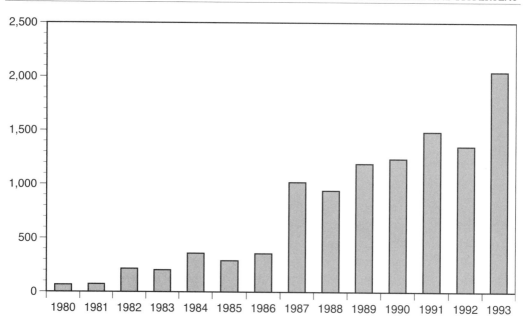

Figure 8.1. *Chart showing the growth in number of entries per year in the HCIbib database of the human–computer interaction literature.*

growth rate of 92% in number of messages posted. These growth rates are largely due to the increase in readership that follows from the annual doubling of the Internet.

I subscribe to an email mailing list of Danes living abroad, and the statistics from this group are a good example of the increasing information overload on the Internet. The number of words of email traffic sent to the group has been growing by 170% per year from about 16,000 words in 1990 to almost 900,000 words in 1994. The number of distribution list members grew by 118% per year over the same period. The must faster growth in traffic than in the number of people is probably related to the fact that the number of potential interactions (person A commenting on person B's postings) grows by the square of the number of members.

Rapidly growing amounts of information can also be found outside electronic systems. According to the January 1990 issue of the journal *Mathematical Review,* the number of mathematical papers published annually has grown from 840 a year in 1870 to about 50,000 in 1989, with an accelerating growth that has doubled the number of papers every ten years since World

War 2. In general, the number of scientific papers across all fields have been doubling every 10–15 years for the last two centuries [Price 1956, as cited in Odlyzko 1995]. In fact, the number of paper research publications has grown so large that many scientists have given up keeping up with all of the literature, even in their own highly specialized fields, and many journals now have the reputation of being "write-only," meaning that they are not being read very much. The *Science Citation Index* has found that more than half of the papers published in research journals are never cited by anybody else, and even though that does not prove that nobody *read* those papers that were not cited, it certainly means that nobody found them of particular value.

Gary Perlman maintains the "HCIbib" online bibliography of the human–computer interaction literature at the Ohio State University. The number of new articles in the HCIbib database has grown by 30% per year as shown in Figure 8.1. A 30% annual growth rate corresponds to 1,300% growth every ten years, which is much more than the doubling of the research literature per decade seen in more established fields like mathematics.

Even though the growth rates differ among disciplines there is no doubt that the research literature is growing fast enough to present scientists with a major information overload problem. Research publications are edited with a view toward keeping down the number of publications by weeding out less interesting submissions. Unedited publications like the netnews or the Danish email list grow much faster and quickly reach the point where many people have to stop reading them.

There are many different ways of calculating the economic value of information: one can consider the cost needed to produce the information, or one can consider what it can sell for. In a world with information overload, one also needs to consider the *negative* value of information in terms of the resources spent reading or pondering it. If somebody sends an email message to all the employees of a company with a staff of 10,000 then the cost to the company of the time spent on the message can be anywhere from $1,000 (if everybody immediately discards the message) to $15,000 (if everybody reads it). A steady increase in the amount of information risks acting as a time sink that can prevent people from ever getting any real work done.

Fortunately, it is possible to deal with large amounts of information. As an example, Table 8.1 shows an estimate of the amount of information in a

Sunday issue of *The New York Times*.[2] The Sunday paper does include huge amounts of information, and it is sometimes said that a single Sunday *Times* has more information than the average villager would get in a lifetime during the Middle Ages. In fact, I am sure that old-time villagers encountered lots of information when farming the fields since it takes many megabytes to accurately represent data about weather and growth patterns. But if we only consider official "news" in the form of words or images reporting on world events, edicts from the King or Pope, and similar types of newspaper-like information the comparison may in fact be correct.

The estimates of data content in Table 8.1 were made under the following assumptions: Each full page of text is about 31 kB. Each page is about 262 square inches (0.17 m^2). Each page of images is about 1.6 MB of uncompressed data, given that about 10% of the images are in color and that the print resolution is approximately equivalent to 72 pixels per inch, in 8 bits grayscale or 24 bit color. Each page of display ads is about 30% empty space, 40% images, and 30% text, corresponding to 0.6 MB of image data and 9 kB of text.

In total, the sample Sunday *New York Times* contained 7.5 MB of text data and 177 MB of image data.[3] People can get this much information in the door every week and still have time for other activities on Sundays. Admittedly, it takes a long time to read every word and study every image in the Sunday *Times*, but then people don't do that. Instead, every reader selects some parts of the paper that is of interest to that individual and skips the rest. It is feasible to get many times more information delivered than one wants because of the fairly cheap distribution mechanism. And it is feasible to skip the most of the paper because it has been designed to make it easy for readers to find information of interest to them.

In the future, one of the most promising approaches to hypertext journalism is the delivery of individualized electronic newspapers. Since all components of a modern newspaper are edited online, it is possible to replace the delivery of a huge printout with online access to exactly those stories that interest the individual reader. An online newspaper would also deliver the latest version of all stories as of the exact time the reader asked for them.

---

[2] Printing the daily and Sunday editions of *The New York Times* required 301,000 metric tons of newsprint in 1993.

[3] For sake of comparison, this book contains about 1.0 MB of text and 13 MB of image data.

Section Number and Title	Pages	Editorial Text	Editorial Illustrations	Display Ads	Text Ads
1. News	32	37%	13%	47%	3%
2. Arts & Leisure	40	24%	15%	60%	1%
3. Business	42	39%	7%	30%	26%
4. The Week in Review	22	24%	14%	20%	42%
4A. Education Life (actually 52 half-size pages)	26	23%	15%	58%	3%
5. Travel	38	16%	13%	62%	9%
6. The New York Times Magazine (actually 68 half-size pages)	34	32%	26%	33%	9%
7. Book Review (actually 32 half-size pages)	16	54%	9%	38%	1%
8. SportsSunday	24	31%	14%	39%	16%
9. Styles of the Times	10	35%	40%	27%	1%
10. Real Estate	42	7%	8%	34%	51%
11. Help Wanted	42	0%	0%	13%	87%
12. Television listings (actually 56 quarter-size pages)	14	75%	7%	18%	0%
13. New Jersey Weekly (distributed to suburban subscribers as a replacement for the City Weekly that was distributed in New York City)	24	26%	11%	62%	2%
Total for the entire Sunday paper	406	26%	12%	40%	22%
Equivalent number of full pages	**406**	**105**	**50**	**161**	**91**
Information in Megabytes		**3.2**	**77**	**102**	**2.8**

Table 8.1. *The sections in the Sunday* New York Times, *January 9, 1994. In addition to total page count, the table lists the proportion of the pages that was devoted to editorial text and illustrations and to display advertising and text and classified ads. These proportions have been calculated relative to the amount of space taken up by each category of information. The page count excludes several advertising supplements without editorial content that cannot be considered part of the newspaper proper.*

Figures 8.2 and 8.3 show an example of an individualized electronic newspaper developed at GMD in Germany [A. Haake et al. 1994]. The newspaper interface, designed by Klaus Reichenberger, can automatically lay out the current stories that match the user's stated interests, resulting in interesting and appealing displays that invite further exploration and reading.

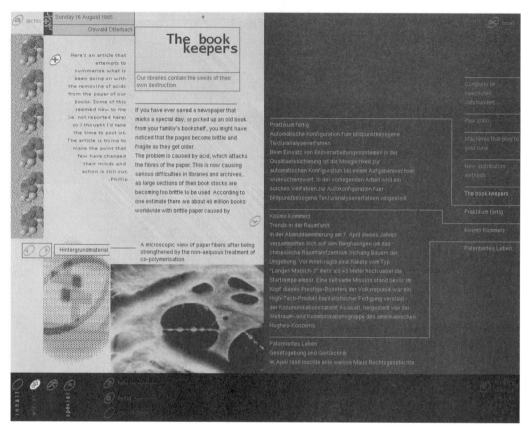

Figure 8.2. *The experimental individualized electronic newspaper (IEN) from GMD in Germany showing a page customized for a reader with an interest in science. Compare with Figure 8.3 showing a page from the same newspaper customized for a reader with an interest in sport. Copyright © 1992 by Klaus Reichenberger and GMD-IPSI, reprinted by permission.*

As can be seen from comparing Figures 8.2 and 8.3, different sets of stories can be assembled for readers with different interests.

Utilizing hypermedia linking, each part of the electronic newspaper can follow the well-established principle from printed newspaper with front pages and cover stories for each of the main sections of the newspaper.

Current attempts at putting newspaper stories online on services like America Online use much more boring menu interfaces where the user gets very little information about the stories before having to decide which ones to

Figure 8.3. *The experimental individualized electronic newspaper (IEN) from GMD in Germany showing a page customized for a reader with an interest in sport. Copyright © 1992 by Klaus Reichenberger and GMD-IPSI, reprinted by permission.*

read. There is no doubt that better systems for automated layout (like the ones shown in the figures here) will be necessary for online newspapers to have a chance of competing with printed ones that are based on hundreds of years of typographical and editorial experience.

There are three main approaches to addressing information overload. The first (and often the most successful) is good user interface design and good editorial preparation of the data, resulting in an ability for the user to rapidly skim the information and pick out the exact pieces that interest him or her. Paper newspapers like *The New York Times* exemplify this solution to the information overload problem. If I am really busy one day, I can just scan the front page of the newspaper and know that I have not missed being informed about any really important event.

The two other solutions are information retrieval and information filtering [Belkin and Croft 1992]. The difference between the two is that retrieval is normally done actively by the user in specific cases where the user is looking for a certain piece of information, whereas filtering is done continuously in cases where the user wants to be kept informed about certain events. For example, a typical retrieval task would be to find the name of the president of IBM and a typical filtering task would be to be informed every time IBM announced a new workstation but not when it announces a new mainframe or PC.

Information Retrieval

A search for information in a hypertext might be performed purely by navigation, but it should also be possible for the user to have the computer find things through various query mechanisms. Navigation is best for information spaces that are small enough to be covered exhaustively and familiar enough to the users to let them find their way around. Many information spaces in real life are unfortunately large and unfamiliar and require the use of queries to find information.

The simplest query principle is the full text search which finds the occurrences of words specified by the user. Some hypertext systems simply take the user to the first occurrence of the search term, but it is much better to display a menu of the hits first as shown in the example from Intermedia in Figure 8.4. The problem with jumping directly to the first term occurrence is that the user has no way of knowing how many other hits are in the hypertext. The general usability principle of letting the user know what is going on leads to a requirement for an overview, even in the case of query results. Figure 8.5 shows the search method from Storyspace which provides a list of all the nodes with hits without indicating the number of times the search terms were found in each nodes. Storyspace has a preview facility which the user can activate by clicking "View current text" to quickly see the beginning of the various nodes before deciding where to jump.

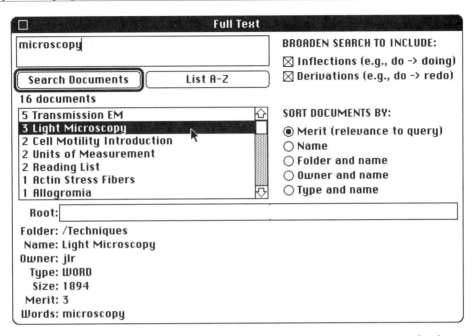

Figure 8.4. *Intermedia's full-text interface allows users to search the entire Intermedia database to find every occurrence of the specified text in all documents, regardless of type. The list of retrieved documents can be sorted according to five different criteria. Clicking on the document name in the list will allow the user to view information about the document. Double-clicking on the document name will open the document. Copyright © 1989 by Brown University, reprinted with permission.*

Normally search is done in stages where the user first specifies the query and then has to wait for the system to return the set of found objects. With faster computers it is becoming possible to perform dynamic queries where the users manipulate sliders or other controls to specify desired search values and get immediate feedback from the system as they do so. In one study the subjects were able to find information in a database 119% faster (i.e., in less than half the time) when they were given dynamic feedback as they constructed their query than when they did not get any feedback until after they had submitted a complete query to the system [Ahlberg et al. 1992].

Figure 8.6 shows the use of dynamic queries in the FilmFinder from the University of Maryland [Ahlberg and Shneiderman 1994]. The user can specify that only films of a certain running length are of interest by moving the range

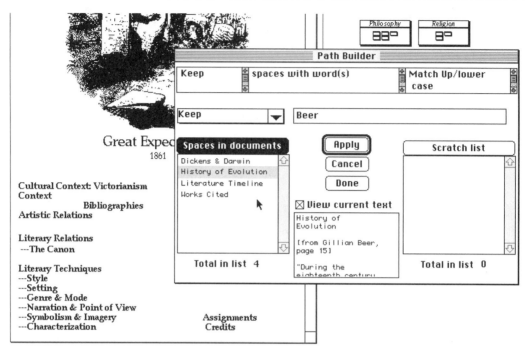

Figure 8.5. *Searching for the name "Beer" in the Storyspace version of the Dickens Web [Landow and Kahn 1992]. Copyright © 1992–94 by Paul Kahn, George P. Landow, and Brown University, reprinted by permission.*

selector slider, and the display will update in real time while the user moves the slider, making it very clear whether reasonable values are being specified. The overview diagram in the FilmFinder is a so-called starfield display where each of the retrieved objects is shown as a "star" in a two-dimensional scatterplot. The two dimensions of the scatterplot can be chosen by the user to represent particularly meaningful object attributes, and a third dimension can be used to color-code the dots (in the figure, genre like Sci-Fi or Western was the attribute used to color-code the films). Note in Figure 8.6 how zooming and panning the scatterplot in effect is the same as specifying query intervals for the attributes represented by the diagram axes.

Figure 8.6 also illustrates the output-as-input interaction technique. When the user has found an interesting film (here *Murder on the Orient Express*), the user can click on the dot representing that object and link to a box with more detailed information about the film. The user can then link further by taking

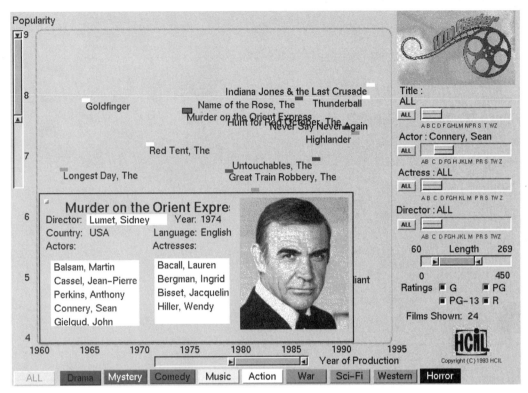

Figure 8.6. *The Maryland FilmFinder uses dynamic queries to allow users to search for films with various attributes. Here, the user has specified a search for films starring Sean Connery with a running length between 60 and 269 minutes. The user has furthermore used the zoom control sliders for the* x *and* y *axes to display only the part of the diagram with films after 1960 that are rated more than 4 in popularity. Copyright © 1993 by University of Maryland Human–Computer Interaction Lab., reprinted by permission.*

this query output as input for the next query: in our example, the user has chosen Sean Connery's name as a search term and transferred it from the initial search result to a new query specification to see only films starring Sean Connery.

Even though most query systems perform text searches or select objects based on numeric attribute values, it is also possible to search on other types of media. Since humans are very visually oriented, they often rely on images to remember things, and image-based searchers might well be a very useful

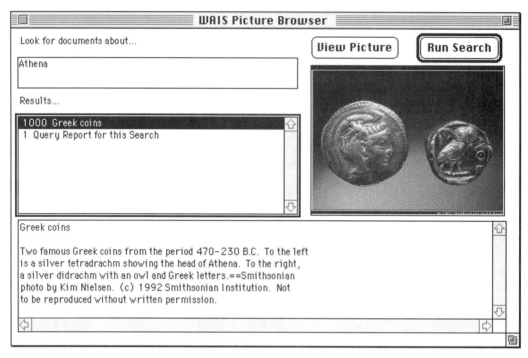

Figure 8.7. *Screendump from a session where the user has connected to a WAIS (wide area information service) server with photographs from the Smithsonian Institution to search for images of the Greek goddess Athena. The system uses a full text search in the caption to retrieve the image. Copyright © 1992 by the Smithsonian Institution, reprinted by permission.*

supplement to text and attribute-based search. Unfortunately, current computer capabilities in the pattern recognition area are very limited, and computers cannot really understand pictures well enough to deal with them as well as with text. Therefore, the traditional way to search image databases has been the one shown in Figure 8.7, where each picture has to be annotated with a text caption or keywords for search purposes.

Searching the captions is a much better way to find a picture than flipping through thousands of photos but it does not work in all cases. In the example in Figure 8.7 it might have been the case that the user wanted a coin with the picture of a woman or that the user remembered approximately how the coin looked but not exactly what it represented.

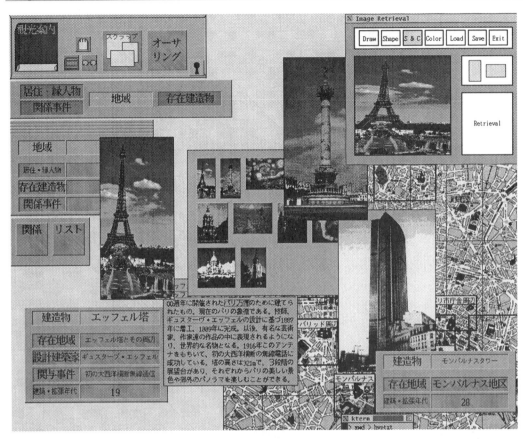

Figure 8.8. *Hypermedia navigation by image retrieval. This experimental system shows a tourist guide to Paris where the user has asked the system to show all other images that look somewhat like the photo of the Eiffel Tower in the upper right window. In the middle of the screen, the system displays miniatures of its pictures of tall thin things, and the user has selected some of these images for full-scale display. The images again have hypertext links to the maps and to textual descriptions of the sights of Paris. Copyright © 1993 by NEC Corporation, reprinted by permission.*

Some experimental systems have been developed that allow computers to deal with image understanding in a rudimentary manner. For example, Figure 8.8 shows a system that understands the general shape of the major objects depicted in an image [Hirata et al. 1993]. In order to find pictures, the user can

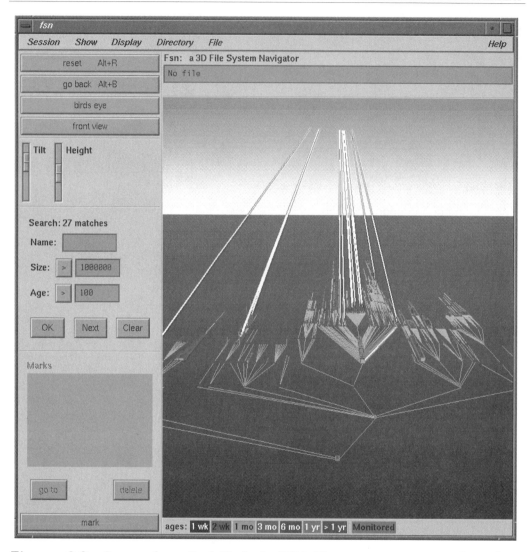

Figure 8.9. *Screen from Joel Tesler's FSN file system navigator [Fairchild 1993]. Here, the user has performed a search on the file system to find files that are larger than one million bytes and older than one hundred days. Copyright © 1994 by Silicon Graphics, Inc., reprinted by permission.*

either sketch the approximate composition of the image or select an existing picture and use it to link to more of the same.

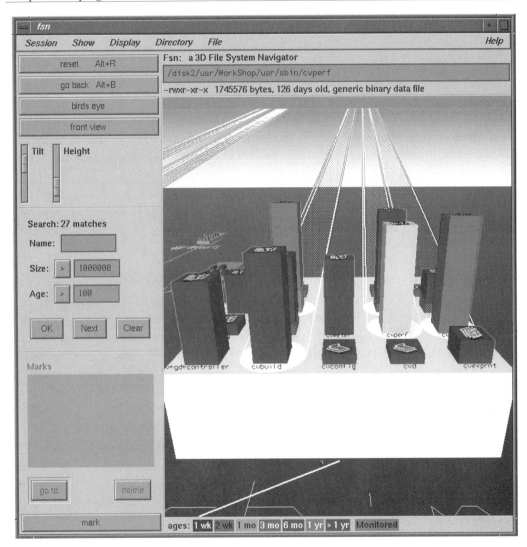

Figure 8.10. *Revised view of the file system from Figure 8.9. Here, the user has used FSN's three-dimensional navigation system to move in to a close-up of one of the directories in order to get a better view of the individual files. Copyright © 1994 by Silicon Graphics, Inc., reprinted by permission.*

A very promising way of showing search results is to integrate them with the overview diagram by highlighting those nodes that contain "hits."[4] Figures 8.9 and 8.10 show how the FSN[5] system highlights search hits in a three-dimensional overview of an information space. SuperBook [Egan et al. 1989] annotates the names of nodes with the number of hits to allow users to see not just *where* there is something of interest but also *how much* there is. It would be possible to use this type of search result to construct fisheye views since the number of hits in a given region of the information space would indicate how interesting that region must be to the user.

One can also use more sophisticated methods from the field of information retrieval. This brief section cannot do justice to that field, which is an active research area in its own right, so the interested reader should read a good textbook like Salton's *Automatic Text Processing* [1989] or at least a full survey article like [Bärtschi 1985].

Information retrieval can be integrated with hypertext navigation to deliver powerful means of finding information. Figure 8.11 shows a hypertext system [Andersen et al. 1989] for reading the Usenet network news, which is a world-wide bulletin board system with a huge number of messages about various computer-related topics. Since there are far too many nodes in the system to rely on manually constructed links, we use a full text similarity rating calculated by counting the overlap in vocabulary between any two nodes. A list of the articles that are rated as the most similar to the current article is displayed when the user clicks on the "similarity" button.

In a case where we have a hypertext available in which the links have already been constructed, we should be able to utilize the information inherent in the linking structure to perform more semantically meaningful searches than just plain full text searches. This step is possible because a hypertext can be considered as a "belief network" to the extent that if two nodes are linked, then we "believe" that their contents are related in some way.

---

[4] "Hits" indicate the number of the user's search terms that can be found in the node. It is possible to use more advanced query facilities and also add to the hit score if words are found which are synonyms or otherwise related to the search terms.

[5] Movie aficionados will be interested in knowing that FSN (pronounced "fusion") was the system used in the film *Jurassic Park* in the memorable scene where a child sees a workstation and happily declares "This is Unix; I can use that" (and saves the day by rapt navigation of the FSN interface). Most of the time, though, the goal of FSN is not to fight dinosaurs but to manage large file systems.

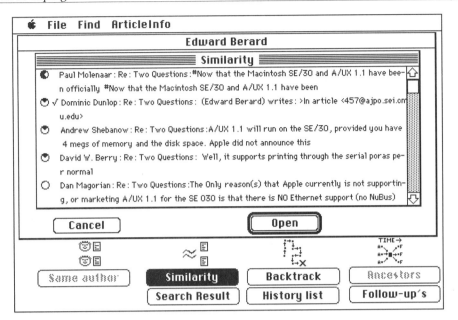

Figure 8.11. *A screen from the HyperNews system showing pie icons rating the links to other articles.*

Thus if a node matches a search, then we should also assign a higher score for the other nodes it is linked to since our "belief" that the connected nodes are related justifies the propagation of scores among them. One way of calculating this score is by assigning the final search result for a node as the sum of the number of hits in the node itself (called the *intrinsic* score) and some weighted average of the scores for the nodes it is linked to (called the *extrinsic* score). As a simple example, we could assign the final query score as the intrinsic score plus half the extrinsic score.

In the example in Figure 8.12, we see that the central node ends up getting the highest query score even though it does not contain any of the search terms (as can be seen from the fact that it has an intrinsic score of zero). This is because the central node sits in the middle of a lot of information related to the user's query and is therefore probably also highly relevant.

In addition to just finding information, query mechanisms can also be used to filter the hypertext so that only relevant links are made active and only relevant nodes are shown in overview diagrams. Even though the "raw" hypertext may be large and confusing, the filtered hypertext can still be easy to

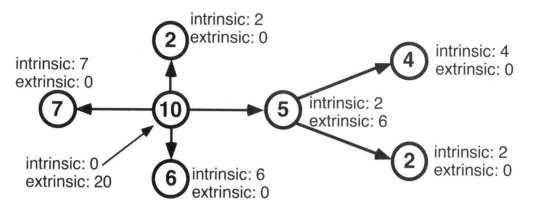

Figure 8.12. *An example of a calculation of query scores as a combination of* intrinsic *scores (how well the individual node* itself *matches the user's query) and* extrinsic *scores (how well the nodes it is* linked *to match the query). Here we have used a rule that gives a node a search score equal to its intrinsic score plus half its extrinsic score (the sum of the scores of the nodes it is linked to).*

navigate. Such a combination of query methods to select a subset of the hypertext and traditional navigation to look at the information might be the best of both worlds if done right.

Human Editing

Despite much work on automated ways of reducing information overload, the most promising approaches will probably be the ones that rely on human judgment to some extent. Some authorities on the human factors of information believe that it is impossible to achieve sufficiently usable information filtering without having a human in the loop somewhere to make individual judgments as to the quality and relevance of each information object. As long as computers are not intelligent enough to be able to actually understand the content of the information they are processing, they will never be able to provide true quality ratings. In fact, perfect information filtering is likely to be an "AI complete problem" in the sense that solving it will be equivalent to solving the complete set of intelligent computing

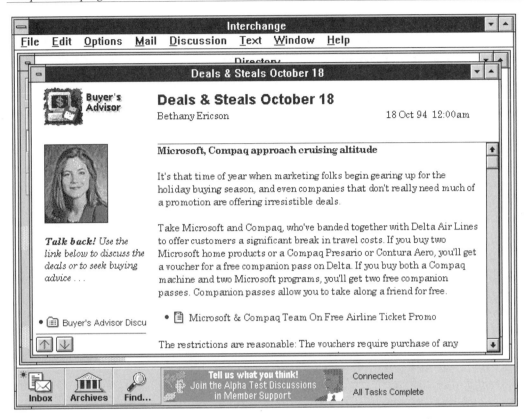

Figure 8.13. *Edited column on the Interchange service with hypertext links to other articles that are available on the service. Copyright © 1994 by Interchange Network Company, reprinted by permission.*

problems.[6] An alternative approach to reducing information overload is the time-honored approach of an editor with a firm hand.

Figure 8.13 shows an example of an edited column from the Interchange online service [Perkins 1995]. The human editor has selected a number of

---

[6] Maybe some day we will achieve sufficiently good artificial intelligence to allow the computer to understand the content of information objects, but quality judgments seem to be beyond the scope of AI for the next many years. Whether it is impossible or just currently infeasible to get computers to rate quality is a philosophical discussion that is fairly irrelevant for anybody wanting to ship product during the next ten or twenty years since the two positions are equivalent within this time horizon.

articles which she believes will be of relevance to readers with an interest in the stated topic of the column (shopping tips for computer buyers). She annotates the links with her own comments and then provides a link to the source material. Note how the personality of the editor is emphasized by showing her picture and by the style of her writing. In fact, it is likely that the information explosion will increase users' desire to feel that they are in touch with real humans and not just with some mass of Internet data. In his book *Megatrends*, John Naisbitt talked about a trend he called High Tech–High Touch, and the edited column in Figure 8.13 is an example of this trend. In a series of user tests I conducted of various WWW sites, people were invariably thrilled about a page with a picture of Microsoft's webmaster standing in front of their server: users enjoyed seeing the guy who was brining them the information as opposed to having it come from a faceless bureaucracy.

Note how the "Deals & Steals" column in Figure 8.13 has a hypertext link to the "Buyer's Advisor Discussion" where the users can add their comments to the topics discussed in the column. By offering this facility, Interchange makes it easier for users to find comments by other users on topics they are interested in, since these comments will often be linked to specific columns or articles. A Bellcore research project called ephemeral interest groups had very similar goals [Brothers et al. 1992]. In the ephemeral interest group system, people could indicate their interest in a topic by "joining" postings to a bulletin board system in order to get sent follow-up messages to the postings. Every single message posted was a potential seed for an ephemeral interest group, and the groups only lived for as long as members posted additional follow-ups. This scheme was very successful in increasing the value of the messages seen by any individual participant: on a 1–5 scale (where 1 indicated completely irrelevant material and 5 indicated very relevant material), users rated messages sent to them by the ephemeral interest group system as 3.9 on the average, whereas the same messages only received a 2.7 rating when we tried sending them to a control group.

Editing can also be done collaboratively where a group of users build up information structures to help each other. Figure 8.14 shows a sample information digest constructed at Lotus Development Corporation [Maltz and Ehrlich 1995]. Because people who work in the same organization know and trust each other, they can assume that information recommended by their colleagues will be of much higher-than-average relevance to them. Information digests can exist on the corporate net for a variety of topics, and

INFORMATION OVERLOAD *Info Digest, vol 1*

Subject: *Information Overload*
Sections: *Information Filtering, Mediators, Business Implications*

Information Filtering

This section summarizes some of the tools and techniques that are available for filtering information.

→ Document Topic: FILTERING AGENTS STREAMLINE GROUPWARE TASKS "Agents for doing filtering" in database IRG Industry Newswire '94

Mediators

This section provides examples of people acting as information mediators

→ Document Topic: INFORMATION GATHERER NEWSLETTER PUBLISHED "Useful list of types of information gatherers" in database IRG Industry Newswire '94

Business Implications

This section looks at business opportunities for products to manage information overload.

→ Document Topic: Advanced On-Line Products Far Off

Figure 8.14. *An Information Digest written in Lotus Notes by Kate Ehrlich at Lotus Development Corp. Copyright © 1994 by Kate Ehrlich, reprinted by permission.*

employees who find interesting information on the Internet or elsewhere can add the information with an annotation and a hypertext link.

Maltz and Ehrlich refer to the system shown in Figure 8.14 as "active filtering" in contrast to the passive filtering discussed in the following section where there is no direct connection between a person casting a vote for some information and the readers who come later and filter the documents based on these votes. In the "active" filtering approach, there is an intent on the part of the person who finds some information to share it with his or her colleagues. The person finding the information may even recommend the information for particular colleagues who are known to have an interest in a particular area, and the Lotus information digest system has a feature for sending announcements of new and interesting information to specific individuals in addition to adding the information to a digest for public consumption.

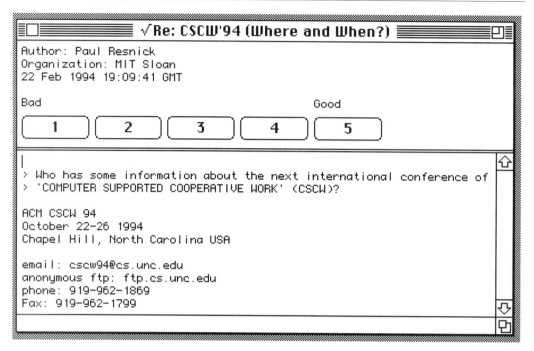

Figure 8.15. *Reading a netnews article with a modified front end in GroupLens. The user can click on one of the five ratings buttons with the mouse, or type a number from 1 to 5 on the keyboard. Copyright © 1994 by Paul Resnick, Neophytos Iacovou, Mitesh Suchak, Peter Bergstrom, and John Riedl, reprinted by permission.*

Interest Voting and Readwear

Even though human editing is ideal, there are many cases where it is infeasible to rely solely on individual editors. The two main problems with human editors are that nobody can cover the full extent of information available on the Internet and other rich sources and that any individual reader only has a partial degree of agreement with the judgment of any individual editor.

An alternative approach is to rely on aggregate judgments by a larger group of editors. Figures 8.15 and 8.16 show an approach to reducing information overload in netnews suggested by Paul Resnick and colleagues from MIT and the University of Minnesota. Their GroupLens system [Resnick et al. 1994] collects quality ratings from anybody who happens to read a netnews article.

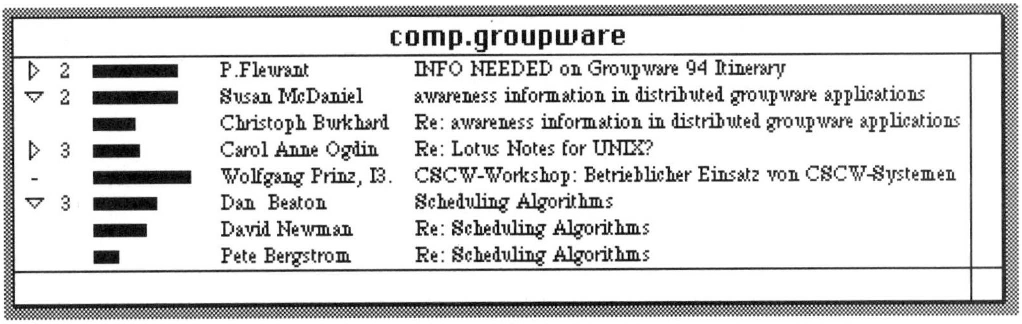

Figure 8.16. *Quality rating scores integrated into a netnews reading interface. The bars represent quality grades as retrieved from the Better Bit Bureau server. Copyright © 1994 by Paul Resnick, Neophytos Iacovou, Mitesh Suchak, Peter Bergstrom, and John Riedl, reprinted by permission.*

These ratings are forwarded to special servers called Better Bit Bureaus from which they are made available to future readers. As Figure 8.16 shows, having ratings available can help people decide what articles to choose from a menu.

So far, quality ratings are only used in research projects like GroupLens. If they become more widely used, one could imagine several different ways of using them. The simplest approach would be to collect ratings from anybody who happens to read an article and just compute its quality as the mean of the individual ratings. Given that netnews was estimated to have seven million readers in 1994, sufficient ratings to form a reliable mean should be available in a few minutes no matter when an article is posted, especially considering that the readers are scattered in all timezones around the world. A major problem with this approach is that it is not clear that you share interests with a group of geeks in New Zealand or whoever happens to be the first to rate an article. It is likely that the early ratings will come to dominate the quality score for an article since very few other users will bother reading an article once it has gathered a string of poor ratings.

A second potential problem with world-wide ratings is the potential for "ratings wars" where people would stuff the ballot box so to speak and seek out postings from their friends or enemies and rate articles without really having read the content. Indeed, netnews articles can be processed automatically as proven, e.g., by the Norwegian hacker who released a "cancelbot" on the Internet to hunt down and erase messages from a certain pair of lawyers who had "spammed" inappropriate ads for their office to thousands of unrelated newsgroups (and who do not deserve further publicity by having their name mentioned here).

An alternative approach to quality voting would be to collect only votes from people within your own organization. The downside of doing so would be that more people would have to read irrelevant articles before it was determined that they were irrelevant, but in return the ratings would be more directed toward the specific needs of the individual organization. It would also be possible to collect votes world-wide but only count the ones from people who in some way had been deemed responsible or who were known to have the same taste as the user who wanted to review the quality ratings.

Hill et al. [1995] experimented with interest voting where the users actively had to indicate their interest in each of 500 films. The system collected votes from 291 people who provided more than 55,000 ratings and then constructed a statistical model of which users had similar interests to which other users. In other words, instead of assuming that everybody had the same taste, the system recognized that people are different and that the same film may be a favorite of some people while being hated by others. The trick is to find a group of other people who share taste with the user for whom the system is trying to find relevant information. Luckily, if the system can aggregate information across a large enough population (e.g., the users of the Internet), there will always be others who have similar tastes, no matter how eclectic you may think you are. Hill et al.'s system was fairly successful in generating recommendations of new films for the users, with a correlation of 0.62 between the system's prediction of how well people would like a film and the actual rating given by the users. In comparison, the correlation between ratings from nationally-known movie critics and the users' own ratings was only 0.22. In other words, one can find much better information objects for users if one knows their taste and ratings of other objects than if one just rely on ratings of the intrinsic quality of the objects.

No matter how quality votes are gathered and distributed they have the distinct disadvantage that they require active decisions on the part of the users. In Figure 8.15, the user has to make up his or her mind as to what rating on a five-point scale to assign to the article, after which the user has to move the mouse to the chosen button to enter the vote. People might be motivated to vote on things that particularly upset them as being bad or that they find exceptionally good, but it will be difficult to get people to spend the time to rate everything they read. Just consider the many publications that have reader

Figure 8.17. *The link dialog box from HyperTED. The system keeps track of how often each link has been followed and displays this count when the user selects a link. Copyright © 1994 by Adrian Vanzyl, Monash University Medical Informatics, reprinted by permission.*

reply cards where you are asked to rate all articles in a given issue. How many of these cards have you sent back? And how often did you provide ratings for *all* the articles?

An alternative to voting is to rely on information that is gathered unobtrusively by the computer in the background as the user goes about his or her normal activities. This approach is called readwear [Hill et al. 1992] because the notion is that reading things on the computer will cause them to be "worn" in the same way as a physical book is worn by repeated reading. In fact, a book that has been used a lot will often open by itself to the pages that have been read the most even if the user has not left a bookmark. Figure 8.17 shows an example of readwear in the HyperTED system: the system keeps track of how many times each link has been followed, and users can use this information to help decide which of several links they want to follow themselves.

In the case of netnews, readwear might be collected by an instrumented system that recorded how long each user spent reading each article. The assumption might be that articles that people spent a long time on would be those that had some inherent quality. Of course there is no guarantee that this is true every time. For example, a user might spend a long time looking at something that was upsetting or potentially false—or the user may just have left the window open while taking a phone call. On the average, though, it does seem plausible that people would invest their time wisely and spend the most time on the best information, and a study of eight users reading 8,000 netnews messages found a strong correlation between the time the users spent reading each message and their subjective rating of the message [Morita and Shinoda 1994].

The n of $2n$ Approach

It is possible to combine automated and human methods for information filtering. Susan Dumais and I have experimented with doing so for assigning submitted conference papers to members of the review committee [Dumais and Nielsen 1992]. Our method is called "n of $2n$" and involves having the computer pick about twice as many papers for each reviewer as that person actually is asked to review. The reviewer thus uses his or her individual judgment to pick n information objects from a selection of $2n$ objects presented by the system. By adding this last element of human judgment, any wildly wrong guesses by the computer are removed from the final set of information objects actually read by the user.

The "n of $2n$" method can be used for many other applications than conference paper reviews. It requires just one additional attribute of the information objects: it should be possible for the human user to pick the most relevant n objects in substantially less time than it would take to read all $2n$ information objects. In the case of conference submissions, it is usually possible for a reviewer to read the abstract in much less time than it would take to read the full paper and it is usually possible to assess the topic of a paper from its abstract, so conference papers are ideal for the "n of $2n$" method.

The assignment of submitted manuscripts to reviewers is a common task in the scientific community and is an important part of the duties of journal editors, conference program chairs, and research councils. Finding reviewers for journal submissions and some types of grant proposals can normally be done for a small number of submissions at a time and at a more or less leisurely pace. For conference submissions and other forms of grant proposals, however, the reviews and review assignments must be completed under severe time pressure, with a very large number of submissions arriving near the announced deadline, making it difficult to plan the review assignments much in advance.

These dual problems of large volume and limited time make the assignment of submitted manuscripts to reviewers a complicated job that has traditionally been handled by a single person (or at most a few people) under quite stressful conditions. Also, manual review assignment is only possible if the person doing the assignments (typically the program chair for the conference) knows all the members of the review committee and their respective areas of expertise. As some conferences grow in scope with respect to number of submissions and reviewers as well as the number of sub-domains of their fields, it would be desirable to develop automated means of assigning the submitted manuscripts to appropriate members of the review committee.

The actual application of assigning manuscripts to reviewers involves two further considerations in addition to the matching of manuscripts and reviewers. First, one needs to guard against conflicts of interest by not assigning any reviewers their own papers or those of close colleagues. Second, there is a need to balance the review assignments to ensure that no single reviewer is overworked just because that person happens to be an appropriate choice for many papers, and that each paper gets assigned a certain minimum number of reviewers. All these constraints can be expressed as linear inequalities that can be handled by a linear programming package, so the entire review assignment can be done automatically.

Dumais and I tried automatic assignment of manuscripts to reviewers for the *Hypertext'91* conference as a pilot project where a human program chair made the final assignments. We also did actual automated assignments for the *INTERCHI'93* and *CHI'94* conferences where we were papers co-chairs ourselves. *Hypertext'91* was a fairly small conference with 117 manuscripts submitted and 25 members of the review committee. *INTERCHI'93* and *CHI'94* were larger conferences with 330 and 263 submitted papers, respectively, and 307 and 276 members of the review committee, respectively.

For *Hypertext'91* the members of the review committee had been asked to review an average of 26 papers each by the program chair. The program chair had received help from our automated method and thus the actual review assignments could not be seen as representative of the work of an unaided human. We simulated the result of purely human review assignments by asking three other hypertext experts to manually assign papers to reviewers.

The human experts assigned an average of 28 papers to each reviewer, achieving a mean rated relevance[7] of 3.6 on a 1–5 scale where 5 was best.[8] In comparison, our automated n of $2n$ method achieved a mean rated relevance of 3.8 on the same scale, thus doing slightly better.

For *INTERCHI'93* each reviewer was sent ten papers and was asked to review five of them. In order to make sure that each paper was read by at least some reviewers, we had pre-assigned three papers to each reviewer, meaning that the reviewer had the freedom to pick two additional manuscripts from the remaining seven that had not been pre-assigned. On a 1–5 scale (with 5 best), the reviewers rated the relevance of the papers they ended up reviewing as 4.1 on the average. For *CHI'94* each reviewer was sent eleven papers and actually reviewed seven,[9] and the mean relevance rating was 3.9 on the 1–5 scale.

For the *INTERCHI'93* and *CHI'94* conferences we do not have data from simulated human manuscript assignments because the job was too large to be done when it was not absolutely necessary. However, data exists from the very similar *CHI'92* conference where a human program chair made the review assignments with help from several experts in different subfields. For the 1992 conference, the mean rated relevance of the manuscripts sent to the reviewers was 4.1 on the 1–5 scale. This is exactly the same as the relevance achieved by our automated method for *INTERCHI'93* and slightly better than the result of the automated method for *CHI'94*.

An interesting aspect of the automated review assignment compared with manual assignment is that some of the more famous reviewers expressed satisfaction with getting papers that were more in line with their current interests than they were used to. Normally, such famous people continue getting papers in areas for which they are famous for many years after they have stopped working in those areas, simply because human committee chairs think, "Oh, a paper on XX, that must be just the thing for Dr. YY." With automated assignment, all the computer knows is what the reviewers told it

---

[7] Relevance ratings were gathered by asking each reviewer to rate how closely each manuscript matched his or her expertise as a reviewer.

[8] The rating scale was 1=how did I get this one?; 2=I'm following it, sort of; 3=somewhat relevant; 4=good match; and 5=right up my alley.

[9] Note that even though we refer to our approach as "n of $2n$" it also works when people can choose some other proportion of the selected information object (e.g., 7 of 11).

themselves when defining their interest profile, so they mainly get papers in the areas they specifically indicated as their current interests.

9. Navigating Large Information Spaces

When users move around a large information space as much as they do in hypertext, there is a real risk that they may become disoriented or have trouble finding the information they need. To investigate this phenomenon, we conducted a field study where users were allowed to read a Guide document at their own pace [Nielsen and Lyngbæk 1990].

Even in this small document, which could be read in one hour, users experienced the "lost in hyperspace" phenomenon as exemplified by the following user comment: "I soon realized that if I did not read something when I stumbled across it, then I would not be able to find it later." Of the respondents, 56% agreed fully or partly with the statement, "When reading the report, I was often confused about 'where I was.'"

Users also had problems using the inverse operations of the Guide hypertext buttons to return to their previous system states, as can be seen from the 44% agreement with the statement, "When reading the report, I was often confused about 'how to get back to where I came from.'" One reason for the confusion felt by many users is probably that Guide uses different backtrack mechanisms depending on which type of "button" (link mechanism) was used originally. Several users complained that Guide does not reestablish a completely identical screen layout when returning to a previous state after a backtrack operation. This change makes it more difficult to recognize the location one has returned to and thus complicates the understanding of the navigational dimensions of the hyperspace.

There are several possible solutions to the navigation problem. The most simple from the user's perspective may be to remove the requirement for navigation by providing guided tours [Trigg 1988] through the hypertext somewhat like the original "trails" suggested by Vannevar Bush in 1945. A guided tour may be thought of as a "superlink" that connects a string of nodes

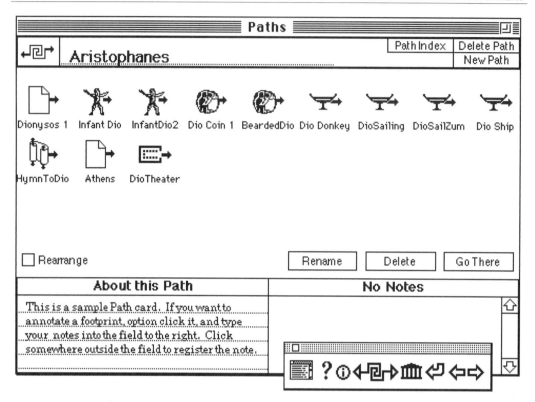

Figure 9.1. *The path editor in Perseus. Each icon (called a "footprint") is a reference to a node in the hypertext. Copyright © 1989 by the President and Fellows of Harvard University and the Annenberg/CPB Project, reprinted with permission.*

instead of just two nodes. As long as users stay on the guided tour, they can just issue a "next node" command to see more relevant information. The Perseus system (see Figures 4.16 and 4.17) have a "path" icon for use in moving back or forth along the selected guided tour. The system also provides the path editor shown in Figure 9.1 listing the names of all the nodes in a path and allowing users to add new nodes or remove or rearrange the existing nodes. Path navigation may be done manually by the user, or the system may automatically forward to the next node on the path after a specified wait [Zellweger 1989]

Guided tours can be used to introduce new readers to the general concepts of a hypertext, and one can also provide several different guided tours for various special-interest readers. The advantage of hypertext guided tours compared to tourist guided tours is that the hypertext reader can leave the guided tour at any spot and continue browsing along any other links that seem interesting. When the reader wants to get back on the tour, it suffices to issue a single command to be taken back to the point where the tour was suspended. The "guide" will be waiting as long as it takes.

Guided tours are nice, but they really bring us back full circle to the sequential linear form of information. Even though guided tours provide the option of side trips, they cannot serve as the only navigation facility since the true purpose of hypertext is to provide an open exploratory information space for the user.

Backtrack

Probably the most important navigation facility is the backtrack, which takes the user back to the previous node. Almost all hypertext systems provide some form for backtrack but not always very consistently, and we found in the Guide study mentioned above that inconsistency in backtracking could give users trouble. The great advantage of backtrack is that it serves as a lifeline for the user who can do anything in the hypertext and still be certain to be able to get back to familiar territory by using the backtrack. Since backtrack is essential for building the user's confidence it needs to fulfill two requirements: It should always be available, and it should always be activated in the same way. Furthermore, it should in principle be possible for the user to backtrack enough steps to be returned all the way to the very first introduction node. Even though much of the functionality of backtrack can be achieved by a hypertext design where the user can see the previous nodes (e.g., in a table of contents), there are great benefits to being able to go back without having to spend time on figuring out how to do so [Vargo et al. 1992].

Electronic Art's multimedia version of *Peter Pan* includes a special form of backtrack in the form of a replay option accessed through an hourglass icon. This interactive fiction is aimed at 3–8 year old children who often like to repeat the same actions over again, and clicks on the replay icon will move back in the story to allow the child to reexperience fun animations or other special scenes. Alternatively, a child can use the hypermedia aspects of the system during replay to see what would happen if he or she chose an alternative course of action at a branching point in the story.

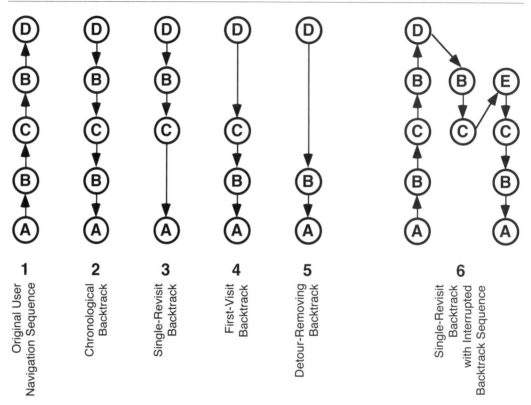

Figure **9.2.** *Various backtrack models. Sequence 1 represents the user's initial navigation and sequences 2–5 represent possible backtrack movement. Sequence 6 shows a more complicated example of sequence 2.*

Backtrack is conceptually very simple: the user clicks on a button and is returned to the previous node. The problem arises when the user backtracks more than once and when the user has visited certain nodes more than once. Sequence 1 in Figure 9.2 shows an example of a navigation sequence where the user has started in node **A**, moved to node **B** and **C**, then revisited node **B**, and finally moved on from **B** to **D**. The simplest backtrack model is chronological backtrack as shown in sequence 2, where all the nodes are visited again in the opposite order.

The main problem with chronological backtrack is that it is inefficient for the users to spend time on revisiting the same node multiple times just because they originally went through it several times. In our example in Figure

9.2, node **B** is the only one to be revisited, but users often move back and forth between a few nodes several times before deciding to backtrack out, and chronological backtrack would involve too many visits to the same nodes. To avoid this problem, several alternative backtrack models have been proposed.

My favorite backtrack model is the single-revisit backtrack shown in sequence 3 in Figure 9.2. Single-revisit backtrack works like chronological backtrack, but the computer keeps track of what nodes have already been revisited during the current backtrack sequence and does not show them a second time. A backtrack sequence is a sequence of user navigation actions that includes nothing but backtrack commands (and possibly local movement within the current node in systems with features like panning or scrolling). As soon as the user navigates to another node using any command other than backtrack, the backtrack sequence is interrupted. There are two ways of dealing with interrupted backtrack sequences. My preference is to reset the backtrack sequence and start a new one the next time the user initiates a backtrack command. I will call this approach simple single-revisit backtrack. The alternative, strict single-revisit backtrack, is to have the system remember the backtrack sequence and continue to add to it the next time the user backtracks.[1]

Sequence 6 in Figure 9.2 shows an example of an interrupted backtrack sequence. The user first moves **ABCBD** and then backtracks to node **C**. At this time, the backtrack sequence contains nodes **D**, **B**, and **C**, and a subsequent backtrack command would have moved the user back to node **A** (as shown in sequence 3) since the single-revisit backtrack model will skip the first occurrence of node **B**. In sequence 6 the user has chosen to move from **C** to **E**, however, thus interrupting the current backtrack sequence. When the user issues a backtrack command from node **E**, the system will first move back to node **C**. A second backtrack command will move to node **B** in the simple single-revisit backtrack model (as shown in sequence 6 in Figure 9.2) and all the way to node **A** in the strict single-revisit backtrack model.

First-visit backtrack (sequence 4 in Figure 9.2) is related to single-revisit backtrack but probably harder to understand and less useful for most applications. In both cases, each node is only revisited once, but nodes that

---

[1] Unfortunately, strict single-revisit backtrack involves a further complication since it is necessary to remove the current node from the remembered backtrack sequence at the time when the user interrupts the backtrack sequence. Otherwise, users would not be able to revisit this node, and backtracking from node **E** in sequence 6 in Figure 9.2. would take the user directly to node **A** without stopping at node **C**.

have been visited multiple times are treated differently. In first-visit backtrack, only the first visit to a node is considered a backtrack candidate, whereas in single-revisit backtrack it is the last visit to a node that is the backtrack candidate.

Detour-removing backtrack (sequence 5 in Figure 9.2) was suggested by Bieber and Wan [1994] as a way to avoid backtracking through nodes that were visited by mistake. The notion is to detect when the user has been on a detour through hyperspace and returns to a main navigation sequence. The detour can then be eliminated from any subsequent backtrack. In Figure 9.2, the user's movement from **B** to **C** and back to **B** would suggest that the visit to **C** was a mistake and should be treated as a detour. The difficulty in detour-removing backtrack is obviously to detect the detours and there is currently no empirical evidence to suggest that this is possible in the general case.

The backtrack models so far are all identical with respect to the required user action: the user simply clicks on the "go back" button.[2] The button may be generic, or it may include the name of the node to which the user will be returned. This latter approach is taken in General Magic's Magic Cap interface [Knaster 1994] where the name of the previous location is consistently listed in the upper right corner of the screen (e.g., **☞Hallway**). A more advanced, but also more complicated, option is to offer parameterized backtrack [Garzotto et al. 1995] where the user can specify some condition and backtrack to the most recently visited node for which the condition holds. In hypertext systems with typed nodes, the most common use of parameterized backtrack is to backtrack to nodes of a certain type. For example, in a banking system, the user might want to backtrack to the last time a "customer" node was visited.

History Lists

Some hypertext systems provide more general history mechanisms than the simple backtrack. For example, some systems have history lists like Figure 9.3 to allow users direct access to any previously visited node. Figure 9.3 shows a best-case user interface for a history list where it is possible to combine pictures and text for each object. A combination of the two is to be preferred because the two media complement each other (see, for example, the two different meanings of the word "paint" in Figure 9.3) and make it easier for users to

---

[2] Sometimes "back," "backtrack," "previous," or other terms are used for the backtrack command, but our user studies suggest that "go back" is the easiest to understand.

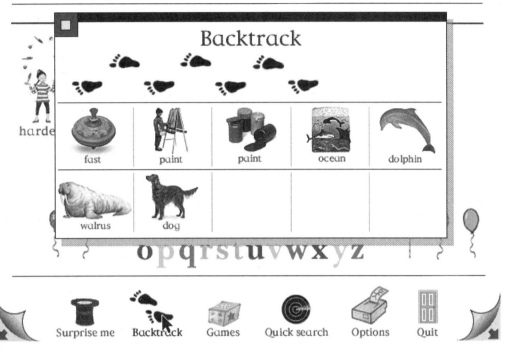

Figure 9.3. *The history list in* My First Incredible, Amazing Dictionary *(a children's dictionary). The system shows the ten most recently visited nodes and allows the user to return directly to any one of them. Note that even though the dialog box is called "Backtrack," it is actually a history list in the terminology used in this book. Copyright © 1994 by Dorling Kindersley, reprinted by permission.*

understand the meaning of each element in the list [Egido and Patterson 1988]. The two obvious alternatives for history lists are text alone (often the node name, as shown in Figure 2.10) or pictures alone (shown in Figure 9.5). The choice between the two will depend on the visual nature of the content of the nodes, since pictures only make sense if they are sufficiently distinct and characteristic to be recognized quickly. Finally, it is of course possible to use some other representation like the miniatures shown in Figure 9.4.

Since users are most likely to want to return to nodes they have visited relatively recently, it is possible to display the top part of the history list as a "visual cache" like Figure 9.4 where a small number of nodes are kept

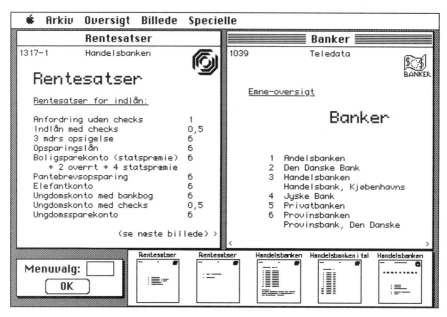

Figure 9.4. *A "visual cache" of miniatures of the five most recently visited nodes. From a prototype window-oriented videotex system designed at the Technical University of Denmark in 1989 (implementation by Flemming Jensen).*

permanently visible on the primary display. The design in Figure 9.4 represents the nodes by miniatures [Nielsen 1990f] of their graphic layout, but it is also possible to use icons or just the names of the nodes. Compare with Figure 9.5 to see how much better miniatures work when representing graphical nodes than the mostly text-oriented nodes in Figure 9.4. When the visual cache is shown as a horizontal list it is also sometimes referred to as a "visit shelf" because it stores the places that have been visited recently.

Bookmarks

Hypergate and some other systems allow users to define bookmarks at nodes they might want to return to later. The difference between bookmarks and history lists is that a node gets put on the bookmark list only if the user believes that there might be a later need to return to it. This condition means that the bookmark list is smaller and more manageable, but it also means that it will not include everything of relevance. It frequently happens that you do

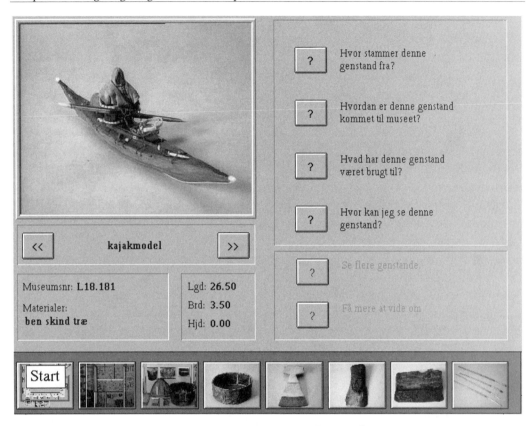

Figure 9.5. *Museum information system from the National Museum of Denmark. Users can navigate back to the eight most recently visited nodes by touching the miniatures at the bottom of the screen. Note that the miniatures do not represent the entire screen but only the photograph of the artifact, making them easier to recognize. Miniatures of illustrations instead of the full screens are sometimes referred to as a comic book interface [Lesk 1991]. Buttons link to information about the use and origin of the artifact and to a diagram showing where the object is exhibited in the room, thus providing a simple kind of augmented reality [Wanning 1993]. Copyright © 1994 by the National Museum of Denmark, reprinted by permission.*

not classify something as relevant until a later time, when its connection with something else suddenly becomes apparent. Then it is nice to be able to find it on the history list, which the system has automatically been keeping for you.

When the user defines a bookmark, the system may put the node's name on the bookmark list, or it may prompt the user for a small text to remember the node by. Bookmarks are more useful in hypertexts than in regular books because it is possible to use more of them. It is easy for a user to scan a menu of twenty node names that have been marked, whereas the same number of physical bookmarks in a book would be a complete mess to handle.

A special kind of bookmark would allow a user to resume the session with a hypertext system after an interruption and keep the state of the hypertext unchanged. A "smart bookmark" might even show some additional context to reorient the reader in the information space.

The Symbolics Document Examiner offers a special feature where users can build a list of references to nodes that they might want to remember to look at later. These references might be picked up from links in previously visited nodes and thus alleviate the problem of only being able to navigate to one new node at a time in most hypertext systems. This feature is called a bookmark list but might more appropriately be called a "shopping list."

Bookmarks have classically been seen as list elements in a bookmark list. The main advantage of this approach is that a single centralized bookmark list makes it easy for the user to determine how to get to the bookmarks (just open the list with the single command dedicated to that purpose) and how determine what bookmarks exist (just scan the list). A variant of this approach is used in the Netscape WWW browser (a variant of Mosaic). Users tend to collect a very large number of bookmarks pointing to WWW pages because of the difficulty of finding locations on the Web (due to the lack of overview diagrams or other navigational aids). These bookmark collections are normally referred to as hotlists, and it is quite common for WWW hotlists to contain 50 or more items. In order to manage these large lists, Netscape uses a hierarchical bookmark list, where the user can add dividers and a nested set of named categories. Users can then add new bookmarks to the general list, or they can place them in the appropriate category.

Bookmarks can also be seen as objects in their own right, meaning that they can have an existence outside the bookmark list. The advantage of this approach is obviously the added flexibility to move bookmarks around and to build different kinds of collections of bookmarks for different purposes. The downside is that the added features complicate the user interface and make it less clear what bookmarks exist in the system. Object-oriented bookmarks are used in General Magic's Magic Cap user interface. When the user defines a

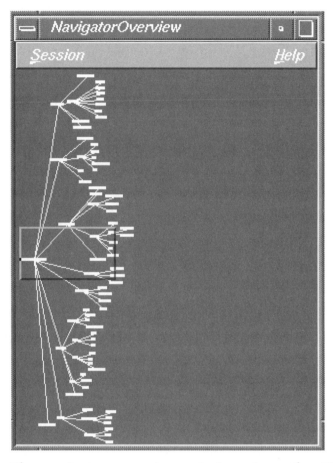

Figure 9.6. *The navigator overview window from the SGI Topic/Task Navigator (see Figure 9.21). The rectangular "viewport" indicates the part of the tree currently visible in the main window and the user can move to other views by dragging the viewport with the mouse. Copyright © 1994 by Silicon Graphics, Inc., reprinted by permission.*

bookmark, it is visualized with a paper clip icon (a fairly common icon for bookmarks). The user can peel off copies of the bookmark icon and drag them to other places in the interface from which they act as links to the bookmarked page.

Overview Diagrams

Since hypertext is so heavily based on navigation, it seems reasonable to use a tourist metaphor and try to provide some of the same assistance to hypertext users as one gives to tourists. One option is the guided tour as mentioned above, but as hypertext users are mostly supposed to find their own way around the information space, we should also give them maps. Since the information space will normally be too large for every node and link to be shown on a single map, many hypertext systems provide overview diagrams to show various levels of detail.

The system described in Chapter 2 uses both a global and a local overview diagram and displays both of them on the screen at the same time. An alternative is to acknowledge that the overview diagram has to be large and then provide a second layer of navigational mechanisms to move within the overview. This "meta-navigation" might be represented as an orthogonal dimension to the main information space through a zoom facility to allow users to see more or less detail. There have also been a few attempts to design three dimensional overview diagrams [Fairchild et al. 1988; Fairchild 1993; Robertson et al. 1991]. Finally, meta-navigation may be accomplished by moving a viewport indicator over a reduced representation of the main diagram as shown in Figure 9.6. Viewports (sometimes called panners) can be moved by direct manipulation and thus allow the user to quickly access other parts of the main diagram at the same time as the reduced view provides an indication of the structure of the data in the main view.

Overview diagrams can be particularly useful for students who can use them not just to navigate the hypertext but also to understand the domain matter. Figure 9.7 shows an example of use of overview diagrams to bring out literary structures in English literature in the *Dickens Web* developed at Brown University. The "Literary Relations" overview shows authors that influenced Dickens above his name and authors that were influenced by Dickens below his name. Each name is linked to articles about the various authors, so the diagram serves as an overview of the part of the hypertext that talks about various authors. Actually, not only is the "Literary Relations" a local overview of the "author" part of the hypertext, it has been filtered to a specialized local overview of only those authors who are relevant for an understanding of the novel *Great Expectations*.

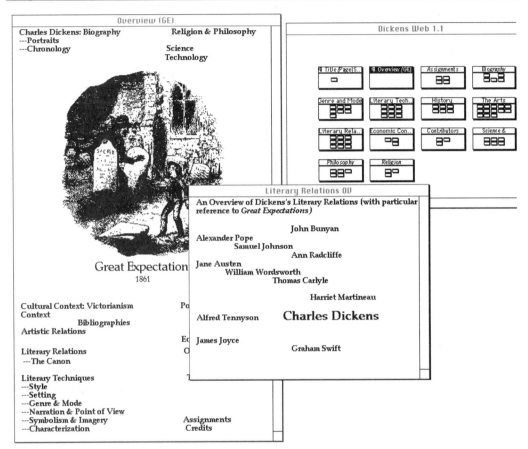

Figure 9.7. *Use of multiple overview diagrams in the* Dickens Web *[Landow and Kahn 1992]. The "Literary Relations" overview gives students an understanding of the relation between Charles Dickens and other authors and the "Great Expectations" overview shows the various issues relevant for a discussion of that novel. In addition, the figure shows a structural overview of the hypertext generated automatically by the Storyspace system. Copyright © 1992–94 by Paul Kahn, George P. Landow, and Brown University, reprinted by permission.*

An alternative to multilevel overviews is to use a fisheye view [Furnas 1986] like the one in Figure 9.8 that can show the entire information space in a single overview diagram using varying levels of detail. A fisheye view shows great detail for those parts of the information that are close to the user's current

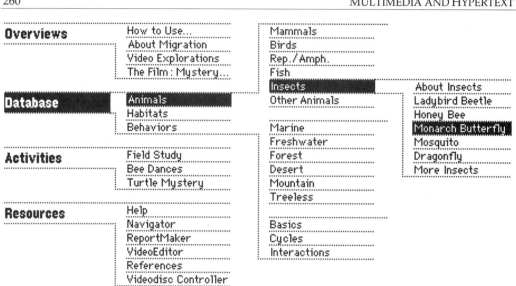

Figure 9.8. *A fisheye view-like browser from* Interactive NOVA. *Copyright ©
1989 by Apple Computer, Inc., WGBH Educational Foundation, and Peace
River Films, Inc., reprinted with permission.*

location of interest and gradually diminishing amounts of detail for those parts
that are progressively farther away. The use of fisheye views therefore requires
two properties of the information space: It should be possible to estimate the
distance between a given location and the user's current focus of interest, and it
should be possible to display the information at several levels of detail. Both
conditions are met for hierarchical structures like that shown in Figure 9.8, but
they may be harder to meet for less highly structured hypertexts.

   In addition to showing users the layout of the information space, overview
diagrams can also help users understand their current location and their own
movements. To achieve this understanding, the overview diagram should
display the user's "footprints" on the map to indicate both the current location
and the previous ones.

   If the information space in a hypertext has an underlying structure, that
structure may be used to make the overview diagram easier to interpret. For
example, Figure 9.9 shows parts of the overview diagram for the online
proceedings of the 23rd International Congress of Applied Psychology. Along
the left part of the diagram is a listing of the different areas of psychology
covered by the congress and across the top are the various categories of

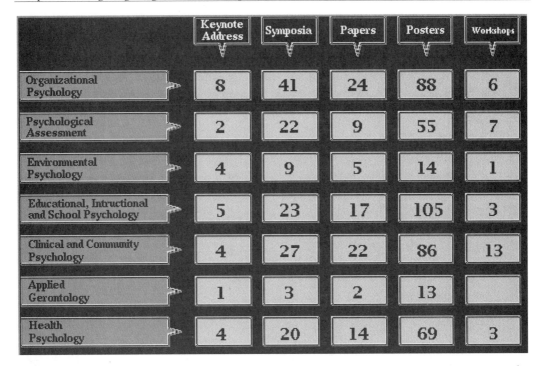

	Keynote Address	Symposia	Papers	Posters	Workshops
Organizational Psychology	8	41	24	88	6
Psychological Assessment	2	22	9	55	7
Environmental Psychology	4	9	5	14	1
Educational, Intructional and School Psychology	5	23	17	105	3
Clinical and Community Psychology	4	27	22	86	13
Applied Gerontology	1	3	2	13	
Health Psychology	4	20	14	69	3

Figure 9.9. *Part of the contents overview in the online proceedings of the 23rd International Congress of Applied Psychology (the full overview has several additional entries.* http://www.ucm.es/23ICAP/23icap.html). *Copyright © 1994 by the 23rd International Congress of Applied Psychology, reprinted by permission.*

presentations. The cells in the diagram show the number of objects one would see by going to that combination of topic and format.

Figure 9.10 shows a review grid from the Interchange online service. The review grid nicely summarizes the content of a large number of reviews and provides hypertext links to the original reviews. Notice how the typed hypertext anchors give a preview of each review: solid anchors are used for links to positive reviews and hollow anchors are used for links to negative reviews, thus allowing the user to dismiss products that have been negatively reviewed without having to navigate to the actual review. This ability of the hypertext overview diagram to summarize the content of the individual reviews highlights the power and responsibility of the hypertext editor since

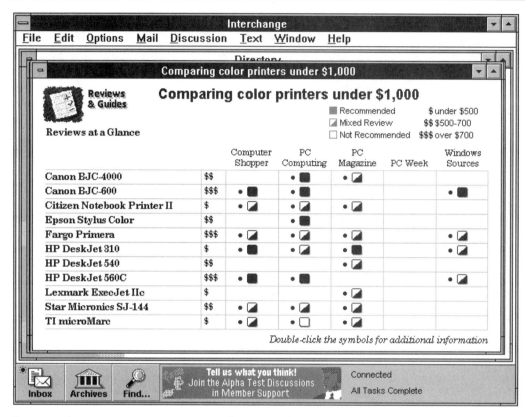

Figure 9.10. *Review grid from the Interchange online service. By clicking on one of the review markers, the user can jump to the full review. Copyright © 1994 by Interchange Network Company, reprinted by permission.*

users probably *will* skip reading about products that are linked to by negative anchors.

If the information space can be structured in multiple ways, some research suggests advantages from making several different overview diagrams available to the users. For example, Vora et al. [1994] studied a hypertext about nutrition that could be structured in three different ways: according to vitamins (Vitamin A, Vitamin B, etc.), according to food source (fruit, vegetables, grains, etc.), and according to the diseases and other health problems that can be caused or prevented by eating various food and vitamins. Users performed search tasks 21% faster in a system with overview diagrams for all three structure schemes than in a system where the only overview diagram was one for the vitamins. On the other hand, other studies suggest that multiple organizational schemes may make it more difficult for learners to construct their own mental models of the information space because they do not consistently get reinforcement from a single diagram. In the nutrition hypertext, the three different perspectives on the data were familiar to the users and were probably easy to distinguish, and this may have been the cause of the positive result in Vora et al.'s experiment.

Guided tours and map are both known to help tourists, and to continue the tourist metaphor for hypertext, another facility that often helps users navigate is the use of landmarks in the form of especially prominent nodes. Tourists who visit Paris quickly learn where the Eiffel Tower is and how to use it and a few other landmarks for orientation. Almost all hypertext systems define a specific node in a document as the introductory node and allow fast access to it, but one can also define additional local landmarks for special regions of the information space and make them stand out on the overview diagrams. Landmarks are usually defined by the author of a hypertext system as part of the process of providing a usable structure for the readers. It might be possible for the hypertext system to define landmarks automatically by the use of connectivity measures (see the example in Table 11.1), but it is probably better to have the author choose the landmarks. As an authoring aid, the choice might be made starting from a list of candidate nodes calculated on the basis of connectivity.

Contextual information can also be conveyed by more subtle contextual cues like the use of different background patterns in different parts of the information space. Even though such methods will not eliminate the disorientation problem, they are still needed to solve the *homogeneity* problem in hypertext. Traditional text is extremely heterogeneous as can be seen by comparing a mystery novel with a corporate annual report. You do not need actually to read the text to distinguish between the two. But the same two texts would have looked exactly the same if they had been presented online on a traditional computer terminal with green letters.

Printed books look different depending on their quality and age. They even automatically change to reflect how often they are used by being more or less worn [Hill et al. 1992]. Modern graphic computer screens allow us to utilize similar principles to provide additional information to the user, but we still have to discover the best ways of doing so.

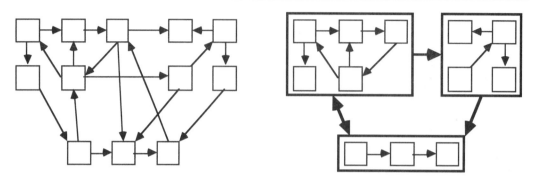

Figure 9.11. *Link inheritance during a clustering operation.*

The main hypertext control structure is the `goto` statement in the form of a jump. In an analogy with software engineering, it might be possible to use alternative methods that are more similar to structured programming such as the nested hierarchies of Guide.

Another example of structured hypertext mechanisms is the use of link inheritance [Feiner 1988] to allow simplified views of an information space without having to show all the links. As shown in Figure 9.11, link inheritance replaces the individual links between nodes in an overview diagram with lines connecting clusters of nodes, thus simplifying the diagram considerably.

Figure 9.11 shows a conceptual view of link inheritance but Figures 9.12 and 9.13 show an actual example from a medium-sized hypertext. It is immediately apparent from the pictures that the structure of the hypertext is impossible to understand in the full overview diagram whereas it is much clearer from the diagram where the nodes have been nested according to the hierarchical structure of the information space and where only the connecting links are shown.

Even though the nested view in Figure 9.13 provides a great overview of the structure of the Free Trade Agreement, the individual parts of the diagram are much too small to allow the user to use them to understand specific sections of the Agreement. This is where fisheye views come into play to show the user's current focus of attention at a greater scale. In turn, the other parts of the overview diagram will have to be scaled down given a fixed amount of screen real estate for the diagram. Figure 9.14 shows a fisheye view of the Free Trade Agreement assuming that the user's current interest is in the

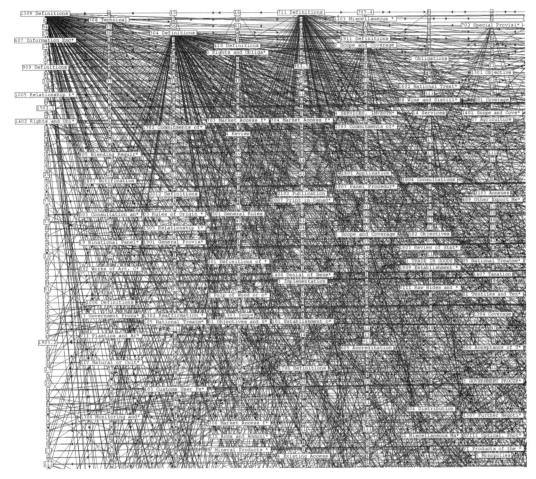

Figure 9.12. *A hypertext version of the Canada–U.S. Free Trade Agreement with all nodes and links visible. Actually, to save space, the figure only shows 32% of the total image, which has 1860 nodes and 3852 links. Copyright © 1993 by Emanuel G. Noik, reprinted by permission.*

"definitions" section (possibly because the user is currently viewing a node from that section).

Fisheye views belong to the class of so-called "distortion-oriented" presentation techniques [Leung and Apperley 1994] because they have to move some of the information around in order to fit everything into a single picture.

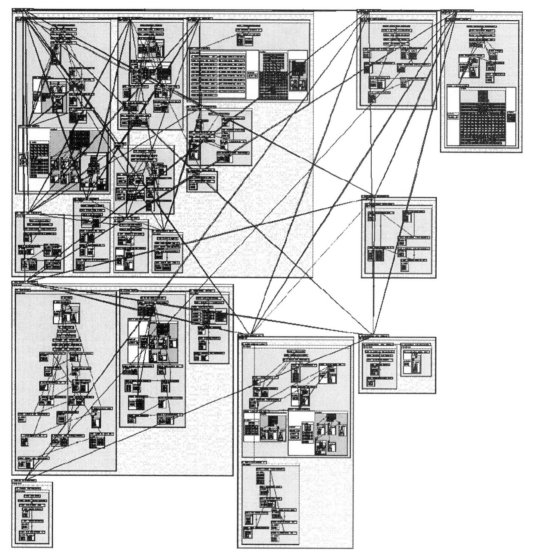

Figure 9.13. *View of the Free Trade Agreement with nesting and link inheritance to clarify the picture. This time, the figure* does *show the full hypertext. Notice now grayscales are used to indicate the hierarchy of the nesting. Copyright © 1993 by Emanuel G. Noik, reprinted by permission.*

In calculating the view in Figure 9.14, some of the sections have been moved around from their location in Figure 9.13.

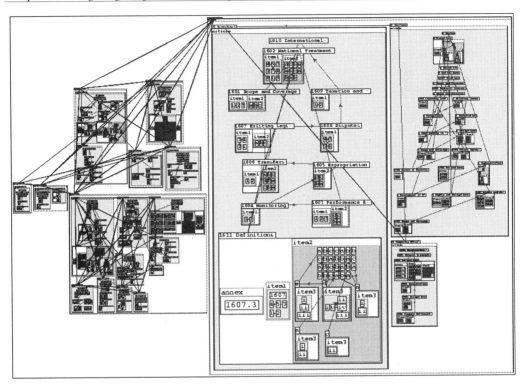

Figure 9.14. *Fisheye view of the Free Trade Agreement centered on the definitions. The fisheye view was calculated using Noik's layout-independent algorithm for node placement [Noik 1993], meaning that the placement of each section of the hypertext was determined with an eye to maximize the understandability of the diagram and not just from a rescaling of the original layout. Copyright © 1993 by Emanuel G. Noik, reprinted by permission.*

Obviously, one wants to minimize the changes in the diagram as the user moves through the information space, but given that the two-dimensional representation of the N-dimensional hyperspace is somewhat artificial anyway, it is more important to preserve the relationships and approximate shapes of the sections than their exact placement.

Most graphical fisheye views use straight geometric distortion to scale a drawing at multiple levels and in doing so balance local detail and global context.

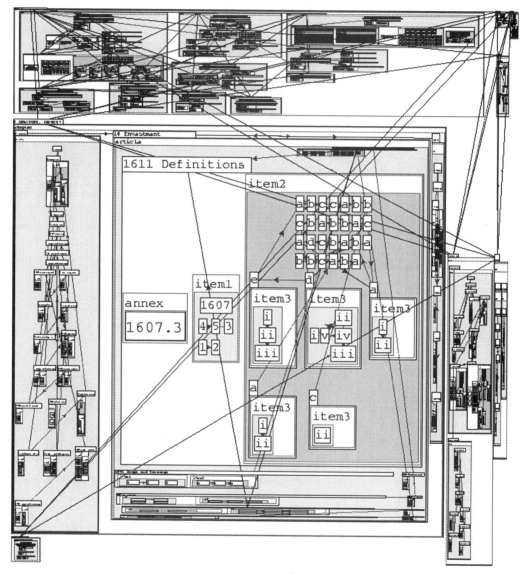

Figure 9.15. *Fisheye view of the Free Trade Agreement centered on the definitions. This time, the fisheye view was calculated by simple geometric distortion from the base view in Figure 9.13 Note how the structure of the hyperspace is much harder to understand than in the layout-independent fisheye view with the same focus in Figure 9.14 Copyright © 1993 by Emanuel G. Noik, reprinted by permission.*

Distorted views tend to be difficult to understand (especially of nested graphs) because the technique uses geometric notions of distance (which is not appropriate for hyperspace) and because geometric distortion alters the shapes of nodes too much (which is bad for nested nodes). Figure 9.15 shows what would happen to the Free Trade Agreement if the fisheye view was calculated by a simple geometric distortion that scaled each level at some proportion to its original size in the full nested overview diagram in Figure 9.13. Clearly, the view in Figure 9.15 is much harder to understand and to use as an overview of the hypertext than the more appropriately scaled fisheye view in Figure 9.14.

Link inheritance and nesting both require the hypertext to have a structure. At the same time, the ability to write and generate ideas freely is one of the most attractive aspects of hypertext systems as an intellectual tool. Having to define a structure before one has created the materials feels constaining and also constitutes a barrier to writing. The famous "writer's block" of staring at a blank sheet of paper and not knowing what to write first is a classic indication of the difficulties inherent in any requirements for early structure. It is much easier to start writing and generating ideas as they flow and then later reorganize and link the material as it emerges.

Premature structuring has been found to be a serious problem for hypertext authors [Monty 1986], and much work has therefore been devoted to schemes for structure discovery. The basic goal is to allow authors to develop the hypertext more or less as they please and then to have the system generate suggestions for ways of structuring the material. For example, the VIKI system [Marshall et al. 1994] was explicitly designed to support emerging structure through the use of spatial hypertext where users can associate nodes by placing them near each other on a canvas.

Figure 9.16 shows a screen from Xerox' Aquanet system which is often used to develop argumentation structures [Marshall et al. 1991]. In Aquanet, users get a large canvas on which they can place hypertext nodes spatially as they add information to their knowledge base. Aquanet uses typed nodes and displays different types in different colors. From the screen in Figure 9.16 it is apparent that the hypertext has four major components, each of which seems to be structured very differently with different node types (as indicated by color and shape) in the four corners of the window. It is almost certainly the case that the user has thought of the problem domain as having four parts, even though this may only have become apparent after the fact. Marshall and Shipman

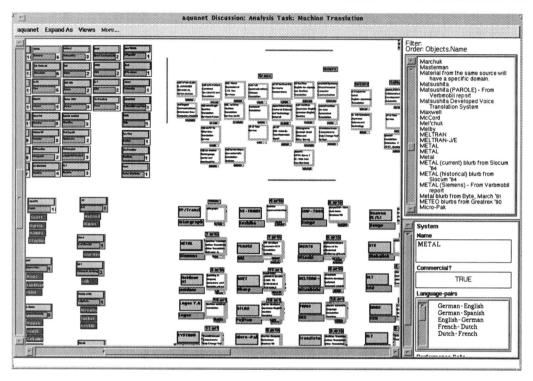

Figure 9.16. *Screen from Aquanet showing a user-constructed layout of hypertext nodes that can be used for discovery of structure by pattern recognition. Copyright © 1994 by Catherine C. Marshall, reprinted by permission.*

[1993] have developed a program to automatically detect such implicit structures by pattern recognition.

Each of the larger structures in Figure 9.16 has its own internal substructure. For example, the lower left structure is made up of composite nodes, each of which has a two-element box on the top and a list of smaller nodes below that box. The two-element boxes are composite nodes constructed explicitly in the system as a special type. The example in Figure 9.16 is a representation of a writer's notes about machine translation. The full hypertext has 2,000 nodes and took two years to develop as part of a project assessing the state of machine translation [Marshall and Rogers 1992]. The two-element boxes in the lower left corner actually represent links to collections of articles about specific systems. The top element in the box holds the name of the

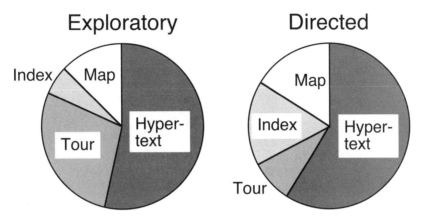

Figure 9.17. *Distribution of the methods used to transfer to new screens in hypertext on the history of York when users were asked to explore the information space and when they performed a directed search to answer specific questions. Data replotted from Hammond and Allinson [1989].*

system and the lower element holds the name of its vendor. In addition to this information about the specific systems (and links to backup materials), the user has placed smaller, single-element nodes next to the two-element boxes. These smaller nodes contain further notes about the systems, and it is quite obvious to the human eye what notes go with what system-nodes. The pattern recognition software can also recognize many of these patterns and can build up higher-level composite nodes. In the example, a new type of composite node would be defined with one slot for a two-element system node and a variable number of slots for note-nodes.

Hammond and Allinson [1989] have studied users of a hypertext history of the city of York. Some subjects used the system for an *exploratory task* wherein they first read the hypertext on their own and were later given a test to see how much they had learnt. Other subjects were given a *directed task* wherein they were given a set of questions that they were to answer using the hypertext system. Several different navigational methods were provided in addition to the plain hypertext links between associated parts of the text. One test compared the use of an overview map to the same system without the map and found that users performed slightly better (but insignificantly so) in both the exploratory and directed tasks when they had the use of the map. The same was true for an index mechanism. There were large, significant differences in both task conditions, however, in the ratio of new, different hypertext nodes visited compared to previously visited hypertext nodes being revisited. Both the map and the index led to users seeing a significantly larger proportion of new nodes.

Furthermore, users in the exploratory task also visited more new nodes than users in the directed task. This difference is understandable since the exploratory users could not know what questions they would be asked and therefore would feel encouraged to cover as much of the information base as possible in the time given.

Hammond and Allinson also tested a system wherein users had an overview map, an index, and a guided tour facility available. As shown in Figure 9.17, it turned out that users' use of these facilities varied significantly depending on their task, with the guided tour being used 28% of the time for the exploratory task but only 8% of the time for the directed task, the index being used 6% of the time for the exploratory task compared to 17% for the directed task, and the map being used about the same (12% vs. 16%).

Navigational Dimensions and Metaphors

Navigational dimensions and metaphors can help users better understand the structure of the information space and their own movements.

For example, the interactive fiction *Inigo Gets Out* mostly uses a navigational metaphor related to Laurel's [1989] definition of *personness* in interactive systems. Most of the story has a *first-person* feel wherein the user identifies with the cat and clicks at those points in the environment where the cat wants to go. See the screen in Figure 9.18 where the user would click on the tree if that is where the cat "wants" to go at that point in the interactive fiction.

In a few locations, however, the story changes to a *second-person* feel where the user orders the cat around by clicking on *it* rather than on the environment. For example, in Figure 9.19 (one of the last screens of the story), the cat is shown running along the path to the house where it lives. Because of the general first-person feel of the story, many users click at the end of the path, thus expressing the sentiment "Now let's run in this direction." The system, however, requires the user to click on the cat itself, which leads to a sentiment more like "OK you cat, move along now."

We conducted a field study of children in a Copenhagen kindergarten using *Inigo Gets Out* [Nielsen and Lyngbæk 1990] and mostly found that the children had great fun reading the story and could navigate easily. But from

Figure 9.18. *A central screen from* Inigo Gets Out. *This screen has a first-person perspective: To get the cat to climb the tree, you click the tree. Copyright © 1987 by Amanda Goodenough, reprinted with permission.*

logging user interactions in our field study we know that users in total made 30 clicks on the screen in Figure 9.19 from the (erroneous) first-person perspective and 38 clicks from the second-person perspective. Any first-person click on this screen must have been made before a second-person click, since users would not be moved to the next screen until they realized the need for a second-person click. These data do not prove that first-person stories in general are more intuitive than second-person stories, but they do indicate the need for consistent navigational metaphors in hypertexts.

The hypertext system described in Chapter 2 is based on two navigational dimensions. One dimension is used to move back and forth among the text pages within a given node, and another dimension is used for hypertext jumps. To reinforce users' understanding of these two dimensions, two different animation techniques are used when shifting from one screen to another.[3]

---

[3] Other studies have confirmed that animated transitions help users understand their movements through an information space [Merwin 1990].

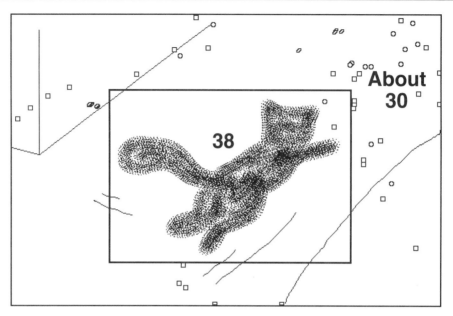

Figure 9.19. *Screen from* Inigo Gets Out. *This screen has a second-person perspective: To get the cat to run to the right, you click on the cat itself. The actual image from* Inigo Gets Out *has been overlaid with data from a field study of the use of the system in a Copenhagen kindergarten (the heavy border showing the button on the cat, the small symbols denoting mouse clicks outside the button, and the numbers counting clicks in various regions of the screen). Click markers inside the button rectangle denote cases where the user moved the mouse in between pressing down the mouse button and releasing it. Copyright © 1987 by Amanda Goodenough, reprinted with permission.*

Movement between pages within a node is seen as a linear left–right dimension, corresponding to the orientation of the scroll bars at the bottom of the screen and to the way printed books are read in Western society. A change to a new page along this dimension is visualized by an animated right or left wipe, using built-in visual effects from HyperCard that look quite like the turning of a page.

Hypertext jumps are seen as being orthogonal to the left–right page turning and are visualized as an in–out dimension using an animated iris that *opens* for anchored jumps and *closes* for return jumps. The opening iris gives users the impression of diving deeper into the hyperspace when they take a

Figure 9.20. *Preliminary (top) and final icons (bottom) from HP's SynerVision. User interface by Jafar Nabkel (Software Engineering Systems Division, Hewlett-Packard Company) and Eviatar Shafrir (User Interaction Design, Hewlett-Packard Company). Copyright © 1993 by Hewlett-Packard Company, reprinted by permission.*

hypertext jump, and the closing iris for return jumps gives the inverse feeling of pulling back again.

Another example of orthogonal navigational dimensions is the "season knob" in the *Aspen Movie Map* described in Chapter 3. It could be operated independently of the navigation through the streets, and navigation in time and geographical navigation were thus done along orthogonal dimensions.

Even though navigational metaphors are usually beneficial in helping users understand their options and movements, it is not always appropriate to tie a design to a single metaphor that may be too constraining. For example, the top row of icons in Figure 9.20 shows an initial design using a book metaphor for all aspects of navigation. User testing revealed that people had trouble distinguishing the subtle differences in the uses of books, and the designers therefore chose to engage a variety of metaphors for the final design shown in the bottom row in Figure 9.20 [Shafrir and Nabkel 1994]. In the final SynerVision design, pictures of books represented real, physical books (for example, "directions to all information, both online and printed" for the middle icon and "cross-reference to the printed manuals" for the rightmost icon). A geography and travel metaphor was used for the table of content (branching road with road sign in the leftmost icon) and the guided tour (map with highlighted path, second from right), and an office metaphor was used for the index (box of index cards, second from left).

It is possible to provide alternative navigational dimensions that are optimized for specific user needs in cases where the fundamental structure of the information space is unsuited for some user tasks. For example, many online manuals are written from the perspective of the experienced user who needs to know everything about a system. Therefore, they are often structured in ways that make sense for people who want to understand the scope and conceptual nature of the full system. A user who just wants to accomplish a specific task (e.g., installing a printer or changing the background screen color) without understanding the full system may be better served by an alternative navigation mechanism.

Figure 9.21 shows the Silicon Graphics Topic/Task Navigator which provides an alternative way of navigating the IRIS InSight library of online manuals. The original information base has two underlying navigational dimensions: a hierarchical structure of books, chapters, and sections, and a full text search capability. Novice users may not appreciate the book structure and they also sometimes have difficulty in coming up with appropriate search terms. After all, when you are new to a system you don't always know what things are called. The Topic/Task Navigator alleviates these two problems by providing hierarchical navigation that is structured around tasks users may want to perform, instead of being structured according to the way the computer system is built. By presenting possible tasks and subtasks, the Topic/Task Navigator helps users to understand the way it has structured the information space in much the same way that window-based user interfaces use pull-down or pop-up menus to make their functionality visible to the user. Field feedback shows that the Topic/Task Navigator is also used by many experienced users when desired information exists across a number of books.

Because the Topic/Task Navigator acts as an alternative navigational dimension, there is no one-to-one mapping between its categories and the text units in the underlying information base. Therefore, instead of linking directly from the nodes in its overview diagram to the content nodes, the Topic/Task Navigator uses a fat link in the form of a menu of relevant nodes from which the user can select the final destination.

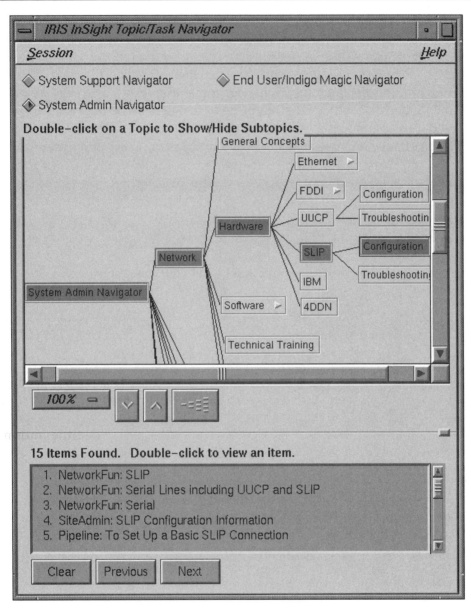

Figure 9.21. *In the Topic/Task Navigator interface to IRIS InSight users can click their way through a topic hierarchy. For each node the system lists a number of links into the online documentation. Copyright © 1994 by Silicon Graphics, Inc., reprinted by permission.*

In cases where the hypertext does not have an underlying structure or easily comprehensible dimensions it may difficult to present meaningful overviews. One can still give the user an idea of the content of the full system by using a technique called "flying" [Lai and Manber 1991]. Flying through a hypertext is done by flashing each node on the screen for a very brief time (possibly half a second). If the hypertext is fairly small, all nodes can be displayed (unless the user chooses to interrupt the fly-through), but if the hypertext is large the system may only display, say, every tenth node. Flying through a hypertext is analogous to flipping the pages of a book and may also be helpful as a supplemental overview tool in cases where the hypertext does have a structure.

10. Hypertext Usability

Usability is traditionally associated with five usability attributes [Nielsen 1993a (chapter 2)]:

1) *Easy to learn:* The user can quickly get some work done with the system.

2) *Efficient to use:* Once the user has learned the system, a high level of productivity is possible.

3) *Easy to remember:* The casual user is able to return to using the system after some period of not having used it, without having to learn everything all over.

4) *Few errors:* Users do not make many errors during the use of the system, or if they do make errors they can easily recover from them. Also, no catastrophic errors must occur.

5) *Pleasant to use:* Users are subjectively satisfied by using the system; they like it.

Since most hypertext systems are not used for such critical applications as process control, medical applications, or financial asset management, the subcriterion of preventing catastrophic errors is of less importance. To the extent that hypertext is used for authoring, we would still like users to be prevented from easily wiping out their entire work, however. Except from this qualifying comment, it seems that usability of hypertext systems really fits the general definition of computer system usability quite well, so it will also be used in this chapter.

Several methods exist for evaluating how well a given user interface scores on each of these primary usability parameters and for refining them to even more precisely measurable secondary parameters. See, e.g., Gould [1988], Whiteside et al. [1988], Landauer [1988], and Nielsen [1993a] for lists of such methods and for issues to study in a general usability evaluation process and see Nielsen [1990d] and Perlman et al. [1990] for a discussion of hypertext usability evaluation.

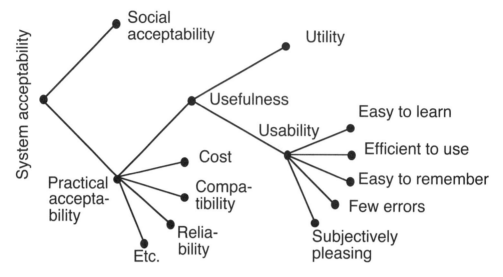

Figure 10.1. *The various parameters associated with system acceptability.*

It turns out that most discussions of hypertext usability are not founded in measurements of the usability parameters but are more in the nature of conjectures based on personal experience. Some empirical evaluations of hypertext systems do exist, however, and are reviewed here. First I try to refine the definition of the usability parameters for the purpose of evaluating hypertext; I then survey research that has resulted in benchmark measures comparing the performance of different systems, and the chapter ends with a discussion of non-benchmark studies.

Usability Parameters for Hypertext

Figure 10.1 shows a simple model of system acceptability. The overall acceptability of a computer system is a combination of its *social acceptability* and its practical acceptability. As an example of social acceptability of hypertext systems, consider the French LYRE system [Bruillard and Weidenfeld 1990] for teaching poetry. LYRE allows the students to see the poem from various "viewpoints," each highlighting certain parts of the poem as hypertext anchors to relevant annotations and allowing the student to add new annotations. LYRE does not, however, allow the student to add *new* viewpoints since that capability is reserved for the teacher. The premise is that students should work within the framework set up by the teacher and not construct completely new ways to analyze the poem. This premise is obviously socially acceptable in the southern European tradition in France, and indeed an alternative design might well have been deemed socially *un*acceptable in that country because it would have undermined the teacher's authority. On the other hand, many people in Denmark where Scandinavian attitudes are more prevalent would view the current design of LYRE as socially unacceptable because it limits the students' potential for independent discovery.[1]

Given that a system is socially acceptable, we can further analyze its practical acceptability within various categories, including traditional categories such as cost, support, reliability, compatibility with existing systems, etc., as well as the category of *usefulness,* which is of special interest to us in this chapter. Usefulness is the issue of whether the system can be used to achieve some desired goal. It can again be broken down into the two categories of *utility* and *usability*, where utility is the question of whether the functionality of the system in principle can do what is needed and usability is the question of how well users can use that functionality. Note that the concept of "utility" does not necessarily have to be restricted to the domain of hard work. An educational hypertext has high utility if students learn from using it, and an entertainment product has high utility if it is fun to use.

Consider the two additional examples of international usability shown in Figure 10.2. To depict the concept of a report generator, the designers' first idea was to call it a "Reporter" and use an icon inspired by old films showing a 1930's camera with a reporter pass in a man's hat. This icon is not particularly offensive, so it would pass the "social acceptability" test in most countries, but people who do not speak English (or who had not seen countless old American films) might not make the connection between report generators and journalists or the connection between journalists and the icon. In general, it is dangerous to design icons that depict[2] things that *sound* like the concept one

---

[1] See [Nielsen 1990g] for further information about international user interfaces.

[2] The "report generation" icons discussed here are reference icons and not resemblance icons because they show *other* concepts that are supposed to act as references to the actual item of interest. An icon showing a report being generated would be a resemblance icon and would have a better chance of being universally recognized (but might be more difficult to depict). With reference icons, the added level of indirection increases the probability that some people will not make the connection between the reference concept and the target concept. The third, and most difficult, class of icons is arbitrary icons.

Figure 10.2. *Initial and final versions of icons from HP SynerVision showing changes made during iterative design to improve international usability. The two icons on the left represent the report generation tool and the two icons on the right represent the glossary. User interface by Jafar Nabkel (Software Engineering Systems Division, Hewlett-Packard Company) and Eviatar Shafrir (User Interaction Design, Hewlett-Packard Company). Copyright © 1993 by Hewlett-Packard Company, reprinted by permission.*

wants to communicate in one language because the words may be completely different in other languages. Using a typewriter[3] to represent report generation preserved the connection between "report generation" and "Reporter" for the American users while being much easier to recognize for users in other countries, thus proving that it is often not necessary to sacrifice usability for one group in order to improve it for others. The icons on the right of Figure 10.2 represent the highly abstract concept of a glossary. Both icons have about equal usability but the one with a cat risks being socially unacceptable in cultures where such animals carry religious or social significance. In either case, the text in the icons should be translated to the local language.[4]

For a discussion of the usability of specifically hypertext systems, we can refine the primary usability parameters somewhat. The first point is that the usability of a hypertext system is determined by a combination of the usability of the underlying hypertext system *engine* (i.e., the basic presentation and navigation support available) and the usability of the *contents* and *structure* of the hypertext information base, and by how well these two elements fit together. From the user's perspective, all of these elements are of course seen

---

[3] Of course, the typewriter will eventually be hard to recognize for users who have grown up without ever having seen one, but that will take many years.

[4] Normally one avoids text in icons in order to eliminate the need for translators to learn and use drawing programs during localization, but for the concept of a glossary it would be very difficult to design a good icon without including some words.

as one single interface, and the user will not care whose "fault" it is if something is not usable. But from an analytical perspective, this distinction between the underlying system and the information base is probably an advantage. Furthermore, the relevant secondary parameters will be different for readers than for authors in many cases. Normally, the "easy to learn" parameter will be of less importance for a hypertext author who will spend a lot of time with the system.

1) Easy to learn: The hypertext engine itself is easy to learn. Users are quickly able to understand the most basic commands and navigation options and use them to locate wanted information.

When users enter an information base for the first time, they are immediately able to understand the first screen and to browse from it. Users are quickly able to learn the basic structure of the hypertext network and where or how to look for specific information.

Users of educational or entertainment hypertexts can learn something or enjoy the session without having to familiarize themselves with the entire hypertext structure.

The contents of the hypertext information base are easy to understand: Each node contains text (or other information) that is easy to read.

For authors: Authors who are editing an information base constructed by somebody else can easily understand the basic structure of this hypertext and are able to modify it without knowing the entire contents of the information base.

2) Efficient to use: Given that users want to find a certain piece of information, they either get to it quickly or soon discover that it is not in the information base. When users arrive at a node, they are quickly able to orient themselves and understand the meaning of the node in relation to their point of departure.

For educational hypertext: Users learn the facts or concepts that are most relevant for their purpose without having to learn or go through non-relevant material or material they already know more than necessary.

For authors: Authors can quickly construct a hypertext structure to reflect their understanding of the domain. It is easy to modify and maintain this structure.

3) Easy to remember: After a period of not having used the hypertext engine, users have no problems in remembering how to use and navigate in the hypertext.

After a period of not having used an information base, users can remember its general structure and are still able to find their way around the hypertext network and to recognize landmark nodes. Users can remember any special conventions or notations for special anchors, links, and nodes.

Users can transfer their knowledge of the use and navigation of one information base to the use of another information base with the same engine.

For authors: When a hypertext structure needs revision after some time, it is easy for the author to return to the information base and update it. The author can remember or is reminded about the basic structure of the information and does not need to remember details in order to update it.

4) Few errors: Users will rarely follow a link only to discover that they really did not want to go to wherever the link leads. In case users have erroneously followed a link, it is easy for them to return to their previous location. Users can in general easily return to locations where they have been, in case they decide that some lengthy digression should be abandoned.

For authors: The hypertext has very few links that erroneously lead nowhere or somewhere else than where they are supposed to go. The information contained in the nodes is correct.

5) Pleasant to use: Users prefer using the hypertext system to existing alternative solutions such as paper or other, non-hypertext computer systems. Users are rarely frustrated with using the hypertext engine or disappointed about the result of following links. Users feel that they are in control with respect to the hypertext and that they can move about freely rather than feeling constrained by the system.

For non-work related hypertext such as interactive fiction, users find using the hypertext an entertaining and/or moving and/or enriching experience.

A Semantic Differential Scale for Usability

Guillemette [1989] asked users to evaluate traditional (non-hypertext) documentation and found that their replies could be characterized by the following seven factors, which explained 65% of the variance:

- *Credibility* (correct–incorrect, reliable–unreliable, believable–unbelievable)
- *Demonstrative* (precise–vague, conclusive–inconclusive, strong–weak, complete–incomplete)
- *Fitness* (relevant–extraneous, meaningful–meaningless, appropriate–inappropriate)

• *Personal affect* (varied–monotonous, interesting–boring, active–passive)

• *Systematic arrangement* (organized–unorganized, orderly–chaotic, structured–unstructured)

• *Task relevance* (useful–useless, informative–uninformative, valuable–worthless)

• *Understandability* (clear–confusing, understandable–mysterious, readable–unreadable)

The terms in parentheses after each factor are the semantic differential scales associated with each factor. These seven factors are of course somewhat related to the five usability parameters but can also be viewed as a new set of dimensions according to which one could evaluate hypertext. They have the advantage of matching the way users view documentation but the disadvantage of overlooking that hypertext can be used for many other applications than online documentation. It is not clear whether the factors will cover other application areas too.

To use semantic differential scales to assess the users' subjective satisfaction with a system, they are presented with a questionnaire showing the chosen scales, with the endpoints written over each end of a 1–7 scale. Each user is then asked to place the system on each of the scales according to what that user feels about the system [Nielsen 1993a]. For example, on a 1–7 scale, where 1=orderly and 7=chaotic, a user might choose to rate the system a 6, meaning that it felt very chaotic to that user, but not extremely chaotic.

Survey of Benchmark Research

A fair amount of research has resulted in benchmark numbers comparing the usability of various approaches to accessing text online. Rather few studies exist that have looked at the hypertext problem as such, but there are some studies of non-hypertext systems that are relevant for the usability of hypertext and which are also reported here.

Impact of User Interface System Software

Online information systems can be implemented using several different kinds of common user interface system software. One of the most common at the moment is the use of multiwindow systems, and Tombaugh et al. [1987] have conducted a test of the impact of such systems on users' abilities to once again find information they have previously read. The test was conducted both with novice subjects who had not used window systems before and with subjects who already had skills in the use of the windows themselves. For both novice and experienced users, the plain reading of the text was slightly slower when it was presented split up into several windows than when it was presented in one scrolling window (17 min. vs. 15 min. for novices and 17 min. vs. 16 min. for experienced users). But when it came to retrieving parts of the previously read text in order to answer questions about it, novices continued to do slightly worse in the multiwindow interface (85 sec. vs. 72 sec. per question) whereas the experienced users performed better with the multiwindow system than with the single scrolling window (50 sec. vs. 65 sec.). The slower reading time for the multiwindow condition is probably because it is slower to shift between windows than simply to keep the mouse on the scroll bar and scroll the text in a single window. For the novice users, the multiwindow situation was also slower for rereading the text to answer questions because of unfamiliarity with the skills for window manipulation. But for the experienced users, having multiple overlapping windows allowed faster access to more text, and the window title bars probably helped in locating previously seen information in the deck-of-cards window layout used in this experiment.

Considering the two very different conclusions about whether multiple windows help people relocate information, this study also demonstrates the importance of using a group of test subjects who are representative of the intended users of the system. In this case, one can probably assume that most users will be familiar with multiwindow interfaces if they have a personal computer or workstation using such an interface. But for systems to be used by the general population, one should probably pay more attention to the results from the novice subjects in this study.

The impact of system response time on users' browsing behavior was studied by Patterson and Egido [1987], who found that users (not so surprisingly) solved problems faster when the system response time was fast but also that they looked at more nodes before making decisions to change the active set of objects they were browsing in the image database (1.6 vs. 1.0 nodes on average). Patterson and Egido do not know whether the users made *better* decisions because they looked at more nodes, but they do conclude that response time affects the way information is collected to make a decision to the extent that users explore more when it can be done faster.

Hypertext vs. Scrolling Text Files

Hypertext should be compared with traditional means of accessing text on a computer. This method is mainly scrolling text files in ordinary word processors, and Monk et al. [1988] performed such an experiment with the comprehension of the text of a Pascal program. They found that the subjects performed faster with the traditional scrolling files than with a hypertext system (13.2 min. vs. 18.3 min. to answer 15 questions about the program). The hypertext system they originally used did not include an overview diagram of the structure of the information base, so they conducted a simple follow-up experiment by drawing such a diagram by hand and pasting it to the computer used in the experiment. This addition improved the performance with the hypertext system to 13.0 min. so that it was slightly better than the scrolling text file. Of course there are two problems with this experiment. One is that by using an added paper diagram to simulate hypertext overview diagrams, they actually also simulated using a larger screen, which is normally seen as an advantage in itself. Secondly, the improved performance may not have been due to any advantage of overview diagrams in hypertext in general, but could instead be based on the specific advantage an overview of a program structure gives in comprehending that program. So the overview may help with this specific task but not with others.

A different kind of comparison was made by Gordon et al. [1988]. They used a hypertext system that is not named in the paper but seems to be a home-made design somewhat similar to Hyperties but with fewer browsing facilities. They tested four existing magazine articles, two on general interest topics ("Falling in Love" and "Reverse Sterilization") and two on technical topics ("Attentional Factors in Jet Aircraft Crashes" and "Speech Synthesis and Recognition"). Subjects read the articles on a computer screen using either a hypertext format or the original linear format and were then asked to recall as many concepts as possible from the article. Readers of general interest articles performed significantly worse on the hypertext system than on the linear file system (17% vs. 31% of concepts recalled) while readers of the technical articles performed about the same (22% vs. 21% recall). The authors speculate that one reason for this difference could be that readers of technical material would apply more effort to learning the material while readers of general interest material would tend to be distracted by the hypertext system. Another reason for the poor performance of the general interest hypertext might have been that the text had been written for the linear format and was probably not well

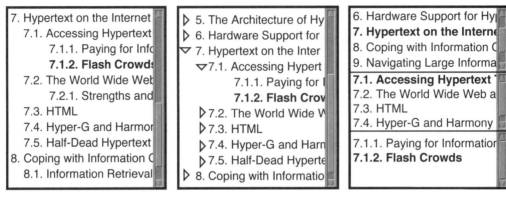

Figure 10.3. *Three different designs for tables of contents. The left design uses simple scrolling of one long ToC, the middle design uses expansion and contraction (similar to the operations found in outliners), and the right design uses a multipane display. The three designs are described further in [Chimera and Shneiderman 1994]. Also note that the exact graphics used by Chimera and Shneiderman were different from the ones used in this conceptual diagram.*

suited to being split up into smaller nodes of information while the technical texts might have been more structured, even if they too were originally written for the linear format. Furthermore, the subjects in the experiment had not received any training in the use of the hypertext system, which in itself would be enough to make them more negative towards it.

Chimera and Shneiderman [1994] studied the three different designs for tables of contents shown in Figure 10.3 to see whether scrolling lists were better or worse than structured views. Subjects were asked to do nine different search tasks, using three different tables of content (two small ones with 118 and 174 elements and a large one with 1,296 elements). The average time to find a specific section in the table of contents was 63 seconds with the scrolling ToC and 41 and 42 seconds with the two structure-oriented ToC designs (expanding and multipane), respectively. The only task for which the scrolling list was fastest was "what is the title of Section 1.1?," so it seems safe to recommend the use of non-scrolling tables of content where information is shown and revealed as the user manipulates the various objects and their links.

Hypertext vs. Other Traditional Computer Systems

Information could be made available through a set of traditional menus instead of by hypertext. Shneiderman [1987a] studied access to a small data set through either Hyperties or a traditional menu selection system and found that subjects answered significantly more questions when using Hyperties than when using the menu system (15.2 vs. 12.2 questions answered in 15 min.). The subjects' subjective preferences were also significantly in favor of the hypertext system (5.9 vs. 4.2 on a 1–7 scale).

Since hypertext is very similar to the database concept, comparisons between hypertext and traditional, command-based database access are also of interest. Canter et al. [1985] compared the strategies with which users moved around in the data in a hypertext-like system and in a command-based database. They found that users visited about the same number of different nodes of data but that the hypertext users revisited these nodes more, leading to a lower proportion of different nodes visited to total number of nodes visited for the hypertext users (33% vs. 68% of all visits were to previously unvisited nodes). Hypertext users had significantly more rings (returning to a previously visited location) and spikes (returning by exactly retracing a backtrack path through the locations visited) in their navigation than did the command-based users (61 vs. 28 and 17 vs. 5). So Canter et al. conclude that users move through the same data in different ways when they gain hypertext-like access capabilities.

Some applications of hypertext are very similar to expert systems, and Peper et al. [1989] compared an internal IBM hypertext system to a commercial expert system shell for the representation of information needed to diagnose problems in a world-wide computer network. The same information was represented in both forms and tested with a set of sample problems to be solved by twelve users who were either involved in network problem determination or had had such responsibilities earlier in their careers. These test users solved 81% of the problems correctly when using the hypertext system compared to only 67% when using the expert system. Using the expert system was faster, however, with 4 min. per problem compared to 5 min. when using the hypertext system. When asked what systems they would prefer to use on the job, 50% of the subjects chose the hypertext system, and 25% chose the expert system. From the authoring perspective, Peper et al. claim that it is "a very simple task" to update the information in the hypertext system while it is "difficult" to maintain the knowledge base in the expert system. Unfortunately they give no further results from this aspect of comparing hypertext with expert systems except to note that the operators themselves were able to update the hypertext on the spot with annotations.

Hypertext vs. Paper

Perhaps the most important comparison is that between complete hypertext implementations of a set of information and a paper implementation of the same information in the form of a book or an article. Shneiderman [1987a] compared two versions of a set of historical articles taking up 138 pages in the printed version. The electronic version was implemented in Hyperties. When subjects answered questions for which the answer could be found at the start of an article, they did worse in Hyperties than on paper (42 sec. vs. 22 sec.), whereas they were only insignificantly slower when the answer was in the body of an article (58 sec. vs. 51 sec.) and took the same time when the answer had to be found by combining facts from two articles (107 sec. in both conditions). These results seem to indicate that hypertext is of some help in situations where the user has to jump around in the information, and that hypertext slows the user down in situations where the information can be found by a glance on a page.

Users' Subjective Judgments

I asked a group of computer science students to judge whether they would prefer having their manuals, their textbooks, and fiction available in an online form instead of in a printed form [Nielsen 1986]. The question was asked both for online systems including the possibility for user annotations (a form of hypertext) and for plain online text without an annotation feature. Users were asked to rate their agreement with the statement that the online system would be an advantage on a scale from 0 to 4 (disagree much, disagree a little, neutral, agree a little, agree much). We should note that the validity is fairly low when one asks people to rate the usefulness of systems with which they do not yet have any experience since people often change their minds once they have tried something. But users' preconceived opinions about hypertext are still of interest since they will determine the speed with which the new technology can penetrate the market. The group studied here (computer science students) is not typical of the general population, which will probably tend to be more negative towards technological innovations.

For the questions assuming a facility for user annotations, results showed that the students viewed online manuals as a big advantage and online textbooks as a small disadvantage, whereas online fiction was viewed as a very big disadvantage. Comparing the responses for questions about systems with and without an annotation facility shows that users found annotations to be a small advantage for online manuals and a big advantage for online textbooks, but not to be any advantage for online fiction.

In another study, Marchionini [1989] had sixteen high school students use the *Grolier's Academic American Encyclopedia* in both print form and electronic form. The subjects were then asked to compare the print and electronic encyclopedias. Half said that the electronic version was faster, three said that it contained more information than the printed version, and one said that it was more up to date. This result was in spite of the facts that the two versions of the encyclopedia actually contained the *same* text and that the subjects were measurably slower with the electronic version. This indicates some of the problems with subjective evaluations and the seductive qualities of novel technology.

Finding Information

Fox [1992] asked groups of user interface designers to select appropriate rules for a specific design project from a document with a large number of guidelines. When using a printed version of the document, the subjects selected 91% of the rules that had been determined to be appropriate. When using a hypertext version, they only selected 83%. One of the reasons for the poorer performance with the hypertext system may have been that users tried to avoid reading the full text and selected guidelines based on their titles to a great extent. The users selected more than five times as many guidelines based on title only when using the hypertext than when using the printed book. This result indicates the need to design information differently for the online medium than for printed text. For example, one might want to use illustrations to a greater extent or one might rewrite the body text to be shorter and thus less likely to be skipped.

Egan et al. [1989a; 1989b] have conducted tests of the use of a statistics book in a hypertext version in the SuperBook system and in its traditional printed version. The book was originally written with printed publication in mind, so it might be possible to design a version specifically for hypertext that would do better than the one tested here. Users were asked to find the answers to certain questions about statistics, which could be answered from the book, and they were timed. When key words from the question were words occurring in the headings of the book, users performed best in the printed book (3.5 min. vs. 4.4 min.). This result is probably because queries using words from a book's headings match the author's structuring of the book pretty well. The typographical nature of the printed book also supports access to the text in that structure in the form of quick scanning of the table of contents and running headings when flipping through the pages of the book. When the relevant page has been found, it is easy to locate the subheading that starts the section the user is to read.

The situation was the opposite, however, when the questions used words that did occur in the running text of the book but not in its headings. Then the online version was faster (4.3 min. vs. 7.5 min.), probably because it included a full text index.

Egan et al. also measured whether the users gave correct responses to the questions and found that the hypertext version was better than the printed book. The users were then asked to write an essay based on the book, and those essays were graded by an impartial judge who was not informed about what version of the book each writer of an essay had used. These ratings were significantly higher for the hypertext version (5.8 vs. 3.6 on a 7-point scale). To investigate why users performed better even when it came to the contents of the book, Egan et al. conducted another experiment [1989a]. They identified a number of key facts about statistics that ought to be represented in an essay of the type the subjects had been asked to write. The essays were then scored for any mentioning of these facts, and it turned out that there were more facts in the essays written by hypertext users (8.8 vs. 6.0 out of 15). Upon closer analysis, it turned out that most of the difference in number of facts could be seen by looking at just three facts that were discussed in the same single paragraph of the statistics book. The hypertext users included almost all of these so-called "discriminating facts" in their essays whereas the paper book users included rather few (2.7 vs. 1.2 out of 3).

Egan et al. then videotaped users while they read the book and wrote the essays to find out why users of the paper book did not find the discriminating facts. All the users in both conditions actually looked at the page containing the critical section of text with the discriminating facts. The problem with the printed version was that it did not specifically highlight the critical section any differently from the rest of the page and this section appeared approximately two-thirds of the way down the page. The hypertext system, in contrast, highlighted the user's search terms, thus pointing out that the critical section contained something of special relevance.

The results reported here were derived from studies of a revised version of SuperBook. Egan et al. [1989c] have also reported results from conducting the same studies with the original version of SuperBook. The redesign was done on the basis of observations from usability studies of the first version, and the results show that the revised version was indeed the best, since the mean search time for answering all types of questions was 5.4 min. with the revised version and 7.6 min. with the original. The proportion of correct responses to the questions also rose (75% vs. 69%).

The value of iterative design was confirmed by studies of a hypertext version of a Sherlock Holmes encyclopedia, HyperHolmes [Instone et al. 1993; Mynatt et al. 1992]. When using the initial hypertext user interface, users spent 236 seconds answering questions about Sherlock Holmes, which was slower than the paper version of the encyclopedia where the same tasks only took 201 seconds. When using a user interface revised based on the usability problems found in the first user test, users were able to perform the test tasks in 178 seconds. The users' accuracy in answering the questions was also improved.

The initial version of HyperHolmes is shown in Figure 10.4 and the redesign is shown in Figure 10.5. One obvious difference between the versions is that version 1 used overlapping windows whereas version 2 used tiled windows which are known to be faster for many tasks [Bly and Rosenberg 1986]. The outgoing links tool in version 1 was not really needed since all links were indicated by capitalized words in the primary window. In order to simplify the interface, the outgoing links tool could therefore be removed from version 2. The interface was also simplified by removing features from the search system. Users were originally provided with the option to search for word beginnings, whole words, contiguous words, or exact strings, but if the users' first search was unsuccessful they typically gained nothing by spending additional time changing these options. Thus, by removing features, the designers followed the "less is more" design principle: fewer search options may lead users to try more different search terms and therefore lead them to find more relevant material. A final change was to elevate the overview node to landmark status and provide direct access to it from an icon on the screen. In the first version, users could only get to the overview by first going to the home page.

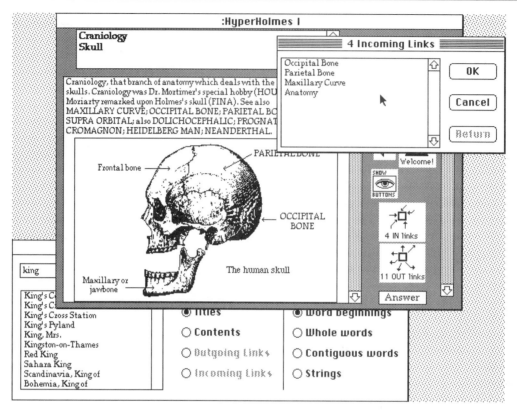

Figure 10.4. *HyperHolmes version 1. Copyright © 1993 by Bowling State University, reprinted by permission.*

Use of Hypertext in Education

Catano [1979] used one of the first hypertext systems, FRESS, to teach poetry. Results were measured by giving students a poem for analysis in essays that were graded by an external evaluator. This test was done both before and after the class, and for students in both a class using the hypertext system and a class taught by the same teacher using printed materials. The ability of students to analyze poems increased slightly more for the students taking the hypertext class (1.2 vs. 1.0 points). When the experiment was repeated the following year, the hypertext class improved less than the regular class, however (1.4 vs. 2.5 points), so this study is not conclusive. In any case, this study of a pioneering system may not be indicative for the current generation of modern hypertext

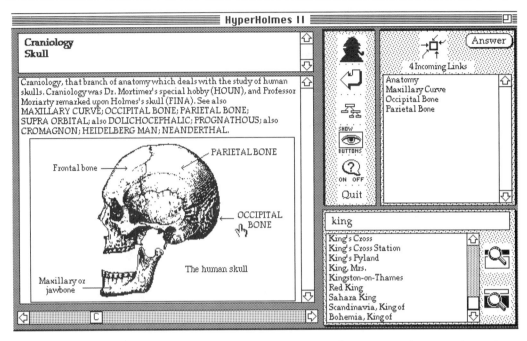

Figure 10.5. *HyperHolmes version 2. Copyright © 1993 by Bowling State University, reprinted by permission.*

systems. The study is interesting, however, because it actually tried to measure what students learned from using a hypertext system while comparing them with a control group taught by the same teacher using traditional materials.

In a newer study, Christel [1994] compared two versions of a hypermedia course in code inspection. The course included several recordings of meetings and other aspects of the method where the student could interact with simulated participants in a software project. One version used full-motion video (30 frames per second) and the other version presented the same sound but only one image every 4 seconds (using a slide-show design). After the course the students were asked to identify information that had been taught, and students who had seen the full-motion video did significantly better than students who had used the slide show interface. The full-motion users remembered 89% of the information and the slide-show users only remembered 71% of the information. This study indicates that higher-quality visuals may indeed help instructional hypermedia perform better.

The use of the Perseus Project hypertext to teach classics (see Chapter 4) has been subjected to intensive evaluation studies [Marchionini and Crane 1994], with data collected from 12 courses with a total of 640 students. Most of the courses were evaluated by observation and by interviews with the professors and students. For example, one student praised the use of hypermedia during lectures and noted: "If we are talking about a certain site and [the instructor] can put a picture of the site up behind him, it makes his explanation much clearer; and it is something that you can remember more than just what he said." Other students complained about some confusion stemming from the concurrent activities in lectures where the instructor would both talk and access Perseus. Observations of students reading Greek texts in Perseus indicated that looking up words took about the same time whether it was done on the system or manually in a dictionary but that the students could use the time while the system analyzed the text to reread or read ahead.

These interviews and observations are qualitative and do not indicate whether the students actually performed better with Perseus. A comparative study was conducted where students were asked to write essays about the ancient Greeks' concept of honor. Students using Perseus used 22 citations on the average, whereas students without access to the hypertext used 15 citations on the average. The use of hypertext thus promoted student use of quotations and references to the primary texts, which is desirable in the field of classics. Also, other statistics showed that students using Perseus developed their arguments from a wider range of texts than students who did not have access to Perseus. The same assignment had been given in earlier years (before the introduction of Perseus), and essays from those students contained 16 citations on the average. The fact that the results were essentially the same from pre-Perseus students and from students in the Perseus class who did not have access to Perseus is promising for the ability to conduct comparative research on educational use of hypertext without having to teach completely differently courses.

As a final measure of the educational value of Perseus three professors were asked to grade essays from students who had been given Perseus and from students who had not been given Perseus. The professors did not know what essays were written by which students, and the two groups of students received the same grades. Thus, the bottom line seemed to be that Perseus added something to the students' experience but did not result in a better end product (at least not if you believe that exam results are the best measure of education).

Field Studies

The main difference between field studies and laboratory studies is that field users use the system for a real-world reason (not because an experimenter has set up the system for them to try) to solve self-defined tasks (rather than tasks defined by the experimenter). Since one of the main ideas behind hypertext is to empower users to navigate an information space according to their own individual wishes and at their own speed, it is important to look at people using hypertexts in their own natural environments.

Nielsen and Lyngbæk [1990] had users read a hypertext document in Guide on their own time and report back on the usability of the three forms of hypertext used in Guide. On the question whether the hypertext facility was easy to understand, the Guide note button (used for pop-up) and replacement button (used for in-line hierarchical expansion) scored significantly higher than the reference button (used for goto): 1.5 vs. 1.5 vs. 2.2 on a 1–5 scale with 1 being best. On the question whether the hypertext facility improved the document, the note button scored significantly better than the replacement and reference buttons (2.0 vs. 2.5 vs. 2.8). So these users view the reference goto button as the poorest form for hypertext support and the note pop-up button as the best.

Conklin and Begeman [1988] had 32 people use the gIBIS hypertext tool for one year to build argumentation structures about various design decisions. gIBIS uses typed links between nodes, and for links to nodes commenting on a previous position there was a strong trend to having more of the type "supports" than of the type "objects to" (450 vs. 190), so users like to be positive towards their colleagues.

Many aspects of system use can be observed only in the field. Baird et al. [1988] observed the use of the *Glasgow Online* hypertext, which was made available to the general public at the Glasgow Garden Festival where about 500 people looked at it, corresponding to 11% of the total number of visitors to the university pavilion where it was displayed. Of these 500 people, about 70 were young people of 20 years of age or less, while about 430 were older than 20 years. Yet, of the about 50 people who went from the passive status of looking at the system to the active status of actually using it, about 32 came from the small, younger group and only 17 came from the much larger, older group.

The ultimate field studies look at the impact of the hypertext on the users' performance in the real world task, which is their reason for having the hypertext system in the first place. Unfortunately, very few such studies exist, possibly because hypertext systems have not been used all that much for real tasks yet. Nielsen and Lyngbæk [1990] studied children in a kindergarten who played with the interactive fiction *Inigo Gets Out* (see Figures 9.18 and 9.19) and found that they enjoyed doing so. For this system, enjoyment is its reason for existing, so it must be said to have been successful. Unfortunately, we could not *measure* the children's enjoyment on a quantitative scale.

Peter Brown [Brown 1989b] has reported on the use of Guide at the British computer company ICL for the task of diagnosing the fault when a customer calls ICL for service. This task is called "laundering" and is used to determine whether or not a visit by a repair technician is needed and what spare parts the technician should bring to the customer site. Making the right diagnosis therefore has real financial implications since it is expensive to send technicians bringing the wrong spare parts or to discover some trivial problem that the customers could have corrected themselves. It turned out that the proportion of customer calls handled correctly was 68% when the launderers used a paper representation of the information and 88% when they used hypertext (rising to 92% after six weeks of use).

Individual Differences

The users' level of expertise will have a large impact on how they use the system. Tombaugh et al. [1987] had users answer questions about texts that were displayed in several windows on a screen. Users who had been given just 30 minutes of practice in manipulating the very simple window system performed much better even at the end of a 90 minute experiment than users who had started the experiment as complete novices with regard to windows (50 sec. vs. 85 sec. to answer each question about the text).

In a study of an online engineering manual, Joseph et al. [1989] found that users changed their relative frequency of use of the various access mechanisms as they became more experienced. On the first day of using the online manual, users would use the table of contents quite a lot (20% of their information access was through the table of contents). This volume was probably because of their expectations based on having used similar engineering manuals in paper form. But the online table of contents was not very usable in this system because it displayed only chapter names and not the section listings that are found in the printed manual's table of contents. Going by the names of the chapters alone, information about arch bridges could have been in at least three of the chapters listed, and users selecting chapters from a table of contents actually made the wrong choices 80% of the time. Because of this poor experience, users changed to using the table of contents for only 5% of their information access on the third day of using the system.

Some people are more active in discussions than others, whether due to motivation, knowledge of the field, energy, extroverted nature, or whatever. In a study of the use of the gIBIS hypertext system for shared group-wide discussion of design issues, Conklin and Begeman [1988] found a huge individual variability in the number of hypertext nodes created by various users. Discussion group B had only two participants, and one created 190 nodes while the other created only 30. Discussion group A had four participants, and the most active created 221 nodes whereas the second most active participant created only 22. In the other discussion groups studied, the variability was less extreme but still very large.

Campagnoni and Ehrlich [1989] tested the Help Viewer online help system for the Sun*386i.* The subjects were given a standard test of spatial visualization ability, which showed that users with higher visualization scores needed less time to locate the answers to the questions, mostly because they had less need to return to the top level table of contents. This result indicates that users with good visualization abilities were better able to construct a conceptual model of the structure of the information space. There was a good regression fit between visualization scores and performance in the use of the hypertext system (correlation 0.75), indicating that people with high visualization scores could answer a given set of questions in 700 seconds while people with poor visualization scores needed 1,350 seconds.

Just being fatigued can change a user's work. As mentioned above, Wilkinson and Robinshaw [1987] had subjects proofread a traditional text file from computer screens continuously over periods of one hour and found that performance was significantly better during the first ten minutes than during the last ten minutes (error rate 25% vs. 39%).

Conclusions about Benchmark Studies

One of the very interesting questions one could ask about these studies is whether hypertext is in fact any good. The answer is simply, "It depends," since it seems that some studies indicate advantages to hypertext while others indicate disadvantages. It depends on the hardware and system software used, it depends on the design of the hypertext system, and it depends very much on the user's task and individual characteristics.

It is also interesting to consider the most extreme ratios between the conditions studied. The unqualified winner is the factor of more than 11 for proportion of young people compared to the proportion of older people who went from looking at Glasgow Online to actually using it. This difference between the two age groups of more than an order of magnitude makes all the 20% to 50% differences so carefully measured in other studies pale in comparison. This indication of the importance of age in the acceptance of new technology is a lesson we should take seriously, especially when considering that most of the studies reported here have been conducted with young college students as subjects.

Non-Benchmark Studies

Several studies of hypertext usability have avoided coming up with measurable comparisons of two or more conditions. This avoidance has typically been either because only a single system has been tested or because qualitative approaches have been judged more relevant for the purpose of the study.

Users' Conceptual Models of Domain Knowledge

Teshiba and Chignell [1988] measured the fit between the structure of students' conceptual model of the U.S. Constitution and related issues and an ideal model of this domain generated by experts. The models were found by having the students sort cards with various terms by perceived similarity into piles that they grouped hierarchically. The hierarchies generated by the students were then compared with the ideal hierarchy by Hubert's [1978, 1979] gamma measure of proximity between two hierarchies, and the authors found that this proximity measure increases slightly (but not significantly) over time with the use of the hypertext. These results are actually useless for an assessment of the usability of the authors' hypertext system since we do not know whether a larger increase would have resulted from having the students spend the same time on studying constitutional issues in a more traditional way. But the paper is interesting because it shows a way to measure the conceptual model-building effect of using hypertexts.

Logging User Interactions

Computer systems can be instrumented to monitor automatically users' interaction behavior. The advantages of this approach are that no human experimenter is needed to collect the data, that the data is collected unobtrusively without influencing the user's working style (but with the associated problems relating to privacy), and that because of these two characteristics data can be collected in the field and over long periods of time.

Some studies exist of logging data from hypertext. Egan et al. [1989a] logged readers' use of the SuperBook system in their study discussed above of why more facts were found by SuperBook readers than by readers of a printed book. In a typical use of logging data, Egan et al. [1989c] used knowledge of which operations users performed frequently to improve the average response times of SuperBook by tuning a redesigned version. Yoder et al. [1984] logged the use of the ZOG system on board the aircraft carrier USS *Carl Vinson* to determine which tasks the users performed with the system and what errors they made. Since ZOG (now known as KMS) is strictly frame-based, it was easy to record the time spent by users at each node in the hypertext as a set of discrete data. This approach is somewhat harder in hypertext systems based on the scrolling file paradigm.

Shneiderman et al. [1989] logged the navigation behavior of users of Hyperties at three museums. One information base was used at two of the museums and another information base was used at the third. A computer with an information base on the photographer David Seymour was exhibited at both the International Center for Photography and the B'nai B'rith Klutznick Museum, and a total of 734 user sessions were logged. It was possible for users to start from the welcome screen by reading either an introductory article or by going to the index. At both museums, about 80% of the users started by reading the introductory article, and of these users about 50% then went directly on to the index from the introductory article rather than following the hypertext links leading out from the introduction. For the approximately 20% of the users who went to the index first, the most popular article to select from the index was an article about Israel for the visitors to the B'nai B'rith Klutznick Museum and an article about the photographer for visitors to the International Center for Photography, thus showing that different groups of users may access an information base in different ways.

Shneiderman et al.'s third study logged 4,461 user sessions with an information base about archaeology at the Smithsonian Institution. The list of articles (Hyperties nodes) sorted by frequency of access was topped by most of the articles mentioned in the introductory article, indicating that a listing in such a central location is a good way to attract user attention. The list of articles accessed by selection from the index indicated a strong preference for articles having names in the beginning of the alphabet: Of the 20 top articles, 18 had names beginning with A, B, or C, probably revealing that the index mechanism was not very usable since it was long and arranged alphabetically instead of by topic. Shneiderman et al. also comment that the very names of articles (which are used as anchors in Hyperties) seemed to impact their popularity among users who were most attracted to articles with names indicating that they contained specific information. Finally, Shneiderman et al. comment that they actually got the most useful information for their own design of the hypertext interface from more informal observations of the users and not from the logging data.

Nielsen and Lyngbæk [1990] studied the use of nonverbal interactive fiction by children in a kindergarten. A Macintosh running the hyperstory *Inigo Gets Out* was made available for the children for a day where the computer logged all the mouse clicks made by the children while navigating the artificial world of the story. For the analysis of this data, we had the computer draw diagrams of the screens that graphically showed where the users had clicked. An example is shown in Figure 9.19. This data representation provided much more insight into the usability of the hyperstory than a more statistically oriented analysis of the data, but this advantage is of course partly based on the graphic nature of the user interface being studied.

Observing Users

Several studies have been conducted using various variations of observation or thinking aloud methods. Hardman [1989b] studied the usability of *Glasgow Online* using the thinking-aloud methodology and found several problems in its user interface. Most of these problems were actually more related to traditional issues in human-computer interaction, such as readable screen design. But some of Hardman's observations are directly related to the hypertext nature of *Glasgow Online*. She found that users had problems using the "next" operation because it was based on a confused linking paradigm. She also found that many users did not use the backtrack facility but instead started all over from the welcome screen and retraced their path through the information base. This preference was probably because backtrack is inconsistently implemented in *Glasgow Online*.

Iterative Interface Refinement

Current practice in usability engineering [Whiteside et al. 1988; Nielsen 1989c, 1993a] is to refine user interfaces iteratively since one cannot design them exactly right the first time around [Nielsen 1993c].

One example of a usability study that can be used for such a purpose is Hardman's [1989a] evaluation of the understandability of the icons used in *Glasgow Online* to denote various services at hotels in a manner similar to many guidebooks. When test subjects went through the hypertext in the study discussed above, Hardman stopped them when they first reached a screen showing information about a particular hotel (where the hotel service icons were found) and asked them to tell her how they would interpret each of the icons. For each subject she then made a list of the icons guessed correctly as well as the icons the subject could not guess or guessed wrongly. For example, one user thought that an icon showing a globe of the earth meant that the hotel offered facilities for exchanging foreign currency whereas it actually was intended to mean that the hotel had conference facilities (presumably the idea was to induce an association with international meetings). Several other users believed that an icon showing a pineapple meant that the hotel had fresh fruit in the rooms or that it served fresh fruit, whereas the intention was to indicate that the hotel catered to special diets (such as vegetarians).

This information about wrong guesses can be very useful when it comes to redesigning icons to reduce the probability for mistakes. One would especially want to redesign icons where some users make disastrously wrong guesses. Hardman also accumulated the number of correct and wrong guesses for each icon to a list indicating their overall understandability. One would also want to redesign those icons where many subjects made wrong guesses, even if none of the guesses were disastrous.

Many of the other studies discussed in this chapter have also been conducted with the purpose of allowing the experimenters to refine the next version of their system.

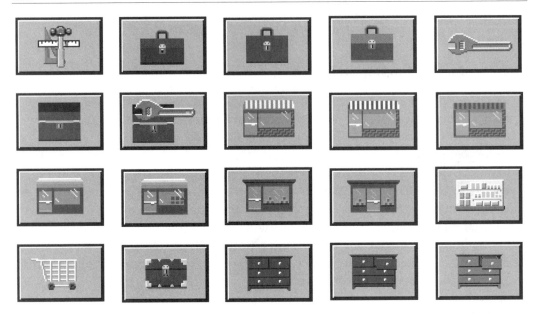

Figure 10.6. *Darrell Sano and I had to go through twenty iterations of icons for the concept of special-purpose applications in the design of the SunWeb user interface.*

Figure 10.6 shows an extreme example of iterative design from the development of the SunWeb user interface [Nielsen and Sano 1994]. SunWeb is a WWW interface to internal information for Sun's employees. One of the concepts we wanted represented in the interface was "special-purpose applications." In total, we designed twenty versions of this icon: seven tool metaphor icons, nine shopping metaphor icons (including a shopping cart and a grocery shelf), and four "application chest" icons. In order to produce our many different designs, ideas were gleaned from a thesaurus, a visual dictionary, and catalogs of international signs and symbols.

For user testing, we simply showed our initial icons to four users without labels and asked the users to tell us what they thought each icon represented. Our initial toolbox icon (number 2 in Figure 10.6) was interpreted as a briefcase by most users, so we opened it up and added a monkey wrench. This redesign worked and users in later studies had no problems recognizing the icon as a toolbox. Unfortunately, the tool metaphor was too strong and users associated a very large number of additional concepts with this icon with the comment that "oh, this is a tool." Essentially, almost any concept that represented an

Original Icon	Intended Meaning	Test Users' Reactions	Final Icon
	Human Resources and Benefits	Health field, money, health care is expensive, Clinton's health plan, hospital, don't know, benefits	
	What's New	Bulletin board, bulletin board, bulletin board, laundry	
	Product Catalog	System oriented, disk, CD, computer, CD-ROM, CD-ROM	
	World Wide Web	Networking on a world scale, map, location, dimensions of the planet, networking around the world, geography, global	

Table 10.1. *Some examples of minor icon changes in the user interface Darrell Sano and I did for SunWeb.*

executable program was considered a tool. An example was the expense report application which should have been grouped with the travel icon but was often placed in the toolbox.

In order to use a weaker metaphor for the special-purpose applications, we next tried a shopping metaphor with icons showing a storefront. When we conducted an icon intuitiveness study and showed one of these icons to a user, he immediately said "this is a circuit board." This user happened to be an engineer, but since we do have a very large number of engineers in the user population for SunWeb, we decided to take this comment seriously and redesigned the icon. This is an example where our judgment as user interface specialists was to rely on a result from a single user since we felt that this user's problems would be frequent in real use of the system.

We tried several alternative storefront and other shopping icons before realizing that a successful shopping icon would interfere with one of our other interface elements: the "product catalog" icon. Therefore, we dropped the application store as the metaphor and we finally settled on the "application chest" icon shown as the last icons in Figure 10.6.

Not all of the icons in Figure 10.6 were subjected to user testing. Many were designed simply as alternatives to try out various ways of representing the

Figure 10.7. *Sample snapshot from a design session using large-scale paper mock-ups of windows, icons, and possible content. The photo was taken with a digitizing camera (an Apple QuickTake) that directly produced an image file that could be uploaded to a Sparc Server for online distribution to team members immediately after the meeting.*

same idea. For example, we feel that the chest icon was made better by pulling out a drawer but we never collected user data to prove this. Many smaller design decisions have to be made on the basis of the experience and gut feeling of the designers.

We did not always have to make that many changes in our icons. Table 10.1 shows some of the icons where user testing revealed very few problems. Our company benefits icon may have been too much oriented toward the cost of the benefits (with the money bag) but all users understood it or interpreted it as something closely related to its meaning. One user did misunderstand the bulletin board icon for "what's new" but we kept it the same except for minor color changes. One should not always take action based on results from a single user, and this is a good example of such a case where we overruled a user.

Sometimes minor changes can improve the usability of an interface. I often say that "details matter" in user interfaces. In our first product catalog icon, the image of the CD-ROM stood out too much and dominated the users' replies. After this observation, we changed the visual balance in the icon and made the computer screen more prominent with a darker color.

In order to be able to get early results from user testing, it is often a good idea to produce mock-ups of the design in the form of paper prototypes. As shown in Figure 10.7, paper prototypes are also useful in design sessions because of their flexibility and it is possible to use photos of large screen mock-ups to communicate design ideas widely before any running systems exists. For multimedia products, prototypes often require some form of video or other time-varying media, but since these are often very expensive to produce, they are normally not available early in a project. An alternative approach that is used often in the advertising industry is to rely on so-called ripomatic footage from earlier productions. Even though video from other titles will not give exactly the impression you are after, there is still often an advantage to being able to show some moving images in a prototype.

The Larger Picture

Among the benchmark studies we see that individual differences have the largest impact on the performance when using hypertext systems. Another major factor is the different tasks users have when they use hypertext systems. These two issues are absolutely the most important when is comes to measuring hypertext usability.

One should take care not to identify usability evaluation with quantitative benchmark studies only, since we have seen that many of the most interesting insights leading to improved hypertext user interfaces have come from more qualitative observational studies.

11.   Multimedia Authoring

Unfortunately, even though you can easily get some ideas about hypertext authoring from your experience as a hypertext reader, we face the general problem that people have not learned how to structure information in hypertext networks the same way they have learnt to write linear reports through writing endless numbers of essays in school. Early experience with the use of NoteCards [Trigg and Irish 1987] indicated the need to give users a "strategy manual" about the design of hypertext networks and the useful conventions they might respect. Just giving users the four types of NoteCards objects and letting them loose was not enough.

Some advice for authors of hypertexts comes from our understanding of the reading situation. For example it is a good idea to keep each node focused on a single topic to make it easier to understand and recognize in overview diagrams, history lists, etc. Having a single topic for each node also makes it easier for the author to know what links to construct. The key things to remember for hypertext authoring is modularize, modularize, modularize.

Because we know that reading speed is slower from screens than from paper, we need to make hypertext nodes shorter than paper articles. The very nature of hypertext helps the author achieve this goal because subsidiary topics, definitions, etc. need not be elaborated in the primary text. One should construct additional nodes to hold this information.

One general strategy is to be critical of the links and to avoid adding every possible link between remotely related concepts. A "clean structure" is easier for users to navigate and many hypertext systems allow the readers to add extra links if they really want them. Remember that it is an author's job to set priorities for the readers (even in hypertext).

I would expect that our knowledge of what constitutes good hypertexts will build as we see more examples of what works or does not work, and maybe even some reviews of well-authored hypertext documents [Nielsen et al. 1991b]. Eventually students might learn hypertext authoring in schools just as they currently learn essay writing, and the problem will go away. For the short term, the best recommendation probably is to pay close attention to the authoring principles implicit in other writers' hypertext and try to emulate the principles you like.

Usability for Authors

It is important to keep in mind that the users who require usable systems are not just the end-users but also the authors who develop the hypertext structures read by these end-users. For some tasks, such as brainstorm support, the readers and the writers are the same people, and certain hypertext systems provide exactly the same user interface for readers and writers. But in many cases, extra facilities are available for information authors, and it is important to ensure the usability of these facilities. Unfortunately, the authoring of hypertext has been even less studied than the reading of hypertext.

One example of an authoring facility is the list of dangling references in Hyperties [Shneiderman 1989] showing links not yet completed by the author. Based on personal experience with developing a hypertext structure in a system *without* such a facility [Nielsen 1989a, 1990b], I am convinced of the need for a dangling reference facility in an authoring system. But this kind of personal experience does not indicate the best way of implementing such a facility or of integrating it with the rest of the system.[1] And to evaluate the usefulness of more advanced or complex types of authoring support, purely personal opinions may not suffice.

Other evidence from informal studies indicates a severe problem with premature structuring [Halasz 1988] because many hypertext systems force the author to structure the information at too early a stage. A simple example is the need to enter a name for a new node before one even knows what it will really be about [Walker 1988b]. This latter problem can be alleviated by a "rename" command that also automatically updates all links. The very distribution of the information over nodes may be harder to change even

---

[1] There are several reasons why a hypertext system might allow (but manage) dangling links and not just prevent them completely from being authored. First, the author might want to refer to future materials before they have been written, and second, one of the users of a multiuser writing system might be editing a part of a hypertext without having access to the whole [Grønbæk and Trigg 1994].

though it is also likely that authors will change their way of thinking about the domain as they write.

In a study of authors revising their works, Haas [1989] asked the test subjects to think aloud, and counted the proportion of their utterances that referred to the editing medium itself rather than to the text being edited. This proportion was only 3% when they used paper but 8% on a mouse-based workstation and a whopping 21% on a keyboard-based personal computer, thus indicating that the use of pen and paper was significantly more transparent even though the test users all had at least four years of computer experience. This study points out the importance of having as transparent authoring tools as possible so that authors are allowed to focus on the task of communicating their domain knowledge to the readers.

Unfortunately hardly any studies exist of the usability of authoring interfaces, possibly because they are harder to study. For a reading interface, specific tasks can be set and one can measure how fast readers solve these tasks. It is also fairly easy to assess how much the readers have learnt by asking them questions about the content of the information. But for writers, we need to assess the quality of the information they create and this judgment is very hard to make as long as we do not have a firm understanding of what makes a good hypertext structure in the first place. A fully valid test would probably need to measure the usability of authoring facilities by having several authors create information bases that would then be measured in use by groups of end-users. This approach leads to exorbitant requirements for end-user test subjects and is probably infeasible in almost all cases.

An alternative is to follow the Hansen and Haas [1988] test of letter writing with various screen sizes (discussed in Chapter 10) and have judges evaluate the quality of the result of the authors' work. This is easier to do as long as the result is linear texts, which we are used to judging, but work on heuristic evaluation techniques for hypertexts could lead to the possibility for also judging non-linear texts such as was done informally by Nielsen [1990a] who evaluated the usability of three systems by using various usability heuristics such as the need for consistent backtracking, history facilities, and support for navigational dimensions.

A field study [Kerr 1989] of the working style of designers doing everyday production of videotex frames showed that, over time, designers tend to be bored since most routine frame creation work is not very interesting. The study revealed a conflict over the place of individual creativity in videotex work where the designers chafe at restrictions imposed by managers because using the hardware and software in unusual and exploratory ways is a principal motivation in designers' daily work.

In contrast, Shneiderman [1989], in his discussion of the lessons learnt from building more then thirty hypertext structures for Hyperties, emphasized the key lesson that each project was different and had to have its information structured according to a principle that was suited for its specific domain. Shneiderman's experience also showed, however, that it is necessary to have a single managing editor to coordinate a project and to copy edit the final result. So there is certainly the potential for tension among the people whose work it will be to create future, large information bases. Just as software developers may feel frustrated by user interface standards restricting their design options, information base developers may be frustrated by having to place consistency over their individual creativity. One hopes that the unique individual needs of each project will provide enough variation to keep this problem to a minimum, but only further experience can tell.

Separate Interfaces for Writers

The fundamental question in relation to hypertext authoring is whether there should be a separate interface to the hypertext for the writers or whether all users should share the same interface.

Several hypertext systems are based on the principle that "readers" also need to write. KMS has no specific reading or writing modes but allows users to add text or links to any frame at any time. This approach eliminates the need for users to remember what mode they are in or to understand the difference between the commands and data representations available in the two modes.

Other systems do allow both reading and writing but in slightly different modes. For example, HyperCard includes a "user level" mechanism that can be set to several different values, allowing more or less radical changes to the document. One of these user levels is a browse-only mode without any authoring capabilities. Even when the user level is set allow authoring, the author needs to enter special modes to add new buttons or fields to a card. The advantage of this approach is to reduce complexity in each of the modes because they can be optimized for a single task. Users maintain the possibility of changing the document, but they do not risk doing so inadvertently.

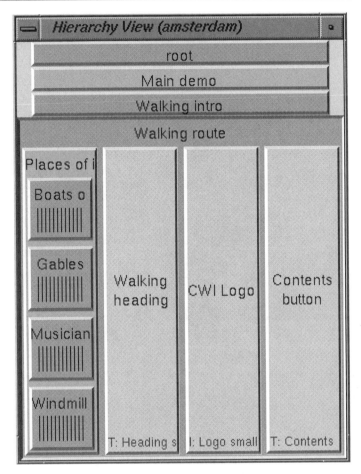

Figure 11.1. *Authoring interface for manipulating complex time-dependent hypermedia structures [Hardman et al 1993]. Copyright © 1994 by CWI, reprinted by permission.*

Finally, a few hypertext systems including the Symbolics Document Examiner and Hyperties provide separate authoring environments, typically because they want to provide extremely simple interfaces for their readers.

The basic model of the WWW is that information on any given site should be authored solely by users at that site. Thus, most of the WWW is a read-only hypertext from the individual user's perspective. Since users often do want to contribute beyond reading, some WWW sites have included functionality that allows readers to add comments and annotations to the basic

Figure 11.2. *Initial view of the hypertext node generated by the structure in Figure 11.1. Copyright © 1994 by CWI, reprinted by permission.*

information on the site. Examples include HotWired and Time Warner's WWW sites, both of which have a letters-to-the-editor-like annotation facility. Hyper-G is based on an access right model, meaning that users with the appropriate rights can even add or edit documents and/or links, on remote sites across the Internet, thus providing a unified system for writers and (some of the) readers.

When authoring a traditional, text-only, hypertext it is easy for the author to specify what should happen as a link is followed. Indeed, normally the author does not specify link actions explicitly but leaves it to the presentation engine to remove the departure node and replace it with the destination node. In time-dependent hypermedia, however, the situation is somewhat more complex. The simplest case again involves removing the departure node and

Walking through the city

The canal houses are famous for their distinctive and
De grachtenpanden zijn beroemd ...

contents   musicians

Figure 11.3. *View of the hypertext node generated by the structure in Figure 11.1. This screenshot was taken while the "Gables" subnode was playing. Note how most of the screen elements are identical to Figure 11.2 because the specification in Figure 11.1 keeps most of the node constant. Copyright © 1994 by CWI, reprinted by permission.*

stopping whatever film, sound clips, etc. were playing there. Even in this simple case, the author will have to specify what should happen upon arrival at the destination node: should the system start playing any video and sound clips immediately or should it give the users a chance to look over the node and orient themselves before they start the multimedia presentation (for example by clicking on a "play" button)?

In more complex hypermedia presentations, a node may contain several components, and links may only affect some of them. For example, Figures 11.1 to 11.3 show various views of a composite node with components of several different media types [Hardman et al. 1993]. The node title in the upper left and the logo in the upper right are kept constant, as is the "contents" button in the lower left. The fact that these three components are displayed throughout is indicated in the authoring view in Figure 11.1 by having the boxes that represent them fill up the entire duration of the containing "walking route" box. The box for "places of interest," however, is split up into sub-boxes which is a way for the author to indicate that the components should replace each other. In the example in Figure 11.2, having the user click on the "gables" button would cause the picture in Figure 11.3 to appear. Also, the "gables" button would be replaced by a "musicians" button and the subtitles (and any background sounds) would change. All these changes are specified inside the smaller boxes for "Boats," "Gables," etc. in Figure 11.1, but the author would have to enlarge the boxes to see (and edit) that level of detail.

Hardman et al. [1993] introduce the notion of a context to define the part of a hypermedia presentation affected by following a link. In our example, the source context of the "gables" link is the button itself as well as the picture of the boats in the canal and the subtitles and the associated sound effects. This entire source context will be removed when the user follows the link and the destination context will be displayed. The destination context for the link might specify that the "gables" video clip should be displayed on the screen as a still image taken from a representative part of the film. The destination context for the link could also have specified the *first* frame of the video as the still picture to be displayed, or it might have specified that the video should start playing automatically upon arrival. The exact choice is an authoring decision, but the context concept and the associated authoring tools give the author the necessary framework for making those decisions.

Hierarchical views like Figure 11.1 will allow the author added control over the time-varying media found in many hypermedia works. Of course, one would normally not present this authoring information to the readers of the hypermedia since they will not need to modify the connections and constraints between media components, but authors do need this added overview of the composite nodes and their structure.

Concordia

The Symbolics writing environment was called Concordia [Walker 1988a] and was based on the premise that writers have different needs from readers. Also writers have more motivation for learning the hypertext tool itself, so they can be provided with a more full-featured but perhaps more complex user interface.

Concordia was a structure-oriented editor and gave writers templates [Catlin et al. 1991] for their nodes with special slots for standard information like keywords and section headings. It also managed meta-information for each node in addition to the text seen by the readers. This meta-information included auditing data (determining whether the text has been checked) as well as the writers' own notes for future versions. Even though the Symbolics Document Examiner had only one-directional links for the readers, Concordia provided bidirectional links for the writers in the form of a list of incoming links for the current node. This facility was included because writers needed to know what other nodes in the hypertext referred to the one they were working on in order to provide a decent "rhetoric of arrival" by making their text understandable in the context of the reader's potential navigation paths.

Concordia used a generic markup language to separate form from content in the text. A special "book design" database defined the appearance on the screen of the various text elements and enabled global formatting changes for the purpose of, say, going from a color screen to a monochrome screen. The structure oriented editor took care of inserting appropriate markup tags, but the writers also had a facility available to change the display to show the text in the final formatting readers would see under a given book design database.

Authoring Toolkits

A toolkit for hypertext authors should obviously first of all contain the basic tools needed by any writer, such as integrated spelling check and drawing packages for making good illustrations that can easily be modified. Unfortunately almost all current hypertext systems are monolithic programs and do not integrate well with the other facilities of the user's computational environment. This means, for example, that users need to construct illustrations in external graphics programs and import them to the hypertext, where they are considered static images. If an illustration has to be changed, the user has to reexport it back to the graphics program it came from and edit it there.

The lack of integration between stand-alone hypertext programs and the rest of the user's computational environment was one of the major user complaints in several surveys conducted by Leggett et al. [1990]. This sad state of affairs does not necessarily have to continue, however. There is some work being done on providing link services [Pearl 1989] to integrate all applications on a given computer, and that work could well prove to be a great help for the hypertext authoring interface also. Also, it is possible to retrofit hypertext capabilities onto existing document processing tools as was done with, e.g., the Microsoft Word Internet Assistant (an add-on to produce HTML files from Word documents).

The integration of traditional writing aids into hypertext authoring systems may be difficult in practice, but at least we know what to aim for. With respect to specialized tools for writing specifically hypertext, we are less well off because we do not yet know what to aim for.

There is an obvious need for tools to import text from other programs, whether they are other hypertext systems or more traditional text systems. Hypertext interchange is discussed further in Chapter 5, and the conversion from plain text to hypertext is discussed in Chapter 12.

Recommendations for hypertext authors would probably include the traditional advice: to begin with making a synopsis to structure the information in a top-down fashion. In real life, however, many authors seem to prefer a bottom-up approach of writing hypertext nodes as they think of them. This attitude has been found to be the case in a study of HyperCard authors [Nicol 1988] who mostly worked in a "button-up" manner of constructing their hypertext one button (link) at a time.

Because of this phenomenon there is a need for authoring tools to help writers structure their hypertext after the fact. As mentioned above, Hyperties has a nice facility for keeping track of dangling links. Other tools to help the author understand the emerging network would include the overview diagrams that many systems already produce for readers (see Chapter 9), but for authors the diagrams could also be used for dynamic restructuring of the information space.

The system could also give the author helpful statistics calculated from the structure of the hypertext network. Clustering methods can be used to show the underlying structure in the network, and connectivity measures can indicate potential landmarks by listing those nodes that are central in the hypertext.

Table 11.1 shows two calculations of connectivity for the nodes in *Hypertext Hands-On!* by Ben Shneiderman and Greg Kearsley. These calculations were performed using the transitive closure of the links with steadily decreasing weights for nodes that were more than one jump away.

Connectivity scores calculated giving high weight to incoming links and low weight to outgoing links (i.e. nodes that are referred to a lot)	Connectivity scores calculated giving low weight to incoming links and high weight to outgoing links (i.e. nodes from which you can go to a lot of places)
74 Bibliography: References 73 Browsing 59 Hyperties 54 HyperCard 53 Windows 52 Links 51 Authoring Overview 50 Graphics 50 Shneiderman 50 Guide	77 Introduction 58 Systems Overview 49 Guide 49 Authoring Overview 48 Bibliography: References 48 Getting started 48 Hyperties 48 Links 43 Dictionaries 41 Hyper hype?

Table 11.1. *Connectivity of nodes in* Hypertext Hands-On! *by Ben Shneiderman and Greg Kearsley. Only the top ten nodes are listed for each way to calculate connectivity. Numbers calculated using the HyperBook system implemented at the Technical University of Denmark by Michael H. Andersen and Henrik Rasmussen.*

This means that the connectivity score for a given node is calculated by counting all those other nodes in the network that are connected to it by paths of one or more links, taking the length of this path into account. The left column was calculated by giving the highest weight to incoming links while the right column shows the result of putting the emphasis on the outgoing links.

Five nodes (Bibliography, Hyperties, Links, Authoring overview, and Guide) actually occur on both lists, indicating that they have a truly central location in the information space of this hypertext. For the calculations in Table 11.1 we have given all links and nodes equal weight but it would be possible for the author to assign different importance ratings to the links and nodes in a hypertext and have those values reflected in the connectivity scores. A node would get a higher score if the links connecting it with other nodes were deemed to be especially important or if those other nodes had a high importance rating.

Cooperative Authoring

Much work with modern computer systems is collaborative in nature and involves groups of people working together. This is certainly true of most large writing projects such as the writing of the text for the Symbolics Document Examiner online manual. Fortunately hypertext is quite well suited for supporting collaboration since its linking structure allows the coordination of nodes written by multiple authors. Hypertext annotation facilities and the possibilities for linking through distributed networks also offer support for group work. Actually some hypertext systems like gIBIS (see Figure 4.2) have group support as their main purpose.

Several problems arise when more than one user works on a shared hypertext. The disorientation problem discussed in Chapter 9 could well become much worse when the information space changes behind the back of the individual user because of the activities of other writers. In one case of collaborative use of NoteCards [Trigg et al. 1986], the solution to this problem was to establish a special area of the hypertext for communication among the authors and to use a different typeface for the text written by each author.

In general, the hypertext system might keep the identity of the authors as attributes of nodes and links and use that information to determine authorizations to change or delete the information. It could also be possible for a user to ask the system to filter the hypertext with respect to the author IDs to see only nodes and links added by particular categories of users and to make the information "owned" by that user especially prominent in overview diagrams.

In some cases the users can be divided into two or more categories with different access privileges. A typical example is the use of Intermedia for teaching where the professor would be authorized to add or change the "canonic" hypertext structure whereas the students would be authorized only to add links and annotations.

Version control [Delisle and Schwartz 1986] is a final problem that becomes even more serious in multi-author hypertexts even though it is also present in single-user systems. What should happen if node **A** links to node **B** and someone suddenly changes **B**? For example, the text in **B** might be split over two new nodes and the link from **A** could be redirected to the more appropriate of them. The choice of "more appropriate" is probably impossible to make automatically, so the best we can hope for is a hypertext system that informs the person making the change that there is a need to update the links.

The SEPIA system [Streitz et al. 1989, 1992] supports collaborative authoring of hypertexts by providing a set of different "activity spaces" for the various stages in the authoring process. The system is based on a cognitive theory of writing, resulting in activity spaces to support planning, structuring the content domain and relevant background information, creating an argumentation structure, and formatting and revising the final document from a rhetorical perspective. Each of these activities require specific types of nodes and links, and the use of this richer structure helps the individual authors understand what the other authors are doing.

The Authority of the Author

Hypertext basically destroys the authority of the author to determine how readers should be introduced to a topic. From the readers' perspective, this is one of the great advantages of hypertext since it means that they are free to explore the information as they see fit. Remember the SuperBook study described in Chapter 9 showing that readers could access the information in the hypertext just as easily when they approached it with questions that had not been included in the author's original structuring of the text.

It might also be good news from the author's perspective. Authoring takes on an entirely new dimension when your job is changed to one of providing opportunities for readers rather than ordering them around. These opportunities should not be endless, however. The author still has the responsibility to provide certain priorities for the readers and to point them in relevant directions.

The old saying "more is less" is also true of hypertext linking: If you add every conceivable link to your hypertext, readers will benefit less than if you add only those links that are truly important and relevant. Every extra link is an additional burden on the user who has to determine whether or not to follow it. And if there are too many links leading to uninteresting places (because "they might be relevant for some readers") then readers will quickly become disappointed and learn not to trust your judgment.

In writing fiction in hypertext [Howell 1990], the loss of the absolute authority of the author leads to the loss of a single narrative stream of action which again destroys most traditional ways of writing in Western civilization. Instead the role of the author becomes much more closely connected to the tradition from science fiction of "building worlds" that the reader can explore.

12.   Repurposing Existing Content

The ideal situation with respect to hypertext would be to write all the nodes from scratch since the text is to be presented in a new medium. Just as the best films are not made by putting a camera in the best seat of a theater, the best hypertexts are not made from text that was originally written for the linear medium. But in the real world we have to respect that large amounts of extremely useful text and other content materials already exist and can be converted to hypermedia form much more cheaply than the same information could be rewritten or recreated. This chapter first covers some of the issues in the conversion of existing text to hypertext and then gives more detail about two concrete conversion projects: a medical handbook and a large dictionary.

The worst type of repurposing is the so-called shovelware, consisting of content that has been "shoveled" onto a CD-ROM or other hypertext medium without any real conversion. Repurposing is an honorable activity if it aims at making important pre-hypertext information available online, but it is usually necessary to do more than simply putting the materials on a computer without *any* further work. The obvious problem is that pre-hypertext have been designed for a linear presentation medium, no matter whether the information is a book, a movie, a radio program, or some other non-hypertext medium.

I must confess to being as guilty as anybody at producing shovelware. Darrell Sano and I wrote a paper on our experience in designing the SunWeb user interface to internal WWW at Sun. This paper was intended for presentation at the Second International WWW Conference and was published in the proceedings of that conference. Because of these two linear presentation media (talk and book), we wrote the paper as a traditional, linear manuscript. Once we had written the paper, many people started asking for ways to access it over the WWW, and I finally gave in and put copies on Sun's internal and external Web servers. Unfortunately, I did not have time to rewrite the paper for hypertext, so the resulting file was a simple conversion from FrameMaker into HTML.

A few months later, I was conducting a user test of Sun's external WWW server, and during the exploratory part of the study the test participant happened to access my SunWeb paper. He was (rightly) quite upset that the icons in the paper were not linked to any additional information and that he could do nothing but scroll through masses of text and figures. Better luck next time, Dr. Nielsen.

Conversion

To avoid the shovelware curse, people who want to repurpose existing content have to come up with ways of adding value to the online version compared with the pre-hypertext version. Figure 12.1 shows a good example of how this was done in converting Art Spiegelman's comic book *Maus* to the hypertext *The Complete Maus.*

The main window contains a scanned image of the original comic book, and icons in the left margin provide links to audio and video clips with additional information that could not be provided in the printed format. In the example in Figure 12.1, the top icon links to a tape recording where the protagonist (the artist's father) discusses the incident depicted on the page, and the second icon links to a statement from the artist himself. Most of the pages are also linked to several sketches showing the evolution of the page layouts and/or the individual panels. In the example in Figure 12.1, four different versions are available for the panel where the protagonist announces his engagement. These earlier versions can be seen as a form of the "temporal scrolling" envisioned by Ted Nelson and provide significant insights into the artist's creative process.

Conversion projects have to split the existing text into nodes and come up with links and their anchors. This process may be done automatically if the text is already suitably encoded or is regular enough to allow the writing of a simple pattern recognizing program. But in many cases it is necessary to do at least some of the conversion manually. Link structures can often be derived from existing sources like a printed index or table of contents, whereas node structures are often defined as the smallest named units of the text (typically sections).

Figure 12.1. *Page from* The Complete Maus. *Copyright © 1994 by Art Spiegelman and The Voyager Company, reprinted by permission.*

Sometimes a small software development effort can result in a customized system to generate hypertext structures automatically. As an example, the software mail order company the Savings Zone distributed several versions of their price list in a hypertext format. The first few versions were produced by hand, but they quickly realized that they spent about 30–40 hours for each new version on updating information by hand. The problem was solved by writing a HyperCard program that could take a dump of the information in their product database and produce the hypertext version automatically. This conversion program was fairly easy to implement because of the fixed data format in the database dumps.

To the extent that the conversion from text to hypertext is not done completely automatically, the converter has the option of adding new links to the information structure. Kahn [1989b] distinguishes between "objective links" derived directly from the original text and "subjective links" that are added because the converter feels they are relevant. Objective links would include cross references in the text or a link from the name of a city to its location on a map. Subjective links, in contrast, are located in concepts seen by the converter as being associated.

Obviously many of the "objective" links are only objective as far as the converter is concerned. For the original author, the decision of which other works to reference and which internal cross-references to add to the rest of the author's own document was mostly subjective. As more text is written in hypertext from the start, subjective links will probably tend to outnumber objective links. There are still some objective links left, such as the link from a person's name to the biography of the person if such a biography is present on the system. Many of these links may tend to become implicit, however.

The addition of new links or hypertext structure to an existing text gives rise to a problem similar to that of "colorizing" old black-and-white films. There is a risk that the hypertext version of the information will be subtly altered by the new structure or new way of connecting things and that the original author's intentions are violated. One example was the conversion of an issue of the journal *Communications of the ACM* to the "Hypertext on Hypertext" product. The KMS version had to include new structure because its frame-oriented nature could not accommodate an entire journal article in a single node. This specific modification does not seem to have caused any problems, but one should be aware of the potential risks.

In many cases one probably needs a different information structure for hypertext than the structure of the existing document. If an automatic conversion is deemed necessary anyway, one should at least allow the readers more freedom than they would normally get to add their own links and to annotate or customize the information.

The reverse problem of converting a traditional text to hypertext is to linearize a hypertext structure for printing. There are several reasons for doing so, including the pragmatic one that a lot of material is still distributed on paper. Even in the remote future when computers may have replaced paper completely there will still be a need to give oral presentations to an audience. And presentations simply *have* to be linear in time.

It is fairly easy to linearize a hypertext having a strict hierarchical structure by performing a depth-first tree traversal, meaning that you start by printing the first chapter and all the sections it contains before moving on to the second chapter. Another easy way out is to follow any guided tours the author may have defined through the hypertext. But in the general case where the hypertext is a highly connected network without any special order, it is very difficult to produce a good linearization. Experience with the use of NoteCards to write traditional reports [Trigg and Irish 1987] showed that many writers had to perform a final round of editing on the linear document after it had been generated by a conversion of the NoteCards hypertext structure.

Because of the extensive need to repurpose linear text in hypertext form, several tools are available for automatic conversion. One class of conversion tools can be categorized as simple page-turners and should be avoided for reasons of usability. It is certainly easy to produce an online document from a traditional document by simply displaying images of the pages on the computer screen, but doing so produces a "worst of both worlds" solution, where the user suffers from the lower readability of computer screens compared with paper without gaining the computer's benefits of flexible information presentation and navigation.

Luckily, many solutions exist that produce true hypertext, moving beyond the page-turning model. Microsoft offers an extension to Word that converts Word files into HTML format for delivery over the WWW, and there are several shareware solutions for producing HTML files from other formats like FrameMaker. Figure 12.2 shows a screen from Lotus SmarText, a commercial tool for hypertext conversion on the Windows platform [Rearick 1991].

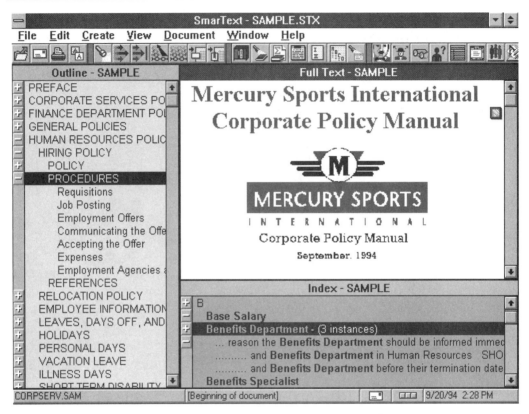

Figure 12.2. *Screen from Lotus SmarText. Copyright © 1994 by Lotus Development Corporation, reprinted by permission.*

SmarText reads files in most popular word processor formats, including Microsoft Word, Lotus Ami Pro, and WordPerfect. It then builds a table of contents from paragraphs formatted as headings and uses this information to construct an outline structure for the document to allow hierarchical navigation. SmarText also constructs a keyword-in-context (KWIC) type index for the document by collecting all specialized terms (and eliminating stop words and words that occur so frequently in the specific document as to be useless for an index). Of course, the elements in the table of contents and the index are hyperlinked to the main document. The outline and index views of the document are shown in the example in Figure 12.2.

SmarText also tries to construct hypertext links between parts of the document by inferring parts of text that seem related to other parts. It looks for tightly packed clusters of index words within the text. These clusters are assumed to correspond to nodes that are particularly relevant for those index terms, and SmarText proceeds by constructing hypertext links from other, isolated, occurrences of the terms to the clusters.

The Manual of Medical Therapeutics

The Washington University *Manual of Medical Therapeutics* is a 500-page book with guidelines for medical diagnosis and therapy that has been converted into hypertext in a variety of research prototypes [Frisse 1988] in NoteCards and HyperCard, and on the NeXT machine.

The printed book had a highly hierarchical structure as can be seen from the following example of a series of steadily more deeply nested section headings:

Chapter 6. Heart Failure
  V. Digitalis
    D. Digitalis Toxicity
      3. Treatment
        c. Ventricular Arrhythmias

This regular structure made it easy to construct a hypertext representation of the text automatically. Each subsection was made into a node that was given an identifier corresponding to the section number in the printed text. In the above example, the section number and node identifier is 6.V.D.3.c. Since this section number is basically incomprehensible for anybody who is not extremely experienced in using the *Manual*, each node was also given a title consisting of the first six words in its text. These names are certainly not optimal, but given the specialized nature of the medical terminology and the way the sections were written, they are nevertheless still quite readable for physicians. The names are shown as labels for hypertext links and as the search results after user queries.

Furthermore, the system can automatically construct hypertext links between a section and all its subsections and from a subsection to its parent node. Readers can use these hypertext links to browse the book, but they can also perform queries based on a combination of keyword search and hypertext navigation.

Assume that we have to find information about how to cure a patient having certain heartbeat irregularities. A physician knowing the correct terminology might give the computer a command like the following:

find "treatment of digitalis-induced ventricular arrythmias"

Even though subsection 6.V.D.3.c of the *Manual* contains the answer (as can be seen from the above example of the section hierarchy), it would not be found because it does not contain all the keywords specified by the user. Several of the keywords only occur in the higher-level sections of which 6.V.D.3.c is a subsection. This way of writing the nodes made sense when the text existed in a printed form since the author could assume that the reader knew the context of a given piece of text in the chapter-section-subsection hierarchy.

Therefore the hypertext version of the text must provide a more context-dependent search facility if it is to reuse the text from the printed book. This is done by computing search results as a combination of the intrinsic and extrinsic query scores as explained in Chapter 8. In other words, the degree to which a given node is said to match a user query takes into account how well the match is for other nodes it is connected to by hypertext links. In the example, the node for section 6.V.D would match "digitalis," the node for section 6.V.D.3 would match "treatment," and the node for section 6.V.D.3.c would match "ventricular arrythmias." These three nodes would be listed in a menu of search results in an order determined by the exact search weights, and the user could browse through them using the hypertext links until all the necessary information was found.

Oxford English Dictionary

The *Oxford English Dictionary* (*OED*) is one of the largest texts to be converted to a hypertext format [Raymond and Tompa 1988]. The printed version was originally published in twelve volumes from 1884 to 1928, and a four volume supplement was published in the period 1972–1986. Because it is so old, the *OED* did not exist in machine-readable form but had to be rekeyed manually in a process taking eighteen months.

It might have been possible to scan in the text from the printed books by optical character recognition but that would have generated a fairly "stupid" representation of the text. By having humans type in the text it was possible to have the basic text supplemented by tags to indicate the nature of the various text elements. For example it was desirable to distinguish among the actual dictionary entries, their definitions, their etymologies, and the quotations from other literature.

The data is stored as one contiguous 570 megabyte stream of text, recorded using these descriptive SGML-style markup tags. Thus there are no nodes explicitly stored as separate units and there are no explicit links stored as pointers. The software used to access the text is based on indexes stored externally to the main data stream. Therefore one can view this software as converting a flat text file to hypertext every time it is used.

The original *OED* contained 252,259 entries (words that can be looked up), and the supplement contained 69,372 entries. To complicate matters further, there was some overlap between the original dictionary and the supplement since some words had acquired new meanings or quotations. Just merging the two sets of entries was thus in itself a service to users and the new edition furthermore includes an additional 5,000 new or revised entries.

One reason hypertext is a good access mechanism for the *OED* is that it contains 569,000 cross references within the dictionary itself. Many of these references link to variant forms of a word, to words with a similar meaning, or to entries about prefixes or suffixes. Since the *OED* contains definitions of almost every word in the English language, it also contains an astronomical number of implicit links since users may jump from every word in the complete text to that word's entry even if the editors have not included an explicit link.

The *OED* contains 2.4 million quotations to illustrate the way various authors have used words throughout the history of the English language. These quotations can really be seen as references to other literature, so a "universal hypertext" like Ted Nelson's Xanadu would replace them with links to the full text of the original sources, allowing the user to see not just the sentence in which a word was used but also the broader context of that use.

Unfortunately it was not possible to design a single simple hypertext interface to the *OED*. The stumbling block was the great variability in the size of entries and the different uses to which the dictionary might be put. The distribution of the length of dictionary entries is extremely skewed. Only 5% of the entries in the *OED* are larger than 4,000 characters but they account for 48% of the total text. As an example, the entry for the verb "to set" is almost half a megabyte. At the same time, 20% of the entries are smaller than 50 characters. Obviously one cannot use the same principles for access to 50 character entries as for 500,000-character entries.

The larger entries can normally be structured according to the various meanings and sub-meanings of the word. These "senses" form a hierarchical structure that is suited for hypertext browsing since users often only care about a word in a few of its main meanings. The hypertext version of the *OED* automatically constructed this hypertext hierarchy from the encoding of the raw text with tags. The other types of information had tags that mostly followed a flat structure such as the year for various quotations. Therefore one form of hypertext support for browsing quotations could be a timeline.

Finally, the interface to the *OED* needed to allow alternative displays of entries according to the user's task since some users are very interested in the linguistic evolution of the words and ancient quotations whereas others only need the word definitions. This difference can again be supported quite well by hypertext. Instead of having a system that automatically formats the text in a single predefined way, the *OED* hypertext interface allows dynamic restructuring of the text according to the individual user's specification.

We should also note that the *OED* is one of the few examples where hypertext is actually more readable than paper. Most people who have the *OED* on paper do not have the full-sized twenty volumes but a three-volume edition in microscopic print.[1] The hypertext version can of course have as large a display font as the user wants and is therefore easier on the eyes. The variable font size is a real benefit for many handicapped readers.

---

[1] The microprint edition has two volumes corresponding to the original sixteen volume *OED* as well as a further single volume containing the supplement.

13. The Future of Multimedia and Hypertext

It is very hard to forecast the future of hypertext. Of course, as the saying goes, prediction is hard—especially of the future—but it is particularly difficult in the case of hypertext because we do not have enough experience yet with real-life use of hypertext to know what the trends are going to be. One thing that is fairly certain is that hypertext is going to grow in use over the years as the technology spreads to progressively more applications and more markets.

Hypertext is not the first new technology in the world, and previous innovations have been studied extensively leading to several mathematical models for technology transfer and the spread of innovations, some of which are suitable for modeling the increased use of hypertext [Kain and Nielsen 1991]. The most basic model is based on the Bass curve for product innovation diffusion which has been used successfully to model the spread of many new products. Mahajan et al. [1990] provide a major survey of the Bass model and its applications.

The Bass model gives the following equation for the cumulative number of adopters of the innovation at time t,　N_t:

$$N_t = N_{t-1} + p(m - N_{t-1}) + q\frac{N_{t-1}}{m}(m - N_{t-1})$$

The three parameters of the model are:

- m = the market potential; the total number of people who will eventually use the product
- p = the coefficient of external influence; the likelihood that somebody who is not yet using the product will start using it because of mass media coverage or other external factors

333

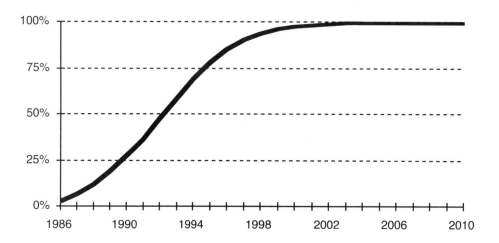

Figure 13.1. *The standard Bass curve for hypertext market diffusion with p=.03 and q=.38. The figure shows how much of the eventual market penetration might be achieved for each year after the introduction of the first commercial hypertext product, Guide, in 1986.*

- q = the coefficient of internal influence; the likelihood that somebody who is not yet using the product will start using it because of "word-of-mouth" or other influence from those already using the product.

The number of new adopters in the interval from time $t-1$ to time t who are due to external influence is therefore proportional to p and the number of non-adopters in the potential market. The number of new adopters due to internal influence is proportional to q and the number of non-adopters, but it is also proportional to the relative number of previous adopters since they are the source of the influence.

For analyses of traditional products, market diffusion models are mostly concerned with actual unit sales of the product. Here, we are discussing a concept rather than a specific product, and we are therefore talking about adopters "using" hypertext rather than "buying" it. "Use" could come from actually buying a hypertext system or from having regular access to one through, e.g., the Internet. We will require *regular* use of hypertext to consider a person as having adopted hypertext. Just browsing through a few Hyperties screens during a single museum visit would not count as having adopted hypertext but would be seen as exposure to a case of external influence.

Based on a meta-study of 213 applications of the Bass model, Sultan et al. [1990] report average values of .03 for *p* and .38 for *q*. Assuming that Year 1 for the hypertext market was 1986 (the introduction of the first shrinkwrap hypertext product, Guide), the basic Bass curve for these *p* and *q* estimates is shown in Figure 13.1.

For traditional products, such as a new computer model, it may be reasonable to consider *p* as a fixed parameter, even though it should really vary depending on the vendor's advertising budget. Hypertext, however, is more in the nature of a concept than a product and there is no centralized media planning to determine the mass media coverage of hypertext and the external influence on people to adopt hypertext. It has clearly been the case over recent years that hypertext has been getting steadily more media coverage, with front page articles on Mosaic in *The New York Times'* business section in 1994 and with many other stories on CD-ROM publishing and the Internet.

Easingwood et al. [1983] argue that the internal influence is not necessarily linear and instead suggest the non-uniform-influence (NUI) model with the equation

$$N_t = N_{t-1} + p(m - N_{t-1}) + q\frac{N_{t-1}^{\delta}}{m}(m - N_{t-1})$$

This model is identical to the basic Bass model except that the impact of the other adapters is not proportional with their number. Their influence may grow more slowly than their number if $\delta < 1$, or it may grow faster if $\delta > 1$. Easingwood et al. [1983] estimated δ to be between 0.3 and 1.5 for a variety of innovations. Here we will use the upper value of $\delta = 1.5$ because the spread of many forms of hypertext seems to depend heavily on having a large number of users. In this regard, hypertext is similar to music compact discs [Bayus 1987], where the sales of players and records are interdependent; many people will not want to use hypertext until there is a wide variety of good hypertext documents available on the market, but at the same time publishers will not invest resources in releasing information in a hypertext format until there are many hypertext users. Furthermore, certain types of hypertext rely on combining hypertext networks generated by groups of users and can therefore also be expected to increase as a function of the number of users with a power greater than one, since the number of possible links grows as the square of the

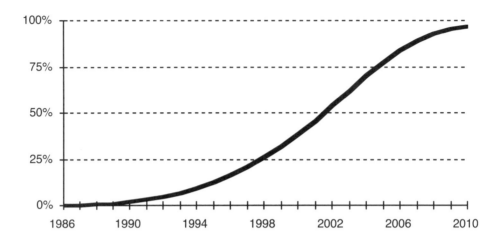

Figure 13.2. *The market diffusion curve for hypertext under changed assumptions: the external influence coefficient (p) is assumed to grow over time and there is non-uniform internal influence with δ=1.5. Other parameters as in Figure 13.1.*

number of nodes. Figure 13.2 shows the revised curve, taking these considerations into account. Initially, the curve grows more slowly, but after a certain "critical mass" of users have been reached, the synergistic effect comes into play and the curve rises rapidly.

The growth of the World Wide Web (shown in Figure 7.1) has definitely been faster than indicated by the Bass curves in Figure 13.1 and Figure 13.2, but then the WWW is only one type of hypertext. For all kinds of hypermedia combined it would be reasonable to expect the growth curves to look somewhat like those shown in this chapter. One of the main reasons to believe in sustained, but slower, growth than that experienced on the Internet is that most potential users still do not have computers that are powerful enough to support multimedia. With the introduction of new 64-bit game home computers in 1995 this is changing, but these new computers will take some time to penetrate the market. Looking at the business market, transitions to technologies like SGML also take time and are not complete yet, meaning that business users will also see substantially increased use of online documents and hypermedia in the coming years.

The conclusion from these considerations is that we are most likely still in the early stages of hypertext adoption though the curve is starting to bend to the part where it goes up very fast. Most likely, the people who started using hypertext during the period until about 1995 were the early adopters who like to try out new technology. The majority adopters will embrace hypermedia during the period from now until about the year 2002 and there will still be a fairly large group of laggards who will not start using hypertext until well into the next century.

What Happened to the Predictions from my Earlier Book?

My book, *Hypertext and Hypermedia*, was published in 1990 so it is appropriate to consider how the predictions in that book compare to reality five years later. In 1990 I predicted that "three to five years later" (that is, at the time of this writing), we would see the emergence of a mass market for hypertext. Indeed, this has more or less come to pass with CD-ROM encyclopedia outselling printed ones and with large numbers of hypermedia productions available for sale in computer shops. This "mass market" is still fairly small, though, compared with the market for printed books, magazines, and newspapers, but it is getting there.

I also commented on the fact that most hypertext products in 1990 ran on the Macintosh and predicted a shift to the IBM PCs as a natural consequence of the mass market trend I discussed. This shift has certainly come to pass and most new hot hypermedia products ship for the PC[1] long before they come out in Mac format (many are never converted).

My second main prediction for 1995 was the integration of hypertext with other computer facilities. This has mostly not come to pass, even though the PenPoint operating system did include hypertext features as a standard part of the system. Most computer systems still have impoverished linking abilities and make do with a few hypertext-like help features like the Macintosh balloon help that allows users to point to an object on the screen and get a pop-up balloon to explain its use.

More generally integrated hypertext features must await the fully object-oriented operating systems that are currently being developed by most leading

---

[1] Of course, these computers are normally called "Windows machines" these days and not "IBM PCs," since IBM only manufacturers a very small percentage of the hardware.

computer vendors. It turned out to be too difficult to add new elements to the computational infrastructure of existing systems and expect the mass of applications to comply with them. We are currently living through the last years of the Age of Great Applications with hundreds or thousands of features. These mastodons are ill suited to flexible linking and have too much momentum to adjust to fundamentally new basic concepts like universal linking and embedded help. I predict that in another five to ten years a fundamental change will happen in the world of computing and that integrated object-oriented systems will take over. This will happen slowly, though, because the current generation of Great Applications is powerful indeed. It will take some time for the smaller, more agile mammals—sorry, modules—to win.

A final prediction failed miserably only a few years after it was made: I predicted that universities would start exchanging Intermedia webs on a regular basis to build up extensive curricula across schools. In fact what happened was that the Intermedia project got its funding canceled and the system does not even run on current computers since it has not been maintained for years. I stand by my original conviction that Intermedia was the best hypertext system available in 1990. It *deserved* to have succeeded, but short-sighted funding agencies are of course nothing new.

Short-Term Future: Three to Five Years

In the short term of three to five years, I don't really expect significant changes in the way hypertext is done compared to the currently known systems. Of course new stuff will be invented all the time, but just getting the things we already have in the laboratory out into the world will be more than enough. I expect to see three major changes:

- the consolidation of the mass market for hypertext
- commercial information services on the Internet
- the integration of hypertext and other computer facilities

Consolidating the Mass Market for Hypertext

Hypermedia products are already selling fairly well even though it is still only a minority of personal computers that have sufficiently good multimedia capabilities to do them justice. I would expect very few personal computers to be sold in the industrialized world from now on without multimedia capabilities, so the market for hypermedia should get much larger in the next few years.

We already have one product category, encyclopedias, that is selling better in hypermedia form than in paper form. I would expect a few more such product categories to appear, but I would expect most product categories to be dominated by traditional media in the short term. One product category that is a prime candidate for initial multimedia dominance is movie guides. The moving images and the ease of updating make this domain a natural for a combination of CD-ROM and online publishing, and several large studios have indeed started to distribute trailers for their films through America Online and other services. Microsoft Cinemania was one of the first hypermedia movie guides and I would expect many more to appear. TV guides will also move from print to hypermedia for much the same reasons. Furthermore, cable TV services with 500 or more channels are just too much for a printed guide to describe in any kind of usable format. Instead of scanning TV listings, users will have to start using a combination of search methods and agent-based program recommendations [Isbister and Layton 1995]. For example, if my TV guide knows that I normally watch Star Trek and that most other Star Trek fans seem to like a certain new show on channel 329, then it might prompt me with a recommendation to watch that show one day.

I also expect the emergence of many more engaging interactive multimedia games and entertainment products as the convergence of Hollywood and Silicon Valley shakes out. Current computer games have a paucity of storytelling talent and production values and thus have to make progress through the story needlessly difficult to draw out the experience enough to make it worth the purchase price for the buyer. With more powerful computers and with more talented writers, directors, and other creative talent, computerized entertainment should become much smoother to navigate and should present richer worlds for the user to explore without being killed every few turns. Truly new entertainment concepts will have to await the next century, though: I don't expect to see really intelligent environments that change the story to fit the individual user until after the year 2000.

Commercial Hypertext on the Internet

We will definitely start seeing charging mechanisms on the Internet. In order to get good quality information, people will have to pay something for the necessary authoring and editing efforts. It will only be a matter of a very short time before a NetCash system gets established to allow people to pay for their consumption of information over the Internet.

Integrating Hypertext with Other Computer Facilities

The reader will probably have noticed that I am quite enthusiastic about the possibilities of hypertext. Even so, it must be said that many of the better applications of hypertext require additional features to plain hypertext.

We are currently seeing a trend for hypertext systems to be integrated with other advanced types of computer facilities. For example, there are several systems that integrate hypertext with artificial intelligence (AI).

One such system was built by Scott M. Stevens [Stevens 1989] at the Software Engineering Institute at Carnegie Mellon University for teaching the software engineering technique called *code inspection*. Code inspection basically involves discussing various aspects of a program during a meeting where the participants each have specified roles such as reviewer, moderator, or designer of the program. It turns out that it is impossible to teach people this method without first having them participate in a number of meetings where they are assigned the various roles. This process can be quite expensive if the other meeting participants have to be experienced humans.

It is possible, however, to simulate the other participants on a computer by the use of artificial intelligence. By doing so, the person learning the code inspection method can have as many training meetings as necessary, and the student can even go through the same meeting several times to take on the different roles. The major part of the meeting simulation system is therefore an AI method for finding out how the other meeting participants would react to whatever behavior the student exhibits. But the system also includes a lot of text in the form of the actual program being discussed, its design specifications, and various textbooks and reports on the code inspection method. These texts are linked using hypertext techniques.

Another example of the integration of hypertext with other techniques is the commercial product called *The Election of 1912* from Eastgate Systems running in their Hypergate system on the Macintosh. Whereas the code inspection meeting simulator was primarily an AI system with hypertext thrown in for support, *The Election of 1912* is primarily a hypertext system but also includes a simulation.

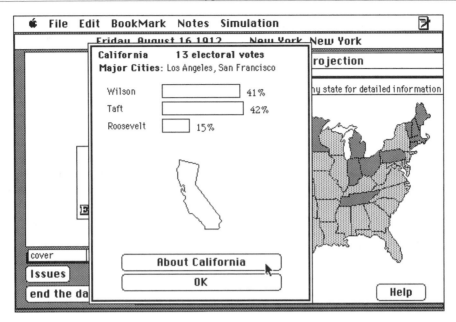

Figure **13.3.** *Screen from* The Election of 1912 *showing the simulation part of the system. The user has called up a map showing the results of a (simulated) opinion poll and has asked for further information about one of the states. Copyright © 1987 by Eastgate Systems, Inc., reprinted with permission.*

Most of the *1912* system is a hypertext about the political events in the United States in 1912 with special focus on the presidential election of that year. It is possible to read the hypertext in the normal way to learn about this historical period and its people. There is also a political *simulation* to increase student motivation for reading through the material.

Basically the simulation allows the user to participate in "running" for president in 1912 by "being" the campaign manager for Teddy Roosevelt. The user can plan the travel schedule for the candidate, what people he should meet with, and what issues he should speak out on in which cities. During the simulation, the user can call up a map showing the "result" of opinion polls for each state as shown in Figure 13.3.

The simulation is hooked into the hypertext system in such a way that the user can jump from the simulated information about a state to the actual historical information about a state (as shown in Figure 13.4) to understand

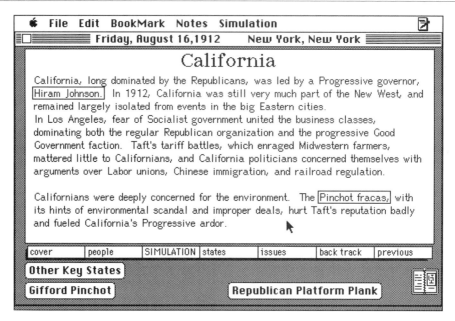

Figure 13.4. *Screen from* The Election of 1912 *hypertext showing the result of following the "About California" link from the simulation part of the system. Copyright © 1987 by Eastgate Systems, Inc., reprinted with permission.*

why the voters in that state have reacted as they have to the candidate's speeches.

There are also hypertext links from the meetings with various possible supporters and famous people in the simulation to the hypertext's information about these people and from the issues in the simulation to the discussion about these issues in the real election.

Medium-Term Future: Five to Ten Years

Toward the turn of the century we should expect to see widespread publishing of hypertext material. It is also likely that the various forms of video, which are currently quite expensive, will be part of the regular personal computers people have in their homes and offices. So we should expect to see true hypermedia documents for widespread distribution.

Within this timeframe there is also some hope for a solution to the practical problems of data compatibility between systems. Currently it is impossible for a user of, say, an IBM OS/2 system to read a hypertext that has been written on, say, a Unix Sun in KMS. In the world of traditional, linear text, the data compatibility problem has been more or less solved some time ago, with the possibility to transfer word processor and spreadsheet documents between Windows and Macs being just one of the more spectacular success stories.

Current work on the "hypertext abstract machine" (HAM)[2] or similar ideas for interchange formats will almost certainly succeed to the extent that it will be possible to consider publishing the same hypertext on several different platforms. This change will increase the size of the market even more and will therefore add to the trend toward focusing on content. Of course there will still be many hypertexts that will need to take advantage of the special features available on some specific platform like the Macintosh, and these hypertexts will then not be universally available.

The availability of hypertext documents on several platforms is not just a commercial question of the size of the market for the seller. It is also a social issue for the readers of hypertext. Just imagine how you would feel as a reader of traditional printed books if there were some mechanism which restricted you to reading books printed in a specific typeface like Helvetica. But this is exactly the current situation with hypertext: If you own Hyperties, then you can read hypertext documents written in Hyperties but not those written in KMS, HyperCard, Guide, Intermedia, NoteCards, ...

An interchange format will partly resolve this problem. But the problem will be solved only *partly* because of the special nature of hypertext, which involves dynamic links to other documents. It is not even remotely likely that we will see Ted Nelson's original Xanadu vision of having all the world's literature online in a single unified system fulfilled in the medium-term future. Therefore hypertext documents will get into trouble as soon as they start linking to outside documents: Some readers will have them, and others will not. It is likely that most hypertexts in the medium-term future will remain as isolated islands of information without a high degree of connectedness to other documents. This has been called the *docuislands* scenario.

Even to the extent that many documents are served over the WWW, they may still be isolated from a hypertext perspective since inter-document linking lacks much to be desired. People mostly link between documents on their own

---

[2] See Chapter 5.

server and under their own control since cross-site links are subject to become dangling without any warning as the remote site changes its file structure.

Several of the current practical problems with hypertext documents should be expected to be solved in the medium-term future. For example, there is currently no standard way to refer to a hypertext document the way there is with traditional books, which have a standard ISBN numbering system and recognized publishers with established connections to bookshops. If you want a book, you go to the bookshop and buy it. And if they don't have it, they can get it for you.

Hypertexts are published by a strange assortment of companies to the extent that they are published at all. Many a good hypertext is available only from the individual or university who produced it. And the sales channels for hypertexts are either nonexistent or a mixture of mail order and computer shops, many of which do not carry hypertext.

In a similar way, regular libraries almost never include hypertexts in their collections and wouldn't know how to deal with electronic documents anyway. There are a few online services that store a small number of electronic documents, but since there is no systematic way to determine where a given document is stored and since most hypertext documents are not available online anyway, these services cannot substitute for traditional libraries.

It is very likely, however, that the medium-term future will see established publishers and sales channels for hypertext documents. Whether they will be the same as the current system for printed books remains to be seen and would depend on the level of conservatism in the management of publishers and major booksellers. Libraries will certainly have to handle electronic documents, and many of the better and larger libraries are already now starting to invite hypertext specialists to consult on ways to deal with these issues.

Intellectual Property Rights

I expect major changes in the way intellectual property rights (e.g., copyright) are handled. These changes really ought to happen within my short-term time frame since they are sorely needed, but realistically speaking, changes in the legal system always trail technological changes, so I don't expect major changes until the year 2000.

There are two major problems with the current approach to copyright: first, "information wants to be free" as the hackers' credo goes, and second, the administration of permissions and royalties adds significant overhead to the efforts of people who work within the rules. Under current law, hypermedia authors are not allowed to include information produced by others without explicit permission. Getting this permission is estimated to cost about $220 on the average in purely administrative costs such as tracking down the copyright owner, writing letters back and forth, and possibly mailing a check with the royalty payment. If you are negotiating the rights to the large-scale reproduction of an entire book or all the paintings in a museum then $220 for administration is negligible, but that is not so if you want to assemble a large number of smaller information objects.

To overcome the problem with administrative overhead, it is possible that information objects will start to include simplified mechanisms for royalty payment. Each object could include attributes indicating the copyright owner, the owner's NetCash account number, and the requested royalty for various uses of the material. This approach would be similar to the Copyright Clearance Center codes often found printed in each of the articles in a research journal. With the current system, every time somebody copies an article from one of the journals associated with the Copyright Clearance Center, they (or their library management) can send the Center the article code and a check for the $2.00 or so that are the requested royalty for that article. The Copyright Clearance Center codes require manual interpretation and would not be suited for information objects costing a cent or less per copy, but an object-oriented data representation would allow computers to process the payments automatically. If each data object came with payment information, the holders of intellectual property rights should not mind wanton distribution of copies of their materials since they would get paid every time somebody actually *used* the information.

The more basic problem, though, is that "information wants to be free." Once you know something, it is very hard to pretend that you don't. Thus, it is difficult to charge people every time they use some information. Also, information does not get worn or diminished by being copied. This is in contrast to traditional goods like a cake: if I let you have a bite of my cake, there is less left for me to eat, but if I let you look at the front page of my newspaper, I will not suffer any adverse effects.

It is possible to establish barriers to information dissemination, either by legal and moral pressure ("don't copy that floppy") or by actual copy protection. Users tend to resent such barriers and have been known to boycott vendors who used particularly onerous copy protection mechanisms. An alternative would be to eliminate copyright protection of the information itself and let information providers be compensated in other ways. It is already the case that software vendors generate most of their revenues from upgrades and not from the original sales of the software, so it might be feasible to give away the software and have the vendors live off upgrades and service. Moving software from a sales model to a subscription model (possibly with weekly or daily upgrades) would make it similar in nature to magazines and newspapers where people pay to get the latest version delivered as soon as possible.

It is also possible for intellectual property owners to get compensated, not from the information itself, but from a derived value associated with some other phenomenon that is harder or impossible to copy. This is the way university professors currently get compensated for their research results. They normally give away the papers and reports describing the results and get paid in "units of fame" that determine their chance of getting tenure, promotions, and jobs at steadily more prestigious institutions. Fame may also provide a reasonable compensation model in many other cases. For example, people visit the Louvre to see the real Mona Lisa even though they already have seen countless reproductions of the image. In fact, the more the Mona Lisa is reproduced, the more famous it gets, and the more people will want to visit Paris and go to the Louvre. Therefore, the Louvre should welcome hypermedia authors who want to use Mona Lisa bitmaps and should allow them to do so for free. Similarly, a rock band might make its money from tours and concerts and give away its CDs (or at least stop worrying whether people duplicate the CD with DAT recorders), and a professional society could get funded by conference fees instead of journal sales. The trick is to use the information (e.g., music CDs and tapes) to increase the value of the physical or unique event for which it is possible to charge.

Long-Term Future: Ten to Twenty Years

What will happen in the *really* long-term future, more than twenty years from now? That is for the science fiction authors to tell, and I recommend that you look at the references listed under "Far Out Stuff" at the end of the bibliography in the Appendix.

In the computer business, ten to twenty years counts as long term future indeed, so I will restrict myself to that horizon in the following comments.

Some people like Ted Nelson expect to see the appearance of the global hypertext (e.g. Xanadu) as what has been called the *docuverse* (universe of documents). I don't really expect this to happen completely, but we will very likely see the emergence of very large hypertexts and shared information spaces at universities and certain larger companies.

Already we are seeing small shared information spaces in teaching applications, but they are restricted to the students taking a single class. In the future we might expect students at large numbers of universities to be connected together. Another example of a shared information space is a project to connect case workers at branch offices of a certain large organization with specialists at the main office. The staff at the branch office does not follow the detailed legal developments in the domain that is to be supported by the system since they also have other responsibilities. Therefore the specialists would maintain a hypertext structure of laws, court decisions, commentaries, etc., which would be made available to the case workers at the branches. Also, these local people would describe any cases falling within this domain in the system itself with pointers to the relevant hypertext nodes. In this way they would in turn help the specialists build an understanding of practice and they would also be able to get more pointed help from the specialists regarding, for instance, any misapplication of legal theory.

So given these examples which are already being implemented, I would certainly expect to see the growth of shared information spaces in future hypertext systems. There are several social problems inherent in such shared spaces, however. If thousands or even millions of people add information to a hypertext, then it is likely that some of the links will be "perverted" and not be useful for other readers. As a simple example, think of somebody who has inserted a link from every occurrence of the term "Federal Reserve Bank" to a picture of Uncle Scrooge's money bin. You may think that it is funny to see that cartoon come up the first time you click on the Bank's name, but pretty soon you would be discouraged from the free browsing that is the heartblood of hypertext because the frequency of actually getting to some useful information would be too low due to the many spurious links.

These perverted links might have been inserted simply as jokes or by actual vandals. In any case, the "structure" of the resulting hypertext would end up being what Jef Raskin has compared to New York City subway cars painted over by graffiti in multiple uncoordinated layers.[3]

---

[3] In recent years, the New York subway has cleaned up most of the graffiti. Let us hope that this is a positive sign, also for hypertext.

Even without malicious tampering with the hypertext, just the fact that so many people add to it will cause it to overflow with junk information. Of course the problem is that something I consider to be junk may be considered to be art or a profound commentary by you, so it might not be possible to delete just the "junk."

A likely development to reduce these problems will be the establishment of hypertext "journals" consisting of "official" nodes and links that have been recommended by some trusted set of editors. This approach is of course exactly the way paper publishing has always been structured.

An example of such a development can be seen at Carnegie Mellon University where there is a very lively flow of electronic information on the Andrew electronic message system. Most people don't have the time to read all the messages and instead subscribe to electronic magazines [Borenstein and Thyberg 1988], which are put out by human editors who read through the mass of messages to find those of interest for whatever is the topic of their magazine.

It would also be possible to utilize the hypertext mechanism itself to build up records of reader "votes" on the relevance of the individual hypertext nodes and links. Every time users followed a hypertext link, they would indicate whether it led them somewhere relevant in relation to their point of departure. The averages of these votes could then be used as a filter by future readers to determine whether it would be worthwhile to follow the link.

Another potential social problem is the long-term effects of nonsequentiality. Large parts of our culture have the built-in assumption that people read things in a linear order and that it makes sense to ask people to read "from page 100 to 150." For example, that is how one gives reading assignments to students. With a hypertext-based syllabus students may show up at exam time and complain about one of the questions because they never found any information about it in the assigned reading. The professor may claim that there was a hypertext link to the information in question, but the students may be justified in their counter-claim that the link was almost invisible and not likely to be found by a person who was not already an expert in the subject matter.

The reverse problem would occur when the professor was grading the students' essays, which would of course be written in hypertext form. What happens if the professor misses the single hypertext link leading to the part of the paper with all the goodies and then fails the student? Actually the solution to this problem would be to consider hypertext design part of the skills being tested in the assignment. If students cannot build information structures that clearly put forward their position, then they *deserve* to fail even though the information may be in there in some obscure way.

A further problem in the learning process is that novices do not know in which order they need to read the material or how much they should read. They don't know what they don't know. Therefore learners might be sidetracked into some obscure corner of the information space instead of covering the important basic information. To avoid this problem, it might be necessary to include an AI monitoring system that could nudge the student in the right direction at times.

There is also the potential problem that the non-linear structure of hypertext as being split into multitudes of small distinct nodes could have the long-term effect of giving people a fragmented world view. We simply do not know about this one, and we probably will not know until it is too late if there is such an effect from, say, twenty years of reading hypertext. On the other hand, it could just as well be true that the cross-linking inherent in hypertext encourages people to see the connections among different aspects of the world so that they will get *less* fragmented knowledge. Experience with the use of Intermedia to teach English literature at Brown University [Landow 1989b] did indicate that students were several times as active in class after the introduction of hypertext. They were able to discover new connections and raise new questions.

Attribute-Rich Objects

Most current hypermedia systems are based on the notion that each information object has one canonical representation, meaning that a given node should always look the same. The WYSIWYG (what you see is what you get) principle has actually been fundamental for almost all modern user interfaces, whether for hypertext systems or for traditional computer systems. There is something nice, safe, and simple about this single-view model, and it is certainly better than the previous model where all information on the computer screen was presented in monospaced green characters no matter how the document would look when printed.

The single-view model is best suited for information objects that have an impoverished internal representation in the computer because the computer will have no way to compute alternative views and thus has to faithfully reproduce the layout given by the human user. It may take more than ten years to get to the next model, but eventually I expect the computer to process information objects with significantly more attributes than it currently has. Once the computer knows more about each information object, it will be able to display them in various ways depending on the user's specific needs for the user's current task.

One example of a multi-view hypertext is the SIROG (situation-related operational guidance) project at Siemens [Simon and Erdmann 1994]. SIROG contains all parts of the operational manual for accidents in a Siemens nuclear power plant and is connected to the process control system and its model of the state of the plant. The hypertext objects have been manually encoded by the authors with SGML attributes that inform SIROG about the part of the plant and the kind of situation they describe. The system can match these attributes with the actual situation of the plant and present the relevant parts of the manual to the operators. Obviously, unexpected situations can occur and the system may not have a perfect understanding of the plant state. Therefore, SIROG relies on the operators' abilities to read and understand the content of the manual: it is not an intelligent system to diagnose nuclear power plant problems; it is a system that tries to display the most relevant part of the manual first rather than having the manual always look the same every time the operators bring it up.

Program code is another example where multiple views are both relevant and possible[4] [Østerbye and Nørmark 1994]. Sometimes a programmer wants to see only the executable code, sometimes a commented view is better, sometimes an overview of the program's structure is most helpful, and sometimes a view annotated with debugging or performance metering will be needed. For third-party programmers who want to reuse a program through its API simplified views of the interface structure will suffice (and indeed, a view of the internal structure would be harmful).

---

[4] Multi-view representations of program code are particularly easy to produce because so many software development tools exist to parse the code and interpret it in various ways. For other kinds of information objects we still need better ways of letting the computer manipulate structure and meaning.

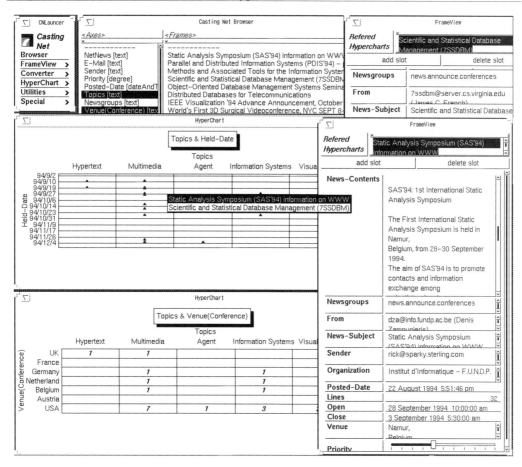

Figure 13.5. *Views of the highly structured CastingNet system where the nodes are structured as frames with slots. Copyright © 1994 by the Science and Technology Agency of the Japanese Government, reprinted by permission. The study was performed by Special Coordination Funds of the Science and Technology Agency of the Japanese Government.*

Figures 13.5 and 13.6 show two views of the CastingNet system [Masuda et al. 1994] which uses a frame-based model with highly structured nodes. Each node is a frame with a number of named slots that represent its properties and the type of the node determines what frame will be used to represent its content. Each slot has a mapping function that maps each possible value of that slot onto an axis. In the example in Figure 13.5, hypertext nodes that represent

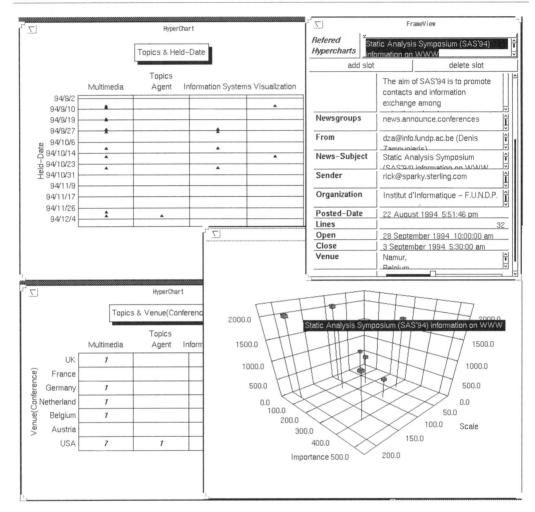

Figure 13.6. *Example of a view of three axes in CastingNet. Copyright © 1994 by the Science and Technology Agency of the Japanese Government, reprinted by permission. The study was performed by Special Coordination Funds of the Science and Technology Agency of the Japanese Government.*

research conferences may have slots for the country in which the conference is held, the date of the conference, some classification of the topic of the conference, and many more attributes of conferences and conference announcements.

The conference-venue slot would map onto a country axis that could be represented as a linear list (as shown in Figure 13.5), as a world map, or in many other ways. As shown in Figures 13.5 and 13.6, the attribute axes can be used to construct many different two- or three-dimensional overview diagrams of the hypertext according to criteria that are of interest to the user. The frame-based representation also allows the system to construct links between nodes that are that have identical or closely related values along one or more axes. For example, it would be possible to link from a given conference node to nodes representing other conferences taking place in the same location at the same time (or the following or previous week) as a conference a user was thinking of going to. Also, due to the mapping functions, it will be possible to link to nodes that have different, but compatible, slots. For example, instead of linking to other conference nodes with similar venue slots, it would be possible to link to the user's personal information base of friends and contacts to see what people lived in the same town and might be visited in connection with a conference trip. This link would be possible because the address nodes for each friend would have slots for city and ZIP code that could be mapped to the same axis as the venue slot in the conference frame.

The frame-axis model of CastingNet provides flexible ways for the user to restructure the views of the hypertext and to link the information in new ways as new needs are discovered. This type of flexibility will be very important in the future as people start accumulating large personal information bases, but it will only be possible if the computer has ways of representing the same information in multiple ways depending on the interpretations that are currently of most value to the user.

Hypermedia Publishing: Monopoly or Anarchy?

Assume that in fact most information will migrate online and that it will be published in hypertext form with substantial multimedia components. What will this change imply for the publishing industry and the dissemination of information in the future?

Two opposite trends might be possible: either information publishing will be concentrated in a few, near-monopolistic companies, or the ability to publish information will be distributed over many more companies than are now involved. Both trends actually seem plausible due to different characteristics of hypermedia publishing.

Information publishing currently involves five different stages:

- Creating the content
- Editing the content, including the selection of the authors
- Manufacturing copies of the resulting product
- Distributing copies of the product through the sales channels
- Advertising and promoting the product

The middle stage, manufacturing physical copies of the information product, will more or less go away for hypermedia publishing because the users will be creating their own copies on demand as they download information from the Internet. Even for non-Internet hypermedia products, the physical duplication of CD-ROMs or floppy disks will account for an increasingly small part of the overall cost of the information products. Currently, the cost of printing and binding books (or newspapers or other information products) is one of the factors that limit the number of publishers of information products. The widespread availability of desktop publishing and photocopies have changed the picture somewhat and has made it economically feasible for people outside the established publishing houses to produce information products in small numbers.

Even though anybody can print, say, 100 copies of a booklet, the last two stages of the publishing process, distribution and promotion, have limited the actual sale and utilization of small-scale information products with pre-hypertext technology. What do you do after you receive the 100 copies of your booklet back from the QuickPrint shop? To get any sales you would have to get bookstores to carry it, newspapers to review it, and you would need a way to ship a copy to the one resident of New Zealand who might happen to be one of your customers.

Production, distribution, and promotion limitations have caused the publication of paper-based information products to be concentrated in the hands of a number of publishers that is much smaller than the number of potential authors or providers of information. At the same time, the barriers to setting up a new publishing company are fairly low and there is in fact a large number of publishers in business all over the world, some of which have very small market shares but are still profitable.

With the move to distributing information products over the Internet, distribution will go away as a limiting factor for information publishing, supporting a trend towards having more publishers. Essentially everybody with a workstation and an Internet subscription can become a publishing house and sell information products over the net. Indeed, with the WWW, the trend so far has been for a large number of people to set up their own individual "publishing houses" in the form of their home pages and associated hyperlinked material. Promotion and advertising will still tend to favor larger publishers with more resources, but the most effective type of promotion for Internet hypertext will be having others link to your material, and an author can potentially be linked to by many others without being affiliated with a major publisher.

The trends discussed so far in this section would seem to favor a kind of information anarchy where many more authors get published than is currently the case and where the publishing gets done by a larger number of companies. There are several opposing trends, though. The first is the information overload that is already taking its toll on people's ability to check out new WWW sites. With more and more information placed on the Internet, a backlash might cause many users to stay within safe Web sites that are known to offer high-quality material. As a parallel consider the way many people get highly aggravated by junk mail and deliberately try to avoid it.

Information monopolies are encouraged by three phenomena: production values, fame, and critical mass. With the move from simple text-based hypertext to multimedia-oriented hypermedia production values become steadily more important. For a text-only hypertext product, an individual author can craft a good product, but a full-scale multimedia product with video and animation takes a crew of graphic artists, set designers, actors, make-up specialists, camera-people, a director, etc. It may still be possible for a small company like Knowledge Adventure to produce a better dinosaur CD-ROM than Microsoft[5] by including 3-D dinosaur attack animations, but material produced by the average dinosaur enthusiast pale in comparison with either CD-ROM. Professionally produced multimedia titles with good production values look so much better than amateur productions but they require much higher capitalization and thus can only be produced by a fairly small number of

---

[5] To be fair, I should mention that I don't know for sure whether Knowledge Adventure's *3-D Dinosaur Adventure* is better than *Microsoft Dinosaurs*. I just know that *3-D Dinosaur Adventure* got the best review of the two in a magazine I was reading, and since I thought that one dino CD would be enough, I only bought *3-D Dinosaur Adventure*. This proves my main point, though: when there are too many dinosaur hypermedia titles available, people tend to concentrate on a few published by reputable sources (Microsoft) or that have particularly good production values (3-D animations). I do not have time to fully research the market for dino CDs; I just read reviews of the two that seemed the best bets.

companies. We are already seeing a trend to higher production values on the WWW with the major computer companies hiring specialized production staff and graphic artists to dress up their home pages and smaller companies with boring pages (or worse, ugly graphics designed by a programmer) will lose the production-value battle for attention.

Fame is the second factor that tends to support monopoly in information products. By definition, fame favors a few people or companies that are particularly well known, and the more people read or hear about someone famous, the more famous that person becomes. Consider two hypothetical new film releases, one starring Arnold Schwarzenegger and one with another hunk with equal acting talent whom nobody has heard of before. Which film will attract the largest audience? Why, Arnold's, of course. Thus, after these two films have played the world, Schwarzenegger will be more famous than before (since many people will have seen him) and the unknown hunk will remain unknown.[6] Similarly, because Microsoft is a famous company, all magazines and newspapers review every new release of *Encarta* and other Microsoft hypermedia titles, making Microsoft even more famous and increasing their sales compared to smaller publishers. Also, Microsoft by mailing publications like *Microsoft Magazine* to their customers' home, Microsoft is pursuing a brand-name strategy to build up customer loyalty in a way that would be impossible to emulate by smaller brands.[7]

Even though production values and fame both tend to favor a small number of large hypermedia producers, the third factor, critical mass, may be the killer monopoly enhancer. Hypertext products derive significant added value from links and add-on information. Consider again the example of dinosaurs. Microsoft *Encarta* (a hypertext encyclopedia) could have hypertext links to *Microsoft Dinosaurs,* thus simultaneously increasing sales of *Microsoft Dinosaurs* and adding value to *Encarta.* Of course, a third-party hypertext encyclopedia could have a link to *3-D Dinosaur Adventure* but depending on

---

[6] The movie star example is not entirely irrelevant to a discussion of hypermedia markets. *Compton's Interactive Encyclopedia* is using Patrick Stewart (British actor famous for his role as the captain in *Star Trek—The Next Generation*) as a narrator in the hope that some of his star quality will rub off on the hypermedia product.

[7] In fact, hypermedia offered by smaller companies will tend to be viewed as un-branded and seen as individual, stand-alone products. Only the very largest hypermedia vendors will be able to achieve brand-name status in the market, and these vendors will thus gain significant benefits from brand-name recognition.

the way distribution and royalty mechanisms play out, there may not be much synergy to doing so. Also, independent software vendors (ISVs) may produce add-on modules to widely sold products like *Encarta* to provide special effects such as an animated physics simulation to better explain, say, gravity. All experience from the PC market shows that ISVs only port software to the most popular platforms, so the availability of add-on modules will tend to favor hypermedia titles that have already established critical mass with respect to market share.

It is currently impossible to predict which of the two opposing trends to anarchy and to monopoly will prove the strongest. It is possible that a third way will emerge where the hypermedia market is dominated by a small number of near-monopoly players who set standards and mainline directions while a much larger number of garage-shop publishers add variety and have the ability to explore new options faster than the giants.

It is possible that a new phenomenon will emerge in the form of "temporary monopolies" that dominate for a short period only to be replaced virtually overnight. The Internet seems to encourage temporary monopolies because of its ability to instantly distribute software to millions of users who all are part of the same discussion groups and rumor mills. Consider two examples discussed further in Chapter 7: the Netscape browser for the WWW increased its market share from 0.1% to 64% during the four-month period from August to December 1994 (and the previous market leader, Mosaic, dropped from 73% to 21% in the same period), and usage of the Lycos search server increased at an annualized rate of 130 million percent during the fall of 1994.

Creative Centers

For printed materials, there has not traditionally been a single city or geographic area that dominated world market. Books and newspapers are published throughout the world and it is not particularly advantageous for an author to move to a specific location in order to be published. Many countries have a concentration of large book publishers and newspapers in their capitals but traditionally most provincial towns have had their own newspaper(s). In the U.S., New York City serves as the closest approximation to a creative center for word production. Two of the three national newspapers in the U.S., *The New York Times* and the *Wall Street Journal*, are published in New York (the third, *USA Today*, is published in Arlington, Virginia). However, the combined circulation of the three national newspapers is only 4.5 million copies which is 7% of the circulation of all newspapers in the U.S. In other words, 93% of newspaper circulation in the U.S. is due to local papers.[8]

In contrast to the print industry, the film and computer industries have had a disproportionate part of their most important companies located in a very small number of geographic areas. The film industry is concentrated in the Los Angeles area[9] not just with respect to the U.S. market, but with respect to the world market: 80% of the box office receipts in Europe go to American films[10] and all major top-grossing blockbuster releases[11] for the last several years have been American.[12] The computer industry is not quite as concentrated as the film industry,[13] but the Silicon Valley area between San Francisco and San Jose still serves as the main creative center for this industry with a very large number of established and start-up companies. In order to benefit from the availability of skilled staff, suppliers, customers, and other

[8] The influence of New York as a creative center for the print industry is larger than the market share of its newspapers indicates: *The New York Times* and the *Wall Street Journal* are read disproportionally by influential decision makers and opinion leaders and the city publishes magazines accounting for nearly half of the magazine industry's national revenues.

[9] Only one of the six major studios, Paramount, is physically located in Hollywood. Two (Disney and Warner Bros.) are in Burbank, and three (Universal, Columbia/Sony, and 20th Century Fox) are in other Los Angeles suburbs.

[10] For comparison, European films only have a 1% market share of the U.S. film market.

[11] All films grossing more than $100 million outside U.S. in 1993 were American: *Jurassic Park* ($530M), *The Bodyguard* ($248M), *Aladdin* ($185M), *The Fugitive* ($170M), *Indecent Proposal* ($152M), *Cliffhanger* ($139M), *Bram Stoker's Dracula* ($107M), and *Home Alone 2* ($106M). The only non-U.S. film to come close was *Les Visiteurs*, which scored a $90M non-U.S. box office. But since *Les Visiteurs* had zero dollars in U.S. sales in 1993, it ended as number 27 on the list of world-wide box office receipts—all the top 26 films were American.

[12] For the week before Christmas in 1994, only 26 of the 110 films on the top-10 lists in Belgium, Brazil, Denmark, France, Italy, The Netherlands, Norway, South Africa, Spain, Sweden, and Switzerland were non-American according to *Variety* magazine. Disney's *The Lion King* was number one in seven of the eleven countries and number two in two more (*Variety* article "Lion king over Euro holiday B.O.," January 8, 1995, p. 18).

[13] The top-five companies only account for 33% of the software market, whereas the top-five film companies have an 81% market share.

partners in the creative center, 20% of the largest 50 software companies that were founded in Europe have since moved their headquarters to the U.S.[14]

The existence of internationally dominant creative centers for the film and computer industry serves to motivate high-caliber personnel to relocate to those areas from all other parts of the world, leading to further centralization of activity. By concentrating so many people who work in the same field, creative centers ensure an extraordinary degree of cross-fertilization which again leads to rapid refinement and dissemination of ideas [Saxenian 1994]. Technology transfer by warm bodies is known to be much more effective than technology transfer by technical reports, and the extensive job hopping that takes place in a creative center therefore benefits all the companies in the area by increasing their exposure to new ideas and techniques.

It is currently too early to predict whether the multimedia and hypermedia industry will be dominated by creative centers in the way the film and computer industries are, or whether it will follow the less centralized precedent set by the publishing industry. In principle, the Internet allows people to work together on a multimedia project without the need for them to live in the same area, but in practice intensely creative work, brainstorming, design, and the informal contacts that lead to most business still require people to be colocated in the same physically proximate reality (PPR). Virtual reality and cyberspace are not the same as dinner at Il Fornaio.

Since the two main components of the multimedia industry are the computers and moviemaking, the most likely candidates for a creative center for multimedia are Silicon Valley and Hollywood. Whether the resulting "Siliwood" will form around San Francisco's "multimedia gulch" or around the Hollywood studios is currently the topic of much debate, but there is no doubt that California is a very likely home for one or more creative centers for multimedia. Of course, if the monopoly scenario outlined above turns out to happen, there will be definite advantages to be located close to Microsoft headquarters in Redmond, WA, and the Seattle area is already attracting a large number of highly creative multimedia companies.

---

[14] Classified by the location of their headquarters, the distribution of the 30 software companies with the largest sales in Europe is as follows: U.S. 19, France 5, Germany 4, Italy 1, U.K. 1.

A Summary: Hypertext versus the Competition

As can be seen from the discussion of the empirical usability research in Chapter 10, there is no clear evidence for whether hypertext is in fact superior to paper. For some applications hypertext tested better, but for other applications paper tested better than the current generation of hypertext. It seems clear that hypertext is indeed superior in some cases even now. But for many other applications we will have to wait for better technology and better user interface designs to get any hope of replacing paper.

Furthermore, we have very little experience with really big hypertexts. Almost all the hypertexts that have been tested in formal usability experiments have been very small and have contained only about a hundred nodes or less. Only a few larger hypertexts have been constructed, such as *The Electronic Whole Earth Catalog* with its approximately ten thousand nodes (see Chapter 4), and even they can only be considered as medium-large.

A really large hypertext would contain at least a hundred thousand nodes, and we should expect to see some hypertexts with millions of nodes in the future. The only current example of hypertext of this magnitude is the World Wide Web but is it doubtful whether this collection of disparate information can be considered as a single hypertext structure. It may well be that many of the major advantages of hypertext will not become apparent until we have such great hypertexts integrating major fields of human knowledge. But we are guaranteed to discover new usability and implementation problems as we move to such huge information structures.

Table 13.1 gives a summary of the advantages and disadvantages of hypertext.[15] Obviously hypertext has enough advantages to ensure it a bright future if we can design sufficiently usable interfaces to at least partly overcome

---

[15] It is interesting to note that Table 13.1 was taken almost unchanged from a similar table in my 1990 book, *Hypertext and Hypermedia*. I decided to make only two changes. The first change was to delete "not portable" as a disadvantage of hypertext compared with paper. Laptops are now sufficiently small that many people travel with their computer wherever they go, and the PDAs (personal digital assistants) are even smaller and will soon have wireless connectivity to the Internet. The second change was to add cross-platform information exchange via the WWW as an advantage of hypertext compared with traditional computer systems. The remaining advantages and disadvantages remain the same as five years ago, showing that the big picture of technology changes more slowly than it may seem to those of us who are caught up in individual projects on a day-to-day basis.

	Compared with paper	Compared with traditional computer systems
Advantages of Hypertext	Can show moving images, animations, film Easier to update—can permit automatic downloading of changes May be shipped over networks Making single copies is easy Takes up less physical storage space Can be shared by several people User-oriented reading Potentially: The whole world's literature a click away	Data structures have user-oriented semantics A single framework to handle unstructured data (free text), semi-structured data (semantic nets etc.), and structured data (tables etc.) Does not require "programming" skills to be able to construct complex structures On the WWW: A single standard for information transfer across platforms
Disadvantages of Hypertext	30% slower reading speed on current displays Lower resolution graphics Overhead in having to learn system and setting up computer No user interface standard No standard for data transfer No regular publishing channels, bookshops, libraries, ISBN, etc. No "romance"—first editions, leather binding, etc. Computer text "homogenized"	Possible spaghetti structure No central definition of the structure of the data, and therefore no easy way to specify general actions or computations on the data

Table 13.1. *Summary of the advantages and disadvantages of hypertext compared with the competition.*

those disadvantages that have the largest negative impact on our users. But just as obviously, hypertext is not the single answer to all our problems.

Appendix: Annotated Bibliography

The literature on hypertext and hypermedia is very scattered, reflecting the fact that these concepts have not been subjected to a focused research effort until recently. It is thus almost impossible for any individual to get an overview of the literature, and this bibliography is certainly not intended as a complete listing of every paper ever published on hypertext. It includes the papers and books that I have read and found useful and it also reflects my personal interest in specifically the user interface aspect of hypertext.

Surveys

A highly illustrated survey of many recent hypermedia designs is given in *"Understanding Hypermedia: From Multimedia to Virtual Reality"* by Bob Cotton and Richard Oliver (Phaidon Press 1993). The book is essentially a huge collection of design examples without much in the way of analysis so it is best suited for people who already know what they should be looking for as they enjoy the many pretty pictures.

Mike and Sadie Morrison's *"The Magic of Interactive Entertainment"* (second edition, Sams Publishing 1994) is a wide-ranging survey of video games and other kinds of entertainment systems with many historical examples. The book is well-illustrated with game screens as well as photographs of various home and arcade hardware. The book comes with a CD-ROM with demonstrations of many popular games for DOS, Windows, and the Macintosh.

The best short overview of hypertext is probably still the review paper by Jeff Conklin from MCC: Hypertext: An introduction and survey. *IEEE Computer* **20**, 9 (September 1987), 17-41. Even though the paper is somewhat old by now, it is still an excellent source for the basic concepts of hypertext and for descriptions of the classic and pioneering hypertext systems. For a briefer and less conceptually profound survey, see the October 1988 issue of *BYTE* (especially [Fiderio 1988]) which also included a list of vendors of popular hypertext products.

Several broad overview papers covering many aspects of hypertext and many important case studies of practical projects are contained in the *"Hypertext/Hypermedia Handbook"* edited by E. Berk and J. Devlin (McGraw-Hill 1991). The *"CD-ROM Handbook"* edited by Chris Sherman (second edition, McGraw-Hill 1994) contains listings of CD-ROMs on the market and surveys of issues related to the editing and production of CD-ROMs and multimedia.

"Hypertext Hands-On! An Introduction to a New Way of Organizing and Accessing Information" by Ben Shneiderman and Greg Kearsley (Addison-Wesley 1989) is a short and quickly read book covering the basics of hypertext. It is written like a hypertext with lots of cross-references between sections, and does indeed include a true hypertext version of the text on two IBM PC diskettes in Hyperties format.

"Hypertext in Context" by Cliff McKnight and Andrew Dillon (Cambridge University Press 1991) is also fairly short but is much more theoretically inclined. Its specific focus is the academic use of hypertext (for research as well as education) and studies of research of how people read.

"The Way MultiMedia Works" by Simon Collin (Microsoft Press and Dorling Kindersley 1994) is a highly illustrated popular survey of the technology behind multimedia. It also includes screenshots from several current multimedia titles and has a hardware buying guide. Aaron Marcus' book *"Multimedia Interface Design Studio"* (Random House, late 1995) focuses on the the design of user interfaces for multimedia and online services with many case studies.

Societies

The only professional society specifically for hypertext researchers and designers is the Association for Computing Machinery (ACM)'s SIGLINK special interest group. SIGLINK membership includes a newsletter with information about events in the hypertext field and announcements of the leading annual conference (see below). For membership information, contact

ACM Headquarters
1515 Broadway
New York, NY 10036
USA
Tel. +1-212-869-7440, Fax +1-212-944-1318
Email `acmhelp@acm.org`

Compendium

A major collection of hypertext papers (including the collected papers from the most important conferences) is available in hypertext form as the *ACM Hypertext Compendium*, edited by Robert Akscyn. The total size of the hypertext is about 4,500 nodes, covering 128 papers. Three versions are available: KMS for Sun workstations ($495 for non-members and $295 for ACM members), HyperCard for Macintosh ($179 for non-members and $100 for members), and plain ASCII text with or without link markup (also $179/$100). To order, contact ACM Press at ACM Headquarters at the above address or call +1-212-869-7440 for further information.

Conferences

Due to the rapid changes in the hypermedia field, the most interesting information is to be gained at conferences and not from slower publication media like journals.

For in-depth information, the most interesting references on hypertext at the moment are the proceedings from the ACM series of hypertext conferences that started with the **Hypertext'87 Workshop** held at Chapel Hill, NC, November 13–15, 1987. The proceedings from Hypertext'87 contains all the papers presented at the workshop as well as position papers by most of the participants. This workshop was the first formal meeting on hypertext and attracted almost all the people active in the field.

The proceedings were out of print for a long time but can now be obtained for $35 as ACM Order No. 608892 from:

ACM Order Department
P.O. Box 64145
Baltimore, MD 21264
USA
Tel. 1-800-342-6626 or +1-410-528-4261

Selected papers from the Hypertext'87 workshop have been published in the July 1988 issue of the *Communications of the ACM*. This issue is also available in various hypertext formats as *Hypertext on Hypertext* in versions for the IBM PC and Macintosh (about $30 each), and Unix workstations such as Sun (rather expensive).[1] It is worth getting hold of several of the versions to compare how different designers convert the same basic information into hypertext.[2] Order information is available from:

> Marketing Manager Electronics Products
> Association for Computing Machinery
> 1515 Broadway
> New York, NY 10036
> USA

It may be quite natural to have reports on the Hypertext'87 workshop appear in a hypertext format. I am aware of three such reports: one by Lynda Hardman from the Scottish HCI Centre in Edinburgh written in Guide, one from Mark Bernstein from Eastgate Systems written in their own Hypergate system, and one written by myself[3] in a homemade format (described in [Nielsen 1990b]) running under HyperCard. All three reports run on the Macintosh. Generally, the problem with electronic publications at the moment is that there is no organized way of getting hold of them in the way there is with traditional books, so you may want to read the traditional version of my own report, which is printed in the April 1988 issue of the ACM *SIGCHI Bulletin* (vol. 19, no. 4, 27–35). A good workshop report by Esther Dyson appeared in issue 87-11 of her newsletter *Release 1.0*, dated 25 November 1987.

The second ACM hypertext conference was **Hypertext'89** (Pittsburgh, PA, November 5–8, 1989). The proceedings from this conference cost $36 from the

---

[1] Furthermore, these papers are part of the much larger *ACM Hypertext Compendium* (see above).

[2] See [Alschuler 1989] for a comparative review of three versions of the ACM *Hypertext on Hypertext*. Some of the versions have been "colorized" (prettied-up after the fact by somebody other than the author) to some extent by adding new information that was not present in the original publication: The HyperCard version for the Macintosh contains scanned photographs of the authors, the HyperTies version for the IBM PC contains added commentary articles, and the KMS workstation version contains new levels of hierarchical subheadings to better structure the text.

[3] The last section of Chapter 2 describes how you may acquire a copy of this hypertext.

ACM Order Dept. (address above), Order No. 608891. See [Nielsen 1990c] and [Jacques 1990] for conference reports.

The third ACM hypertext conference, **Hypertext'91**, was held December 15–18, 1991 in San Antonio, TX. The proceedings cost $35 and are available from the ACM Order Dept. (Order No. 614910).

In 1991, ACM SIGLINK officially decided to have its annual conference take place in Europe every second year under the name *ECHT'xx.* (European Conference on HyperText) and every second year in North America under the name *Hypertext'xx.* The fourth ACM hypertext conference was therefore **ECHT'92**, held in Milan, Italy, November 30 – December 4, 1992. The proceedings are available for $30 from the ACM Order Dept. (Order No. 614920).

The fifth ACM hypertext conference, **Hypertext'93** took place in Seattle, WA, November 14–18, 1993, and the sixth conference was **ECHT'94** under the slightly changed name "European Conference on Hypermedia Technology" (Edinburgh, Scotland, September 18–23, 1994).

The seventh conference, **Hypertext'96**, will be held in the U.S. in the spring of 1996. At the time of this writing, the location and dates for the ACM hypertext conferences had not yet been determined for 1997 and later years, but in keeping with tradition,[4] 1997 conference will most likely be **ECHT'97** and take place in Europe. For further information about these conferences, contact ACM headquarters by email to acmhelp@acm.org or link to http://acm.org/siglink/conf.html on the Internet.

The Alvey[5] HCI Club sponsored a U.K. workshop on hypertext in Aberdeen, 17–18 March 1988. It was not nearly as widely announced as the North Carolina workshop and the proceedings are considerably thinner, but they give a nice overview of the fairly large hypertext activity in the U.K. The proceedings are published as Ray McAleese (Ed.), *Hypertext: Theory into Practice,* Ablex, 1989.

The second U.K. conference on hypertext, **Hypertext 2**, was held at the University of York on 29–30 June 1989. The proceedings are published as Ray

---

[4] Actually, the ACM "tradition" changed somewhat in 1995 when there was no hypertext conference because they decided to move the conference date from the end of the year to the spring.

[5] British research program in information technology.

McAleese and Catherine Green (Eds.), *Hypertext: State of the Art,* Ablex, 1990. See [Nielsen 1989d] for a conference report.

This conference came close to being a true European conference but the first "official" European hypertext conference was **ECHT'90** (European Conference on Hypertext) in Paris, France, November 28–30, 1990. The ECHT'90 proceedings were published by Cambridge University Press.[6] Because of ECHT'90's role as the major European hypertext conference, Hypertext'3 (Enschede, The Netherlands, 10–12 April 1991) was organized as a special interest workshop on educational use of hypertext. Since 1992, the ECHT series of conferences has been granted status as the official ACM hypertext conference for even years, so ECHT should really be considered an international conference and not just a European one. See the discussion of the ACM conferences above.

Due to the rapid changes in the deployment of the World Wide Web, conferences take place twice a year, with conferences in Europe in the spring and in the U.S. in the fall. The first two conferences were **WWW'94** at CERN (Geneva, Switzerland, May 25–27, 1994) and the **Second International WWW Conference Fall'94: Mosaic and the Web** (Chicago, IL, October 17–20, 1994). The next four WWW conferences are planned for Darmstadt, Germany (spring 1995), Boston, MA (fall 1995), Paris, France (spring 1996) and a location on the west coast of the U.S. (fall 1996).

In keeping with the globalist hypertext tradition of the WWW, the proceedings from these conferences are available in hypertext format on the Internet: URL `http://www1.cern.ch/WWW94/` for WWW'94 and URL `http://www.ncsa.uiuc.edu/SDG/IT94/Proceedings/WWW2_Proceedings .html` for Mosaic and the Web'94. Information about future WWW conferences is made available over the WWW and links to this information will almost certainly be found on CERN's WWW home page (`http://info.cern.ch/hypertext/WWW/TheProject.html`) and the "What's New with NCSA Mosaic" page at the National Center for Supercomputing Applications (`http://www.ncsa.uiuc.edu/SDG/ Software/Mosaic/Docs/whats-new.html`).

---

[6] The ECHT'90 proceedings are published as Rizk, A., Streitz, N., and André, J. (Eds.) (1990), *Hypertext: Concepts, Systems and Applications.* Cambridge University Press, Cambridge, U.K., ISBN 0-521-40517-3.

The National Institute of Standards and Technology (NIST) (formerly known as the National Bureau of Standards) sponsored a **Hypertext Standardization Workshop**. It took place in Gaithersburg, MD, 16–18 January 1990 and is documented in Moline, J., Benigni, D. and Baronas, J. (Eds.) (1990). *Proceedings of the Hypertext Standardization Workshop January 16–18, 1990,* National Institute of Standards **Special Publication 500-178**. This book is for sale at

> Superintendent of Documents
> U.S. Government Printing Office
> Washington, DC 20402
> USA
> Tel. +1-202-783-3238

and

> National Technical Information Service
> 5285 Port Royal Road
> Springfield, VA 22161
> USA
> Tel. +1-703-487-4600

For information about possible future standardization workshops contact:

> Hypermedia Standardization Workshops
> attn: Daniel R. Benigni
> National Institute of Standards and Technology
> Hypertext Competence Project
> Technology Bldg. 225, Room A-266
> Gaithersburg, MD 20899
> USA
> Fax: +1-301-590-0932
> Email: benigni@ise.ncsl.nist.gov

Other conferences that sometimes have papers on hypertext include:

- IFIP **INTERACT** (Human-Computer Interaction) [every two or three years]
- ACM **CHI** (Computer-Human Interaction) [every year]
- ACM **SIGIR** (Information Retrieval) [every year]
- ACM **COIS** (Office Information Systems) [every year]
- the British Computer Society **HCI** (Human-Computer Interaction); proceedings published by Cambridge University Press under the title *People and Computers* [every year]

- the ACM conference on **Document Processing Systems** [December 1988 in Santa Fe, NM]
- the ACM **CSCW** (Computer-Supported Cooperative Work) conferences [every two years in even years]
- **International Online Information Meetings** (proceedings published by Learned Information Ltd.)

Journals and Magazines

The only scientific journal specifically dedicated to hypertext is *Hypermedia,* which was started in 1989.

For subscription information or a free sample copy, contact

> Taylor Graham Publishing
> 500 Chesham House
> 150 Regent Street
> London W1R 5FA
> United Kingdom

To submit a paper to *Hypermedia,* contact the editor,

> Patricia M. Baird
> Scottish Daily Record & Sunday Mail
> Anderson Quay
> Glasgow, G3 8DA
> United Kingdom
> Tel. +44-41-248 3523
> Fax +44-41-242 3527
> Email: `100137.3304@compuserve.com`

In addition to at the conferences listed above, papers on hypertext are also published in several journals in the computer science/user interface/information retrieval area. Wiley is publishing the journal *Electronic Publishing—Origination, Dissemination and Design (EP-ODD),* which started in 1988 and has hypertext as one of its core subjects. Subscription information and a free sample copy may be obtained by writing to

> Dept. AC
> John Wiley & Sons Ltd.
> Baffins Lane, Chichester
> W. Sussex PO19 1UD
> United Kingdom

or

Subscription Dept. C
John Wiley & Sons Inc.
605 Third Avenue
New York, NY 10158
USA

The *Journal of the American Society for Information Science* (JASIS) also covers hypertext to some extent, especially with regard to the search problem and information retrieval issues. The May 1989 issue was a special issue on hypertext and the September 1993 issue was a special issue on digital libraries.

The special issue of *IEEE Computer* (vol. **21**, no. 1, January 1988) on "Electronic Publishing Technologies" included several papers on hypertext, as did the October 1991 (vol. **24**, no. 10) special issue on multimedia information systems. In addition to the special issue on the Hypertext'87 conference discussed above, the *Communications of the ACM* has had several relevant special issues: July 1989 was a special issue on "interactive technology" with emphasis on such hypertext-related issues as interactive video, DVI, and optical disks, December 1992 was a special issue on information filtering, January 1993 was a special issue on multimedia in the workplace (e.g., desktop video conferencing), February 1994 was a special issue on reference models and formal specification of hypertext, July 1994 was a special issue on intelligent agents, and August 1994 was a special issue on the Internet. The *ACM Transactions on Information Systems* had a special issue on hypertext in January 1989 (vol. **7**, no. 1). The *IEEE Computer Graphics & Applications* magazine had a special issue on multimedia in July 1991 (vol. **11**, no. 4) with several articles on hypermedia systems and many pretty color illustrations.

The various personal computer magazines sometimes have coverage of hypertext and related issues such as multimedia developments. *BYTE* magazine has traditionally had the best general coverage from a technical perspective. The June 1982 issue of *BYTE* was an early special issue on interactive videodisks, the November 1986 issue was a special issue on optical storage media, and the October 1988 issue was a special issue on hypertext itself. Magazines such as *PC World*, *MacWorld*, and *MacUser* cover more platform-oriented developments, and magazines like *Internet World* cover the net. Multimedia issues are covered in endless magazines of which *New Media* is one of the better, and there are also several trade magazines specifically about CD-ROMs (e.g., *CD•ROM World*). You can often wing free subscriptions if you are a "qualifying buyer" who specifies or recommends purchases for a large department.

The coolest publication about online events and interactive media is WIRED magazine. It covers nerd culture and the evolving online communities with an emphasis on people and usage implications (for example, an article on the work environment at Microsoft referred to the employees as "microserfs"). The magazine has its own WWW server called HotWired at `http://www.hotwired.com/`. For subscription information contact

> WIRED Magazine
> P.O. Box 191826
> San Francisco, CA 94119-9866
> USA
> Tel.[7] 1-800-SO-WIRED or +1-415-904-0660
> Email: subscriptions@wired.com or info@wired.com

Also, the Usenet has a netnews newsgroup called `alt.hypertext` with online discussion of hypertext issues. Other newsgroups of interest include `comp.infosystems.www.*` (several groups about the World Wide Web) `comp.multimedia`, `comp.internet.net-happenings` (new facilities and events on the Internet), `comp.ivideodisc` (interactive videodisks), `rec.arts.int-fiction` (interactive fiction), `alt.cd-rom`, `sci.virtual-worlds` (virtual reality), and `comp.sys.mac.hypercard`.

Videotapes

Since hypertext systems are dynamic by nature, they can often be explained better on a videotape than in a printed article. A highly recommended tape is the ACM's *Interactive Digital Video,* which costs $50 for members and $75 for nonmembers. This tape covers Palenque, the Carnegie Mellon University intelligent meeting simulation, the Intel DVI (Digital Video Interactive) technology, a system from the Getty Museum for access to medieval manuscripts, VideoWindows, samples from the MIT Media Lab (including the *Aspen Movie Map*), and systems from several other companies and universities. Ordering information (order no. 217890 for VHS and 217891 for U-Matic) is available from

---

7   The 800 number is quite characteristic of the magazine's style.

ACM Press Database and Electronic Product Series
Association for Computing Machinery
1515 Broadway
New York, NY 10036
USA

ACM also has a continuing series of videotapes called the *SIGGRAPH Video Review*, which as the name implies is mostly focused on traditional rendering work in computer graphics and computer animation. But some of the videos in this series are hypermedia-related, including especially issues 13 (the *Movie Manual*), 19 (the Symbolics Document Examiner), 48 (the MIT *Illustrated Neuroanatomy Glossary* and other multimedia applications), 58 (the Apple MacWorld tradeshow information kiosk), 63 (the Guides system), 78 (scenarios for future hypermedia), and 70 (possible future trends for HyperCard and the Knowledge Navigator). Most of these tapes are available in both NTSC (U.S. format) and PAL (European format). The SIGGRAPH Video Review and a free catalog listing all the issues are available from:

SIGGRAPH Video Review
c/o VI&A/First Priority
PO Box 576
Itasca, IL 60143-0576
USA
Tel. (24 hr.) +1-800-523-5503 or +1-708-250-0807
Fax +1-312-789-7185
Email: `svrorders@siggraph.org`

Books about the Internet

I have given up providing literature references about the Internet since there are so many different books available these days (the number of books about the Internet grows at about 290% per year). Any bookstore with just a minimum selection of computer books will have an entire table dedicated to the most recent crop of books, and since the Internet changes so fast there is reason to recommend newer books over older ones. A list of more than 200 Internet-related books is posted bimonthly to the newsgroups `alt.internet.services`, `alt.online-service`, `alt.books.technical`, `misc.books.technical`, `alt.bbs.internet`, `misc.answers`, `alt.answers`, and `news.answers`. The list is available by anonymous FTP as

`ftp://rtfm.mit.edu/pub/usenet/news.answers/internet-services/book-list`

To receive the list by email, send the following message:

```
To: mail-server@rtfm.mit.edu
Subject: <subject line is ignored>
send usenet/news.answers/internet-services/internet-booklist
```

The problem with this list is obviously that you have to be on the net already to be able to find it. Three of the most respected printed books are *"The Whole Internet User's Guide and Catalog"* by Ed Krol (2nd edition, O'Reilly & Associates 1994), *"The Internet Unleashed"* edited by Kevin Kelly (Sams Publishing 1994), and *"Everybody's Guide to the Internet"* by Adam Gaffin (MIT Press 1994). The latter is a printed version of the Electronic Frontier Foundation's famous online file *"The Big Dummy's Guide to the Internet,"* which you can download for free from many Internet servers around the world. In buying the book, you basically pay for the convenience of being able to get an introduction to the Internet without having to be on the net first.

Here is a list of some of the places on the Internet where you can get *The Big Dummy's Guide to the Internet.* My experience with giving links to specific Internet files in my books is fairly poor since most of these addresses change fairly rapidly. Even so, I am listing a large number of links, so you will most likely be able to find at least one that works. Please try sites close to your own location first.

Australia
    http://www.vifp.monash.edu.au/bdgtti

Austria
    http://www.cosy.sbg.ac.at/doc/bdgtti/bdgtti-toc.html
    http://info.archlab.tuwien.ac.at/doc/

Canada
    http://madhaus.utcc.utoronto.ca/bdgtti/bdgtti.html
    http://www.emr.ca/big-dummys-guide/bdgtti-intro.html
    http://www.mta.ca/bdgtti/bdgtti.html

Denmark
    http://www.iesd.auc.dk/system/bdgtti-2.2/bdg_toc.html
    http://www.daimi.aau.dk/bdgtti-1.01_toc.html

Estonia
    ftp://ftp.eenet.ee/pub/guides/bdg/bdg_3.html

France
    http://mistral.enst.fr/~pioch/bigdummy/

Germany

    ftp://ftp.germany.eu.net/pub/books/big-dummys-guide/

    http://www.germany.eu.net/books/bdgtti/bdgtti.html

    http://www.Mathematik.Uni-Marburg.de/doc/bdg/bdg_toc.html

    http://www.cs.tu-berlin.de/bigdummy/

    http://dv.go.dlr.de:8081/misc/doku/bdgtti-2.0/bdg_toc.html

    http://lurker.dfv.rwth-aachen.de/dummy/bdg_198.html

    http://www.artcom.de/help/BDGttI/bdgtti-1.02_toc.html

Italy

    http://www.pi.infn.it/bdgtti-2.2/bdg_toc.html

Japan

    http://www.ntt.jp/bdgtti

Latvia

    http://www.riga.lv/bdgtti/bdgtti.html

Norway

    http://www.oslonett.no/html/bdgtti/bdg_3.html

Singapore

    http://www.iss.nus.sg/public/Internet_Links/BDGNEW/bdg_toc.html

South Africa

    http://www.iaccess.za/bdgtti/index.html

South Korea

    ftp://cair.kaist.ac.kr/doc/EFF/EFF/papers/

Switzerland

    http://cuisg13.unige.ch:8100/bdgtti-1.01.html

Turkey

    http://www.metu.edu.tr/bdgtti/bdg_toc.html

United Kingdom

    http://www.mcc.ac.uk/BigDummy/bdgtti.html

    http://sg1.cc.ic.ac.uk:6680/bdg/bdgtti.html

    http://agora.leeds.ac.uk/WWW/bdgtti/bdgtti-1.02_toc.html

United States

    ftp://ftp.eff.org/pub/Net_info/Big_Dummy/

    http://www.eff.org/papers/bdgtti/bdg_toc.html

    http://soma.npa.uiuc.edu/docs/bdgtti.html

    http://cdr.stanford.edu/html/bdgtti/bdgtti.html

http://rainbow.ldeo.columbia.edu/bdgtti
http://alpha.acast.nova.edu/bigdummy/bdg_toc.html
http://www.gc.cuny.edu/resourcetools/BigDummy.html
http://ageninfo.tamu.edu/bdgtti/bdgtti.html
http://www.hep.net/documents/bigdummy/bdgtti.html
http://gopher.metronet.com:70/1/bdg
http://ucunix.san.uc.edu/bdgtti/bdgtti.html
http://icicle.winternet.com/books/bdg/
http://www.iia.org/bdg-2.2/bdg_toc.html
http://www.umn.edu/bdgtti/bdgtti-1.04_toc.html
http://www.cs.yale.edu/HTML/WORLD/org/eff/bdgtti-1.04/bdgtti-1.04_toc.html
http://www.hcc.hawaii.edu/bdgtti/bdgtti-1.02_toc.html
http://www.cs.byu.edu/bdg/bdgtti-1.01_toc.html

Furthermore, a HyperCard version of *The Big Dummy's Guide to the Internet* is available by anonymous FTP from ftp.eff.org as

/pub/Net_info/Big_Dummy/Other_versions/big-dummys-guide.sea.hqx

Classics

Bush, V. (1945). As we may think. *Atlantic Monthly,* July, pp. 101–108. This was the original paper in which Vannevar Bush proposed his "Memex" device, which is now regarded as the first hypertext system (even though it was never implemented). The paper is reprinted both in the proceedings from the first Microsoft CD-ROM conference (as mentioned in section 3) and in A. Goldberg (Ed.) (1988): *A History of Personal Workstations,* Addison-Wesley. It also exists in a hypertext form on a Guide demo disk called "The Guide to Hypertext" available from OWL. Nyce and Kahn [1989] discuss Bush's early essays in which he developed the Memex idea and reprint two illustrations showing how the Memex would have looked had it been built. Nyce and Kahn [1991] reprint both the original paper and several other essays by Bush together with commentaries linking them to modern hypertext research.

Engelbart, D. C. and English, W. K. (1968). A research center for augmenting human intellect. *AFIPS Conference Proceedings* **33**, 1, 395–410. Engelbart was an early pioneer in actually implementing the hypertext ideas.

Kay, A. and Goldberg, A. (1977). Personal dynamic media. *IEEE Computer* **10**, 3 (March), 31–41. A very influential early paper on multimedia personal computing. Reprinted in A. Goldberg (Ed.): *A History of Personal Workstations,* Addison-Wesley 1988, 254–263.

Lippman, A. (1980). Movie-Maps: An application of the optical videodisk to computer graphics. *Computer Graphics* **14**, 3, 32–42. Paper on the *Aspen* system, which was very likely the first hypermedia system.

Nelson, T. (1974). *Computer Lib/Dream Machines,* first edition self-published by Nelson in 1974, revised edition published by Microsoft Press in 1987. The part called "Computer Lib" was probably the first book published on the subject of personal computing. The other half of the book, "Dream Machines," is to a great extent about hypertext.

Nelson, T.: *Literary Machines,* Mindful Press, 3020 Bridgeway #295, Sausalito, CA 94965, USA ($25 postpaid in the US, $30 rest of world). An abridged version of *Literary Machines* in hypertext form (on a demo disk for the Guide system) was issued by OWL International, Inc., in 1987. This book has been published in several versions, starting in 1981. It describes Nelson's Xanadu system and many of his other original and pioneering ideas in the hypertext area.

Biographies of several of the hypertext pioneers appear in the following popular book: Rheingold, H. (1985). *Tools for Thought: The People and Ideas behind the Next Computer Revolution,* Simon & Schuster, New York.

Alphabetical Listing of Papers and Books

Ahlberg, C., and Shneiderman, B. (1994). Visual information seeking: Tight coupling of dynamic query filters with starfield displays. *Proc. ACM CHI'94,* 313–317 & 479–480.

> Dynamic queries are those where the user interactively manipulates one or more continuous scales of attributes and can see the results immediately. This paper describes two applications: the HomeFinder (where dots representing houses for sale are displayed on a map if the houses are within a specified price range and a specified distance from the user's work) and the FilmFinder (where films can be selected according to criteria like the actors, directors, genres, year of production, running time, and review rating). For the HomeFinder, geography provides a natural spatial layout for the data on the computer screen, but for the FilmFinder, a new mechanism called starfields was used. The starfield is a scatterplot where the user can select what two attributes should be mapped to the axes. A third attribute is used for color coding, and the remaining attributes are available via pop-ups.

Ahlberg, C., Williamson, C., and Shneiderman, B. (1992). Dynamic queries for information exploration: An implementation and evaluation. *Proc. ACM CHI'92 Conf.,* 619–626.

> Subjects could find information in a database 119% faster (i.e., in less than half the time) when they were given dynamic feedback as they constructed their query than when they did not get any feedback until after they had submitted a complete query to the system.

Akscyn, R., and Halasz, F. (Eds.) (1991). *Topics on Hypertext.* Addison-Wesley.

Revised versions of selected papers from the ACM Hypertext'89 conference as well as supplementary material such as a survey of existing research and commercial hypertext systems.

Akscyn, R., McCracken, D., and Yoder, E. (1988). KMS: A distributed hypermedia system for managing knowledge in organizations. *Communications of the ACM* **31**, 7 (July), 820–835.

KMS is a commercial hypertext system for Unix workstations (e.g. Suns) that was designed as a follow-up to ZOG [Robertson et al. 1981]. Its nodes are called workspaces and take up exactly half a screen or a full screen, and since links point to an entire workspace, the system is highly frame-based.

Akscyn, R., Yoder, E., and McCracken, D. (1988). The data model is the heart of interface design. *Proc. ACM CHI'88* (Washington, DC, 15–19 May), 115–120.

A discussion of how the choice of fixed-size frames as the basic data/node structure influenced the design of the KMS system.

Alben, L., Faris, J., and Saddler, H. (1994). Making It Macintosh: Designing the message when the message is design. *ACM interactions* **1**, 1 (January), 10–20.

Making It Macintosh was a CD-ROM edition of Apple's user interface standard that used animation to illustrate the dynamic aspects of the GUI.

Alschuler, L. (1989). Hand-crafted hypertext: Lessons from the ACM experiment. In Barrett, E. (Ed.): *The Society of Text*, MIT Press, Cambridge, MA, 343–361.

A comparative review of three versions of the same underlying text (the *Communications of the ACM* special issue on hypertext) in HyperCard, Hyperties, and KMS. The review is of a fairly non-conceptual nature, mainly listing various usability problems and inconsistencies without analyzing why they occur. Main conclusions are that there are vast differences in the way the same information can be structured and that there are difficulties in converting linear material to hypertext form.

Ambron, S., and Hooper, K. (Eds.) (1988). *Interactive Multimedia: Visions of Multimedia for Developers, Educators, & Information Providers.* Microsoft Press.

Very nice book containing the proceedings of a conference on *Multimedia in Education* sponsored by Apple. Most of the systems described run on Apple computers (mostly the Macintosh). A good feature of the book is that many of the papers are highly illustrated, almost to the extent of storyboarding interactions with the systems described (the second best thing to actually trying them out).

Andersen, M. H., Nielsen, J., and Rasmussen, H. (1989). A similarity-based hypertext browser for reading the Unix network news. *Hypermedia* **1**, 3, 255–265.

The HyperNews system for providing hypertext access to a world-wide bulletin board system in form of the Unix netnews.

Anderson, K. M., Taylor, R. N., and Whitehead, E. J. (1994). Chimera: Hypertext for heterogeneous software environments. *Proc. ACM ECHT'94 European*

Conference on Hypermedia Technology (Edinburgh, U.K., September 18–23), 94–107.

A hypertext system to support software development must allow the user to view objects in many different specialized views. Since each view supports different tasks, the authors advocate associating the anchors with specific views of the nodes and not with the nodes themselves.

Andrews K., and Kappe F. (1994). Soaring through hyperspace: A snapshot of Hyper-G and its Harmony client. *Proc. of Eurographics Symposium and Workshop on Multimedia: Multimedia/Hypermedia in Open Distributed Environments* (Graz, Austria, June).

Hyper-G is a general-purpose, large-scale, distributed hypermedia information system based on the client–server model across the Internet. It is thus similar to the World Wide Web, with the main differences being that Hyper-G supports search and that it uses integrated viewers rather than external viewers for non-textual media. This latter difference means that Hyper-G supports hypertext links to and from multimedia datatypes since it is connected to their viewers. Harmony is a Hyper-G client for X-windows on Unix platforms. This paper is available from

ftp://iicm.tu-graz.ac.at/pub/Hyper-G/papers/egmm94.ps

Andrews K., and Pichler M. (1994). Hooking up 3-space: Three-dimensional models as fully-fledged hypermedia documents. Proc. of East–West International Conference on Multimedia, Hypermedia, and Virtual Reality (Moscow, Russia, September).

This paper examines the incorporation of three-dimensional models into hypermedia systems as fully-fledged documents. Display, linking, navigational, and authoring aspects of 3-D hypermedia documents are discussed and are illustrated with examples taken from the Harmony viewer for the Hyper-G hypermedia information system. This paper is available from

ftp://iicm.tu-graz.ac.at/pub/Hyper-G/papers/mhvr94.ps

Apple Computer (1989). *HyperCard Stack Design Guidelines.* Addison-Wesley.

Recommendations for the usability engineering process to be followed in the design of HyperCard stacks. Contains a summary of the general Apple human interface guidelines and specific advice for the use of graphics, buttons, and sound in HyperCard interfaces and for the navigational structure of stacks. Also includes a good annotated bibliography of graphic design, animation, and related issues.

Arons, B. (1991). Hyperspeech: Navigating in speech-only hypermedia. *Proc. ACM Hypertext'91 Conf.*, 133–146.

An audiotex system connecting snippets of recorded speech accessed with voice recognized commands. As the sounds cannot easily contain embedded anchors, the user navigates mostly by using typed links. For example, after having heard one person's view on a topic, the user can say "opposing" to hear an opposing view.

Baird, P. (1990). Hypertext—towards the single intellectual market. In Nielsen, J. (Ed.): *Designing User Interfaces for International Use*, Elsevier Science Publishers, Amsterdam, 111–121.

On the problems associated with producing hypertexts for international use.

Baird, P., Mac Morrow, N., and Hardman, L. (1988). Cognitive aspects of constructing non-linear documents: HyperCard and Glasgow Online. *Proc. Online Information 88* (London, U.K., 6–8 December), 207–218.

An introduction to the *Glasgow Online* tourist information project and some observations from a field study of the system. Older people tended to look at the system without using it and when using it tended to proceed cautiously through the hyperspace, reading everything on the screen before making a choice. Children, on the other hand, took a much less focused approach and sometimes seemed to click on a random basis.

Baird, P., and Percival, M. (1989). Glasgow Online: Database development using Apple's HyperCard. In McAleese, R. (Ed.): *Hypertext: Theory into Practice*, Ablex, 75–92.

An introduction to the *Glasgow Online* tourist information system and its development process.

Barrett, E. (Ed.) (1988). *Text, Context, and Hypertext: Writing with and for the Computer.* The MIT Press, Cambridge, MA.

An edited collection of papers from a conference on *Writing for the Computer Industry* at MIT in 1987. Readers should be warned that this book is mostly about general skills for technical writers and has only a few papers about hypertext.

Barrett, E. (Ed.) (1989). *The Society of Text: Hypertext, Hypermedia, and the Social Construction of Information.* The MIT Press, Cambridge, MA.

More about hypertext as such than Barrett's 1988 book, this book contains several interesting chapters on various aspects of hypertext as well as some general chapters on online help and technical writing. A few of the chapters are reprints from earlier journal papers.

Barron, D. W. (1989). Why use SGML?. *Electronic Publishing—Origination, Dissemination and Design* **2**, 1 (April), 3–24.

A nice introduction to the SGML Standard Generalized Markup Language, which is used by some systems for automatic conversion of flat text files to hypertext. This paper does not address hypertext issues in the use of markup languages, however.

Bärtschi, M. (1985). An overview of information retrieval subjects. *IEEE Computer* **18**, 5 (May), 67–84.

A short tutorial paper introducing the most important information retrieval concepts and models (vector spaces, fuzzy sets, and probabilistic models).

Bearman, D. (Ed.) (1991). *Hypermedia and Interactivity in Museums.* Archives and Museum Informatics Technical Report 14, Archives and Museum Informatics, Pittsburgh, PA. ISSN 1042-1459.

Proceedings of a conference October 14–16, 1991 with reports on several museum hypertext systems.

Bechtel, B. (1990). Inside Macintosh as hypertext. *Proc. ECHT'90 European Conf. Hypertext* (Paris, France, 28–30 November), Cambridge University Press, 312–323.

The five volumes of the *Inside Macintosh* manual for Macintosh programmers were converted to a hypertext form called *SpInside Macintosh* and were further interlinked with a hypertext version of 265 Apple Technical Notes and a tutorial list of 207 questions (with answers) often asked of Apple's technical support staff. The author claims that his experience from this project confirms Glushko's [1989b] recommendation for the design of multidocument hypertexts, even though the Apple team were not aware of Glushko's paper when they created their product.

Bederson, B. B., and Druin, A. (1995). Computer-augmented environments: New places to learn, work and play. In Nielsen, J. (Ed.), *Advances in Human–Computer Interaction* vol. **5**. Ablex.

Augmented reality refers to systems where the computer in some way projects or adds information to the physical world. The hypertextual concequence of this technology is that it becomes possible to use physical objects as hypertext nodes and link from them to appropriate information. Physical objects may even serve as destination nodes for half-dead links by having the computer project an arrow pointing to a physical object or in other ways indicate that the user is to go to it.

Beeman, W. O., Anderson, K. T., Bader, G., Larkin, J., McClard, A. P., McQuillan, P., and Shields, M. (1987). Hypertext and pluralism: From lineal to non-lineal thinking. *Proc. ACM Hypertext'87 Conf.* (Chapel Hill, NC, 13–15 November), 67–88.

Report on the learning effects from two field studies of educational use of Intermedia. Students were much more active in the English literature class after the introduction of the hypertext system (but note the possibility that this could partly be due to the Hawthorne effect of people working better when they know they are being studied) and were better able to connect concepts in a non-linear way.

Begeman, M. L., and Conklin, J (1988). The right tool for the job. *BYTE* **13**, 10 (October), 255–266.

The gIBIS hypertext system (graphical Issue-Based Information System). This article is practically a subset (edited for slightly higher readability) of the more complete paper [Conklin and Begeman 1988].

Belkin, N. J., and Croft, W. B. (1992). Information filtering and information retrieval: Two sides of the same coin? *Communications of the ACM* **35**, 12 (December), 29–38.

Comparison of information filtering and information retrieval and a discussion of a probabilistic model for information filtering.

Berners-Lee, T., Cailliau, R., Groff, J-F., and Pollermann, B. (1992). World-Wide Web: The information universe. *Electronic Networking: Research, Applications and Policy* **2**, 1 (Spring), 52–58.

Overview of the data model for the World Wide Web.

Berners-Lee, T., Cailliau, R., Loutonen, A., Nielsen, H. F., and Secret, A. (1994). The World-Wide Web. *Communications of the ACM* **37**, 8 (August), 76–82.

Overview of the architecture of the World Wide Web by its designers.

Bernstein, M. (1988). The bookmark and the compass: Orientation tools for hypertext users. *ACM SIGOIS Bulletin* **9**, 4 (October), 34–45.

Rationale for the design of the Hypergate user interface, including "breadcrumbs" marking the user's footprints, user-defined bookmarks, and author-defined thumb tabs (permanently visible links to landmark nodes). The author advocates use of hand-drawn overview maps instead of automatically generated maps.

Bernstein, M. (1990). An apprentice that discovers hypertext links. *Proc. ECHT'90 European Conf. Hypertext* (Paris, France, 28–30 November), Cambridge University Press, 121–223.

A semi-intelligent program that suggests likely hypertext links on the basis of similarity matches between the contents of nodes. The author has the ultimate responsibility for deciding which of the apprentice's suggestions to follow. The apprentice provides the author with easy access to a list of possible nodes to link to the current node and may point out potential links that would otherwise have been overlooked.

Bieber, M., and Wan, J. (1994). Backtracking in a multiple-window hypertext environment. *Proc. ACM ECHT'94 European Conference on Hypermedia Technology* (Edinburgh, U.K., September 18–23), 158–166.

Conceptual models and algorithms for several different kinds of backtrack. The authors specifically consider whether navigation should be treated differently depending on whether it was by done activating a hypertext anchor or whether it was done through the window system (e.g., bringing a window to the front by clicking in it).

Bier, E. A. (1992). EmbeddedButtons: Supporting buttons in documents. *ACM Trans. Information Systems* **10**, 4 (October), 381–407.

Embedded buttons can be used not just for hypertext anchors but also to make documents active. Existing document editors can be modified to use embedded buttons, thus allowing them to serve as hypertext editors.

Bigelow, J. (1988). Hypertext and CASE. *IEEE Software* **5**, 2 (March), 23–27.

On the use of the Tektronix Neptune system for Computer Aided Software Engineering (CASE): The system interconnects specifications, design documents, user and program documentation, and the source code.

Bigelow, J., and Riley, V. (1987). Manipulating source code in DynamicDesign. *Proc. ACM Hypertext'87 Conf.* (Chapel Hill, NC, 13–15 November), 397–408.

The DynamicDesign system and its associated GraphBuild utility can automatically construct a hypertext structure from a C source code file. It then allows the software developer to click on a variable, for instance, and see its definition or to utilize bidirectional links in the reverse direction from a variable to the locations where it is used.

Blake, G. E., Bray, T., and Tompa, F. W. (1992) Shortening the OED: Experience with a grammar-defined database. *ACM Trans. Information Systems* **10**, 3 (July), 213–232.

Automatic extraction of a subset of the *Oxford English Dictionary* for use in publishing an abridged version.

Bly, S. A., and Rosenberg, J. K. (1986). A comparison of tiled and overlapping windows. *Proc. ACM CHI'86 Conf.*, 101–106.

Users were 30% slower when using overlapping windows than when using tiled windows for tasks where the information had a fairly simple structure. To a large extent, the extra time was due to the need for the users to manually move and adjust the windows in the overlapping condition. The authors conclude that windows would be better they could automatically conform to their content and that window systems should relieve the user of window management as far as possible.

Bolt, R. A. (1984). *The Human Interface: Where People and Computers Meet.* Lifetime Learning Publications, Belmont, CA. (The book is now distributed by Van Nostrand Reinhold).

A brief but good book on the work done at the MIT Architecture Machine Group (now part of the Media Lab). Much of this work can be classified as hypermedia.

Bolter, J. D., and Joyce, M. (1987). Hypertext and creative writing. *Proc. ACM Hypertext'87 Conf.* (Chapel Hill, NC, 13–15 November), 41–50.

On interactive fiction and the Storyspace system.

Borenstein, N. S., and Thyberg, C. A. (1988). Cooperative work in the Andrew message system. *Proc. 2nd Conf. Computer-Supported Cooperative Work* (Portland, OR, 26–28 September), 306–323.

A system for electronic mail and bulletin boards with several advanced features: Users can put together edited *magazines* of selected articles from other bulletin boards, users can vote on messages, and the system can automatically filter incoming messages for them.

Borgman, C. L. (1987). The study of user behavior on information retrieval systems. *ACM SIGCUE Outlook* **19**, 2–3 (Spring/Summer), 35–48.

A survey of research on user difficulties in the use of traditional bibliographic databases.

Botafogo, R. A., Rivlin, E., and Shneiderman, B. (1992). Structural analysis of hypertexts: Identifying hierarchies and useful metrics. *ACM Trans. Information Systems* **10**, 2 (April), 142–180.

Authoring tools for improving the degree of structure in a hypertext. One tool tries to identify hierarchies by finding nodes with high outgoing link centrality. Other tools compute metrics like *compactness* (the intrinsic connectedness of the hypertext) and *stratum* (the extent to which some nodes must be read before others).

Bowman, C. M., Danzig, P. B., Manber, U., and Schwartz, M. F. (1994). Scalable Internet resource discovery. *Communications of the ACM* **37**, 8 (August), 98–107 & 114.

Resource discovery is the problem of finding out where on the Internet certain information, software, files, or other services or facilities are available. The article describes the Netfind system and WAIS (wide-area information server), both of which are intended to handle very large amounts of data, and compare them with the smaller scale Veronica and Archie systems.

Boy, G. A. (1991). Indexing hypertext documents in context. *Proc. ACM Hypertext'91 Conf.*, 51–61.

NASA's CID (Computer Integrated Documentation) system used adaptive indexing to collect index entries from user queries: if the user has asked for something and likes what the system shows, the query terms are reinforced as index terms.

Brand, S. (1987). *The Media Lab: Inventing the Future at MIT.* Viking Penguin.

A perhaps somewhat too popularistic survey of the work at the MIT Media Lab and its predecessor, the Architecture Machine Group, including interviews with several of the main researchers.

Brøndmo, H. P., and Davenport, G. (1990). Creating and viewing the Elastic Charles—a hypermedia journal. In McAleese, R., and Green, C. (Eds.) *Hypertext: State of the Art,* Ablex, 43–51.

The *Elastic Charles* is a hyperfilm combination of video recordings of the River Charles made by 15 people. Links between film clips are anchored on the screen by so-called *micons,* which are miniature moving clips of the destination film.

Brothers, L., Hollan, J., Nielsen, J., Stornetta, S., Abney, S., Furnas, G., and Littman, M. (1992). Supporting informal communication via ephemeral interest groups. *Proc. ACM CSCW'92 Conf. Computer-Supported Cooperative Work* (Toronto, Canada, 1–4 November), 84–90.

The ephemeral interest groups allowed users to establish a subscription link to messages posted on a bulletin board such that they would be notified when updated information or new discussions on the topic became available.

Brown, H. (Ed.) (1990). *HyperMEDIA / HyperTEXT and Object Oriented Databases.* Unicom Seminars Ltd., Brunel Science Park, Uxbridge, U.K.

The proceedings from a seminar with speakers mostly from the U.K. but also some from other countries.

Brown, P. J. (1987). Turning ideas into products: The Guide system. *Proc. ACM Hypertext'87 Conf.* (Chapel Hill, NC, 13–15 November), 33–40.

The basic principles behind the design of Guide and their relation to previous research ideas. Brown mentions that he did not have a `goto` link in his original design even though it has been introduced in the commercial version of Guide.

Brown, P. J. (1988). Linking and searching within hypertext. *Electronic Publishing—Origination, Dissemination and Design* **1,** 1 (April), 45–53.

A discussion of how a "find" command (viewed as an unstructured linking mechanism) can be integrated into a hypertext system.

Brown, P. J. (1989a). Do we need maps to navigate round hypertext documents?. *Electronic Publishing—Origination, Dissemination and Design* **2,** 2 (July), 91–100.

Peter Brown restates his argument in favor of hierarchically organized hypertexts with a minimum of "`goto`-like" cross-references.

Brown, P. J. (1989b). Hypertext: Dreams and reality. *Proc. Hypermedia / Hypertext and Object Oriented Databases Seminar* (Brunel University, London, 5–7 December). Reprinted in [Brown, H. 1990].

A description of the use of a specially tailored version of Unix Guide at ICL for the diagnosis of hardware problems reported by customer (so-called "laundering"). The paper also discusses seven issues facing hypertext: integration, authorship, testing, large documents, getting lost (including avoiding `goto`s), abstractions, and the cost of projects.

Brown, P. J. (1990). Assessing the quality of hypertext documents. *Proc. ECHT'90 European Conf. Hypertext* (Paris, France, 28–30 November), Cambridge University Press, 1–12.

Review criteria for hypertext for use mainly in grading student papers in hypertext form.

Brown, P. J. (1991). Higher level hypertext facilities: Procedures with arguments. *Hypermedia* **3**, 2, 91–100.

An idea for extending links with arguments, such that the resulting destination node differs depending on the value of the arguments, in an analogy with the way procedure calls work in programming languages.

Brown, P. J. (1992). Unix Guide: Lessons from ten years' development. *Proc. ECHT'92 Fourth ACM Hypertext Conf.*, 63–70.

Brown, P. J. (1994). Adding value to network hypertext: Can it be done transparently? *Proc. ACM ECHT'94 European Conference on Hypermedia Technology* (Edinburgh, U.K., September 18–23), 51–58.

The author defines two kinds of transparency for networked hypertext systems: authorship transparency and readership transparency. Examples are given from the addition of network support to the Unix version of Guide.

Brown, P. J., and Russell, M. T. (1988). Converting help systems to hypertext. *Software—Practice and Experience* **18**, 2 (February 1988), 163–165.

The Unix man (manual) help information for the fs program was converted to a Guide hypertext by adding button tags to the nroff file. The same underlying help text could then be accessed both as a hypertext (through Guide) and as a traditionally formatted linear text (through man and nroff—because nroff just throws away those tags that it does not recognize).

Bruillard, E., and Weidenfeld, G. (1990). Some examples of hypertext's applications. In Jonassen, D. H., and Mandl, H. (Eds.), *Designing Hypertext/Hypermedia for Learning.* Springer-Verlag, Heidelberg, Germany, 377–386.

Examples of several French hypertext systems, including the LYRE system for teaching poetry (from the authors' company, SOFTIA).

Burger, A. M., Meyer, B. D., Jung, C. P., and Long, K. B. (1991). The virtual notebook system. *Proc. ACM Hypertext 91 Conf.*, 395–401.

A hypertext system for researchers built on the metaphor of a laboratory notebook into which a scientist can paste information gathered from many different sources.

Bush, V. Memex revisited. In Bush, V. (Ed.) (1967), *Science is not Enough,* William Morrow and Co. Reprinted in Nyce, J. M., and Kahn, P. (Eds.) (1991), *From Memex to Hypertext: Vannevar Bush and the Mind's Machine.* Academic Press, 197–216.

Campagnoni, F. R., and Ehrlich, K. (1989). Information retrieval using a hypertext-based help system. *ACM Trans. Information Systems* **7**, 3 (July), 271–291. Also in *Proc. ACM SIGIR'89* (Cambridge, MA, 25–28 June 1989), 212–220.

About the Sun Help Viewer online help system for the Sun386i and the usability testing of this hypertext system. Most test subjects were found to prefer a browsing search strategy over using the index. The subjects were given a standard test of spatial visualization ability, which showed that users with higher visualization scores needed less time to locate the answers to the questions, mostly because they had less need to return to the top level table of contents. This result indicates that users with good visualization abilities were better able to construct a conceptual model of the structure of the information space.

Campbell, B., and Goodman, J. M. (1988). HAM: A general purpose hypertext abstract machine. *Communications of the ACM* **31**, 7 (July), 856–861.

Discussion of a generalized storage medium for hypertext networks, which are seen as collections of contexts, nodes, links, and attributes. The paper shows how HAM can be used to describe the underlying data structures for many different hypertext systems, including Guide buttons, Intermedia webs, and NoteCards FileBoxes.

Canter, D., Rivers, R., and Storrs, G. (1985). Characterizing user navigation through complex data structures. *Behaviour and Information Technology* **4**, 2 (April–June), 93–102.

The authors define four graph theory-like classes of user navigation behavior: *paths* (a route that does not cross any node twice), *rings* (a route that returns to the node where it starts, this node being called the base node of the ring), *loops* (a ring that does not contain any ring as part of itself, i.e., it was a path until the user returned to the base node), and *spikes* (a route where the return journey retraces [i.e. backtracks] exactly the route taken on the outward journey). Based on these elementary structures, the authors characterize five different user navigation strategies: *scanning* (mixture of deep spikes and short loops), *browsing* (many large loops and a few large rings), *searching* (ever-increasing spikes with a few loops), *exploring* (many different paths), and *wandering* (many medium-sized rings). The authors compared users navigating a data set by hypertext and by direct command selection of desired nodes (a combination of `goto` and information retrieval) and found that the hypertext users had many more rings and spikes than the direct access users but had about the same number of paths and loops. The authors also discuss a comparison between their studies of real users and a so-called "random user" in the form of a computer simulation that follows links randomly with equal probability for activating any anchor at a given node.

Canter, D., Powell, J., Wishart, J., and Roderick, C. (1986). User navigation in complex database systems. *Behaviour and Information Technology* **5**, 3 (July–September), 249–257.

Three different access methods were tested for a videotex-like system: direct addressing (command control), linked addressing (hypertext-like links between pages with similar information), and natural language search. Novice users performed best with linked addressing (experts were not tested).

Caplinger, M. (1986). Graphical database browsing. *Proc. 3rd ACM SIGOIS Conf. Office Information Systems* (Providence, RI, 6–8 October), 113–121.

A graphic browser to a 45,000 item information space. A 3D flyby browser was implemented but did not seem useful without hardware support for depth cues.

Carey, T. T., Hunt, W. T., and Lopez-Suarez, A. (1990). Roles for tables of contents as hypertext overviews. *Proc. INTERACT'90 Third IFIP Conf. Human–Computer Interaction* (Cambridge, U.K., 27–31 August), 581-586.

Carroll, J. (1994). Guerrillas in the Myst. *WIRED* **2**, 8 (August), 69–73.

Interview with the creators of the Myst adventure game, Rand Miller and Robyn Miller.

Carroll, J. M. (1990). *The Nurnberg Funnel: Designing Minimalist Instruction for Practical Computer Skill.* The MIT Press.

Book on ways to teach users to use computers without overloading them with information. Topics range from the "minimal manual" to the support of guided exploration. Minimalism is particularly relevant for hypertext authors since users read more slowly from screens than from paper.

Catano, J. V. (1979). Poetry and computers: Experimenting with the communal text. *Computers and the Humanities* **13** , 269–275.

An early experiment in online poetry used with shared hypertextual annotations by students taking a poetry class.

Catlin, K. S., Garrett, L. N., and Launhardt, J. A. (1991). Hypermedia templates: An author's tool. *Proc. ACM Hypertext'91 Conf.*, 147–160.

Templates are a set of pre-defined nodes and links that can be instantiated with a single operation. Templates make authoring easier and also promote consistency in the resulting hypertext structure. This article describes Intermedia's approach to templates.

Catlin, T. J. O., and Smith, K. E. (1988). Anchors for shifting tides: Designing a 'seaworthy' hypermedia system. *Proc. Online Information 88* (London, U.K., 6–8 December), 15–25.

Intermedia [Yankelovich et al. 1988] was extended to accommodate two new types of hypermedia: *InterAudio* for access to CD-audio sound bites and *InterBrowse* for access to information retrieved from external (and heterogeneous) databases. These new media involved some problems with respect to the established Intermedia model for hypertext anchors: e.g., how does one select a piece of sound, and how can the computer highlight a selection (one option might be to play it louder than the rest of the sound, but the option chosen was to play only the selection and then provide users with a command to also play the rest of the context of the selection). For this new kind of medium, it was necessary to extend the Intermedia paradigm to include *proxies* which graphically represent what would otherwise be non-graphic or conceptual, thereby allowing users to make tangible selections.

Catlin, T., Bush, P., and Yankelovich, N. (1989). InterNote: Extending a hypermedia framework to support annotative collaboration. *Proc. ACM Hypertext'89 Conf.* (Pittsburgh, PA, 5–8 November), 365–378.

InterNote provides a general facility for reader annotation in Intermedia.

Cavallaro, U., Garzotto, F., Paolini, P., and Totaro, D. (1993). HIFI: Hypertext interface for information systems. *IEEE Software* **10**, 5 (November), 48–51.

Hypertext can be used as a front-end to a database management system by providing a mapping between the database schema and the hypertext structure.

Charnock, E., Rada, R., Stichler, S., and Weygant, P. (1994). Task-based method for creating usable hypertext. *Interacting with Computers* **6**, 3, 275–287.

Various guidelines for increasing the usability of hypertext. The authors recommend so-called gateways on links that will take the user from the current context to a different one with different conventions (e.g., when jumping to a new WWW site). The gateway link would put up a confirming dialog box to warn the user about the change of context before moving on.

Chen, P. P-S. (1986). The compact disk ROM: how it works. *IEEE Spectrum* **23**, 4 (April), 44–49.

A popular overview of the technology behind CD-ROMs.

Chimera, R., and Shneiderman, B. (1994). An exploratory evaluation of three interfaces for browsing large hierarchical tables of contents. *ACM Trans. Information Systems* **12**, 4 (October), 383–406.

The three interfaces were: stable scrolling (the text did not change and the user had to scroll to see new elements in the ToC), expand/contract (the outliner principle where the user can expand a chapter entry to see the section entries it hides), and multipane (where each new level is displayed in a separate pane). Subjects performed search tasks in 63 seconds on the average with the scrolling ToC and in 41 and 42 seconds with the two non-scrolling ToC designs (expanding and multipane), respectively).

Christel, M. G. (1994). The role of visual fidelity in computer-based instruction. *Human–Computer Interaction* **9**, 2, 183–223.

A hypermedia course in code inspection was tested in two versions: one where full motion video was used with a frame rate of 30 images per second and one with the same sound and slide-show like graphics (a new image every 4 seconds). Subjects remembered 89% of the information when they has seen the motion video and only 71% when they had seen the still photos instead.

Claffy, K. C., Braun, H. W., and Polyzos, G. C. (1994). Tracking the long-term growth of the NSFnet. *Communications of the ACM* **37**, 8 (August), 34–45.

About the methods used to collect statistics about the use of the NSFnet (one of the main Internet backbones).

Coffman, D. R. (Ed.) (1987). *The Guide to Hypertext.* Macintosh diskette, OWL International.

A demo of the Guide system containing interlinked articles on hypertext by several authors.

Collier, G. H. (1987). Thoth-II: Hypertext with explicit semantics. *Proc. ACM Hypertext'87 Conf.* (Chapel Hill, NC, 13–15 November), 269–289.

A system that has a main mode of browsing a graphic representation of a semantic net. From this graph, the user can select a node and enter a special text-reading mode to see its text in a window.

Conklin, J., and Begeman, M. L. (1988). gIBIS: A hypertext tool for exploratory policy discussion. *ACM Trans. Office Information Systems* **6**, 4 (October 1988), 303–331. Also in *Proc. 2nd Conf. Computer-Supported Cooperative Work* (Portland, OR, 26–28 September), 140–152.

Describes the gIBIS system (graphical Issue-Based Information System). gIBIS is used in the MCC *Design Journal* project to provide a computerized record of a software design process with special emphasis on capturing the rationale behind the design decisions through hypertext links among issues, positions and arguments. gIBIS is designed for color workstations and uses color to indicate node and link status (for a color screen shot, see [Begeman and Conklin 1988]). Preliminary empirical observations indicated that users had a greater tendency to add supporting comments than to add objecting ones. Some users complained about the danger of premature segmentation of new ideas and would have liked a "proto-node" simply to record ideas before structuring them. The first half of this paper (describing the system itself but not the empirical evidence about its actual use) can also be found in [Begeman and Conklin 1988].

Conklin, E. J., and Yakemovic, K. C. B. (1991). A process-oriented approach to design rationale. *Human–Computer Interaction* **6**, 2&3, 357–391.
Report on a field trial of gIBIS at NCR. Actually, the system used was itIBIS (indented text IBIS), since the users did not have graphical workstations. The paper discusses the problems stemming from this use of a character-based user interface.

Consens, M. P., and Mendelzon, A. O. (1989). Expressing structural hypertext queries in GraphLog. *Proc. ACM Hypertext'89 Conf.* (Pittsburgh, PA, 5–8 November), 269–292.
GraphLog is a visual query language for finding hypertext subnets that satisfy specified structural properties.

Cook, P. (1988). Multimedia technology: An encyclopedia publisher's perspective. In Ambron, S., and Hooper, K. (Eds.), *Interactive Multimedia: Visions of Multimedia for Developers, Educators, & Information Providers.* Microsoft Press, 1988, 217–240.
A discussion of several prototype ideas for enhancing the electronic version of Grolier's *Academic American Encyclopedia* from its 1986 text-only CD-ROM to a future multimedia system.

Cooke, P., and Williams, I. (1989). Design issues in large hypertext systems for technical documentation. In McAleese, R. (Ed.): *Hypertext: Theory into Practice,* Ablex, 93–104.
On OWL's IDEX system to automatically display large databases of existing text encoded in SGML in a hypertext format. Besides SGML, the product also relies heavily on other standards: SQL for the underlying database, Ethernet for LAN, and the Microsoft Windows and Presentation Manager for the user interface.

Coover, R. (1992). The end of books. *The New York Times Book Review* June 21, pp. 1 & 23–24.
The first major review of hypertext fiction in a leading mainstream publication.

Coover, R. (1993). Hyperfiction: Novels for the computer. *The New York Times Book Review* August 29, pp. 1 & 8–12.
Extensive set of reviews of hypertext fictions.

Crain, J. C. (1993). Storyspace: Hypertext writing environment. *Computers and the Humanities* **27**, 2, 137–141.
Review of the use of the Storyspace hypertext system for the teaching of creative writing. The article is richly illustrated with screendumps.

Crane, G. (1987). From the old to the new: Integrating hypertext into traditional scholarship. *Proc. ACM Hypertext'87 Conf.* (Chapel Hill, NC, 13–15 November), 51–55.
Converting classical Greek literature to hypertext in the Perseus Project.

Crane, G. (1988). Redefining the book: Some preliminary problems. *Academic Computing* (February), 6–11 and 36–41.

About the Perseus Project for hypertext representation of classic Greek literature and history. Also discusses specific problems in the representation of Greek text and online dictionaries. Some of the associated issues are whether the existence of automatic hypertext dictionary lookup will keep students from really learning Greek, and the need for affordable platforms such as HyperCard and the Macintosh to ensure decentralized development: only the researchers actually engaged in various forms of study of ancient history will be able to imagine the tools needed.

Crane, G. (1990). Standards for a hypermedia database: Diachronic vs. synchronic concerns. *Proc. NIST Hypertext Standardization Workshop* (Gaithersburg, MD, 16-18 January), 71–81.

Synchronic standards allow all hypertext systems at any given time to exchange materials, whereas diachronic standards allow a hypertext document to be equally usable now and with future systems many years from now. Crane views diachronic standards as essential for projects like his own Perseus and finds short-lived systems destructive for disciplines where scholars cannot afford to lavish time on creating documents that will not last at least thirty years.

Creech, M. L., Freeze, D. F., and Griss, M. L. (1991). Using hypertext in selecting reusable software components. *Proc. ACM Hypertext'91 Conf.*, 25–38.

The Kiosk system for storing a software library in hypertext form.

Cutting, D. R., Karger, D. R., Pedersen, J. O., and Tukey, J. W. (1992). Scatter/gather: A cluster-based approach to browsing large document collections. *Proc. ACM SIGIR'92 Conf. on Research and Development in Information Retrieval*, 318–329.

Two-step user interface for information browsing: First, the system "scatters" the information base into a small set of clusters, each of which is automatically named, and the user then "gathers" the names of the clusters that are of interest. This process continues recursively, with the system clustering progressively smaller collections, until the clusters match the user's specific interests.

Cybulski, J. L., and Reed, K. (1992). A hypertext based software engineering environment. *IEEE Software* **9**, 2 (March), 62–68.

Using hypertext to integrate the tools of a CASE system (computer-aided software engineering).

Davenport, E., and Baird, P. (1992). Hypertext—A bibliometric briefing. *Hypermedia* **4**,2, 123–134.

A study of which authors in the hypertext field are cited the most (Halasz, Conklin, Yankelovich, Furuta, Nielsen, Trigg, Shneiderman, Schwartz, Meyrowitz, Streitz, Stotts, Salton, Frisse, Akscyn, Croft, Landow) and what subissues are the topic of the most papers (browsing, design, graphics, knowledge, links, models, navigation, structure).

Davis, H., Hall, W., Heath, I., Hill, G., and Wilkins, R. (1992). Towards an integrated information environment with open hypermedia systems. *Proc. ECHT'92 Fourth ACM Hypertext Conf.*, 181–190.

Different levels of support for cross-application hypertext links, including full support by applications that agree to follow a linking protocol and limited support by applications where the hypertext server can insert a datatype it can interpret without help from the application.

Davis, H. C., Knight, S., and Hall, W. (1994). Light hypermedia link services: A study of third party application integration. *Proc. ACM ECHT'94 European Conference on Hypermedia Technology* (Edinburgh, U.K., September 18–23), 41–50.

> Extending the Microcosm system from [Davis et al. 1992] to be able to work with applications that cannot be modified at all.

Delany, P., and Landow, G. P. (1991). *Hypermedia and Literary Studies.* MIT Press.

> Collection of papers on the use of hypertext in literature, creative writing, and English departments, with an emphasis on educational use at the university level.

Delisle, N., and Schwartz, M. (1986). Neptune: A hypertext system for CAD applications. *Proc. ACM SIGMOD'86 Conf.* (Washington, DC, 28–30 May), 132–142.

> The Tektronix Neptune system for working with program code.

Delisle, N., and Schwartz, M. (1987). Contexts—A partitioning concept for hypertext. *ACM Trans. Office Information Systems* **5,** 2 (April), 168–186.

> Version control in a hypertext system to support collaborative writing of large software systems.

DeRose, S. J. (1989). Expanding the notion of links. *Proc. ACM Hypertext'89 Conf.* (Pittsburgh, PA, 5–8 November 1989), 249–257.

> A taxonomy of twelve kinds of links with examples from the CDWord hypertext version of the Bible.

DeRose, S., and Durand, D. (1994). *Making Hypermedia Work: A User's Guide to Hytime.* Kluwer Academic Publishers.

> Hytime is a standard for time-varying hypertext such as movies and audio.

De Young, L. (1989). Hypertext challenges in the auditing domain. *Proc. ACM Hypertext'89 Conf.* (Pittsburgh, PA, 5–8 November), 169–180.

> Auditing is well suited for hypertext because it basically consists of interrelating documents. The links are so important that auditors who define a link take personal responsibility for it by authenticating it with their initials. The paper describes a prototype system at Price Waterhouse called EWP (Electronic Working Papers) giving several screen dumps. They estimate that auditors spend 30% of their time preparing, maintaining, and reviewing these working papers in the current paper-based procedures.

De Young, L. (1990). Linking considered harmful. *Proc. ECHT'90 European Conf. Hypertext* (Paris, France, 28–30 November), Cambridge University Press, 238–249.

> The EWP (Electronic Working Papers) project uses structured hypertext in the form of sets of links, relational links, and finite state sequences.

Deutsch, P. (1992). Resource discovery in an Internet environment—the Archie experience. *Electronic Networking: Research, Applications and Policy* **2**, 1 (Spring), 45–51.

Archie was an attempt to index all the files that could be accessed by anonymous FTP over the Internet.

Dillon, A. (1991). Readers' models of text structures: The case of academic articles. *Intl. J. Man–Machine Studies* **35**, 6 (December), 913–925.

As a first step in designing a hypertext academic journal, the author studied how researchers currently use printed journals. Readers of traditionally structured research papers were able to correctly place paragraphs within a superstructure (introduction, method, results, and discussion) 80% of the time, suggesting that such conventions may help reduce disorientation.

Dillon, A., and McKnight, C. (1990). Toward a classification of text types: A repertory grid approach. *Intl. J. Man–Machine Studies* **33**, 6 (December), 623–636.

Empirical study of how six users perceived various documents (e.g., a newspaper, a manual, and a novel) in terms of their use, content, and structure. Each user was asked to generate a number of dimensions that they would use to distinguish the various types of documents (e.g., written by a single author or by multiple authors), and the resulting similarity grids were subjected to cluster analysis. Some of the findings may not have been surprising (e.g., newspapers and magazines were rated as similar, as were conference proceedings and technical journals), but the paper presents a generally applicable method for eliciting users' mental models of information.

Dillon, A., McKnight, C., and Richardson, J. (1990). Navigation in hypertext: A critical review of the concept. *Proc. INTERACT'90 Third IFIP Conf. Human–Computer Interaction* (Cambridge, U.K., 27–31 August), 587-592.

An analysis of hypertext navigation using psychological research results from studies of geographical maps and route finding.

Dillon, A., Richardson, J., and McKnight, C. (1989). Human factors of journal usage and design of electronic texts. *Interacting with Computers* **1**, 2 (August), 183–189.

A study of how scientists read paper journals and some loose thoughts about the design of hypertext journals. The scientists always started by scanning the table of contents of a new journal issue and they expressed a strong preference for having the table of contents on the cover of the journal so that they did not have to open the journal. In other words, an extremely low overhead is desired for the initial process of scanning to find relevant information.

Dixon, D. F. (1989). Life before the chips: Simulating Digital Video Interactive technology. *Communications of the ACM* **32**, 7 (July), 824–831.

Describes how DVI was simulated before the actual DVI hardware was designed and produced, giving several examples of applications (e.g., the "Galactic Challenge" game) built to test the ideas and provide requirements for the hardware. Interesting both for the historical record and because of the general principle of simulating interactive systems before they are built.

Dougherty, D., and Koman, R. (1994). *The Mosaic Handbook for Microsoft Windows, The Mosaic Handbook for the Macintosh,* and *The Mosaic Handbook for the X Window System.* O'Reilly and Associates.

Three essentially identical books about the World Wide Web viewer Mosaic. Each book includes a disk with Spyglass' enhanced version of Mosaic for the appropriate platform.

Dumais, S. T., and Nielsen, J. (1992). Automating the assignment of submitted manuscripts to reviewers. *Proc. ACM SIGIR'92 Conf. on Research and Development in Information Retrieval,* 233–244.

Using the papers submitted to the Hypertext'91 conference as an example, the authors find that links between peoples' stated interests and a set of potentially interesting papers can be made more relevant by combining automated and human methods.

Dumais, S. T., Furnas, G. W., Landauer, T. K., Deerwester, S., and Harshman, R. (1988). Using latent semantic indexing to improve access to textual information. *Proc. ACM CHI'88* (Washington, DC, 15–19 May), 281–285.

Latent semantic indexing is a method for organizing text nodes into a semantic structure on the basis of the overlap of the words used in those nodes.

Easingwood, C. J., Mahajan, V., and Muller, E. (1983). A nonuniform influence innovation diffusion model of new product acceptance. *Marketing Science* **2**, 3 (Summer), 273–295.

Analysis of the spread of new technology through the market in situations when the pressure to use the innovation is not a linear function of the number of people already using it. Two classic examples are music CDs (described in the paper) and hypertext: both technologies become much more useful to the individual buyer if they are in widespread use (because more CDs and more hypertexts, respectively, will be available).

Egan, D. E., Remde, J. R., Landauer, T. K., Lochbaum, C. C., and Gomez, L. M. (1989a). Acquiring information in books and SuperBooks. *Machine–Mediated Learning* **3**, 259–277.

This is a more in-depth report of the SuperBook experiments described in [Egan et al. 1989b]. This paper also includes logging data of the usage patterns of the SuperBook readers and videotape data of how the readers of the conventional book used it. A comparison showed that readers used the table of contents (overview) much more in SuperBook than in the printed book and that they read about the same number of sections of the text even though they solved the problems in less time. One reason users performed better with SuperBook was that the typographical display of the information was customized to their current needs. The printed page always looked the same, but the SuperBook display highlighted the terms the user had used in the search, thus drawing attention to paragraphs of special importance for the task at hand.

Egan, D. E., Remde, J. R., Landauer, T. K., Lochbaum, C. C., and Gomez, L. M. (1989b). Behavioral evaluation and analysis of a hypertext browser. *Proc. ACM CHI'89 Conf. Human Factors in Computing Systems* (Austin, TX, 30 April–4 May), 205–210.

A SuperBook hypertext version of a statistics manual was compared with a 562 page paper version. Subjects with a background in statistics were able to locate information in SuperBook significantly faster than in the paper book (4.3 min. vs. 7.5 min.) when questions were phrased using words that were present in the running text but not in the section headings. For questions using words taken from section headings, paper was slightly (non-significantly) faster. The authors conclude that their system help users dealing with questions that are not anticipated by an author's organization of a document.

Egan, D. E., Remde, J. R., Gomez, L. M., Landauer, T. K., Eberhardt, J., and Lochbaum, C. C. (1989c). Formative design-evaluation of 'SuperBook'. *ACM Transactions on Information Systems* **7**, 1 (January), 30–57.

SuperBook is a hypertext system using rich indexing and fisheye views integrated such that aggregated hit rates for word searches show up in the fisheye view. The paper describes two stages in the iterative design of the system: Two main improvements were to speed up search time by a factor of ten and to change the interface to make the *word lookup* function more attractive to use as the first part of a search. When compared with paper in two experiments, the revised version performed better whereas the original version performed worse.

Egan, D. E., Lesk, M. E., Ketchum, R. D., Lochbaum, C. C., Remde, J. R., Littman, M., and Landauer, T. K. (1991). Hypertext for the electronic library? CORE sample results. *Proc. ACM Hypertext'91 Conf.*, 299–312.

CORE (Chemistry Online Retrieval Experiment) aims at putting the journals of the American Chemical Society since 1980 into a hypertext form. The 100,000 articles in the collection comprise about half a million densely printed pages in the journals, corresponding to more than two million standard book pages. Storing the text will take 3 GB, and storing the about 20% of the pages that is devoted to graphics will take up an additional 12 GB. The authors describe two interfaces used with a pilot collection of only 1,068 articles: Pixlook (displaying scanned page images) and SuperBook (displaying text and figures in separate windows). An empirical test compared the performance of chemistry graduate students on five tasks (browsing through the journals with some topics in mind, finding a specific article based on a citation, searching for information to answer a given question, finding information to write an essay about a given issue, and finding information about how to transform one chemical into another, where only analogous transformations are described in the journals). The results showed that the two systems excelled on different tasks, with at least one of the systems being as good as or better than print for every task.

Egido, C., and Patterson, J. (1988). Pictures and category labels as navigational aids for catalog browsing. *Proc. ACM CHI'88* (Washington, DC, 15–19 May), 127–132.

Pictures *plus* textual labels are better than either alone.

Ehrlich, K., and Rohn, J. (1994). Cost-justification of usability engineering: A vendor's perspective. In Bias, R. G., and Mayhew, D. J. (Eds.), *Cost-Justifying Usability*. Academic Press, Boston, MA.

Discussion of the various levels of organizational maturity with respect to usability engineering.

Eisenhart, D. M. (1989). 1-2-3 goes TV: Interactive multimedia at Lotus. Boston Computer Society *BCS Update* (September), 14–17.

An interview with Rob Lippincott who is the director of market development for Lotus's Information Services Group on their current hypertext-like products and future directions. Contains several screen shots from the 1-2-3 Multimedia Release 3.0 Demo.

Elrod, S., Bruce, R., Gold, R., Goldberg, D., Halasz, F., Janssen, W., Lee, D., McCall, K., Pedersen, E., Pier, K., Tang, J., and Welch, B. (1992). Liveboard: A large interactive display supporting group meetings, presentations and remote collaboration. *Proc. ACM CHI'92 Conf.* (Monterey, CA, May 3–7), 599–607.

The Xerox Liveboard is a large electronic whiteboard where the user writes on a large projected computer display with a pen looking pretty much like a magic marker.

Embley, D. W., and Nagy, G. (1981). Behavioral aspects of text editors. *ACM Computing Surveys* **13**, 1 (March), 33–70.

Review of much of the early research on the human factors of interactive text.

Engelbart, D. (1988). The augmented knowledge workshop. In Goldberg, A. (Ed.): *A History of Personal Workstations,* Addison-Wesley, 187–236.

Historical review of Engelbart's work at SRI in the period 1963 to 1976, including a discussion of the NLS/Augment system and several photos from the 1968 FJCC real-time demonstration of online structured text.

Engelbart, D. C. (1990). Knowledge-domain interoperability and an open hyperdocument system. *Proc. ACM CSCW'90 Conf. Computer-Supported Cooperative Work* (Los Angeles, CA, Oct. 7–10), 143–156.

Defines three levels of interoperability for open hypertext: interoperability in an individual's information space (e.g., linking from a phone list to a set of notes), interoperability in a group's information space (e.g., from one person's file space to a colleague's), and interoperability across groups (e.g., linking from the marketing organization to the manufacturing or product development organizations). The latter case is an example of interoperability across knowledge domains since the different groups are likely to use very different applications for their specialized work. The paper uses the McDonnell Douglas Corporation as an example to show that one might need even larger scopes of interoperability, e.g., for the entire aerospace industry since the aircraft companies often share suppliers and sometimes work on joint-venture projects with other aircraft vendors.

Erickson, T., and Salomon, G. (1991). Designing a desktop information system: Observations and issues. *Proc. ACM CHI'91 Conf.*, 49–54.

About the design of a graphical interface for browsing and reading a very large information base, using relevance feedback to retrieve additional, similar information. The authors mention certain issues related to working with dynamic information bases such as a newswire, where the same user query will find different information at different times, thus making it impossible to rely on reuse of a search to refind information that was previously identified as being of interest. The prototype interface allows users to annotate the information and shows a reduced overview diagram where the user's annotations are highlighted, thus emphasizing the personalized parts of the information base.

Eriksson, H. (1994). MBone: The multicast backbone. *Communications of the ACM* **37**, 8 (August), 54–60.

The MBone is a facility for video broadcasts over the Internet that go to many recipients without causing too much network load.

Evenson, S., Rheinfrank, J., and Wulff, W. (1989). Towards a design language for representing hypermedia cues. *Proc. ACM Hypertext'89 Conf.* (Pittsburgh, PA, 5–8 November), 83–92.

On the graphic design of hypertexts and the typographical notation needed to indicate anchors and links.

Ewing, J., Mehrabanzad, S., Sheck, S., Ostroff, D., and Shneiderman, B. (1986). An experimental comparison of a mouse and arrow-jump keys for an interactive encyclopedia. *Intl. J. Man-Machine Studies* **24**, 1 (January), 29–45.

An evaluation of two interaction techniques for Hyperties (then called simply TIES). It turned out that arrow-jump keys were slightly faster for selecting anchors for hypertext jumps (arrow-jump keys are traditional arrow keys that are used to jump the cursor to the next possible anchor instead of just moving the cursor one position).

Fairchild, K. M. (1993). Information management using virtual reality-based visualizations. In Wexelblat, A. (Ed.), *Virtual Reality: Applications and Explorations*, Academic Press. 45–74.

Overviews of ways of using 3-dimensional computer graphics to navigate large information spaces. Despite the title, most of the examples are more related to fisheye views and 2-dimensional projections of 3D views than to traditional virtual reality systems. Examples include SemNet, the perspective wall, cone trees, FSN, and VizNet.

Fairchild, K. M., and Poltrock, S. (1986). Soaring through knowledge space: SemNet 2.1 (videotape). *Technical Report* **HI-104-86**, Microelectronics and Computer Technology Corporation (MCC), Austin, TX.

Because of the extremely dynamic nature of the three dimensional user interface, the SemNet browser is best understood by watching this videotape before reading the scientific paper [Fairchild et al. 1988].

Fairchild, K. M., Poltrock, S. E., and Furnas, G. W. (1988). SemNet: Three-dimensional graphic representations of large knowledge bases. In Guindon, R. (Ed.), *Cognitive Science and its Applications for Human-Computer Interaction.* Lawrence Erlbaum Associates. 201-233.

A graphical interface representing an overview diagram of interlinked pieces of information in three dimensions. The user can move among the nodes using a "helicopter metaphor."

Feiner, S. (1988). Seeing the forest for the trees: Hierarchical display of hypertext structure. *Proc. ACM Conf. Office Information Systems* (Palo Alto, CA, March 23–25), 205–212.

A discussion of the use of hierarchical structures in the IGD system (Interactive Graphical Documents). This paper relates IGD somewhat more to the rest of the hypertext tradition than the earlier paper on the same system [Feiner, Nagy, and van Dam 1982].

Feiner, S., Nagy, S., and van Dam, A. (1982). An experimental system for creating and presenting interactive graphical documents. *ACM Trans. Graphics* **1**, 1 (January), 59–77.

Describes the Electronic Document System, an early hypermedia system. This system has also been known as the Brown Browser and as IGD (Interactive Graphical Documents).

Fenn, B., and Maurer, H. (1994). Harmony on an expanding net. *ACM Interactions* **1**, 4 (October), 28–38..

Overview of the Harmony browser for the Hyper-G Internet system. The authors consider it a major benefit that the links are stored separately from the data in Hyper-G, meaning that the system can manipulate the links and produce, e.g., "local overview diagrams" of the links a few levels out from the current node.

Fiderio, J. (1988). A grand vision. *BYTE* **13**, 10 (October), 237–244 and p. 268.

Brief popular introduction to the hypertext concept. This issue of *BYTE* has a list of vendors of popular hypertext products (as of mid-1988) on p. 268.

Fischer, G., McCall, R., and Morch, A. (1989a). Design environments for constructive and argumentative design. *Proc. ACM CHI'89* (Austin, TX, 30 April–4 May), 269–275.

A proposal for a design integrating an AI system that advises on design issues with a hypertext system containing the rationale for the advice given by the AI system. The hypertext system uses an alternative implementation of the IBIS Issue-Based Information System method made famous by the gIBIS system [Conklin and Begeman 1988] to structure the arguments for and against the various design options, and the AI system can then dump the user at the location in this hypertext that corresponds to the user's current undecided design problem.

Fischer, G., McCall, R., and Morch, A. (1989b). JANUS: Integrating hypertext with a knowledge-based design environment. *Proc. ACM Hypertext'89 Conf.* (Pittsburgh, PA, 5–8 November), 105–117.

A follow-up article to [Fischer et al. 1989a].

Flores, F., Graves, M., Hartfield, B., and Winograd, T. (1988). Computer systems and the design of organizational interaction. *ACM Trans. Office Information Systems* **6**, 2 (April), 153–172.

On The Coordinator system for electronic mail, which has slightly hypertext-like typed links. The authors discuss how this kind of structured communication can fit with the organization of work and its social environment.

Florin, F. (1988). Creating interactive video programs with HyperCard. *HyperAge Magazine* (May–June), 38–43.

On the structure of the WorldView prototype electronic atlas and on the practical details of producing interactive videodisks.

Foss, C. L. (1988). Effective browsing in hypertext systems. *Proc. RIAO'88 Conf. User-Oriented Context-Based Text and Image Handling* (MIT, Cambridge, MA, 21–24 March), 82–98.

A critique of the browsing paradigm, which the author claims leads to two problems: The *embedded digression problem* of multiple sidetracks and redefinitions of current interests, leading users to forget the digressions they wanted to make, and the *art museum phenomenon* where you can spend a whole day in a large art museum and not be able to remember any particular painting in detail. To alleviate these problems, the author has implemented four new kinds of browsing support in NoteCards where she did not believe that the original overview diagram mechanism was sufficient: graphic history lists, history trees, summary boxes, and summary trees.

Fox, E. A. (1988). Optical disks and CD-ROM: Publishing and access. In Williams, M. E. (Ed.): *Annual Review of Information Science and Technology (ARIST)* **23**, Elsevier Science Publishers, 85–124.
A general survey of CD-ROM: hardware technology, data storage, authoring, and access mechanisms as well as applications. Includes an extensive bibliography. Recommended for getting an overview of the area.

Fox, J. A. (1992). The effects of using a hypertext tool for selecting design guidelines. *Proc. Human Factors Society 36th Annual Meeting*, 428–432.
A group of user interface designers were asked to select appropriate rules for a specific design project from a document with a large number of guidelines. When using a printed version of the document, the subjects selected 91% of the rules that had been determined to be appropriate. When using a hypertext version, they only selected 83%. One of the reasons for the poorer performance with the hypertext system may have been that users tried to avoid reading the full text and selected guidelines from their titles to a great extent. This result indicates the need to design information differently for the online medium than for printed text.

France, M. (1994). Smart contracts. *Forbes ASAP* (August 29), 117–118.
Case studies of companies using computers to assemble contracts and other legal documents without the use of lawyers.

Franklin, C. (1989). Mapping hypertext structures with ArchiText. *DATABASE The Magazine of Database Reference and Review* **12**, 4 (August), 50–61.
A review of the ArchiText hypertext program from BrainPower, Inc. with an illustrated walkthrough of its use.

Frenkel, K. A. (1989). The next generation of interactive technologies. *Communications of the ACM* **32**, 7 (July), 872–881.
Survey of the potential for future "intertainment." (interactive entertainment) products and of various current videodisk products such as the Getty Museum disk and the ABC *The '88 Vote*. Also contains a comparison of the competing CD-ROM formats DVI, CD-I, and CD-ROM XA (Extended Architecture) with special emphasis on the last. The reader should note that the comparisons are based on the original specifications for moving video in CD-I and not on the new, considerably improved algorithm, which allows full-quality video and will be used in the final product.

Friedlander, L. (1988). The Shakespeare project. In Ambron, S., and Hooper, K. (Eds.), *Interactive Multimedia: Visions of Multimedia for Developers, Educators, & Information Providers*. Microsoft Press, 115–141.
A prototype hypertext for teaching drama theory and Shakespeare through the use of linked film clips of real performances and simulations of the students' own design and staging choices.

Frisse, M. E. (1988a). Searching for information in a hypertext medical handbook. *Communications of the ACM* **31**, 7 (July), 880–886.

On automatically generating a hypertext structure from a popular medical reference book. Also includes discussion of information retrieval techniques that would help physicians find the relevant nodes in the network.

Frisse, M. (1988b). From text to hypertext. *BYTE* **13**, 10 (October 1988), 247–253.
A discussion of some of the issues involved in transforming existing machine readable text to hypertext form.

Frisse, M. E., and Cousins, S. B. (1989). Information retrieval from hypertext: Update on the dynamic medical handbook project. *Proc. ACM Hypertext'89 Conf.* (Pittsburgh, PA, 5–8 November), 199–212.
How to use various forms of indexes in combination with belief networks and other information retrieval models for hypertext.

Frisse, M. E. , and Cousins, S. B. (1992). Models for hypertext. *J. of the American Society for Information Science* **43**, 2 (March), 183–191.
A survey of three basic models for the architecture of hypertext systems: the Dexter model, a rhetorical model (gIBIS), and the Trellis model with its specification of browsing semantics using Petri nets. The article also discusses how to integrate hypertext features in other applications and operation systems (such as a balloon help feature with links from graphical objects in a user interface to the help system).

Furnas, G. W. (1986). Generalized fisheye views. *Proc. ACM CHI'86 Conf.* (Boston, MA, 13–17 April), 16–23.
Fisheye views show the context immediately surrounding the information of interest in greater detail while information farther away is elided. This idea is similar to the poster from *The New Yorker* showing midtown Manhattan in great detail while the rest of the U.S. is shown disappearing into the distance with an island marked "Japan" in the background.

Furuta, R., Plaisant, C., and Shneiderman, B. (1989). A spectrum of automatic hypertext constructions. *Hypermedia* **1**, 2, 179–195.
A discussion of four projects on converting existing text to hypertext, including the Hyperties version of the ACM *Hypertext on Hypertext*, a course catalog, and two bibliographic listings of technical reports. The authors conclude that some of the projects were suited for automatic conversion while others required manual massaging. Even in cases like the course catalog where much conversion can be done automatically, the authors believe that manual addition of further contextual structure to the hypertext can be beneficial.

Gaffin, A. (1993). *Big Dummy's Guide to the Internet.* Electronic Frontier Foundation, Washington, D.C.
Introduction to the Internet, including email, FTP, netnews, MUD games, and hypertext services like Gopher and WWW. The test of this book can be accessed over the Internet through the URL ftp://ftp.eff.org./pub/EFF/papers/big-dummys-guide.txt

Garg, P. K., and Scacchi, W. (1990). A hypertext system to manage software life-cycle documents. *IEEE Software* **7**, 3 (May), 90–98.
A hypertext system called Documents Integration Facility (DIF) to interrelate the various documents (requirements, specifications, design, source code, testing, and manuals) in the "Software Factory" software engineering research project.

Garrett, L. N., and Smith K. E. (1986). Building a timeline editor from prefab parts: The architecture of an object-oriented application. *Proc. OOPSLA'86 Conf. Object-Oriented Programming Systems, Languages, and Applications* (Portland, OR, 29 September–2 October), 202–213.

The *InterVal* editor is a part of Intermedia designed for the specialized purpose of generating dynamic hypertext timelines.

Garrett, L. N., Smith, K. E., and Meyrowitz, N. (1986). Intermedia: Issues, strategies, and tactics in the design of a hypermedia document system. *Proc. 1st Conf. Computer-Supported Cooperative Work* (Austin, TX, 3–5 December), 163–174.

Careful and well-illustrated discussion of some of the user interface issues in hypertexts with overlapping and/or changing link anchors and/or destinations. Also a discussion of other multi-user issues. This paper is substantially the same as some of the sections in [Yankelovich et al. 1988], which has more and better illustrations.

Garzotto, F., Mainetti, L., and Paolini, P. (1995). Navigation in hypermedia applications: Modelling and semantics. *International Journal of Organizational Computing.*

The authors distinguish between three classes of navigation: free navitation, guided tour navigation, and history-based navigation. They also discuss ways of integrating traditional navigation with query-based movements in a hypertext.

Giguere, E. (1989). Electronic Oxford. *BYTE* **14**, 13 (December), 371–374.

Brief description of the project to convert the *Oxford English Dictionary* to an online format.

Gilder, G. (1994). *Life After Television: The Coming Transformation of Media and American Life*, revised edition. W. W. Norton.

Visionary analysis of the future potential of the personal computer to provide personalized information access for households, providing entertainment and education that is considerably more diversified than traditional broadcast and cable TV.

Girill, T. R., and Luk, C. H. (1992). Hierarchical search support for hypertext on-line documentation. *Intl. J. Man–Machine Studies* **36**, 4 (April), 571–585.

Hybrid interface model, where hypertext is used for global navigation, and tree structures are used for local navigation.

Gloor, P. A. (1991). CYBERMAP: Yet another way of navigating in hyperspace. *Proc. ACM Hypertext'91 Conf.*, 107–121.

Automatic generation of overview diagrams through the use of similarity matching techniques to find nodes "close" to the current one.

Gloor, P., and Norbert Streitz, N. (Eds.) (1990). *Hypertext und Hypermedia: Von theoretischen Konzepten zu praktischen Anwendungen*. Springer-Verlag, Heidelberg, Germany.

The proceedings from the first German conference on hypertext.

Glushko, R. J. (1989a). Transforming text into hypertext for a compact disc encyclopedia. *Proc. ACM CHI'89* (Austin, TX, 30 April–4 May), 293–298.

Another paper about the project discussed in [Glushko et al. 1988].

Glushko, R. J. (1989b). Design issues for multi-document hypertexts. *Proc. ACM Hypertext'89 Conf.* (Pittsburgh, PA, 5–8 November), 51–60.

Issues in converting multiple existing documents to a single integrated hypertext.

Glushko, R. J., Weaver, M. D., Coonan, T. A., and Lincoln, J. E. (1988). Hypertext engineering: Practical methods for creating a compact disc encyclopedia. *Proc. ACM Conf. Document Processing Systems* (Santa Fe, NM, 5–9 December), 11–19.

Design tradeoffs involved in converting a multi-volume engineering encyclopedia to hypertext. The authors advocate the use of an index constructed by humans rather than one constructed automatically.

Gonzalez, S. (1988). *Hypertext for Beginners.* Disk with HyperCard stacks, InteliBooks, San Francisco, CA. ISBN 0-932367-10-0.

Yet another "hypertext on hypertext"—it is a good illustration of the more wildly creative use of graphic layout and hyperlinks to form an intertwined and rather undisciplined information base (somewhat in the style of Ted Nelson's *Computer Lib/Dream Machines).* This document surveys the definition of hypertext, its history, and some of its advantages and disadvantages and does so in a typical hypertext manner with lots of literature references and citations. Most of this information will be known to people who have read other works on hypertext. The document also includes short descriptions of about 50 hypertext systems (including some systems that are only "semi-hypertext") as well as addresses of the vendors of most of these systems.

Gordon, S., Gustavel, J., Moore, J., and Hankey, J. (1988). The effects of hypertext on reader knowledge representation. *Proc. Human Factors Society 32nd Annual Meeting,* 296–300.

Subjects reading hypertext versions of 1,000-word articles did worse than subjects reading linear versions in tests of free recall of the contents of the articles even though they had spent the same time reading them. Subjects also subjectively preferred the linear articles. When reading articles of general interest, subjects after reading hypertext generated only about 60% of the terms generated after reading linear text. When reading articles with a more technically oriented content, however, subjects performed as well after hypertexts as after linear texts. One reason for the result in this paper may be just that the novice subjects used in the experiment had not yet learnt how to use hypertexts, but another reason may be that hypertext is less suited for small articles that are to be read in their entirety.

Gould, J. D. (1988). How to design usable systems. In Helander, M. (Ed.): *Handbook of Human-Computer Interaction,* Elsevier Science Publishers, 757–789.

Good general checklist of methods for testing and improving usability.

Gould, J. D., and Grischkowsky, N. (1984). Doing the same work with hard copy and with cathode ray tube (CRT) computer terminals. *Human Factors* **26**, 323–337.

Reading was 22% slower from screens than from paper.

Gould, J. D., Alfaro, L., Finn, R., Haupt, B., Minuto, A., and Salaun, J. (1987). Why reading was slower from CRT displays than from paper. *Proc. ACM CHI+GI'87* (Toronto, Canada, 5–9 April), 7–11.

While most studies find that reading from a screen is about 30% slower than reading from paper, the studies discussed in this paper identified certain conditions under which reading speeds were identical: high resolution, dark characters on light background, and use of an anti-aliased font.

Graham, I. (1995). *The HTML Sourcebook*. John Wiley & Sons. Much of this book is available on the WWW as `http://www.utirc.utoronto.ca/HTMLdocs/NewHTML/htmlindex.html`

Textbook on HTML.

Gray, S. H. (1990). Using protocol analyses and drawings to study mental model construction during hypertext navigation. *Intl.J. Human–Computer Interaction* **2**, 4, 359–377.

User navigation behavior was studied by the thinking aloud method (having them think out loud while they moved through the hypertext). Their mental model of the information space was assessed by having them draw diagrams of the information after they were finished using the hypertext. Initially, novice users had a strictly linear mental model of the information space, but this model changed during their use of the system.

Green, J. L. (1992). The evolution of DVI system software. *Communications of the ACM* **35**, 1 (January), 52–67.

The structure of the software used to implement DVI (Digital Video Interactive).

Grønbæk, K., and Trigg, R. (1992). Design issues for a Dexter-based hypermedia system. *Proc. ECHT'92 Fourth ACM Hypertext Conf.,* 191–200.

Grønbæk, K., and Trigg, R. H. (1994). Design issues for a Dexter-based hypermedia system. *Communications of the ACM* **37**, 2 (February), 40–49.

Experience from a project to design an open hypermedia system that could incorporate data from other applications through a shared database.

Guillemette, R. A. (1989). Development and validation of a reader-based documentation measure. *Intl.J. Man-Machine Studies* **30**, 5 (May), 551–574.

A factor analysis of users' subjective evaluation of documentation found seven factors that explained 65% of the variability: *credibility* (correct, reliable, believable), *demonstrative* (precise, conclusive, strong, complete), *fitness* (relevant, meaningful, appropriate), *personal affect* (varied, interesting, active), *systematic arrangement* (organized, orderly, structured), *task relevance* (useful, informative, valuable), and *understandability* (clear, understandable, readable).

Guinan, C., and Smeaton, A. F. (1992). Information retrieval from hypertext using dynamically planned guided tours. *Proc. ECHT'92 Fourth ACM Hypertext Conf.,* 123–130.

Guided tours are constructed for the individual user, based on a query specifying that user's current interests.

Haake, A., Hüser, C., and Reichenberger, K. (1994). The individualized electronic newspaper: An example of an active publication. *Electronic*

Publishing: Origination, Dissemination and Design (EP-ODD), special issue on active documents.

The individualized electronic newspaper allows different views of a database of news items depending on the reader's interests. The "newspaper" is also interlinked with other hypertext services such as an online dictionary that can be used to look up words which the user does not understand.

Haake, J. M., and Wilson, B. (1992). Supporting collaborative writing of hyperdocuments in SEPIA. *Proc. ACM CSCW'92 Conf.* (Toronto, Canada, 31 October–4 November), 138–146.

SEPIA supports highly structured hypertext documents and allows both synchronous and asynchronous collaborative work. Authors working on any node not currently used by other authors are referred to as doing individual work. The system also provides support for two types of collaborative authoring: Loosely coupled collaborative authoring where authors are working within the same composite node (group of interconnected nodes forming a single structure) and tightly coupled collaborative authoring where coauthors have a shared view of a composite node's content.

Haake, J., Neuwirth, C., Streitz, N. (1994). Coexistence and transformation of informal and formal structures: Requirements for more flexible hypermedia systems. *Proceedings ECHT'94 ACM European Conference on Hypermedia Technology.* (Edinburgh, U.K., September 18–23, 1994), 1–12.

Contrasting different levels of formality in hypertext structures along two dimensions: the extent to which the system understands and represents the types of the objects internally and the extent to which the user explicitly defines the types of objects. Very informal hypertext does not use types but allows users to write what they want where they want, whereas hypertext systems with formal structures knows something about the meaning of each information object. The trade-off is that more highly structured hypertext allows the system to analyze and process the data in more advances ways but in turn normally requires the user to spend time classifying the information. The paper identifies a third alternative where the information is structured internally in the system even though the user has not specified any structure. This is possible if the computer has a way of parsing the information.

Haan, B. J., Kahn, P., Riley, V. A., Coombs, J. H., and Meyrowitz, N. K. (1992). IRIS hypermedia services. *Communications of the ACM* **35**, 1 (January), 36–51.

Well-illustrated survey of Intermedia and its different services. The article stresses how Intermedia was not so much a single hypertext program as it was a framework for hypertext functionality which supported multiple specialized programs, such as traditional hypertext documents, email, timelines, and animations. The paper ends by listing considerations for next-generation hypertext systems that were explored towards the end of the Intermedia project, including the integration of hypertext features with the user's general work environment, the ability to combine multiple webs over a single hypertext base, filtering tools, and hypertext distributed over a wide-area network.

Haas, C. (1989). Does the medium make a difference? Two studies of writing with pen and paper and with computers. *Human-Computer Interaction* **4**, 2, 149–169.

A comparison of text editing on paper and with computers. Users wrote more words when they used a workstation with large screen and a mouse-based editor than when they used a personal computer with a keyboard-based editor or when using pen and paper. The quality of the writings was about the same on the workstation and paper but was significantly worse on personal computers. Finally, when users who revised their works were asked to think aloud, the proportion of their utterances that referred to the editing medium itself rather than to the text being edited was only 3% when they used paper but 8% on the mouse-based workstation and a whopping 21% on the keyboard-based personal computer, thus indicating that the use of pen and paper was significantly more transparent (even though the test users all had at least 4 years of computer experience).

Hahn, U., and Reimer, U. (1988). Automatic generation of hypertext knowledge bases. *Proc. ACM Conf. Office Information Systems* (Palo Alto, CA, 23–25 March), 182–188.

By natural language parsing/semi-recognition, full-text bases are supplied with an abstraction hierarchy of so-called text graph concept browsers with hypertextual links.

Halasz, F. G. (1988). Reflections on NoteCards: Seven issues for the next generation of hypermedia systems. *Communications of the ACM* **31**, 7 (July), 836–852.

Important paper discussing interface and conceptual challenges for designers of future hypertext systems.

Halasz, F. G., and Schwartz, M. (1990). The Dexter hypertext reference model. *Proc. NIST Hypertext Standardization Workshop* (Gaithersburg, MD, 16-18 January), 95–133.

The general architecture of hypertext systems is described according to a three-layer model. The reference model is formalized in the *Z* specification language. This is intended to be a general model for the description of all hypertext systems and the background for implementing a standardized hypertext interchange format. The paper presents a simple, preliminary example of such an interchange format.

Halasz, F., and Schwartz, M. (1994). The Dexter hypertext reference model. *Communications of the ACM* **37**, 2 (February), 30–39.

A slightly revised version of [Halasz and Schwartz 1990] without the formal specification in *Z*.

Halasz, F. G., Moran, T. P., and Trigg, R. H. (1987). NoteCards in a nutshell. *Proc. ACM CHI+GI'87* (Toronto, Canada, 5–9 April), 45–52.

On the basic design of NoteCards and how it can be used as an idea organizer.

Hammond, N., and Allinson, L. (1988). Travels around a learning support environment: Rambling, orienteering or touring? *Proc. ACM CHI'88* (Washington, DC, 15–19 May), 269–273.

Use of metaphors such as guided tours to aid navigation.

Hammond, N., and Allinson, L. (1989). Extending hypertext for learning: An investigation of access and guidance tools. In Sutcliffe, A. and Macaulay, L. (Eds.): *People and Computers V*, Cambridge University Press, 293–304.

An information system that provided several different access methods was tested with users having either an exploratory task (asked to study for an unspecified subsequent test) or a directed task (had to answer specific questions). In both task conditions, hypertext links accounted for slightly more than half of the transitions between screens, and the overview map accounted for 12–16% of the transitions, whereas the index was used much more for directed search (17% vs. 6% in the exploratory case) and a guided tour facility was used more for exploratory search (28% vs. 8% in the directed case). Some subjects were tested with a system which only contained hypertext links and contained none of the other access mechanisms. Those users visited fewer screens during the experiment and had a significantly lower ratio of different screens to total screens seen, indicating that use of other facilities to supplement hypertext links resulted in wider coverage of the materials and more efficient access to new information.

Hansen, W. J., and Haas, C. (1988). Reading and writing with computers: A framework for explaining differences in performance. *Communications of the ACM* **31**, 9 (September), 1080–1089.

Discussion of the factors that impact throughput and quality in reading and writing online text, including reports of several empirical studies indicating the importance of having large screens.

Hapeshi, K., and Jones, D. (1992). Interactive multimedia for instruction: A cognitive analysis of the role of audition and vision. *Intl. J. Human–Computer Interaction* **4**, 1, 79–99.

Survey of usability issues in adding multimedia effects such as sound and video to hypertext for instructional purposes.

Happ, A. J., and Stanners, S. L. (1991). Effect of hypertext cue presentation on knowledge representation. *Proc. Human Factors Society 35th Annual Meeting*, 305–309.

Study comparing hypertext anchors embedded in the text with anchors in the form of icons in the margin. Users in either condition had acquired a better understanding of the underlying structure of the information than had readers of a corresponding hardcopy text, and there was no difference between the users' performance with the two different kinds of anchors.

Hardman, L. (1988). Hypertext tips: Experiences in developing a hypertext tutorial. In Jones, D. M., and Winder R. (Eds.): *People and Computers IV*, Cambridge University Press, 437–451.

Experience from the development of a tutorial on the structure of the brain for physiology students and some general comments on hypertext style. As a practical comment, the reader should note that the pictures shown in Figures 1 and 2 in the paper have accidentally been swapped.

Hardman, L. (1989a). Transcripts of observations of readers using the Glasgow Online hypertext. *Technical Report AMU8835/01H*, Scottish HCI Centre, Edinburgh, February.

Detailed notes on a series of user experiments with *Glasgow Online*. For a conceptual discussion of the actual results of this study, see Hardman's 1989 *Hypermedia* paper.

Hardman, L. (1989b). Evaluating the usability of the Glasgow Online hypertext. *Hypermedia* **1**, 1, 34–63.

Findings from a laboratory study of novice users interacting with a hypertext tourist information system. Most of the usability problems observed seemed to have more to do with traditional user interface issues such as screen design than with hypertext linkage or network navigation. Exceptions were things such as a confused linking paradigm for a "next" button and the lack of a general backtrack command.

Hardman, L., and Sharratt, B. (1990). User-centred hypertext design: The application of HCI design principles and guidelines. In McAleese, R., and Green, C. (Eds.) *Hypertext: State of the Art,* Ablex, 252–259.

On the basis of five general usability principles, the authors derive guidelines for hypertext user interfaces: user action (2 guidelines); information display (6 guidelines); dialogue (5 guidelines); online assistance (2 guidelines). Many of the guidelines are fairly general in nature (e.g. "ordering of lists should be designed to assist readers' tasks") and hard to follow without further analysis. They do provide insights into the special nature of hypertext interfaces (e.g. the matching of list ordering to users' tasks "can be enhanced by having multiple orderings of the same information").

Hardman, L., Bulterman, D. C. A., and van Rossum, G. (1993). Links in hypermedia: The requirement for context. *Proc. ACM Hypertext'93 Conf.,* 183–191.

When authoring time-dependent hypermedia presentations it is difficult to know exactly where a link should lead. The authors introduce the notion of a context to define the part of a hypermedia presentation affected by following a link. For example, the source context of a link might be a video clip that should be stopped and removed from the screen as the user activates the link, and the destination context for the link might be another video clip that should be displayed on the screen as a still image taken from a representative part of the film. The destination context for the link might have specified the first frame of the video as the still picture to be displayed, or it might have specified that the video should start playing automatically upon arrival. The exact choice is an authoring decision, but the context concept (and the associated authoring tools) give the authors the necessary framework for making those decisions.

Harmon, J. E. (1989). The structure of scientific and engineering papers: A historical perspective. *IEEE Trans. Professional Communication* **32**, 3 (September), 132–138.

Brief overview of the development leading to the current rather strict structure of the typical scientific paper. Early papers from the 17th century often were very short (a few paragraphs or so), had no clearly delimited sections (introduction, method, conclusion, etc.), and were written as a personal discourse.

Hewett, T. T. (1987). The Drexel Disk: An electronic 'guidebook'. In Diaper, D., and Winder, R. (Eds.): *People and Computers III,* Cambridge University Press, 115–129.

A custom application to introduce new students to campus. Includes among other things a hypertextually active campus map.

Hill, G., and Hall, W. (1994). Extending the Microcosm model to a distributed environment. *Proc. ACM ECHT'94 European Conference on Hypermedia Technology* (Edinburgh, U.K., September 18–23), 32–40.

An approach to open hypertext across computer networks: each computer can run one or more applications, and these applications can link to objects in other applications on other computers as well as to their own local objects. This model is more flexible than the standard client–server model that is normally used on the Internet.

Hill, W. C., Hollan, J. D., Wroblewski, D., and McCandless, T. (1992). Edit wear and read wear. *Proc. ACM CHI'92 Conf.*, 3–9.

Readwear involves having the computer record what parts of a text are being read the most ("worn by readers" like well-read books are), thus allowing future readers to see what was popular.

Hill, W., Rosenstein, M., and Stead, L. (1994). Community and history-of-use navigation. *Proc. Second Intl. WWW Conf. '94: Mosaic and the Web* (Chicago, Oct. 17–20), available on the Internet as http://www.ncsa.uiuc.edu/SDG/IT94/Proceedings/HCI/hill/home-page.html.

Mosaic was modified to allow users to indicate quality ratings for individual hypertext nodes as they were reading them. Combining quality votes from a large number of users then allowed the modified Mosaic to indicate the expected quality of the destination of a link by placing a number of stars next to its anchor.

Hill, W., Stead, L., and Rosenstein, M. (1995). Recommending and evaluating choices in a virtual community of use. *Proc. ACM CHI'95 Conf.*

A movie recommender was set up over the Internet, where users could send email to videos@bellcore.com to participate. Users were sent a list of 500 films chosen from a database of 1750 films and were asked to provide their ratings of how well they liked those films they had seen. 291 people participated and provided more than 55,000 ratings. The system computed the correlations between ratings provided by different users and constructed a model of which people seemed to like the same things.

Hirata, K., Hara, Y., Shibata, N., and Hirabayashi, F. (1993). Media-based navigation for hypermedia systems. *Proc. ACM Hypertext'93 Conf.*, 159–173.

Pattern recognition is used to establish links between images that look approximately the same (e.g., all photos of tall buildings).

Hitch, G. J., Sutcliffe, A. G., Bowers, J. M., and Eccles, L. M. (1986). Empirical evaluation of map interfaces: A preliminary study. In Harrison, M. D., and Monk, A. F. (Eds.): *People and Computers: Designing for Usability*, Cambridge University Press, 565–585.

On the use of spatially laid out maps as menu interfaces.

Hodges, M. E., Sasnett, R. M., and Ackerman, M. S. (1989). A construction set for multimedia applications. *IEEE Software* **6**, 1 (January), 37–43.

Describes the software platform for the Athena Muse project and includes screen shots from the Philippe system for teaching French.

Hoekema, J. (1990). HyperCard as a development tool for CD-I. *Boston Computer Society New Media News* **4**, 2 (Spring), p. 1 & pp. 14–20.

HyperCard was used to develop storyboards before the implementation of the CD-I product *Treasures of the Smithsonian*. The author gives examples of preliminary screen designs and discusses the advantages and disadvantages of HyperCard for prototyping CD-I's with their somewhat different interaction techniques.

Houghton, R. C. (1984). Online help systems: A conspectus. *Communications of the ACM* **27**, 2 (February), 126–133.

An overview of traditional computer mainframe online help systems.

Howell, G. (1990). Hypertext meets interactive fiction: New vistas in creative writing. In McAleese, R., and Green, C. (Eds.) *Hypertext: State of the Art,* Ablex, 136–141.

An introduction to the concept of interactive fiction with references to some printed works by traditional authors having hypertext-like characteristics.

Hubert, L. J. (1978). Generalized proximity function comparisons. *British J. Mathematical and Statistical Psychology* **31**, 179–192.

Hubert, L. J. (1979). Generalized concordance. *Psychometrika* **44**, 135–142.

Methods that can be used to measure the proximity of two hierarchical structures and that can be applied to the problem of measuring how far the structure of the user's conceptual model is from a hypertext's structure (see [Gordon et al. 1988]).

Instone, K., Teasley, B. M., and Leventhal, L. M. (1993). Empirically-based re-design of a hypertext encyclopedia. *Proc. ACM INTERCHI'93 Conf.* (Amsterdam, the Netherlands, 29–29 April), 500–506.

The HyperHolmes Sherlock Holmes encyclopedia (see [Mynatt 1992]) was subjected to iterative design based on earlier findings of usability problems. The content was the same in HyperHolmes I and II, but the user interface was changed: Overlapping windows were changed to tiled windows, a redundant listing of the outgoing links from each node was removed (establishing a tighter connection between the links and their anchors), the listing of incoming links (a bidirectional link tool) was simplified, the search tool was simplified (several "advanced" features like the search for contiguous words were removed), and the overview node was given landmark status. As a result of these changes, users' accuracy in answering questions increased from 1.4 in HyperHolmes I to 1.7 in HyperHolmes II (compared with 1.2 when using a paper version of the encyclopedia), when measured on a 0–2 scale. The time needed to answer the questions was reduced from 236 seconds to 178 (compared with 201 for paper).

Irler, W. J., and Barbieri, G. (1990). Non-intrusive hypertext anchors and individual colour markings. *Proc. ECHT'90 European Conf. Hypertext* (Paris, France, 28–30 November), Cambridge University Press, 261–273.

A paper lamenting the use of buttons as anchors for hypertext links, arguing that they are too intrusive. Instead, the authors' system (implemented in ToolBook under Microsoft Windows) allows the user to click anywhere in the window, resulting in a pop-up overview diagram of the possible paths from the current location. Also, the system allows individual users to customize the text with color marks (similar to the use of magic markers to highlight text in printed books, see [Nielsen 1986]).

Irven, J. H., Nilson, M. E., Judd, T. H., Patterson, J. F., and Shibata, Y. (1988). Multi-media information services: A laboratory study. *IEEE Communications Magazine* **26**, 6 (June), 27–44.

Survey of a number of research projects at Bellcore, including a video browser with different organizations of images, the Movie Browser which can automatically build a hypertext from a conventional database of move titles, and a telesophy (remote access to multiple sources of information) system with a quarter of a million nodes taken from wire services, Usenet News, etc. The "laboratory study" referred to in the title of the paper is only discussed in a small part of the paper and mainly addresses performance issues of response times in relation to network transmission speeds.

Isbister, K., and Layton, T. (1995). Agents: What (or who) are they? In Nielsen, J. (Ed.), *Advances in Human–Computer Interaction* vol. **5**. Ablex.

Survey of the user interface issues related to the use of agents. Examples are taken from several Microsoft, Apple, and Hewlett-Packard products as well as many research systems.

Jackson, S., and Yankelovich, N. (1991). InterMail: A prototype hypermedia mail system.

An email system built for Intermedia, allowing users to send messages with embedded links to larger hypertexts.

Jacques, W. (1990). The ACM Hypertext'89 conference. *Boston Computer Society New Media News* **4**, 1 (Winter), 1 and 17-20.

Trip report from **Hypertext'89**, including an extensive summary of discussions of links and anchors for temporal data like movies.

Jarvenpaa, S., and Ives, B. (1994). *Digital Equipment Corporation: The Internet Company.* Business school case study available at http://www.cox.smu.edu/mis/cases/dec/internet.html or by sending an email message to cis-fserv@ube.ubalt.edu with a blank subject and the line SEND CASES.DIGITALWWW in the body of the message.

Case study of the initial growth of WWW usage within DEC. Much early work happened as a result of skunksworks-type grassroot efforts and the research labs turned into product entrepreneurs.

Jennings, E. M. (1990). Paperless writing revisited. *Computers and the Humanities* **24**, 43–48.

Teaching online writing at the university level.

Jonassen, D. H., and Mandl, H. (Eds.) (1990). *Designing Hypertext / Hypermedia for Learning.* Springer-Verlag, Heidelberg, Germany.

The proceedings of the NATO advanced research workshop on hypertext in Rottenburg, Germany, 3–7 July 1989. Includes several chapters on various usability issues relating to hypertext as well as many examples of European hypertext projects. Several of the chapters grapple with the issue of assessing the actual impact of hypertext on learning (if any).

Jones, H. W., III (1987a). Developing and distributing hypertext tools: Legal inputs and parameters. *Proc. ACM Hypertext'87 Conf.* (Chapel Hill, NC, 13–15 November), 367–374.

Mostly about the copyright problem but also some discussion of liability, royalties, antitrust matters, and problems with international law and certain Latin American countries.

Jones, W. P. (1987b). How do we distinguish the hyper from the hype in non-linear text? *Proc. IFIP INTERACT'87* (Stuttgart, Germany, 1–4 September), 1107–1113.
Selectivity of access is seen as a major potential advantage of hypertext and the author presents various approaches to achieving greater selectivity.

Jones, W. P., and Dumais, S. T. (1986). The spatial metaphor for user interfaces: Experimental tests of reference by location versus name. *ACM Trans. Office Inf. Syst.* **4**, 1 (January), 42–63.
Retrieval of objects was more accurate by name than by location in situations with large number of objects, but retrieval by the combination of name and location was better than either method in isolation. The authors conclude that purely spatial filing may be most useful in temporary situations involving a small number of recently encountered objects.

Jordan, D. S., Russell, D. M., Jensen, A-M. S., and Rogers, R. A. (1989). Facilitating the development of representations in hypertext with IDE. *Proc. ACM Hypertext'89 Conf.* (Pittsburgh, PA, 5–8 November), 93–104.
The *Instructional Design Environment* (IDE) contains several authoring tools, including "structure accelerators" that speed up the construction of entire hypertext structures from templates.

Joseph, B., Steinberg, E. R., and Jones, A. R. (1989). User perceptions and expectations of an information retrieval system. *Behaviour and Information Technology* **8**, 2 (March–April), 77–88.
A hypertext-like implementation of a bridge engineering manual on the PLATO system. Users selecting chapters from a table of contents made the wrong choices 80% of the time because the table of contents displayed only chapter names and not the section listings that are found in the printed manual's table of contents. Chapters were organized by engineering activity and not by type of bridge, so going by the names of the chapters alone, information about arch bridges could have been in at least three of the chapters listed. Use of the table of contents dropped from being 20% of the information access on the first day of the experiment to about 5% on the third day of the experiment.

Jurgen, R. K. (1992). Digital video. *IEEE Spectrum* **29**, 3 (March), 24–30.
Summary of developments in digital video, including standards issues and the various CD-ROM formats.

Kacmar, C. J., and Leggett, J. J. (1991). PROXHY: A process-oriented extensible hypertext architecture. *ACM Trans. Information Systems* **9**, 4 (October), 399–419.
An approach to providing hypertext as a system-level service to multiple applications. Each application can interact with a hypertext service through interprocess communication, thus allowing links to cross application boundaries.

Kacmar, C., Leggett, J., Schnase, J. L., and Boyle, C. (1988). Data management facilities of existing hypertext systems. *Technical Report* **TAMU 88-018**, Texas A&M University, September.

A comparison of the data models and operations provided by 11 hypertext systems. The hypertext systems only provided about 60%–70% of the database functions found in standard database systems. The focus of this report is on back-end issues rather than on user interface issues.

Kaehler, C. (1988). Authoring with hypermedia. In Ambron S., and Hooper K. (Eds.), *Interactive Multimedia: Visions of Multimedia for Developers, Educators, & Information Providers.* Microsoft Press, 307–311.

An extremely short article (only a single page of actual text) on the ideas behind the online help package in HyperCard by its designer.

Kahn, P. (1989a). Webs, trees, and stacks: How hypermedia system design effect hypermedia content. In Salvendy, G., and Smith, M. J. (Eds.): *Designing and Using Human-Computer Interfaces and Knowledge Based Systems,* Elsevier Science Publishers, 443–449.

A comparative study of Guide, HyperCard, KMS, and Intermedia from an authoring perspective. The following four issues are discussed: Is the meaning located primarily in the links or in the nodes? What is the relationship between documents, nodes, and visible screen units? Will following a link replace the current node or supplement it? What is the distinction between author and reader? As an example, Kahn gives further detail of an Intermedia web on Lunar geology, "Exploring the Moon."

Kahn, P. (1989b). Linking together books: Experiments in adapting published material into hypertext. *Hypermedia* 1, 2, 111–145.

Describes the conversion of a set of books on Chinese poetry into Intermedia format, giving plenty of screen shots. One interesting illustration is an overview diagram of the translators of the poet Tu Fu, which are ordered in two dimensions: Chronologically on the y-axis and according to the translator's emphasis on sinology or poetry on the x-axis. The author distinguishes between *objective links* (those present in the text being converted such as explicit literature references) and *subjective links* (those added because the converter or other hypertext user sees a connection between two items).

Kahn, P., and Landow, G. P. (1992). Where's the hypertext? The Dickens Web as a system-independent hypertext. *Proc. ECHT'92 Fourth ACM Hypertext Conf.*, 149–160.

Transferring a hypertext on Charles Dickens (used to teach English literature at Brown University) from Intermedia to Storyspace.

Kahn, P., Launhardt, J., Lenk, K., and Peters, R. (1990). Design of hypermedia publications: Issues and solutions. *Proc. Electronic Publishing'90* (Gaithersburg, MD, 18–20 September), Cambridge University Press.

Kain, H., and Nielsen, J. (1991). Estimating the market diffusion curve for hypertext. *Impact Assessment Bulletin* 9, 1–2 (Spring), 145–157.

A model for the growth in hypertext use over time is developed based on the Bass curve for product innovation diffusion. The market penetration of hypertext is expected to grow slowly but steadily in the period 1990–2000 and to grow rapidly from the year 2000.

Kaltenbach, M., Robillard, F., and Frasson, C. (1991). Screen management in hypertext systems with rubber sheet layouts. *Proc. ACM Hypertext'91 Conf.*, 91–105.
Idea for automatic layout of hypertext screens with rules for moving windows out of the way as new windows appear.

Kellogg, W. A., and Richards, J. T. (1995). The human factors of information on the Internet. In Nielsen, J. (Ed.), *Advances in Human–Computer Interaction* Vol. **5**, Ablex.
Survey of the reasons information is so difficult to find and use over the Internet. The authors stress that even though the newer graphical user interfaces are somewhat easier to use than the original Unix command line interface, the Internet still has substantial usability problems that remain to be solved.

Kerr, S. T. (1989). Efficiency and satisfaction in videotex database production. *Behaviour and Information Technology* **8**, 1 (January–February), 57–63.
A field study of the working style of designers doing everyday production of videotex frames. Over time, designers tend to be bored since most routine frame creation work is not very interesting. The study revealed a conflict over the place of individual creativity in videotex work where the designers chafe at restrictions imposed by managers because using the hardware and software in unusual and exploratory ways is a principal motivation in designers' daily work.

Kibby, M. R., and Mayes, J. T. (1989). Towards intelligent hypertext. In McAleese, R. (Ed.): *Hypertext Theory into Practice*, Ablex, 164–172.
The StrathTutor hypertext system tries to eliminate the need to rely on exclusively manual methods for creating links between hypertext nodes by generating links based on its knowledge of the connection between the nodes as the user browses.

Knaster, K. (1994). *Presenting Magic Cap: A Guide to General Magic's Revolutionary Communicator Software*; Addison-Wesley.
Survey of the Magic Cap user interface to Personal Digital Assistants.

Knuth, D. E. (1984). Literate programming. *Computer Journal* **27**, 2 (May), 97–111.
A proposal for an intertwined representation of program code and descriptive text.

Koons, W. R., O'Dell, A. M., Frishberg, N. J., and Laff, M. R. (1992). The computer sciences electronic magazine: Translating from paper to multimedia. *Proc. ACM CHI'92 Conf.*, 11–18.
Design issues involved in producing an in-house electronic magazine at IBM.

Koved, L., and Shneiderman, B. (1986). Embedded menus: Selecting items in context. *Communications of the ACM* **29**, 4 (April), 312–318.
Shows that users work faster when selecting items that are embedded in surrounding contextual information.

Krauss, F. S. H., Middendorf, K. A., and Willits, L. S. (1991). A comparative investigation of hardcopy vs. online documentation. *Proc. Human Factors Society 35th Annual Meeting*, 350–353.

Subjects were slower using an online manual than a hardcopy version, mainly due to time spent moving and resizing windows and time spent recovering from letting lost after following wrong hypertext links. Users often did not know how to return to their original location, confirming the need for an easy backtrack feature.

Kreitzberg, C. B. (1989). Designing the electronic book: Human psychology and information structures for hypermedia. *Proc. 3rd Intl. Conf. on Human-Computer Interaction* (Boston, MA, 18–22 September).

Kreitzberg, C. B., and Shneiderman, B. (1988). Restructuring knowledge for an electronic encyclopedia. *Proc. Intl. Ergonomics Association 10th Congress* (Sydney, Australia, 1–5 August), 615–620.

Design issues for writing the content of a hypertext structure.

Lai, K.-Y., Malone, T. W., and Yu, K.-C. (1988). Object Lens: A 'spreadsheet' for cooperative work. *ACM Trans. Office Information Systems* **6**, 4 (October), 332–353.

Object Lens is the second generation of the Information Lens system for information filtering in electronic mail and online communication. It integrates hypertext, object-oriented databases, and the rule-based agents used to classify incoming messages automatically.

Lai, P., and Manber, U. (1991). Flying through hypertext. *Proc. ACM Hypertext'91 Conf.*, 123–132.

Attempt at giving the user an overview of the contents of a hypertext by quickly flashing through the nodes (in an analogy to flipping through a book).

Landauer, T. K. (1988). Research methods in human-computer interaction. In Helander, M. (Ed.): *Handbook of Human-Computer Interaction,* Elsevier Science Publishers, 905–928.

A good introduction to quantitative and statistical methods used to study usability.

Landow, G. P. (1987). Relationally encoded links and the rhetoric of hypertext. *Proc. ACM Hypertext'87 Conf.* (Chapel Hill, NC, 13–15 November), 331–343.

The rhetoric of hypertext involves establishing conventions for the use of links between nodes: Readers may form expectations for how these links work (e.g. if there is a link, then readers will expect it to have some significance).

Landow, G. P. (1989a). The rhetoric of hypertext: Some rules for authors. *Journal of Computing in Higher Education* **1**, 1 (Spring), 39–64.

A set of 19 rules for the design of hypertext with coherent, purposeful, and useful relationships. These rules are called the *rhetoric* of hypertext and aim at providing conventions for what to expect with regard to links and anchors. The "rhetoric of departure" gives rules for how to show outgoing links from a node, and the "rhetoric of arrival" gives rules for how to orient a reader upon arrival at a new node.

Landow, G. P. (1989b). Hypertext in literary education, criticism, and scholarship. *Computers and the Humanities* **23**, 173–198.

The most complete paper on the use of the Intermedia hypertext system for the teaching of English literature at Brown University. The information base is called *Context32* and originally contained 1000 documents and 1300 links, but more are being added. The use of Intermedia for an introductory course proved successful and even improved the quality of the class sessions where the computers were not being used (an ethnographer who observed the course both before and after the introduction of hypertext found that the number of student comments increased by 300% and that the number of students making comments also increased by 300%). The paper also includes the reading list for the course and a complete listing of the first assignment students get when starting to use Intermedia for the study of English literature.

Landow, G. P. (1990). Popular fallacies about hypertext. In Jonassen, D. H., and Mandl, H. (Eds.), *Designing Hypertext/Hypermedia for Learning.* Springer-Verlag, Heidelberg, Germany, 39–59.

The author argues against several current hypertext research directions: He does not believe that one can study the nature and effect of hypertext with small document sets (several of his own problems did not appear until his Context32 hypertext grew large), he does not believe that analogies of navigation, narration, and space will help us think accurately about hypertext (neither temporal nor spatial metaphors tell the entire truth about hypertext), and he does not believe that navigation and orientation poses a serious problem (author-generated overview diagrams normally help point the reader in the right direction). Landow also presents an interesting critique of the analogy between hypertext and traditional publishing.

Landow, G. P. (1992). *Hypertext: The Convergence of Contemporary Critical Theory and Technology.* Johns Hopkins University Press, Baltimore, MD.

Hypertext as a literary medium as seen by an English professor. Johns Hopkins University Press has also published this book in hypertext formats for the Macintosh and for Windows.

Landow, G. P. (Ed.) (1994). *Hyper/Text/Theory.* Johns Hopkins University Press, Baltimore, MD.

Book on the literary theory of hypertext. Chapter titles like "Wittgenstein, Genette, and the reader's narrative in hypertext" and "Physics and hypertext: Liberation and complicity in art and pedagogy" indicate the range of topics covered.

Landow, G. P., and Kahn, P. (1992). Where's the hypertext? The Dickens Web as a system-independent hypertext. *Proc. ACM ECHT'92* Conf. (Milan, Italy, November 30 – December 4), 149–160.

The Dickens Web is a hypertext about Charles Dickens and his authorship. It was originally developed in the Intermedia system but after the untimely demise of that system, the authors transferred it to two other systems, Eastgate System's Storyspace and Interleaf's WorldView. The authors describe some of the difficulties they encountered due to the different conceptual models of hypertext supported by the different systems (for example, WorldView did not support "fat" one-to-many links as was done in Intermedia). After the conversion, an evaluation was performed where fifteen English students used the three versions to perform class assignments. Students were able to complete their assignments in all three versions and had positive and negative comments about all three (no quantitative measures were collected). In their free-form comments, students did express a desire for those features of Intermedia that were not present in the other systems but it is not clear to what extent this is due to the fact that they were using a hypertext that had originally been authored for Intermedia and thus presumably structured to take optimal advantage of its specific features.

Lansdale, M. W., Young, D. R., and Bass, C. A. (1989). MEMOIRS: A personal multimedia information system. In Sutcliffe, A. and Macaulay, L. (Eds.): *People and Computers V*, Cambridge University Press, 315–327.

MEMOIRS (Memory Enhanced Management for Office Information Systems) is a personal information system where the traditional concept of files is replaced with interlinked information nodes tied to a timeline (called a "timebase").

Laurel, B. (1989). A taxonomy of interactive movies. *Boston Computer Society New Media News* **3**, 1 (Winter), 5–8.

After a brief survey of the "projections" for future interactive media in various science fiction films, Laurel presents a number of dimensions for interactivity: frequency (how often does the user get to make a choice), range (number of options available to choose from), significance (effect of the choice), and personness (1st, 2nd, or 3rd person experiences). Based on these dimensions, interactive movies are classified as navigational, narrative, or dramatic.

Laurel, B., Oren, T., and Don, A. (1990). Issues in multimedia interface design: Media integration and interface agents. *Proc. ACM CHI'90 Conf. Human Factors in Computing Systems* (Seattle, WA, 1–5 April), 133–139.

Agents provide an interface to a hypertext by giving the user suggestions for where to go next in a manner similar to guided tours but with the opportunity for more dynamic calculation of the path. The authors also discuss issues in integrating video and other media in a hypertext while avoiding "media ghettoes" with few links between pieces of information of different media types.

Leggett, J. J., and Killough, R. J. (1991). Issues in hypertext interchange. *Hypermedia* **3**, 3, 159–186.

Use of the Dexter model to transfer hypertexts from Intermedia to KMS. The paper distinguishes between dynamic interchange (both hypertext systems are engaged concurrently in achieving the exchange) and static interchange (all other cases) between hypertext formats.

Leggett, J., Schnase, J. L., and Kacmar, C. J. (1989). A short course on hypertext. *Technical Report* **TAMU 89-004**, Computer Science Department, Texas A&M University, College Station, TX 77843-3112, January.

The overheads from what may have been the first university level course on hypertext.

Leggett, J., Schnase, J. L., and Kacmar, C. J. (1990). Hypertext and learning. In Jonassen, D. H., and Mandl, H. (Eds.), *Designing Hypertext / Hypermedia for Learning*. Springer-Verlag, Heidelberg, Germany, 2737.

Brief reports from the use of hypertext to teach three courses, including summaries of student feedback. In all cases, the students wanted annotations, bookmarks, and the ability to integrate hypertext into their normal computing environment.

Lesk, M. (1989). What to do when there's too much information. *Proc. ACM Hypertext'89 Conf.* (Pittsburgh, PA, 5–8 November), 305–318.

Approaches to providing overview diagrams and interactive information retrieval mechanisms to a catalog of 800,000 items.

Lesk, M. (1991). The CORE electronic chemistry library. *Proc. ACM SIGIR'91 Conf.*, 93–112.

Description of several alternative user interfaces developed to represent ten years of the American Chemical Society's journals: Pixlook shows scanned page images on the screen, SuperBook uses a traditional hypertext approach, and the comic book interface represents each article by a strip of its figures (because figures are important to chemists and can often be used to recognize a paper).

Leung, Y. K., and Apperley, M. D. (1994). A review and taxonomy of distortion-oriented presentation techniques. *ACM Transactions on Computer–Human Interaction* **1**, 2 (June), 126–160.

Distortion-oriented presentation techniques like fisheye views are those that transform the data instead of just clipping it (as done in traditional window systems). Non-distorted views have the benefit of providing the full detail of the original data displayed in a well-known layout. Distorted views may initially be harder to understand and may lose some detail, but they have the benefit of potentially showing the information in a fuller context.

Levy, D. M. (1994) Fixed or fluid? Document stability and new media. *Proc. ACM ECHT'94 European Conference on Hypermedia Technology* (Edinburgh, U.K., September 18–23), 24–31.

The author argues that all documents have some fixed aspects and some fluid aspects. Even paper documents (which are normally considered fixed) are changeable (e.g., one of the recipients of a memo may annotate it, meaning that if the memo is copied further, the second-generation recipients will receive different information depending on which instance of the memo was copied). Also, the author distinguishes between the duration of a document and its fixity: a document like the U.S. Constitution may have a long duration while being modified several times, whereas other documents, like a Post-It note, could last for a very short time even though it never changes once written.

Levy, S. (1994). E-money, that's what I want. *WIRED* **2**, 12 (December), 174–179 & 213–215 & 218–219.

Discussion of projects developing digital money transfer methods, with emphasis on David Chaum's DigiCash. In discussing Microsoft's activities in home finance and digital money, Levy asks, "will dollar bills be replaced by Bill dollars?"

Liestøl, G. (1994). Aesthetic and rhetorical aspects of linking video in hypermedia. *Proc. ACM ECHT'94 European Conference on Hypermedia Technology* (Edinburgh, U.K., September 18–23), 217–223.

Video footnotes used to represent link anchors in video clips.

Lippman, A., Bender, W., Salomon, G., and Saito, M. (1985). Color word processing. *IEEE Computer Graphics and Applications* **5**, 6 (June), 41–46.

A prototype word processor that shows the changes made by users in different colors depending on when those changes were made.

Lucas, P., and Schneider, L. (1994). Workscape: A scriptable document management environment. *ACM CHI'94 Conference Companion* 9–10.

A prototype office system that attempts to duplicate the concept of paper objects in a computer. The system supports spatial arrangements of the objects and the use of Post-It notes.

Luther, A. C. (1988). You are there... and in control. *IEEE Spectrum* **25**, 9 (September), 45–50.

A reasonably popular description of the technology behind DVI (Digital Video Interactive), including some discussion of possible hypermedia applications. The article has some nice color pictures of DVI screens, including a four-frame sequence from Palenque (a surrogate travel application, see [Wilson 1988]).

Macedonia, M. R., and Brutzman, D. P. (1994). MBone provides audio and video across the Internet. *IEEE Computer* **27**, 4 (April), 30–36.

The MBone (Multicast Backbone) provides a way of broadcasting video across the Internet to a large number of recipients without having to establish individual connections from the originating site to every recipient site.

Mackay, W. E., and Davenport, G. (1989). Virtual video editing in interactive multimedia applications. *Communications of the ACM* **32**, 7 (July), 802–810.

A discussion of several multimedia projects at MIT (the Media Lab and Project Athena), including the Athena Muse and the Pygmalion multimedia message system with special emphasis on the tools used to build the designs.

Mackinlay, J. D., Card, S. K., and Robertson, G. G. (1990). Rapid controlled movement through a virtual 3D workspace. *Proc. ACM SIGGRAPH'90 Conf.*, 171–176.

Methods for changing the view of objects in a three-dimensional user interface while preserving the user's understanding of what objects are being viewed and how they are changing. The speed of movement is high while the user is far from the destination but slows down as the destination is approached.

Mackinlay, J. D., Robertson, G. G., and Card, S. K. (1991). The perspective wall: Detail and context smoothly integrated. *Proc. ACM CHI'91 Conf.*, 173–179.

The perspective wall displays data objects along two dimensions on a wall. The x-axis (typically a timeline) is used to provide perspective by bending the wall to curve back before and after the part of the axis that is shown in the middle of the screen. Thus, the wall seems to continue (and be visible due to a 3D perspective) indefinitely in both directions.

MacTech Quarterly **1**, 4 (Winter 1990), 8–26 and 112–124.

Special section on *SuperCard* with reasonably detailed technical articles by Andrew Himes, Chris Van Hamersveld and Tony Myles about SuperCard in general, using SuperCard to build stand-alone applications, and the SuperCard runtime editor.

Mahajan, V., Muller, E., and Bass, F. M. (1990). New product diffusion models in marketing: A review and directions for research. *Journal of Marketing* **54**, 1 (January), 1–26.

This article is not specifically about hypertext but reviews marketing models for the market penetration of product innovation, and as such contains background material for the estimation of the spread of hypertext ideas and products.

Malcolm, K. C., Poltrock, S. E., and Schuler, D. (1991). Industrial strength hypertext: Requirements for a large engineering enterprise. *Proc. ACM Hypertext'91 Conf.*, 13–24.

Prospects for the use of hypertext in the aerospace industry as a way to integrate large amounts of data, manuals, technical drawings, etc. The requirements for hypertext use at Boeing are listed as: interoperability between different computer platforms, shared workspaces among multiple users to allow engineering teamwork and concurrent access to the hypertext, opportunities for both authors and readers to create links, support for attributes on links and nodes, rich link anchors that support links to multiple destinations, typed links, coexistence of public links and links that are private for the individual user, templates for creating predefined structures, automatically constructed overview diagrams, query mechanisms, configuration control, and programmability.

Malone, T. W., Lai, K. Y., and Fry, C. (1992). Experiments with Oval: A radically tailorable tool for cooperative work. *Proc. ACM CSCW'92 Conf.* (Toronto, Canada, 31 October–4 November), 289–297.

An object-oriented system for building electronic mail interfaces with hypertext links. The Oval project is a successor to the Object Lens and Information Lens projects. Oval is highly tailorable and is able to emulate the functionality of many different systems, including gIBIS, the Coordinator, Lotus Notes, as well as Information Lens.

Maltz, D., and Ehrlich, K. (1995). Pointing the way: Active collaborative filtering. *Proc. ACM CHI'95 Conf.*

A group of users in an organization can help each other find appropriate information by constructing "digests" of information that has been found to be useful by at least one user. Other users can access these digests to read highly filtered information and they can follow links to the source of the information to explore further.

Mander, R., Salomon, G., and Wong, Y. Y. (1992). A 'pile' metaphor for supporting casual organization of information. *Proc. ACM CHI'92 Conf.,* 627–634.

The authors conducted a field study of how people deal with paper in their physical workspace, finding that much information was stored in loosely organized piles (probably to overcome the premature classification problem found in NoteCards [Monty 1986]). They then designed a computer interface where some piles were collected by the user and some were constructed by the system based on specified rules.

Mantei, M (1982). *A Study of Disorientation in ZOG*, Ph.D. Thesis, University of Southern California.

This usability assessment of user navigation in the pioneering ZOG system (precursor to KMS) may have been the first Ph.D. thesis about hypertext.

Marchionini, G. (1989). Making the transition from print to electronic encyclopedia: Adaptation of mental models. *Intl.J. Man-Machine Studies* **30**, 6 (June), 591–618.

Sixteen high school students used the *Grolier's Academic American Encyclopedia* in both print form and electronic form and used the two versions in about the same way. This result should not be used to conclude that users in general will use hypertext the same way as they use printed books, however, since the subjects in this study used the electronic book only for a very limited amount of time and since the version of *Grolier's* tested had only very limited hypertext capabilities. An interesting side result from this study came from asking the subjects to compare the print and electronic encyclopedias. Half said that the electronic version was faster, three said that it contained more information than the printed version, and one said that it was more up to date. This result was in spite of the facts that the two versions of the encyclopedia actually contained the *same* text and that the subjects were measured to be slower with the electronic version. This experiment indicates some of the problems with subjective evaluations and the seductive qualities of novel technology.

Marchionini, G. (1990). Evaluating hypermedia-based learning. In Jonassen, D. H., and Mandl, H. (Eds.), *Designing Hypertext/Hypermedia for Learning.* Springer-Verlag, Heidelberg, Germany, 355–373.

A discussion of usability evaluation methods with a bias in favor of very careful (but difficult) methods.

Marchionini, G., and Crane, G. (1994). Evaluating hypermedia and learning: Methods and results from the Perseus Project. *ACM Trans. Information Systems* **12**, 1 (January), 5–34.

Report on a range of evaluation studies of use of the Perseus Project to teach Classics. Students and instructors mostly liked the ability to refer to hypermedia materials during lectures, though some found it confusing. Student essays contained more citations when using the hypertext but they were not graded any higher by independent professors.

Marchionini, G., and Shneiderman, B. (1988). Finding facts vs. browsing knowledge in hypertext systems. *IEEE Computer* **21**, 1 (January), 70–80.

The authors present an information seeking model . As examples of how concrete systems fit their model, the authors discuss Hyperties showing an example of the research version with a two-frame display, and the *Grolier's Electronic Encyclopedia* on CD-ROM.

Marshall, C. C., and Irish, P. M. (1989). Guided tours and on-line presentations: How authors make existing hypertext intelligible for readers. *Proc. ACM Hypertext'89 Conf.* (Pittsburgh, PA, 5–8 November), 15–26.

How to use guided tours and narrative structures such as arrows as *meta-information* to make the main information understandable.

Marshall, C. C., and Rogers, R. A. (1992). Two years before the mist: Experiences with Aquanet. *Proc. ACM ECHT'92 Conf.*, 53–62.

Case study of the use of Aquanet to author a hypertext structure with 2,000 nodes over a period of two years (or about five nodes per working day).

Marshall, C. C., and Shipman, F. M., III (1993). Searching for the missing link: Discovering implicit structure in spatial hypertext. *Proc. ACM Hypertext'93 Conf.*, 217–230.

The Aquanet hypertext system allows users to place hypertext nodes spatially on a large canvas. Based on this user-defined layout, the system can use pattern recognition to discover structures in the hypertext under the assumption that nodes that are placed near each other may be related. The system also tries to find repeated incidences of pairs or other groups of node types under the assumption that such repeated groups mean that users may implicitly be using composite nodes with the elements that have repeatedly been found together.

Marshall, C. C., Halasz, F. G., Rogers, R. A., and Janssen, W. C. (1991). Aquanet: A hypertext tool to hold your knowledge in place. *Proc. ACM Hypertext'91 Conf.*, 261–275.

Aquanet is a hypertext system designed to support knowledge structuring, such as the building of representations of complex arguments. Aquanet is based on composite nodes with a number of slots. A slot is a named attribute of the node and is restricted to containing data of certain types.

Marshall, C. C., Shipman, F. M., and Coombs, J. H. (1994). VIKI: Spatial hypertext supporting emerging structure. *Proc. ACM ECHT'94 European Conference on Hypermedia Technology* (Edinburgh, U.K., September 18–23), 13–23.

> VIKI allows users to associate nodes by placing them near each other on a canvas. This low-overhead supports the gradual refinement of structure and helps users interpret the materials by showing more or less connected information in the same view.

Masuda, Y., Ishitoba, Y., and Ueda, M. (1994). Frame-axis model for automatic information organizing and spatial navigation. *Proc. ACM ECHT'94 European Conference on Hypermedia Technology* (Edinburgh, U.K., September 18–23), 146–157.

> Hypertext nodes can be represented as frames with slots of structured data. The slots can be mapped onto axes that allow navigation between nodes with similar slot values.

Maunder, C. (1994). Documentation on tap. *IEEE Spectrum* **31**, 9 (September), 52–56.

> Short overview article on the steps involved in producing online documentation with SGML, using examples from British Telecom.

Mayes, T., Kibby, M., and Anderson, T. (1990). Learning about learning from hypertext. In Jonassen, D. H., and Mandl, H. (Eds.), *Designing Hypertext/Hypermedia for Learning*. Springer-Verlag, Heidelberg, Germany, 227–250.

> Reports from studies of learners using StrathTutor. The most revealing results came from *constructive interaction* studies observing two users constructively helping each other understand the system.

McCracken, D., and Akscyn, R. M. (1984). Experience with the ZOG human-computer interface system. *Intl.J. Man-Machine Studies* **21**, 293–310.

> A frame-based hypertext system developed at Carnegie Mellon University.

McKnight, C., Dillon, A., and Richardson, J. (1989). Problems in hyperland? A human factors perspective. *Hypermedia* **1**, 2, 167–178.

> A review of some human factors studies of relevance for hypertext user interfaces.

McKnight, C., Richardson, J., and Dillon, A. (1990). Journal articles as learning resource: What can hypertext offer?. In Jonassen, D. ., and Mandl, H. (Eds.), *Designing Hypertext/Hypermedia for Learning*. Springer-Verlag, Heidelberg, Germany, 277–290.

> A project to convert eight volumes of the journal *Behaviour and Information Technology* to hypertext.

Merwin, D. H., Dyre, B. P., Humphrey, D. G., Grimes, J., and Larish, J. F. (1990). The impact of icons and visual effects on learning computer databases. *Proc. Human Factors Society 34th Annual Meeting* (Orlando, FL, 8–12 October), 424–428.

Animated visual effects should be used to signify navigational transitions, since they help users understand what is going on.

Metros, S. E. (1994). Investigating Lake Iluka: Graphic design for the interface. *ACM interactions* **1**, 3 (July), 26–40.

Case study of the graphic design of an educational hypermedia package about ecology. Special emphasis is placed on the graphic design and several iterations are illustrated. The author emphasizes the need for consistent use of an interface metaphor to help users navigate and understand the information space and its controls (here, a notebook metaphor was chosen).

Meyrowitz, N. (1986). Intermedia: The architecture and construction of an object-oriented hypermedia system and applications framework. *Proc. OOPSLA'86 Conf. Object-Oriented Programming Systems, Languages, and Applications* (Portland, OR, 29 September–2 October), 186–201.

A discussion of many of the programming issues involved in implementing a hypermedia system using the object-oriented MacApp programming system.

Meyrowitz, N. (1989a). The missing link: Why we're all doing hypertext wrong. In Barrett, E. (Ed.): *The Society of Text,* MIT Press, Cambridge, MA, 107–114.

According to the author, the reason hypertext has not caught on is that existing systems are not integrated with the rest of the user's computing environment. Intermedia has a linking protocol architecture which allows the integration of third party applications if they would implement it. But to see really wide-spread use, the hypertext linking protocol must be part of the standard system software on the computer (e.g. part of the Macintosh Toolbox or the IBM Presentation Manager).

Meyrowitz, N. (1989b). Hypertext—does it reduce cholesterol, too? *Technical Report* **89-9**, Institute for Research in Information and Scholarship (IRIS), Brown University, Providence, RI, November. Reprinted in Nyce, J. M., and Kahn, P. (Eds.) (1991). *From Memex to Hypertext: Vannevar Bush and the Mind's Machine.* Academic Press, 287–318.

The keynote address from the Hypertext'89 conference. Meyrowitz gives his views on various hypertext design issues and also presents a comparison between Vannevar Bush's original Memex vision and our current technical capabilities.

Meyrowitz, N. (1991). Hypertext and pen computing. *Proc. ACM Hypertext'91 Conf.,* 379.

Summary of the hypertext capabilities in GO's Penpoint.

Meyrowitz, N., and van Dam, A. (1982). Interactive editing systems, parts I and II. *ACM Computing Surveys* **14**, 3 (September), 321–352 and 353–415.

Only a very small part of these papers is about hypertext, but they give the best survey available of more traditional techniques for interacting with textual structures on a computer and also include some coverage of principles for structure editing.

Mills, C. B., and Weldon, L. J. (1987). Reading text from computer screens. *Computing Surveys* **19**, 4 (December), 329–358.

A review of an extensive body of empirical evidence on low-level issues in physically presenting text on video displays (e.g. lower case vs. upper case, line spacing, color, scrolling speed, etc.).

Monk, A. (1989). The personal browser: A tool for directed navigation in hypertext systems. *Interacting with Computers* **1**, 2 (August), 190–196.

An idea for customizing the interface to a hypertext by constructing a table of contents listing exactly those nodes that the user has asked to have added to it. The difference between the personal browser and traditional bookmarks is that the system monitors the user's navigation behavior and in an activist manner interrupts the user to ask whether it should add a node to the browser when it has been accessed frequently.

Monk, A. F., Walsh, P., and Dix, A. J. (1988). A comparison of hypertext, scrolling and folding mechanisms for program browsing. In Jones D. M., and Winder, R. (Eds.): *People and Computers IV*, Cambridge University Press, 421–435.

A study of browsing a quite small "literate program" (i.e. program code intertwined with extensive comments). A hypertext interface without a structural map led subjects to significantly worse performance than a hypertext interface with a structural map or more traditional scrolling and folding (holophrast-based) interfaces.

Monty, M. L. (1986). Temporal context and memory for notes stored in the computer. *ACM SIGCHI Bulletin* **18**, 2 (October), 50–51.

NoteCards users had trouble due to premature structuring of information and the homogeneous appearance of the text on the screen.

Monty, M. L., and Moran, T. P. (1986). A longitudinal study of authoring using NoteCards. *ACM SIGCHI Bulletin* **18**, 2 (October), 59–60.

Summary of a study of a graduate student writing a research paper using NoteCards over a period of seven months.

Morita, M., and Shinoda, Y. (1994). Information filtering based on user behavior analysis and best match text retrieval. *Proc. 17th Annual ACM SIGIR Conf.*, 272–281.

A study of eight users reading 8,000 netnews messages found a strong correlation between the time the users spent reading each message and their subjective rating of their interest in the message. In other word, the "readwear" approach to recording time spent reading or otherwise accessing information is a feasible way of automatically estimating the interestingness of information objects.

Moulthrop, S. (1989). Hypertext and 'the hyperreal'. *Proc. ACM Hypertext'89 Conf.* (Pittsburgh, PA, 5–8 November), 259–267.

A literary analysis of interactive fictions with special emphasis on Michael Joyce's "Afternoon" and the Storyspace system.

Mountford, S. J., Mitchell, P., O'Hara, P., Sparks, J., and Whitby, M. (1992). When TVs are computers are TVs. *Proc. ACM CHI'92 Conf.*, 227–230.

On the prospects for interactive television and other ways of combining computers and television.

Mukherjea, S., Foley, J. D., and Hudson, S. E. (1994). Interactive clustering for navigating in hypermedia systems. *Proc. ACM ECHT'94 European Conference on Hypermedia Technology* (Edinburgh, U.K., September 18–23), 136–145.
> Clustering algorithms are used to build up higher-level structures for use in generating overview diagrams.

Mylonas, E. (1992). An interface to classical Greek civilization. *J. of the American Society for Information Science* **43**, 2 (March), 192–201.
> Survey of the Perseus Project as of the publication of the first public CD-ROM version by Yale University Press.

Mylonas, E., and Heath, S. (1990). Hypertext from the data point of view: Paths and links in the Perseus project. *Proc. ECHT'90 European Conf. Hypertext* (Paris, France, 28–30 November), Cambridge University Press, 324–336.
> By encoding the text elements (and other data objects) in Perseus with information about their meaning, the system can automatically construct links between related elements. Specialized object types are typically domain specific, such as the coin catalog and the vase catalog.

Mynatt, B. T., Leventhal, L. M., Instone, K., Farhat, J., and Rohlman, D. S. (1992). Hypertext or book: Which is better for answering questions? *Proc. ACM CHI'92 Conf.* (Monterey, CA, 3–7 May), 19–25.
> The HyperHolmes hypertext encyclopedia about Sherlock Holmes was compared with a paper version of the same text. Users performed about the same, with hypertext users being better at answering questions where the answers were embedded in the text and book users being better at answering questions where the answers were to be found in maps.

Nabkel, J., and Shafrir, E. (1995). Blazing the trail: Design considerations for interactive information pioneers. *ACM SIGCHI Bulletin* **27**, 1 (January), 45–54.
> The user interface design of HP's SynerVision online help and the Access HP WWW site. Particular emphasis is placed on the use of a geographic navigation metaphor.

Nanard, J., Richy, H., and Nanard, M. (1988). Conceptual documents: A mechanism for specifying active views in hypertext. *Proc. ACM Conf. Document Processing Systems* (Santa Fe, NM, 5–9 December), 37–42.
> How to synthesize a document from an underlying information base.

Negroponte, N. (1995). *Being Digital*, Knopf.
> Expanded versions of Negroponte's columns for WIRED magazine. Insightful comments on the implications of the merging of computation and television and the so-called "Negroponte switch" (his prediction that mass media will move over wires and that personal communication will move over wireless connections in contrast to the traditional situation where TV broadcasts were wireless and telephone conversations were wired).

Nelson, T. (1980). Replacing the printed word: A complete literary system. In Lavington, S. H. (Ed.): *Proc. IFIP Congress 1980,* North-Holland, 1013–1023.
> A paper that is perhaps slightly easier to get hold of (from the World Computer Conference) than the publications which Nelson has self-published. It describes his ideas for a universal hypertext repository containing everything anybody ever has written and will write.

Nelson, T. (1988). Unifying tomorrow's hypermedia. *Proc. Online Information 88* (London, U.K., 6–8 December), 1–7.

A warning against the current trend towards "balkanized" hypertext existing in lots of incompatible systems. Instead of these closed hypermedia systems, Nelson advocates a more general scheme for open hypermedia.

Newcomb, S. R., Kipp, N. A., and Newcomb, V. T. (1991). The HyTime hypermedia/time-based document structuring language. *Communications of the ACM 34*, 11 (November), 67–83.

HyTime is a ISO standard (10744) built on SGML, but oriented towards screen-based display of information rather than printouts, meaning that it accommodates hypertext and time-varying media like video. Additional documents about HyTime are available by anonymous FTP from ftp.ifi.uio.no [129.240.88.1], directory SIGhyper, or mailer.cc.fsu.edu [128.186.6.103], directory /pub/sgml.

Nicol, A. (1988). Interface design for hyperdata: Models, maps and cues. *Proc. Human Factors Society 32nd Annual Meeting*, 308–312.

In a study of designers of HyperCard stacks, most said that they tend not to do much systematic planning but instead construct their designs "button-up."[8] The paper contains several guidelines for more organized designs based on metaphors and navigational conventions.

Nielsen, J. (1986). Online documentation and reader annotation. *Proc. 1st Conf. Work With Display Units* (Stockholm, Sweden, 12–15 May), 526–529.

Empirical study of which kinds of annotation are used the most in printed books, including both highlighting with magic markers and free-form written comments.

Nielsen, J. (1988). Trip report: Hypertext'87. *ACM SIGCHI Bulletin* **19**, 4 (April), 27–35.

Report on events at the first scientific conference on hypertext, held in Chapel Hill, NC, 13–15 November 1987. This report also exists in a hypertext form (see Chapter 2).

Nielsen, J. (1989a). Prototyping user interfaces using an object-oriented hypertext programming system. *Proc. NordDATA'89 Joint Scandinavian Computer Conference* (Copenhagen, Denmark, 19–22 June), 485–490.

Technical issues in the use of HyperCard to build user interfaces. Two examples are discussed: a hypertext system with a user interface building on individualized user history and a videotex system.

Nielsen, J. (1989b). Mini trip report: HyperHyper: Developments across the field of hypermedia. *ACM SIGCHI Bulletin* **21**, 1 (July), 65–67.

A report on events at the British Computer Society meeting in London 23 February 1989, including discussions of the cognitive ergonomics of hypertext and the *Glasgow Online* system.

Nielsen, J. (1989c). Usability engineering at a discount. In Salvendy, G. and Smith, M. J. (Eds.): *Designing and Using Human-Computer Interfaces and*

---

[8] "Button-up" is my term; the paper uses the less humorous "bottom-up."

Knowledge Based Systems, Elsevier Science Publishers, Amsterdam, 394–401.

Usability engineering methods that have low complexity and cost.

Nielsen, J. (1989d). Trip Report: Hypertext II. *ACM SIGCHI Bulletin* **21**, 2 (October), 41–47.

Report on events at the second British conference on hypertext, held in York, U.K., 29–30 June 1989.

Nielsen, J. (1989e). The matters that really matter for hypertext usability. *Proc. ACM Hypertext'89 Conf.* (Pittsburgh, PA, 5–8 November), 239–248.

A review of 92 quantitative results from 30 research papers comparing various approaches to online text and hypertext. The conclusions are that the three factors with the largest effects on usability are individual variability among users, variations in users' tasks, and the difference between the way users use hypertext and the way they use printed text or non-hypertext computer systems. Because of the two first factors, the paper also concludes that no single hypertext system is likely to have universal usability.

Nielsen, J. (1990a). Three medium sized hypertexts on CD-ROM. *ACM SIGIR Forum* **24**, 1–2, 2–10.

A review of *The Manhole* (an interactive fiction), the *Time Table of History*, and *The Electronic Whole Earth Catalog*, all of which are hypertext structures implemented in HyperCard and distributed on CD-ROM because of their size. The review evaluates the usability of the systems by using various usability heuristics such as the need for consistent backtracking, history facilities, and support for navigational dimensions.

Nielsen, J. (1990b). The art of navigating through hypertext. *Communications of the ACM* **33**, 3 (March), 296–310.

A description of the design of a hypertext system using the individual user's personal interaction history to provide a greater sense of context in the navigation space and a discussion of human factors problems found in usability testing of earlier versions of the system. The article is illustrated with a large number of screen dumps forming a guided tour of the system.

Nielsen, J. (1990c). Trip report: Hypertext'89. *ACM SIGCHI Bulletin* **21**, 4 (April), 52–61.

Report on events at the second ACM conference on hypertext, held in Pittsburgh, PA, November 5–8, 1989.

Nielsen, J. (1990d). Evaluating hypertext usability. In Jonassen, D. H., and Mandl, H. (Eds.), *Designing Hypertext/Hypermedia for Learning.* Springer-Verlag, Heidelberg, Germany, 147–168.

Methods for measuring or estimating the usability of hypertexts, including a discussion of the usability parameters for hypertext and test plans.

Nielsen, J. (1990e). Review of BBC Interactive Television Unit's Ecodisc. *Hypermedia* **2**, 2, 176–182.

A CD-ROM from the BBC to teach ecology through the simulation of a nature preserve. From a hypertext perspective, the system is interesting because it includes a section providing surrogate travel through the preserve using a technique similar to that of the MIT *Aspen*

Movie Map—complete with a "season knob" to travel in the summer or winter. The disk contains the complete user interface in nine different languages (English, French, German, Spanish, Italian, Danish, Swedish, Norwegian, and Dutch).

Nielsen, J. (1990f). Miniatures versus icons as a visual cache for videotex browsing. *Behaviour & Information Technology* **9**, 6, 441–449.

Miniatures (graphically reduced images of the nodes) and icons can be used to display a short history list of the previously seen nodes such that the user can easily return to the last few navigational locations.

Nielsen, J. (Ed.) (1990g). *Designing User Interfaces for International Use.* Elsevier Science Publishers, Amsterdam, the Netherlands.

Addresses the issues related to international user interfaces (interfaces used in another country than the one in which they were designed), including translation, software support for localization, guidelines for international use, the special considerations relating to Asian user interfaces, and several case studies, including a hypertext system.

Nielsen, J. (1993a). *Usability Engineering.* Academic Press, San Diego, CA.

Textbook on usability engineering methods to ensure usable interface designs, with many examples from hypertext. The paperback edition (published 1994) was somewhat revised and updated.

Nielsen, J. (1993b). Noncommand user interfaces. *Communications of the ACM* **36**, 4 (April), 83–99.

Article about the next generation of user interfaces, including speculations on how hypertext-based interconnected information objects may provide the replacement for file systems as they get unable to handle the users' increasingly large information spaces.

Nielsen, J. (1993c). Iterative user interface design. *IEEE Computer* **26**, 12 (December), 32–41.

User interfaces can be improved considerably through iterative design. In four case studies (one of which was a hypertext system), the median improvement in measurable usability per iteration was 38%.

Nielsen, J. (1995a). Applying discount usability engineering. *IEEE Software* **12**, 1 (January).

How cheap usability methods were used in the design of SunWeb.

Nielsen, J. (1995b). The electronic business card: An experiment in half-dead hypertext. *Hypermedia* **7**, 1.

Half-dead hypertext has links where the user has to do some work beyond simply activating the anchor to retrieve the destination nodes. Half-dead hypertext can be used in cases where live links are technically difficult or impossible to support. On example is the electronic business card, which is a link to further information about its owner. Electronic business cards can be transmitted between personal digital assistants and will allow the recipient to link to much more extensive information than can be transmitted and stored on a PDA platform. Also, electronic business card links can be printed in brochures, research papers, and other non-electronic media from which access to the server can be made with human intervention.

Nielsen, J., and Lyngbæk, U. (1990). Two field studies of hypermedia usability. In McAleese, R., and Green, C. (Eds.) *Hypertext: State of the Art,* Ablex, 64–72.
A general discussion of using field study methodologies to assess the usability of hypermedia systems, and results from two such studies: a study of professionals reading a Guide scientific report and a study of kindergarten children "reading" a non-verbal interactive story about the adventures of the cat Inigo.

Nielsen, J., Frehr, I., and Nymand, H. O. (1991a). The learnability of HyperCard as an object-oriented programming system. *Behaviour & Information Technology* **10**, 2 (March–April), 111–120.
Students could learn HyperCard programming in about two days but still had problems understanding some of its object-oriented features.

Nielsen, J., Hardman, L., Nicol, A., and Yankelovich, N. (1991b). The Nielsen ratings: Hypertext reviews. *Proc. ACM Hypertext'91 Conf.* (San Antonio, TX, 15–18 December), 359–360.
Principles for the reviewing of hypertext documents according to their utility, integrity, usability, and aesthetics. Hypertext should be seen as a medium of expression similar to other media, and hypertext documents should be reviewed by critics just as is literature, film, and music.

Nielsen, J., and Sano, D. (1994). SunWeb: User interface design for Sun Microsystem's internal web. *Proc. Second Intl. WWW Conf. '94: Mosaic and the Web* (Chicago, Oct. 17–20), 547–557 (also available on the Internet as `http://www.ncsa.uiuc.edu/SDG/IT94/Proceedings/HCI/nielsen/sunweb.html` and as `http://www.sun.com/technology-research/sun.design/sunweb.html`).
Case story of the design of a company-wide information system delivered over the World Wide Web. The paper provides several illustrations of the visual design of the interface, including the iterative design of many of the icons. The paper also reports on the usability engineering methods used in developing the design.

Nievergelt, J., and Weydert, J. (1980). Sites, modes and trails: Telling the user of an interactive system where he is, what he can do, and how to get to places. In Guedj, R. A., ten Hagen, P. J. W., Hopgood, F. R. A., Tucker, H. A., and Duce, D. A. (Eds.), *Methodology of Interaction,* North Holland Publishing Company, 327–338.
An early paper about usability issues in navigation.

Noik, E. G. (1993). Exploring large hyperdocuments: Fisheye views of nested networks. *Proc. ACM Hypertext'93* (Seattle, WA, November 14–18), 192–205.
Principles for layout of fisheye views of nested hypertext documents with the goal of maximizing the user's ability to recognize the various elements of the diagram even when they are rescaled.

Nordhausen, B., Chignell, M. H., and Waterworth, J. (1991). The missing link? Comparison of manual and automated linking in hypertext engineering. *Proc. Human Factors Society 35th Annual Meeting,* 310–314.

> The authors suggest that link usability can be measured by comparing users' ratings of the predicted relevance of a link (estimated before they traverse the link) with their estimates of the evaluated relevance of the link (estimated after they have traversed the link and seen what was at the other end).

Nyce, J. M., and Kahn, P. (1989). Innovation, pragmaticism, and technological continuity: Vannevar Bush's Memex. *Journal of the American Society for Information Science* **40**, 3 (May), 214–221.

> A historical review of how Vannevar Bush arrived at his ideas for the "Memex," which is normally viewed as the first expression of the hypertext concept. The paper contains excerpts from Bush's unpublished writings from the period where he developed the Memex idea as well as a brief discussion of later work. The paper reprints two original illustrations of the proposed Memex.

Nyce, J. M., and Kahn, P. (Eds.) (1991). *From Memex to Hypertext: Vannevar Bush and the Mind's Machine.* Academic Press.

> Reprints Vannevar Bush's original paper on the Memex as well as several of his other papers, including both preliminary notes about the Memex and the "Memex II" and "Memex Revisited" essays. The book also contains several interesting chapters by other authors reporting on the influence of Bush and the Memex on more recent hypertext research. Since many of these chapters are reprints from other publications, this entire book can be seen as an example of the "trailblazing" promoted by Bush.

Oberlin, S., and Cox, J. (Eds.) (1989). *Microsoft CD-ROM Yearbook 1989–1990.* Microsoft Press.

> A 935-page monster of a book containing a comprehensive dictionary of available CD-ROM titles and CD mastering and other services. About 650 pages of the book are filled with short articles (about five pages each) on almost all aspects of CD-ROMs, electronic publishing, and hypertext by a lot of people who are mainly practitioners. Many of the articles are reprints from various sources over the last five years, but since the original sources are extremely scattered and often hard to locate, the reprinting should be seen as a service.

Obraczka, K., Danzig, P. B., and Li, S. (1993). Internet resource discovery systems. *IEEE Computer* **26**, 9 (September), 8–22.

> Survey of so-called resource discovery tools like Archie and Veronica that help users find out where on the Internet specific files and information are stored.

Odlyzko, A. M. (1995). Tragic loss or good riddance? The impending demise of traditional scholarly journals. *Intl. J. Human–Computer Studies* **in press**. (reprinted in Peek, R. P., and Newby, G. B. (Eds.), Electronic Publishing Confronts Academia: The Agenda for the Year 2000, MIT Press 1995). Shorter version published in Notices Amer. Math. Soc., January 1995. Available on the Internet as ftp://netlib.att.com/netlib/att/math/odlyzko/tracig.loss.Z

> The author, a Bell Labs mathematician, argues that online publication and dissemination is the only way to handle the growth in the research literature. Traditional journals cannot

keep up with the flow any more. Odlyzko estimates that the cost of a typical mathematics research paper is $20,000 for the research, $4,000 for the refereeing process, and $1,000 for subsequent writeups in review journals, meaning that the costs related to the intellectual product are $25,000. The cost of printing the paper in an average journal is $4,000, or only 14% of the total costs.

Olsen, D. R. (1992). Bookmarks: An enhanced scroll bar. *ACM Trans. Graphics* **11**, 3 (July), 291–295.

Design for placing multiple user-defined bookmarks in the scroll bar.

Oren, T. (1987). The architectures of static hypertexts. *Proc. ACM Hypertext'87 Conf.* (Chapel Hill, NC, 13–15 November), 291–306.

On the special design considerations for hypertexts to be stored on CD-ROMs or other non-changeable storage media. The read-only limitation can even be viewed as an advantage because it ensures the integrity of the original hypertext network while still allowing additions of links, annotations, etc. stored on a magnetic disk and merged by the display front-end at read-time. Most of the paper is really about general user interface issues in hypertext (e.g. overview maps, limiting the connectivity to about 7 ± 2 links per node) and not about CD-ROM-specific issues.

Oren, T. (1988). The CD-ROM connection. *BYTE* **13,** 13 (December), 315–320.

This is a slightly abridged version of [Oren 1987].

Oren, T., Salomon, G., Kreitman, K., and Don, A. (1990). Guides: Characterizing the interface. In Laurel, B. (Ed.): *The Art of Human-Computer Interface Design,* Addison-Wesley, 367–381.

Using anthropomorphic and even explicitly human (videotaped) narrators to guide users through a hypertext. These guides are similar to interaction agents but do not show intelligence in the current system. Even so, users often attributed greater sophistication to the guides than their implementation would seem to justify.

Østerbye, K. (1992). Structural and cognitive problems in providing version control for hypertext. *Proc. ECHT'92 Fourth ACM Hypertext Conf.,* 33–42.

Using software engineering as the prime example, the author discusses the issues involved when one wants to keep multiple versions of the nodes and/or links in a hypertext. The simplest model is to freeze old versions of a node and allow no changes, but the author argues in favor of allowing new annotations to old versions (e.g., to indicate an assumption that has been invalidated by recent changes). Other types of links (referred to as "substance links") should be frozen with the node in which they originate since they form an important part of the original meaning of the version of the node that presumably wants to keep by freezing the node. One can also keep track of the versions of a link by noting what destinations it has pointed to at various times.

Østerbye, K., and Nørmark, K. (1994). An interaction engine for rich hypertext. *Proc. ACM ECHT'94 European Conference on Hypermedia Technology* (Edinburgh, U.K., September 18–23), 167–176.

By "rich hypertext" the authors mean information bases significant semantic structure (whether in the form of attributes or internal structure of the nodes). This is in contrast to the definition used in this book where the term "rich hypertext" refers to a hypertext with a large number of links from each node. As an example of a hypertext with computer-interpretable semantics the authors discuss program code which can be displayed in many different views depending on the programmer's needs. For example, the hypertext system knows how to abstract an outline view of the code and how to produce a view that may be useful for a third-party programmer wanting to interface with an API.

Palaniappan, M., Yankelovich, N., and Sawtelle, M. (1990). Linking active anchors: A stage in the evolution of hypermedia. *Hypermedia* **2**, 1, 47–66.
Discussion of the issues in linking to active documents such as animations or sound clips (as opposed to traditional, static documents that always display the same information). Active documents are classified in three categories: Playback (dynamic view of a stored set of sequential data), recording (streams fed into the application from some external sensing or recording device), and query (subset of a large collection selected according to a user-defined set of criteria). Special synchronization mechanisms are needed in case the anchor points to multiple dynamic destinations, all of which should be played at the same time.

Patterson, J. F., and Egido, C. (1987). Video browsing and system response time. In Diaper, D., and Winder, R. (Eds.): *People and Computers III,* Cambridge University Press, U.K., 189–198.
Users retrieved 50% more frames to solve the same problems when system response time was fast (3 sec.) rather than slow (11 sec.).

Pausch, R., Robertson, G. G., Card, S. K., Mackinlay, J. D., and Moshell, M. (1993). Three views of virtual reality. *IEEE Computer* 26, 2 (February), 79–83.
Survey of different approaches to virtual reality, including comments on the way it has been hyped in the popular press, nonimmersive interfaces, and military applications.

Pearl, A. (1989). Sun's link service: A protocol for open linking. *Proc. ACM Hypertext'89 Conf.* (Pittsburgh, PA, 5–8 November), 137–146.
Hypertext as a system service to support links across other applications.

Pejtersen, A. M. (1989). A library system for information retrieval based on a cognitive task analysis and supported by an icon-based interface. *Proc. SIGIR'89 Twelfth Annual Intl. ACM SIGIR Conf. Research and Development in Information Retrieval* (Cambridge, MA, 25–28 June), 40–47.
The design of the Book House system for finding fiction in a library.

Peper, G. (1991). Hypertext: Its relationship to, and potential impact on, knowledge-based systems. *Impact Assessment Bulletin* **9**, 1–2, 53–71.
Similarities and differences between hypertext and knowledge-based systems. The main differences listed are that hypertext has a more flexible knowledge representation, better user interfaces in currently available systems, and gives control of the session to the user.

Peper, G. L., MacIntyre, C., and Keenan, J. (1989). Hypertext: A new approach for implementing an expert system. *IBM Expert Systems Interdivisional Technical Liason,* November, 305–309. Available from Gerri Peper, IBM, Dept. 77K, Building 026, 5600 North 63rd Street, Boulder, CO 80314, USA.
Comparison between hypertext and expert systems as means for representing knowledge.

Perkins, R. (1995). The Interchange Online Network: Simplifying information access. *Proc. ACM CHI'95 Conf.*

Interchange is an online service where users can access articles from a number of computer magazines and participate in electronic discussion groups.

Perkins, R., and Rollert, D. (1994). Interchange, an online service for people with special interests. In Wiklund, M. E. (Ed.), *Usability in Practice*, Academic Press, 427–456.

Well-illustrated description of the usability engineering efforts behind the design of Ziff-Davis' Interchange service: an online repository of magazine articles. Special emphasis is placed on user testing and iterative design.

Perlman, G. (1989). System design and evaluation with hypertext checklists. *Proc. 1989 IEEE Conf. Systems, Man, and Cybernetics* (Cambridge, MA, November).

The NaviText SAM system is a hypertext interface to a large set of user interface guidelines.

Perlman, G., Egan, D., Ehrlich, S., Marchionini, G., Nielsen, J., and Shneiderman, B. (1990). Evaluating hypermedia systems. *Proc. ACM CHI'90 Conf. Human Factors in Computing Systems* (Seattle, WA, 1–5 April), 387–390.

Several different approaches to usability evaluation are contrasted.

Potter, R. L., Weldon, L. J., and Shneiderman, B. (1988). Improving the accuracy of touch screens: An experimental evaluation of three strategies. *Proc. ACM CHI'88* (Washington, DC, 15–19 May), 27–32.

Potter, R., Berman, M., and Shneiderman, B. (1989). An experimental evaluation of three touch screen strategies within a hypertext database. *Intl.J. Human-Computer Interaction* **1**, 1, 41–52.

Touch screens were more usable when a take-off strategy rather than a land-on (touch-down) strategy was used for registering user selections.

Potter, W. D., and Trueblood, R. P. (1988). Traditional, semantic, and hyper-semantic approaches to data modeling. *IEEE Computer* **21**, 6 (June 1988), 53–63.

Discusses the difference between computer-oriented data models used in traditional databases and more recent user-oriented hypertext-like database approaches that capture inferentional relationships among real-world concepts.

Price, D. J. (1956). The exponential curve of science. *Discovery* **17**, 240–243.

The number of published scientific papers has seen exponential growth over the last two centuries and seems to double every 10–15 years.

Pullinger, D. J., Maude, T. I., and Parker, J. (1987). Software for reading text on screen. *Proc. IFIP INTERACT'87* (Stuttgart, Germany, 1–4 September), 899–904.

Readers read text significantly faster when they were allowed to jump through it rather than just scroll or page.

Quick, W. T. (1989). Bank robbery. *Analog Science Fiction* **109**, 5 (May), 128–143.

Science fiction story about the importance of human editors (and possible AI editorial assistants) in assembling readable sub-information spaces in a future global hypertext system. The protagonist is a editor who creates links to readable material but has his personalized scanning software stolen. This software is used to search the information space for suitable nodes for reference through the editor's recommended links.

Rada, R. (1991). *Hypertext: From Text to Expertext.* McGraw-Hill, London, U.K.

General introduction to hypertext with special emphasis on the use of hypertext as a knowledge representation medium and as part of artificial intelligence systems and expert systems (the somewhat fanciful term "expertext" refers to this latter issue).

Rada, R. (1992). Converting a textbook to hypertext. *ACM Trans. Information Systems* **10**, 3 (July), 294–315.

Experience from converting [Rada 1991] to hypertext in four formats: Emacs-Info, Guide, Hyperties, and SuperBook. As an intermediate step, the text was transformed to a semantic net which was augmented manually, and special traversal programs were then written to transform these nets into the desired hypertext systems' internal format.

Rada, R., and Murphy, C. (1992). Searching versus browsing in hypertext. *Hypermedia* **4**, 1, 1–30.

Comparison of a book converted into several hypertext systems, showing that browsing was better when users were using a paper version of the book, whereas some of the hypertext systems were better for searching. Some hypertext features, such as having multiple alternative outlines did not help users.

Rafeld, M. (1988). The LaserROM project: A case study in document processing systems. *Proc. ACM Conf. Document Processing Systems* (Santa Fe, NM, 5–9 December 1988), 21–29.

Hewlett-Packard distributes more than 8,000 different publications annually and experiments with putting them on CD-ROM to cut costs. The paper discusses problems in converting existing documents to the new format and integrating illustrations.

Ragland, C. (1988). Guide 2.0 and HyperCard 1.1: Choices for hypermedia developers. *HyperAge Magazine* (May–June), 49–56.

One of the better comparative reviews of the two leading (as of 1988) popular hypertext products.

Rao, R., Card, S., Jellinek, H., Mackinlay, J., and Robertson, G. (1992). The information grid: A retrieval-top-level extension to the desktop user interface metaphor. In *Proc. ACM UIST'92 User Interface Software and Technology* (Monterey, CA, 15–18 November), 23–32.

Conceptually important article viewing information finding as a structuring principle for computer functionality. This perspective may lead to operating systems based on hypertext.

Rao, U., and Turoff, M. (1990). Hypertext functionality: A theoretical framework. *Intl.J. Human–Computer Interaction* **2**, 4, 333–357.

Somewhat complicated taxonomy of hypertext based on a psychological model (Guilford's theory of the structure of the intellect).

Raskin, J. (1987). The hype in hypertext: A critique. *Proc. ACM Hypertext'87 Conf.* (Chapel Hill, NC, 13–15 November), 325–330.

The author suggests that there may be serious problems with user interfaces to the hypertext principle of linked text, whereas interfaces to linear text can be made excellent and simple.

Raymond, D. R., and Tompa, F. W. (1988). Hypertext and the Oxford English Dictionary. *Communications of the ACM* **31**, 7 (July), 871–879.
On automatically converting existing documents to hypertext form.

Rearick, T. C. (1991). Automating the conversion of text into hypertext. In Berk, E., and Devlin, J. (Eds.), *Hypertext/Hypermedia Handbook*, McGraw-Hill.
Discussion of the various stages in converting existing linear text files from preprocessing to computer-assisted linking with emphasis on the methods used in Lotus SmarText.

Rein, G. L., and Ellis, C. A. (1991). rIBIS: A real-time group hypertext system. *Intl. J. Man–Machine Studies* **34**, 3 (March), 349–367.
A further development of gIBIS, allowing multiple users to develop a hypertext simultaneously.

Reinhardt, A. (1994). Managing the new document. *BYTE* **19**, 8 (August), 90–104.
Survey of document management issues with a focus on object-oriented and compound documents. Issues addressed include the architecture of document management from the document repository (e.g., the proposed Shamrock standard) through middleware like Lotus Notes to the applications. A major point is that the applications will have to change from having direct access to the file system to accessing individual document component objects in a database.

Reisel, J. F., and Shneiderman, B. (1987). Is bigger better? The effects of display size on program reading. In Salvendy, G. (Ed.): *Social, Ergonomic and Stress Aspects of Work with Computers,* Elsevier Science Publishers, 113–122.
Bigger *was* better.

Remde, J. R., Gomez, L. M., and Landauer, T. K. (1987). SuperBook: An automatic tool for information exploration—hypertext? *Proc. ACM Hypertext'87 Conf.* (Chapel Hill, NC, 13–15 November), 175–188.
The design of SuperBook was based on principles from human-computer interaction research, including full-text indexing, user-defined aliasing (several terms for the same concept), and dynamic hierarchical views.

Resnick, P., Iacovou, N., Suchak, M., Bergstrom, P., Riedl, J. (1994). GroupLens: An open architecture for collaborative filtering of netnews. *Proc. ACM CSCW'94 Conf.*
As they read netnews articles, users are given the option to vote on the quality of each article. The combined votes are distributed over the Internet and can be used by other users to decide what articles to read.

Rheingold, H. (1993). *The Virtual Community: Homesteading on the Electronic Frontier,* Addison-Wesley.
Popular book on multi-user aspects of computer networking, including MUDs (multi-user dungeons), IRL (Internet relay chat), and online discussion groups, whether on the Internet or private nets.

Riley, V. A. (1990). An interchange format for hypertext systems: The Intermedia model. *Proc. NIST Hypertext Standardization Workshop* (Gaithersburg, MD, 16-18 January), 213–222.

An interchange format for Intermedia links.

Ripley, G. D. (1989). DVI: A digital multimedia technology. *Communications of the ACM* **32**, 7 (July), 811–822.

Well-illustrated article on DVI. Includes both technical information about hardware architecture and disk capacity for various media, and examples of several applications (e.g. Palenque and games such as a WWII Spitfire flight simulator).

Robertson, C. K., McCracken, D., and Newell, A. (1981). The ZOG approach to man-machine communication. *Intl. J. Man-Machine Studies* **14**, 461–488.

ZOG was an early and influential system having linked frames of online text.

Robertson, G. G., Mackinlay, J. D., and Card, S. K. (1991). Cone trees: Animated 3D visualizations of hierarchical information. *Proc. ACM CHI'91 Conf.*, 189–194.

Cone trees represent each level of a hierarchical tree as a circle under its parent node. Thus, some child nodes (and their descendants) are in the foreground and others (including their descendants) are in the background, generating an automatic fisheye view with a focus on the items of interest. Users can focus on other parts of the tree by rotating it at any level.

Robertson, G. G., Card, S. K., and Mackinlay, J. D. (1993). Information visualization using 3D interactive animation. *Communications of the ACM* **36**, 4 (April), 57–71.

By using three-dimensional views it is possible to display significantly more information objects in a window than when using two-dimensional views. Of course, not all the objects can be in the foreground at the same time, animated transitions allow the user to track changes by engaging the perceptual system and not the cognitive system, meaning that users can keep thinking about their task as they manipulate the view.

Russell, D. M. (1990). Alexandria: A learning resources management architecture. In Jonassen, D. H., and Mandl, H. (Eds.), *Designing Hypertext/Hypermedia for Learning*. Springer-Verlag, Heidelberg, Germany, 439–457.

Outline of a project at Xerox PARC to build an integrated learning environment with many tools and resources (e.g. simulations, tests, a video library, and linguistic aids such as dictionaries). The architecture is based on a *kernel* to link many different forms of information and applications. Each of these "resources" is expected to obey the kernel's hypermedia protocol. Russell gives a brief analysis of how IDE [Jordan et al. 1989] fits the Alexandria model.

Salomon, G. B. (1990). Designing casual-use hypertext: The CHI'89 InfoBooth. *Proc. ACM CHI'90 Conf. Human Factors in Computing Systems* (Seattle, WA, 1–5 April), 451–458.

The design of Apple's information kiosk at the ACM CHI'89 conference, including screen shots of several stages in the iterative design. During the conference, attendees entered personal information and digitized photos into the system, and the complete "yearbook" was later distributed to them on a CD-ROM.

Salomon, G., Oren, T., and Kreitman, K. (1989). Using guides to explore multimedia databases. *Proc. 22nd Hawaii International Conference on System Sciences* (Kailua-Kona, HI, 3–6 January), 3–12.

Using anthropomorphic human guides to lead users through a hypertext. See also [Oren et al. 1990].

Salton, G. (1989). *Automatic Text Processing: The Transformation, Analysis, and Retrieval of Information by Computer.* Addison-Wesley.

Only has three pages specifically on hypertext, but this book is a good introduction to information retrieval and similar issues of interest for some hypertext systems.

Samuelson, P., and Glushko, R. J. (1991). Intellectual property rights for digital library and hypertext publishing systems: An analysis of Xanadu. *Proc. ACM Hypertext'91 Conf.*, 39–50.

An analysis of the relation between current copyright law and the proposed Xanadu royalty structure. A main difference is that traditional copyright rules have related to the handling of individual copies of the copyrighted works without regard to how the buyer used those works (and specifically without regard to *how much* the buyer used the works), whereas Xanadu is based on charging on a per-use basis. The article also discusses the charging mechanisms and copyright inclination of services like Prodigy and CompuServe and users of the Internet. Finally, the article speculates on how the Xanadu royalty mechanism might impact the behavior of authors and readers.

Sarkar, M., and Brown, M. H. (1992). Graphical fisheye views of graphs. *Proc. ACM CHI'92 Conf.*, 83–91.

Graphical transformations to produce fisheye views of two-dimensional structures, with more detail in the center of the image.

Savoy, J. (1989). The electronic book Ebook3. *Intl. J. Man-Machine Studies* **30**, 5 (May), 505–523.

Ebook3 is a hypertext system with emphasis on the ability to print the entire document (which is structured as a strict hierarchy) and on being sufficiently open to allow the integration of any external system with the text. Executable programs are typically used for training exercises which may check a student's understanding of the text, and for simulation models of the concepts discussed in the text. Experience with the use of Ebook3 for teaching operations research in Switzerland indicates that students at first print out chapters they want to read but later turn to a more dynamic reading style, including creating their own models. Unfortunately this experience is only documented very sporadically at the end of the paper.

Sawhill, R. (1994). A crazy shade of Winter. *WIRED* **2**, 12 (December), 168–171 & 220.

Portrait of Robert Winter, the author of Beethoven's *Ninth Symphony*, Stravinsky's *The Rite of Spring*, and Dvorack's *From the New World* as annotated music CD-ROMs.

Saxenian, A. (1994). *Regional Advantage: Cultural and Competition in Silicon Valley and Route 128.* Harvard University Press.

Silicon Valley (the area around Palo Alto in California) beat Route 128 (the area around Boston in Massachusetts) to become the center of the computer industry because of its higher degree of flexibility in transferring technology and staff members between companies.

Schnase, J. L., and Leggett, J. J. (1989). Computational hypertext in biological modeling. *Proc. ACM Hypertext'89 Conf.* (Pittsburgh, PA, 5–8 November), 181–197.

Use of hypertext to support biological research by integrating a hypertext structure with raw data and a program to calculate various results from the data.

Schnase, J. L., Leggett, J., Kacmar, C., and Boyle, C. (1988). A comparison of hypertext systems. *Technical Report* **TAMU 88-017,** Hypertext Research Lab, Texas A&M University, September.

Presents a three-level layered model for hypertext system architecture (front-end, hypertext, back-end) and gives definitions of common hypertext terms. This framework is used to discuss ten of the better-known hypertext systems.

Schuler, W., Hannemann, J., and Streitz, N. (Eds.) (1995). *Designing User Interfaces for Hypermedia.* Springer Verlag, Heidelberg, Germany.

Collection of articles from a workshop on hypermedia design at GMD-IPSI in Germany. The emphasis is on hypermedia authoring and user interface design, and on the use of metaphors to assist these two activities.

Schwabe, D., Caloini, A., Garzotto, F., and Paolini, P. (1992). Hypertext development using a model-based approach. *Software—Practice and Experience* **22**, 11 (November), 937–962.

Automatically constructing a HyperCard] stack from a relational database representation of a hypertext document using the HDM hypertext design model.

Scott, J. R. (1994). Library information access client. *ACM CHI'94 Conference Companion* 143–144.

DEC's Library Information Access Client supports a card catalog metaphor and represents individual searches as objects that can be moved and stored. The search results are color coded to let the user know which results go with which searches.

Scragg, G. W. (1985). Some thoughts on paper notes and electronic messages. *ACM SIGCHI Bulletin* **16**, 3 (January), 41–44.

Post-It notes have several advantages over current computer systems: They are applicable in a uniform way in many different situations, have very low overhead, and can be added to existing information tools even where no annotation facility has been planned for.

Sculley, J. (1989). The relationship between business and higher education: A perspective on the 21st century. *Communications of the ACM* **32**, 9 (September), 1056–1061.

A rather broad article by the Apple CEO about possible (and needed) changes in the educational process due to technological progress. Sculley identifies two current core technologies for educational software; hypermedia and simulation, and mentions AI and intelligent "agents" as a future third core technology. The article is illustrated with several color shots from the *Knowledge Navigator* video scenario. It also includes an example of the ALIAS hypertext authoring environment from Stanford for historical simulation.

Seabrook, R. H. C., and Shneiderman, B. (1989). The user interface in a hypertext, multiwindow program browser. *Interacting with Computers* **1**, 3 (December), 299–337.

The HYBROW system for working with program code. The paper briefly considers various alternative interface designs with respect to windows in hypertext systems such as how to replace earlier windows with new ones. The user can designate a window as "frozen. meaning that it will never be overwritten by new windows.

Shafrir, E., and Nabkel, J. (1994). Visual access to hyper-information: Using multiple metaphors with graphical affordances. *ACM CHI'94 Conference Companion* 142 & 483.

Use of metaphor in the visual design for HP's SynerVision. Initial attempts to rely on a book metaphor proved confusing to users and a solution was chosen that used multiple metaphors to communicate different parts of the interface.

Sherman, C. (1994). *The CD-ROM Handbook*, second edition. Intertext Publications/McGraw-Hill.

As the name says: a handbook about CD-ROMs, covering both hardware and software.

Sherman, M., Hansen, W. J., McInerny, M., and Neuendorffer, T. (1990). Building hypertext on a multimedia toolkit: An overview of Andrew toolkit hypermedia facilities. *Proc. ECHT'90 European Conf. Hypertext* (Paris, France, 28–30 November), Cambridge University Press, 13–37.

A hypertext implemented on top of a general multimedia platform.

Shneiderman, B. (1987a). User interface design and evaluation for an electronic encyclopedia. In Salvendy, G. (Ed.): *Cognitive Engineering in the Design of Human-Computer Interaction and Expert Systems*, Elsevier Science Publishers, 207–223.

About TIES (the predecessor of Hyperties), including reports on a number of empirical studies of design details: effect of screen size, embedded vs. explicit menus, and electronic vs. paper versions of the same information.

Shneiderman, B. (1987b). User interface design for the Hyperties electronic encyclopedia. *Proc. ACM Hypertext'87 Conf.* (Chapel Hill, NC, 13–15 November), 189–194.

The basic paper on Hyperties.

Shneiderman, B. (1989). Reflections on authoring, editing, and managing hypertext. In Barrett, E. (Ed.): *The Society of Text*, MIT Press, Cambridge, MA, 115–131.

Surveys several Hyperties applications, including one about the Hubble Space Telescope implemented in a two-frame version on a Sun workstation. The chapter also contains a discussion of the authoring aids in Hyperties. A large part of the chapter is dedicated to the lessons learnt from building more then 30 hypertext structures for Hyperties. One key lesson is that each project was different and had to have its information structured according to a principle that was suited for its specific domain. Experience shows that it is necessary to have a single managing editor to coordinate a project and to copy edit the final result.

Shneiderman, B., Brethauer, D., Plaisant, C., and Potter, R. (1989). The Hyperties electronic encyclopedia: An evaluation based on three museum installations. *J. American Society for Information Science* **40**, 3 (May), 172–182.

Data from more than 5,000 sessions showed that museum visitors using Hyperties used the hypertext embedded menus far more than they used the traditional index facility also available. On a methodological note, the authors conclude that direct observation and iterative refinement were more useful for improving their hypertext systems than were simple logging data of user navigation behavior. The authors also observe that a user interface that was usable in the laboratory as soon as users had seen a 15-second demo still gave many users problems in the museum environment where they were on their own. To avoid these problems in the field, the user interface was redesigned to have, for instance, larger touchable zones for the selection mechanism.

Shneiderman, B., Plaisant, C., Botafogo, R., Hopkins, D., and Weiland, W. (1991). Designing to facilitate browsing: A look back at the Hyperties workstation browser. *Hypermedia* **3**, 2, 101–117.

A review of the design of the Unix version of Hyperties. Facilities include showing link anchors in graphics by having them appear to pop out from the rest of the illustration, the use of pie menus for navigation support, and the use of multiple tiled windows.

Simon, L., and Erdmann, J. (1994). SIROG—A responsive hypertext manual. *Proc. ACM ECHT'94 European Conference on Hypermedia Technology* (Edinburgh, U.K., September 18–23), 108–116.

SIROG is a manual for nuclear power plant operators that matches the content of the manual with a model of the plant's state and tries to present the most relevant parts of the manual to the operators. The manual uses typed links between the sections (e.g., "is-subactivity-of" and "consumes") describing different aspects of the plant.

Slaney, M. (1990). Interactive signal processing documents. *IEEE Acoustics, Speech, and Signal Processing Magazine* (April).

A discussion of a Mathematica notebook with a signal processing model and the advantages and disadvantages of interactive scientific documents, which are compared to "literate programming."

Starker, I., and Bolt, R. A. (1990). A gaze-responsive self-disclosing display. *Proc. ACM CHI'90 Conf. Human Factors in Computing Systems* (Seattle, WA, 1–5 April), 3–9.

About an interactive fiction system based on eyetracking. The application is a children's story based on the book *The Little Prince*. The computer screen shows a 3-D graphic model of the miniature planet where the Prince lives, and synthesized speech gives a continuous narration about the planet. As long as the user's pattern of eye movements indicates that the user is glancing about the screen in general, the story will be about the planet as a whole, but if the user starts to pay special attention to certain features on the planet, the story will go into more detail about those features. For example, if the user gazes back and forth between several staircases, the system will infer that the user is interested in staircases as a group and will talk about staircases. The user never explicitly instructs the computer about what to say.

Instead, links to additional text are activated implicitly based on the computer's observations of the user and its conclusions about the user's probable interests.

Stein, M. J., and Sheridan, C. R. (1990). Hypertext and the identity link. *Online Review* **14**, 3, 188–196.

A project setting up links between bibliographies and full text databases, using MEDLINE and CCAL as examples. The main conclusion is that simple identity links do not work because of errors in the underlying data as well as differences in document construction.

Stevens, S. M. (1989). Intelligent interactive video simulation of a code inspection. *Communications of the ACM* **32**, 7 (July), 832–843.

Use of integrated AI techniques and hypermedia presentation to allow users to simulate taking part in a meeting. The system is used to teach the software engineering review technique of code inspection. This is a technique best learnt through practice and participation in inspection meetings so the main teaching approach is to allow the student to act as a meeting participant in a simulated 1–2 hour meeting. The user "participates" in the meeting by assembling sentence fragments from a menu based natural language interface. In addition to the meeting simulation, the DVI disk also contains motivational and instructional films on the importance of software quality and a hypertext library including the NASA Ada style guidelines, about 1,000 traditional course visuals, and 12 important papers on inspection. Finally the system contains two tools to allow the student to see the code that is the topic of the inspection meeting: a traditional source level debugger and a hypertext browser linking code segments and the relevant sections of the specifications. All these various tools and techniques are integrated in a single instructional environment.

Stiegler, M. (1989). Hypermedia and the singularity. *Analog Science Fiction* **109**, 1 (January), 52–71.

Includes a discussion of "hyperstyle" issues in writing hypertext fiction as well as examples from the hypertext science fiction novel *David's Sling* written by Stiegler.

Stotts, P. D., and Furuta, R. (1988). Adding browsing semantics to the hypertext model. *Proc. ACM Conf. Document Processing Systems* (Santa Fe, NM, 5–9 December), 43–50.

A model of hypertext based on Petri nets, which includes security possibilities for "enforcing browsing restrictions": Certain links are active or not, depending on a hypertext state, which again can depend on the individual user's access privileges or interaction history.

Streitz, N. (1994). Putting objects to work: Hypermedia as the subject matter and the medium for computer-supported cooperative work. Invited talk at the 8th European Conference on Object-Oriented Programming (ECOOP'94), Bologna, Italy, (July 4-8, 1994). In Tokoro, M., and Pareschi, R. (Eds.), *Object-Oriented Programming*. Lecture Notes in Computer Science, Springer, Berlin, Germany, 183–193.

Objects and hypertext support each other well.

Streitz, N. A., Hannemann, J., and Thüring, M. (1989). From ideas and arguments to hyperdocuments: Traveling through activity spaces. *Proc. ACM Hypertext'89 Conf.* (Pittsburgh, PA, 5–8 November), 343–364.

Hypertext authoring environments should provide active support to the authors' cognitive problem solving. A system based on Toulmin argumentation schemas is described.

Streitz, N., Haake, J., Hannemann, J., Lemke, A., Schuler, W., Schütt, H., and Thüring, M. (1992). SEPIA: A cooperative hypermedia authoring environment. *Proceedings ECHT'92 4th ACM European Conference on Hypertext* (Milan, Italy, November 30 – December 4), 11–22.

A multiuser hypertext system that explicitly supports a highly structured writing process by the use of a series of activity spaces (windows with slightly different features): The *planning* space is used for the authors to map out their writing plans and to establish an agenda for the writing activity. The *argumentation* space supports the development of an argumentative structure through Toulmin diagrams linking the pros and cons. The *content* space is used to develop information about the topic of the manuscript with brainstorming, random notes, and background materials (possibly through external links). Finally, the *rhetorical* space is used to develop the actual manuscript for delivery to readers.

Streitz, N., Geissler, J. Haake, J., and Hol, J. (1994). DOLPHIN: Integrated meeting support across LiveBoards, local and remote desktop environments. *Proceedings CSCW'94 ACM Conference on Computer-Supported Cooperative Work* (Chapel Hill, NC, October 22–26), 345–358..

A meeting room is equipped with an electronic whiteboard that can display hypertext nodes linked to workstations operated by the individual meeting participants.

Sultan, F., Farley, J. U., and Lehmann, D. R. (1990). A meta-analysis of diffusion models. *Journal of Marketing Research* **27**, 1 (February), 70–77.

Summary of 213 studies of innovation diffusion and technology transfer.

Talbert, M. L., and Umphress, D. A. (1989). Object-oriented text decomposition: A methodology for creating CAI using hypertext. In Maurer, H. (Ed.): *Computer Assisted Learning*, Lecture Notes in Computer Science **vol. 360**, Springer-Verlag, Berlin, Germany, 560–578.

A set of principles for partitioning knowledge into hypertext nodes based on looking at the key concepts in the domain as interrelated objects. The authors used the method to convert an existing article on the Ada programming language from linear form to hypertext in the KnowledgePro system and then conducted a test in which computer science students read the article in either hypertext form or as a plain text file. The results showed that the hypertext readers had improved their conceptual understanding of the structure of the article more than the plain text file readers. The paper does not explain the experimental methodology or results in sufficient detail, however, to enable us to evaluate their validity. The authors do report that several of the students were frustrated with problems with the KnowledgePro engine used to display their hypertext structure (e.g. strange inverse video).

Tang, J. C., and Rua, M. (1994). Montage: Providing teleproximity for distributed groups. Proc. ACM CHI'94 Conf. (Boston, MA, April 24–28), 37–43.

A video telephone system that works from the user's computer. If a user tries to call another user who is not in, the first user can leave a window with a "stickup" note on the second user's screen. This note window contains some text written by the first user and a button that links back to the first user's video telephone, making it simple to return the call.

Teshiba, K., and Chignell, M. (1988). Development of a user model evaluation technique for hypermedia based interfaces. *Proc. Human Factors Society 32nd Annual Meeting*, 323–327.

Users sorted cards with terms from the domain described in the hypertext into piles based on their perceptions of the similarity between the terms, and then they sorted the piles into a hierarchy. This procedure provided the experimenters with a way of measuring the structure of the users' conceptual models of the domain knowledge described in the hypertext and to assess the differences between the two structures. The authors use the Hubert gamma measure of proximity between two hierarchies for this comparison and find that the proximity increases slightly with extended use of the hypertext.

Thüring, M., Haake, J. M., and Hannemann, J. (1991). What's Eliza doing in the Chinese room? Incoherent hyperdocuments—and how to avoid them. *Proc. ACM Hypertext'91 Conf.*, 161–177.

Sorry, I am not telling; you will have to read the paper to find out what Eliza was doing. The paper is mainly about how to expose the structure of a hypertext to the reader to make it more easily comprehensible.

Timpka, T., Padgham, L., Hedblom, P., Wallin, S., and Tibblin, G. (1989). A hypertext knowledge base for primary care—LIMEDS in LINCKS. *Proc. ACM SIGIR'89* (Cambridge, MA, 25–28 June), 221–228.

A hypertext structure for medical general practitioners which is implemented in a distributed architecture with the database residing on a Sun and the user interface running on a Macintosh.

Tognazzini, B. (1994). The "Starfire" video prototype project: A case history. *Proc. ACM CHI'94 Conf.*, 99–105.

Starfire is an 18-minute videofilm that takes place in the year 2004 and shows a scenario of how people may use several futuristic Sun computers. Predictions include the use of desk-sized displays, chorded input devices, the widespread use of multimedia presentations as part of decision-making meetings, and the availability of hypertext-linked archives of magazines and newspapers on the net. The predictions are have deliberately been restricted to ideas that have already been demonstrated in the lab since it is not realistic to expect anything else to appear in products in a ten-year period.

Tombaugh, J., Lickorish, A., and Wright, P. (1987). Multi-window displays for readers of lengthy texts. *Intl. J. Man-Machine Studies* **26**, 5 (May), 597–615.

Two studies were conducted comparing a single-window system (having the entire text in one big file) and a multi-window system (having the text split into one segment in each window): The first study using untrained users indicated an advantage for the single-window system. In the second study, users were trained in the use of the window-system before their use of it was measured and this experiment indicated some advantage for the multi-window system. An additional insight from this study was that some novices had difficulties in using the mouse (this could be a problem for some hypertext systems in walk up and use situations if they do not use, say, a touch screens instead of a mouse).

Trigg, R. H. (1983). A Network-Based Approach to Text Handling for the Online Scientific Community. *Ph.D. thesis*, Department of Computer Science, University of Maryland (University Microfilms **#8429934**).

One of the first Ph.D. theses about hypertext. Describes the TEXTNET system, which had a highly developed taxonomy of link types.

Trigg, R. H. (1988). Guided tours and tabletops: Tools for communicating in a hypertext environment. *ACM Trans. Office Information Systems* **6**, 4 (October), 398–414.

Two tools to allow an author to convey the meaning of hypertext documents to future readers. *Guided tours* are related to the original Vannevar Bush idea of "trails." through a linked medium and provide an author-specified path through the hypertext. Each stop on the tour is a full set of NoteCards cards (rather than just a single hypertext node). The layout of these cards are determined by the *Tabletop* tool, which allows authors to specify an entire screen full of open windows/cards (including the spatial position) as the destination for a hypertext jump. This paper also appears in *Proc. 2nd Conf. Computer-Supported Cooperative Work* (Portland, OR, 26–28 September 1988), 216–226.

Trigg, R. H., and Irish, P. M. (1987). Hypertext habitats: Experiences of writers in NoteCards. *Proc. ACM Hypertext'87 Conf.* (Chapel Hill, NC, 13–15 November), 89–108.

Observations from 20 writers who used NoteCards to prepare text for later linearizing. The paper includes observations on how authors take notes, structure these notes, and maintain references and bibliographies.

Trigg, R. H., and Weiser, M. (1986). TEXTNET: A network based approach to text handling. *ACM Trans. Office Inf.Syst.* **4**, 1 (January), 1–23.

Trigg, R. H., Suchman, L. A., and Halasz, F. G. (1986). Supporting collaboration in NoteCards. *Proc. 1st Conf. Computer-Supported Cooperative Work* (Austin, TX, 3–5 December), 153–162.

A discussion of the issues involved when several people want to use a hypertext system to write a collaborative work.

Trigg, R. H., Moran, T. P., and Halasz, F. G. (1987). Adaptability and tailorability in NoteCards. *Proc. IFIP INTERACT'87* (Stuttgart, Germany, 1–4 September), 723–728.

Examples of how NoteCards has adapted to different users through flexibility, parametrization and integration with other products and how it has been tailored through its programmer's interface and by design of new card types through object-oriented specialization.

Utting, K., and Yankelovich, N. (1989). Context and orientation in hypermedia networks. *ACM Transactions on Information Systems* **7**, 1 (January), 58–84.

An excellent survey of the issues related to various forms of overview diagrams with examples from several hypertext systems and a detailed discussion of the design of the web view mechanism in Intermedia.

Valdez, F., Chignell, M., and Glenn, B. (1988). Browsing models for hypermedia databases. *Proc. Human Factors Society 32nd Annual Meeting*, 318–322.

Empirical methods for constructing distance measures and indicators of salience (or "landmark quality") for use in the construction of fisheye views. The distance measures were constructed by having subjects sort cards by similarity. Salience indicators were constructed by asking users whether the term being tested would be on the path between two randomly selected nodes. The more times users say that a term associated with a given node would be on the path between two other nodes, the higher "landmark quality" is awarded to the given node. Of the measures that could be derived from non-user testing inspection of the hypertext network, the one having the highest correlation with the empirical landmark quality measure is that of second-order connectivity, i.e. the number of other nodes that can be reached from a given node in two jumps. The correlation between these two measures was $r=0.62$.

van Herwijnen, E. (1994). *Practical SGML*, Second Edition. Kluwer Academic Publishers.

Textbook about the Standard Generalized Markup Language.

van Dam, A. (1988). Hypertext'87 keynote address. *Communications of the ACM* **31**, 7 (July), 887–895.

The history of hypertext (especially at Brown University) and a discussion of some of the issues facing designers of future hypertext systems. Contains a description of the Hypertext Editing System from 1967 and the FRESS system from 1968.

Vargo, C. G., Brown, C. E., and Swierenga, S. J. (1992). An evaluation of computer-supported backtracking in a hierarchical database. *Proc. Human Factors Society 36th Annual Meeting*, 356–360.

Users who were provided with backtrack command performed tasks about twice as fast as users who had to return to previous locations by selecting them from a table of contents.

Ventura, C. A. (1988). Why switch from paper to electronic manuals? *Proc. ACM Conf. Document Processing Systems* (Santa Fe, NM, 5–9 December), 111–116.

A military perspective on the documentation problem. Current fighter aircrafts need 300,000 to 500,000 pages of documentation, and this quantity is impossible to deal with in a paper format. The author details the practical problems of these big piles of paper and hopes that going electronic will solve them (but offers no evidence that it will actually do so).

Vertelney, L., Arent, M., and Lieberman, H. (1990). Two disciplines in search of an interface: Reflections on a design problem. In Laurel, B. (Ed.), *The Art of Human-Computer Interface Design*, Addison-Wesley, 45–55.

Two alternative redesigns of the Macintosh "map" control panel.

Vora, P. R., Helander, M. G., and Shalin, V. L. (1994). Evaluating the influence of interface styles and multiple access paths in hypertext. *Proc. ACM CHI'94 Conf.*, 323–329.

Subjects performed a task 42% faster when overview diagrams had labels on the arcs that represented the links. They performed the task 26% faster when textual nodes had the links anchored within the text (embedded menus) as opposed to when the anchors were listed in a separate part of the text (separate menus). Both results indicate the benefits of integrating structure and content information in a unified interface. The experiments concerned a hypertext about nutrition that could be conceptualized in three different ways: vitamins, food sources, and medical problems. A second experiment showed 21% faster performance when subjects were given access to multiple overview diagrams, one for each of the three main ways of conceptualizing the information base, instead of just a single overview diagram structured by vitamins.

Walker, J. H. (1987). Document Examiner: Delivery interface for hypertext documents. *Proc. ACM Hypertext'87 Conf.* (Chapel Hill, NC, 13–15 November), 307–323.

The Symbolics Document Examiner is an online manual that was the first major hypertext system to see real world use.

Walker, J. H. (1988a). Supporting document development with Concordia. *IEEE Computer* **21**, 1 (January), 48–59.

The authoring interface to documents for the Symbolics Document Examiner.

Walker, J. H. (1988b). The role of modularity in document authoring systems. *Proc. ACM Conf. Document Processing Systems* (Santa Fe, NM, 5–9 December), 117–124.

Authoring environments viewed as an analogy to software development environments: Support for the writing process should involve support for explicit modularity. Good and recognizable node names are essential for abstraction but at first the writers had difficulties in assigning highly specific names because they were used to standard names like "introduction." Over the years this changed, and the writers actually found that specific node names helped them clarify their writing.

Walker, J. H., Young, E., and Mannes, S. (1989). A case study of using a manual online. *Machine-Mediated Learning* **3**, 3, 227–241.

An analysis of the logging of 34,700 user interactions with the Symbolics Document Examiner. 40% of user actions were devoted to finding information (20% keyword search, 19% hypertext jumps from overview diagrams, and 1% jumps from a table of contents) while 60% were devoted to displaying information.

Wanning, T. (1993). Ethnographic treasuries in the computer: Electronic access to a total museum collection. *Proc. ICHIM'93 Second Intl. Conf. Hypermedia and Interactivity in Museums* (Cambridge, England, Sept. 20–24), 26–31.

The National Museum of Denmark is designing a system to allow visitors access to information about all the 80,000 artifacts in the Collection of Ethnography.

Watters, C., and Shepherd, M. A. (1991). Hypertext access and the New Oxford English Dictionary. *Hypermedia* **3**, 1, 59–79.

An interface based on so-called transient hypergraphs (consisting of links that are generated as a response to the user's search and navigation behavior, meaning that they need not take up storage space). Two types of links were used for the NOED: "match links" linking any word to dictionary entries containing that word, and "entry links" linking any word to dictionary entries for which that word is the headword.

Weyer, S. A. (1982). The design of a dynamic book for information search. *Intl.J. Man-Machine Studies* **17**, 1 (July), 87–107.

Weyer, S. A. (1988). As we may learn. In Ambron, S., and Hooper, K. (Eds.): *Interactive Multimedia: Visions of Multimedia for Developers, Educators, & Information Providers,* Microsoft Press, 87–103.

Advocates a more knowledge-oriented view of hypertext instead of the more widely used book and library metaphors, which according to the author can overshadow the dynamic nature of information and its uses. Instead of being static, information should be adaptable to the learner's preferences, and links should depend on the user's previous actions and current goals.

Weyer, S. A., and Borning, A. H. (1985). A prototype electronic encyclopedia. *ACM Trans. Office Information Systems* **3**, 1 (January), 63–88.

A knowledge-based system where the text is encoded in a concept network and the actual output to the user is custom generated based on a model of different attributes of the user. Access to the information is through browsing: "navigating through a neighborhood of information and referencing items by pointing or recognizing. i.e., hypertext. Filters control such things as whether metric or English measurement units should be displayed. This work was done at Atari, but they terminated the project before more than a prototype could be built.

Whalen, T., and Patrick, A. (1989). Conversational hypertext: Information access through natural language dialogues with computers. *Proc. ACM CHI'89* (Austin, TX, 30 April–4 May), 289–292.

A line oriented interface to a hypertext information base. Users move to new hypertext nodes by typing questions in natural language, and the system then interprets these natural language utterances in relation to what would make sense in that location of the hypertext network.

Whiteside, J., Bennett, J., and Holtzblatt, K. (1988). Usability engineering: Our experience and evolution. In Helander, M. (Ed.): *Handbook of Human-Computer Interaction,* Elsevier Science Publishers, 757–789.

Good introduction to generally applicable methods for the lifecycle of usable products.

Wilkinson, R. T., and Robinshaw, H. M. (1987). Proof-reading: VDU and paper text compared for speed, accuracy and fatigue. *Behaviour and Information Technology* **6**, 2 (April–June), 125–133.

The effect of fatigue on reading speed and errors while proofreading: Over a period of one hour of continued use, the relative performance of screen users dropped even more than the performance of paper users did.

Wilson, E. (1990). Links and structure in hypertext database for law. *Proc. ECHT'90 European Conf. Hypertext* (Paris, France, 28–30 November), Cambridge University Press.

On the automatic conversion of legal texts into the Justus hypertext system built on top of the Unix version of Guide at the University of Kent. Justus integrates primary law sources with secondary ones, such as a legal dictionary. Unfortunately, some laws use other definitions of terms than the ones in the dictionary, so one has to be careful in making automatic links.

Wilson, K. S. (1988). Palenque: An interactive multimedia digital video interactive prototype for children. *Proc. ACM CHI'88* (Washington, DC, 15–19 May), 275–279.

A DVI system developed at Bank Street College of Education for teaching Mexican archaeology. Users may move around images and film from Maya ruins and collect a personalized "album" with annotated snapshots. Unfortunately, the paper is not illustrated (a nice videotape of the system was shown at the conference where the paper was presented), but a sequence of four nice color screen shots of Palenque may be found in [Luther 1988].

Wolf, G. (1994). The (second phase of the) revolution has begun. *WIRED* **2**, 10 (October), 116–121 & 150–156.

The story behind the development of Mosaic and the start of the Mosaic Communications Corporation, including interviews with Jim Clark (founder of Silicon Graphics and Mosaic Communications Corp.) and Marc Andreessen (the lead programmer for the original release of Mosaic.

Wright, P. (1989). Interface alternatives for hypertext. *Hypermedia* **1**, 2, 146–166.
A classification of hypertext design options from five categories: linking, jumping, visual appearance of the destination, navigation, and reader tasks. For each category, the design options are ordered according to how much they constrain readers, thereby indirectly indicating what user categories they are suited for.

Wright, P. (1991). Cognitive overheads and prostheses: Some issues in evaluating hypertexts. *Proc. ACM Hypertext'91 Conf.*, 1–12.
User overhead when using hypertext include having to make decisions about whether and where to jump and the need to remember what they can do where, and how they have navigated. Results are presented from several experiments, including one showing that users only followed definition links for 61% of the words they did not understand when the words had a familiar ring to them. This link-following frequency increased to 93% when such new words were provided with a visible anchor.

Wright, P., and Lickorish, A. (1983). Proof-reading texts on screen and paper. *Behaviour and Information Technology* **2**, 3 (July–September), 227–235.
Reading from a computer screen was 27% slower than reading from paper.

Wright, P., and Lickorish, A. (1984). Ease of annotation in proof-reading tasks. *Behaviour and Information Technology* **3**, 3 (July–September), 185–194.
Proofreaders performed faster when their annotations were integrated with the main text.

Wright, P., and Lickorish, A. (1988). Colour cues as location aids in lengthy texts on screen and paper. *Behaviour and Information Technology* **7**, 1 (January–March), 11–30.
Color might be a solution to the problems users have in remembering where in lengthy texts they have previously read something. An experiment showed that this was indeed the case when reading a printed document on colored paper, but three additional experiments failed to show any advantage of using different colors of characters on a computer screen. The authors speculate that color might work better as borders or strips or if it was assigned by the readers rather than by the writers (as in highlighting, cf. [Nielsen 1986]).

Wright, P., and Lickorish, A. (1990). An empirical comparison of two navigation systems for two hypertexts. In McAleese, R., and Green, C. (Eds.) *Hypertext: State of the Art*, Ablex, 84–93.
A comparison of so-called page navigation (traditional hypertext with link anchors on the same display as the text) and a so-called index navigation (where users could only jump to new locations in the hypertext by first going to a special display giving an overview of the entire information). These designs were tested on two different hypertexts with the result that index navigation was best for one text while page navigation was best for the other. The general conclusion is that different navigation mechanisms may be needed for different text structures and reader tasks.

Wurman, R. S. (1989). *Information Anxiety*. Doubleday.

A famous book designer (creator of the ACCESS guide books) presents his philosophy on how to structure information. If ever a book was suited for hypertext publication, this is it. It is full of sidebars and quotes from other work and the table of contents is an extended abstract of each chapter in outline form. This is a good book, even if he never mentions usability testing (is a good designer always right?).

Yankelovich, N., Meyrowitz, N., and van Dam, A. (1985). Reading and writing the electronic book. *IEEE Computer* **18**, 10 (October), 15–30.

A discussion of FRESS, Intermedia, and other Brown systems as well as a very good survey of the issues at the point in time just before hypertext hit the market for real.

Yankelovich, N., Landow, G. P., and Cody, D. (1987). Creating hypermedia materials for English literature students. *ACM SIGCUE Outlook* **19**, 3–4 (Spring/Summer), 12–25.

About the goals for a course on English literature from 1700 to the present taught with the support of the Intermedia hypertext system: Explain historical and cultural context in more depth than possible in a literature class and teach "critical thinking" to let students perceive any phenomenon or event as potentially multidetermined or subject to multi-causation. As their final assignment, students will add information about an author to system and link it to the existing corpus of information.

Yankelovich, N., Haan, B. J., Meyrowitz, N. K., and Drucker, S. M. (1988a). Intermedia: The concept and the construction of a seamless information environment. *IEEE Computer* **21**, 1 (January), 81–96.

A good survey article about the major aspects of Intermedia, including a twelve-screen example session and some amount of implementation detail.

Yankelovich, N., Smith, K. E., Garrett, N., and Meyrowitz, N. (1988b). Issues in designing a hypermedia document system: The Intermedia case study. In Ambron, S., and Hooper, K. (Eds.): *Interactive Multimedia: Visions of Multimedia for Developers, Educators, & Information Providers,* Microsoft Press, 33–85.

The chapter starts with a richly illustrated walkthrough of an example session with Intermedia. It continues with a careful and well illustrated discussion of some of the user interface issues in hypertexts with overlapping and/or changing link anchors and/or destinations. Also contains a discussion of other multi-user issues. Most of this chapter is really an edited version of [Garrett et al. 1986] with more illustrations.

Yoder, E., and Wettach, T. C. (1989). Using hypertext in a law firm. *Proc. ACM Hypertext'89 Conf.* (Pittsburgh, PA, 5–8 November), 159–167.

The HyperLex system used to support work on patent cases and intellectual property law at the largest law firm in Pittsburgh, Reed Smith with 385 attorneys.

Yoder, E., McCracken, D., and Akscyn, R. (1984). Instrumenting a human-computer interface for development and evaluation. *Proc. IFIP INTERACT'84* (London, U.K., 4–7 September).

Instrumenting the frame-based ZOG system to record user behavior. Data for user time spent at each node was fairly easy to collect because of the frame-based nature of the system.

Yoder, E., Akscyn, R., and McCracken, D. (1989). Collaboration in KMS: A shared hypermedia system. *Proc. ACM CHI'89* (Austin, TX, 30 April–4 May), 37–42.

> The authors advocate using the same system for individual work and collaborative work and claim that KMS is suited for such a role. KMS supports "non-disruptive" annotation by providing a specific annotation-type of link (anchors prefixed with an "@") which is ignored by formatting programs.

Zellweger, P. T. (1988). Active paths through multimedia documents. In van Vliet, J. C. (Ed.): *Document Manipulation and Typography*, Cambridge University Press, U.K., 19–34.

> So-called scripts are used to provide a mechanism for guided tours and other predefined directed (but still non-linear) paths (sequences of links) through documents.

Zellweger, P. T. (1989). Scripted documents: A hypermedia path mechanism. *Proc. ACM Hypertext'89 Conf.*, 1–14.

> The author argues that path mechanisms need to become an integrated part of hypertext systems. Several kinds of paths are defined: sequential paths (an ordered progression through a sequence of nodes), branching paths (containing choice points and thus essentially just a subnet of the complete hypertext), and conditional paths (paths that branch but where the choice is made by the computer). Playback controls covered include single-stepping (the traditional "next node" command), automatic control (forwarding after a specified interval), and browsing control where the path is given its own user interface view.

Zizi, M., and Beaudouin-Lafon, M. (1994). Accessing hyperdocuments through interactive dynamic maps. *Proc. ACM ECHT'94 European Conference on Hypermedia Technology* (Edinburgh, U.K., September 18–23), 126–135.

> The SHADOCS hypertext system uses overview diagrams as the central navigation mechanism, adapting real-world conventions about the design of geographical maps. For example, the size of a region in the map reflects the number of documents in that region.

Far Out Stuff

One of the best works of art so far to utilize the principle of parallel story lines is the classic film *Rashomon* (1951) by the famous Japanese director Akira Kurosawa. The film tells four different versions of a violent incident in which a bandit attacks a nobleman in the forests in medieval Japan (one of the versions is told by the ghost of a person who was killed in the incident). The film won the Academy Award for best foreign film. If you cannot find an opportunity to see the film, you can read an English translation of its manuscript together with assorted comments in book form: A. Kurosawa and D. Richie: *Rashomon,* Rutgers University Press, New Brunswick, 1987.

Several of the so-called "cyberpunk" science fiction authors have depicted a future computer system wherein users navigate interlinked highly visual three-dimensional data structures. One of the first and most famous novels in this genre is William Gibson: *Neuromancer*,[9] Ace 1984, which won both the Hugo and Nebula awards for best science fiction novel of 1984. Other relevant science fiction books are Vernor Vinge: *True Names* (Bluejay 1984) and Neal Stephenson: *Snow Crash* (Bantram Spectra 1992). *Snow Crash* is fairly heavily based on hypertext concepts, including electronic business cards (referred to as "hypercards" in the book).

Apple Computer has produced some videotapes narrated by its then-CEO, John Sculley, showing scenarios of how future versions of HyperCard and the "Knowledge Navigator" (using intelligent agents in the interface) would look. These very detailed and professionally produced scenarios are very convincing in their demonstrations of how future hypermedia systems might work. Both of these videos are included in the *ACM SIGGRAPH Video Review* **Tape 79**. There is no substitute for actually watching the video, but you can get at least some idea of the Knowledge Navigator by reading Sculley [1989] and looking at the illustrations in that article.

Bruce Tognazzini at Sun Microsystems has produced a videotape entitled *Starfire* with a scenario of computer use in the year 2004 [Tognazzini 1994]. The protagonist ("Julie") is shown developing a multimedia presentation for an executive committee meeting using projected future hardware like a screen the size of a desk. In the meeting, her opponent pulls a surprise by showing a magazine article that supposedly shows that her product will fail, and she uses her laptop computer to establish a wireless connection to a large library from which she not only retrieves the article in question but also later articles linked to it by bidirectional links. These articles proved that there would in fact not be a problem with Julie's proposal, thus having hypertext save the day.

---

[9] *Neuromancer* is also available in comic book form as a so-called graphic novel by Tom De Haven and Bruce Jensen (Epic Comics, New York 1989, ISBN 0-87135-574-4). It seems to me, however, that Gibson's original written form communicates the cyberspace idea better.

Index

Note: References in square brackets [ ] point to the alphabetical listing in the bibliography in the Appendix. The index does not list the authors of the books and papers mentioned in the alphabetical listing in the bibliography.

Proper indexing is closely related to the hypertext navigation issue. In some cases the number of index entries for a term is large enough to cause disorientation and I have chosen to highlight the one or two most important entries through the use of **bold** page numbers. See for example the entry for "Anchors."

F